Majorities, Minorities, and Future of Nationhood

The design of democratic institutions includes a variety of barriers to protect against the tyranny of the majority, including international human rights, cultural minority rights, and multiculturalism. In the twenty-first century, majorities have re-asserted themselves, sometimes reasonably, referring to social cohesion and national identity, at other times in the form of populist movements challenging core foundations of liberal democracy. This volume intervenes in this debate by examining the legitimacy of conflicting majority and minority claims. Are majorities a legal concept, holding rights and subject to limitations? How can we define a sense of nationhood that brings groups together rather than tears them apart? In this volume, world-leading experts are brought together for the first time to debate the rights of both majorities and minorities. The outcome is a fascinating exchange on one of the greatest challenges facing liberal democracies today.

LIAV ORGAD is an international researcher working at the European University Institute in Florence, WZB Berlin Social Science Center, Peking University School of Transnational Law, and Reichman University in Israel.

RUUD KOOPMANS is Research Director at the WZB Berlin Social Science Center, and Professor of Sociology at Berlin's Humboldt University.

Majorities, Minorities, and the Future of Nationhood

Edited by

LIAV ORGAD
Reichman University
European University Institute
WZB Berlin Social Science Center
Peking University School of Transnational Law

RUUD KOOPMANS
WZB Berlin Social Science Center
Humboldt University Berlin

CAMBRIDGE
UNIVERSITY PRESS

University Printing House, Cambridge CB2 8BS, United Kingdom

One Liberty Plaza, 20th Floor, New York, NY 10006, USA

477 Williamstown Road, Port Melbourne, VIC 3207, Australia

314–321, 3rd Floor, Plot 3, Splendor Forum, Jasola District Centre, New Delhi – 110025, India

103 Penang Road, #05–06/07, Visioncrest Commercial, Singapore 238467

Cambridge University Press is part of the University of Cambridge.

It furthers the University's mission by disseminating knowledge in the pursuit of education, learning, and research at the highest international levels of excellence.

www.cambridge.org
Information on this title: www.cambridge.org/9781009233347
DOI: 10.1017/9781009233378

First published 2023

A catalogue record for this publication is available from the British Library.

ISBN 978-1-009-23334-7 Hardback
ISBN 978-1-009-23335-4 Paperback

Contents

Figures

Tables

Contributors

RAINER BAUBÖCK, European University Institute; Austrian Academy of Sciences

MICHAEL DA SILVA, University of Southampton

DAVID GOODHART, Policy Exchange Think Tank

CHRISTIAN JOPPKE, University of Bern

ERIC KAUFMANN, Birbeck, University of London

RUUD KOOPMANS, WZB Berlin Social Science Center; Humboldt University Berlin

WILL KYMLICKA, Queen's University, Kingston

TARIQ MODOOD, University of Bristol

LIAV ORGAD, WZB Berlin Social Science Center; European University Institute; Reichman University; Peking University School of Transnational Law

CLARA SANDELIND, University of Manchester

YAEL TAMIR, Beit Berl College

CHARLES TAYLOR, McGill University

MAYA TUDOR, University of Oxford

DANIEL M. WEINSTOCK, McGill University

DANIEL ZIBLATT, WZB Berlin Social Science Center; Harvard University

Preface

The chapters in this volume start with an important observation: that discussion in liberal democracies about recognizing and defending group rights centers overwhelmingly on the rights of minorities. Widely invoked formulae, like multiculturalism or interculturalism, are meant to address questions in this domain. They are intended to define and protect the rights of immigrants who do not share the culture of the majority in the societies they are entering.

But concentrating on these matters leaves an obvious question unanswered: What about the right of majorities, for instance, to defend their language and culture? And if there are such rights, how should one balance them against the rights of minorities when the two seem to clash? The laudable aim of this book is to cast light on these important and timely issues.

There are clear cases where the culture of a historic majority is endangered by migration. Small populations, such as the Polynesian Fijians, or the Kanaks of New Caledonia, are obviously endangered by a large influx of people of another culture, as the editors mention in Chapter 1. And then there is the vulnerability of certain languages, where a small population base, coupled with the power of a regional lingua franca, can pose a real challenge. This is the situation faced by Quebecois in the anglophone ocean of North America, where the threat comes from a language that is already a global lingua franca. It is not that French is in danger of extinction globally, but locally its survival is not assured. Or, we can cite the case of Latvian, the native medium of a small country descended upon by a substantial population of Russophones, dominant in the entire region, during the period of Soviet control. These predicaments are also discussed in this volume.

These are special situations, but they raise important issues of principle, which have wide application, concerning the historic role of migration in constituting the population of a given society. A long-standing cultural majority that is later overwhelmed by mass migration describes the plight of aboriginals in a host of contemporary states. Just about all Western hemisphere countries, plus Australia, fit into this category, as arguably does Russia (in Siberia) and perhaps also India (taking Adivasis into account). Here, there are strong grounds for according minorities a special status, and in many cases the right to substantial reparations.

But the situations that are most often discussed and hotly debated in our contemporary world concern advanced democracies, which, for one reason or another, are admitting large numbers of people from outside, either as refugees or as regular immigrants and participants in the labor force. Once again, this class includes many Western hemisphere states, and since the Second World War, Western European states. But countries on other continents, like India and South Africa, also fit this pattern. Resolving majority–minority tensions in these societies is a really challenging task.

One source of difficulty comes from the elusive nature of the majority culture, which may defy resolution in a non-question-begging way. A line from Chapter 1 offers an interesting illustration: "Calls have been made for France to abandon the principle of *laïcité* to accommodate the reality of multiculturalism." Even this way of describing the issue is not neutral. It has a strong ring of the defenders of a hard *laïcité* in France (and also in Quebec), who have diabolized the term *multiculturalisme* in a way that defenders of this principle in (anglophone) Canada find unrecognizable. The big unresolved issue in this debate, on both sides of the Atlantic, is: What exactly is *laïcité* (roughly translated as "secularism," or "the separation of church and state")? One can identify three different kinds, or purposes, of secularism in modern Western history: in one form (a) it exists to defend religion against the state. This is the separation defined in the First Amendment to the US Constitution, which declares that Congress shall adopt no law establishing religion or impeding the "free exercise thereof." Opposed to this, we have (b) *laïcité* that defends the state from religion. We can understand why this played a role in 1904–5 in France, where a powerful movement of monarchist Catholics wanted to abolish the Republic. Then between these two, we have (c) a secularism that takes neither side, but calls for neutral public institutions and defends the freedom to practice whatever religion, or non-religion, or anti-religion subscribed to by citizens.

People often identify secularism (b) with France; but in fact, what happened in 1904–5 is more complicated, and the laws were passed by people who supported both (b) and (c). We can see how many questions are begged in the sentence I quoted above opposing "French" *laïcité* and "multiculturalism." In fact, the issue as I see it, on both sides of the Atlantic pits (b) against (c). Still, I am not a neutral observer, but rather a strong partisan of (c).[1]

This is just one example of why the task of weighing majority and minority rights can be complex and difficult and that means that we are all the more indebted to the well-informed and clear-sighted authors of this volume for undertaking it.

Charles Taylor

Note

1 See Maclure, J. & Taylor, C. (2012). Laïcité et Liberté de conscience. Montréal: Boréal.

Acknowledgments

The idea to put together this volume started in 2019. We had the privilege to host Will Kymlicka at the WZB Berlin Social Science Center and seized the moment to organize our 7th Annual Conference on Migration and Diversity on the topic of "Majority and Minority Rights" in April 2019. The conference raised an exceptionally high interest and yielded a thought-provoking exchange among proponents and opponents of majority and minority rights. This was a perfect time to initiate an academic debate on one of the most urgent issues of our time.

The volume is an offshoot from this conference, but not a classical conference volume. Conference attendants who are included in the volume wrote entirely new pieces. In addition, we invited several contributors who had not been able to attend the conference. To make the discussion more engaging, we have chosen a format not of separate, stand-alone articles but an interactive debate among four leading chapters with two responses for each, one generally "for" and another generally "against" the main thesis of the lead chapter. The outcome is a fascinating dialogue, empirical and normative, on fundamental concepts in law and political theory.

We wish to thank the authors for their willingness to enter into this exchange. We are also grateful for the conference participants whose contributions were not included in the volume, but shaped and sharpened our thinking on the topic: David Abraham, Peter Balint, Christoph Baumgartner, Paul Cliteur, Netta Barak-Corren, Măriuca-Oana Constantin, Ayaan Hirsi Ali, Matthias Hoesch, Ryoko Ishikawa, Roberta Medda-Windischer, Tamar de Waal, and Alex Yakobson. A special thanks is due to John Haslam, Cambridge University Press, who had faith in this project all the way through, Rahel Rimon, the language editor, for excellent editorial feedback, and two anonymous reviewers, whose comments improved the volume remarkably. The project could not have been realized without the financial support of the European Research Council Starting Grant (# 716350) and the WZB Berlin Social Science Center.

A Note on the Cover

The cover illustrates the painting *Netherlandish Proverbs* by Pieter Bruegel the Elder (ca. 1559), exhibited in the Gemäldegalerie in Berlin. It displays a village scene filled with people, animals, and objects that express about 120 Medieval proverbs and idioms. One can learn that people in the Netherlands loved to have fun while the master was away, were ready to take on a challenge but did not try to change the unchangeable, spread gossip, did not give up until a task was complete, and were indecisive. Some proverbs still exist, while others have fallen into disuse.

The painting illustrates that political communities, imagined as they are, have some common customs, traditions, and identities. Identifying a community's core identity is a difficult task. While countries try to define today "how to be British / Dutch / French?", Bruegel the Elder's painting brilliantly caught the way of life in the Netherlands at his time. Looking at it 450 years later demonstrates that concepts like identity are dynamic, as some of the proverbs have faded away.

The painting represents some of the majority-minority dilemmas analyzed in this volume. Is there a local way of doing things in a political community? Should newcomers and minority populations adjust to it, be exempted from some of it, or perhaps ask the majority group to accept or adopt a new way of life? Mutual integration also requires differentiating between the particular and universal, distinguishing between essential and absurd, and figuring out how to welcome newcomers peacefully even though, as one of the proverbs says, "peers get along better with each other than with outsiders." This volume attempts to answer these conundrums.

1 Majority–Minority Constellations

Toward a Group-Differentiated Approach

RUUD KOOPMANS AND LIAV ORGAD

Introduction

Tensions between minority and majority groups are among the most pressing issues of our time. The changing patterns of global migration and the growing diversity of Western societies have shifted the dynamics between groups within the state. On one side, the rise of majority nationalism and the backlash against multiculturalism raise new concerns over the tyranny of the majority. On the other side, fears over the erosion of majorities' cultural identity have emerged due to the accelerated pace of migration and the creation of new minorities. These changes call for the reexamination of fundamental assumptions in human rights law and liberal political theory. To what extent can arguments in favor of minority rights apply to majorities? How can cultural demands of majority and minority groups be balanced? How should the "majority" be defined? And what type of rights should it be granted?

Policies aiming to defend the cultural identity of national majorities suffer from a low level of normative legitimacy, certainly among liberal scholars and minority rights advocates. Actors advocating cultural majority rights are often denoted with negative labels, such as "populists," "nativists," and "racists." The lack of a common normative ground on which the legitimacy of minority and majority claims can be negotiated fairly leads to a dynamic of "right" versus "might," a major structural force behind increasing political polarization. On the one hand, there is the argument that majority groups have no legitimate "right" to claim privileges for their culture over others. On the other hand, there is the argument that the majority right is absolute because, in the populist view, democratic legitimacy is a matter of "might," reduced to whatever the majority decides. Neither of these extreme positions is tenable. Instead, a normative consideration of the legitimacy of majority claims, which identifies conditions under which such claims can be normatively defensible, is urgently needed. Existing concepts are unfit to address the challenges posed to majority cultures. In fact, the concept of the "majority" does not even exist in international law, which centers on "peoples" and apparently assumes that the right of peoples to self-determination is sufficient to protect the culture of the majority.

This chapter develops a new framework for the adjudication of majority and minority claims. It advances a relational approach to majority and minority rights, according to which the normative solution to cases of conflicting norms should depend on the historical rootedness of groups, distinguishing between homeland and migratory groups. Based on this framework, the chapter provides liberal justifications to defend aspects of the majority culture. The ramifications of this approach for the fields of immigration, access to citizenship, and public life have yet to be explored in greater detail in future studies. Here we offer a rather general framework to address majority–minority constellations.

The chapter proceeds as follows. The first part asserts that the moral justifications for cultural minority rights can and should also apply to majority groups. The second part explains the historical reasons, rooted in democratic theory, for granting cultural group rights only to minority groups. The third and fourth parts challenges the validity of these historical reasons, claiming that the rapidly changing reality requires reassessing majority–minority relations in liberal democracies. It shows that such reassessment has already been started in academic and political circles. The fifth part presents two policy areas in which majorities may become vulnerable and need cultural protection – immigration control and domestic affairs. The sixth part is the core of the essay, offering a first-of-its-kind framework to address majority–minority constellations. It first distinguishes between two types of majority groups, homeland and migratory, and then claims that a fair consideration of majority and minority interests should take into account not only the type of the minority (i.e., indigenous/national, migratory) but also the type of the majority (homeland, migratory); we call it an intergroup differentiation approach to majority–minority constellations. The seventh part provides two practical examples for a possible implementation of our approach, while the last, eighth part explains the different faces and meanings of cultural majority rights.

Justifications for Cultural Group Rights

The starting point of any discussion on cultural group rights is the human need for recognition. The plea for recognition is fundamental; it is related to happiness, self-realization, and well-being. It entails a need to belong, as humans are social creatures. The "great cry for recognition," to cite Isaiah Berlin (1969: 142) in his classic essay *Two Concepts of Liberty*, is "one of the greatest forces that move human history." Berlin shows that individuals seek not only freedom from tyranny, equal opportunities, or "a rational plan of life," but also "proper recognition." People wish to avoid a reality in which one's unique identity is "simply being ignored" or "being taken too much for granted … even if this means to be unpopular and disliked." This is as true for individuals as it is for groups. It is group membership that provides a person with personality ("the sense of being someone"), meaningful life, and the liberty to fulfill his/her life goals. What people want "is simply recognition (of their class or nation, or color or race)," and to live and act together with "members of the society to which, historically, morally, economically, and perhaps ethnically" they feel attached (1969: 142–43). Berlin reminds us of self-evident truths about human nature: "For what I am is, in large part, determined by what I feel and think; and what I feel and think is determined by the feeling and thought prevailing in the society to which I belong." Social belonging, in essence, is "the heart of the great cry for recognition on the part of both individuals and groups" (1969: 143–44).

These plain and simple truths have guided liberal theory and human rights law in the past decades with regard to cultural minority rights. In *The Politics of Recognition*, Charles Taylor explains how the demand for recognition has motivated some of the greatest movements in international law and politics. A major focus has been the development of multiculturalism and minority rights to secure the recognition of minorities' cultural identity. Taylor (1994: 38) claims that "*Everyone* should be recognized for his or her unique identity," yet adds that, in a majoritarian democracy, demands for recognition of being different should only apply to minority cultures. This is because their distinct personality "has been ignored, glossed over, assimilated to a dominant or majority identity." International human rights law has entrenched the demand of minority groups for cultural recognition in a long list of documents (Kymlicka 2008). Indeed, the rise of cultural minority rights (and multiculturalism) has been one of the most important developments in human rights law and liberal theory in the past five decades.

The moral validity of the argument supporting recognition, identity, and self-worth is not limited to cultural minorities. If one accepts that "persons belonging to national or ethnic, religious and linguistic minorities have the right to enjoy their own culture" (UN Declaration on Minority Rights 1992: art. 2), and that "persons belonging to such minorities shall not be denied the right, in community with the other members of their group, to enjoy their own culture" (ICCPR 1966: art. 27), then equal recognition requires that majority groups can enjoy such rights too – as a fundamental human need. If Quebecois, native American Pueblo peoples, and Frisians can claim cultural rights, so too should the Danes, the Dutch, and the Italians. Majorities, like minorities, have an interest in adhering to their culture and preserving core elements of it – maintaining a meaningful, yet distinctive, collective way of life. The justifications for this are based on personal autonomy, individual liberty, and social identity. In a political and normative reality in which cultural minority rights exist, there should be, in appropriate cases, cultural majority rights of some scope (Koopmans 2018). The human need for political recognition is not the monopoly of minority groups and should not be contingent on whether the group is a "minority" or a "majority." The same applies to the hopes to preserve a specific culture, and the aspirations for its continuity, in some form, throughout future generations.[1]

Majority Rights in Democratic Theory

A liberal theory of majority rights may seem paradoxical. In liberal political philosophy, majorities have been associated with "evils against which society requires to be on its guard" and, consequently, "precautions are as much needed against this, as against any other abuse of power" (Mill 1859: 3–4). The concern of liberal democracies has traditionally been the tyranny of the majority because democracy is based on a majoritarian rule of some kind, implemented by an electoral system of some sort (direct or representative, presidential or parliamentary, national or regional[2]). Democracy represents the "rule of the people," yet the phrase "the people" is essentially a majority population (Mill 1859: 3–4). In such a system, there is a constant threat that the majority population will "do whatsoever it pleases" to tyrannize the minority (de Tocqueville 1835: vol. II, part 2, ch. 7; Constant 1815: book II, chs. 1 and 2). This threat exists particularly in a democracy, in which a majority has a privileged status.[3] Majorities matter less in authoritarian regimes; numbers matter, especially in a democracy, which is based on the rule of numbers (Burke 1790: 53–57, 103–04). However, in a Democracy the majority is regarded as able to "take care of itself" (Margalit & Halbertal 2004: 530). It can dominate the public sphere by controlling entry into the community and by utilizing the forces of democratic decision-making.

Because of these majority privileges, the design of democratic institutions included, at the very outset, a variety of barriers to restrict their power: judicial review, supermajority requirements, checks and balances, inalienable rights from which no majority can deviate, and federalism. These barriers are needed "to correct the errors of democracy" and, although they are never "able to stop the movements of the majority," they can still "succeed in slowing and directing them" (de Tocqueville 1835: vol. II, part 2, ch. 8). The traditional liberal response to the tyranny of the majority has been tolerance – "letting minorities conduct themselves as they wish ... so long as they do not interfere with the culture of the majority" (Raz 1996: 172). As a result of the Second World War and the human rights movement in the 1960s, antidiscrimination laws on the grounds of race and religion have become part of human rights law and an additional limitation on the power of the majority. During the 1980s and 1990s, a third liberal response became common – the rise of minority rights. Cultural minority rights intend to compensate minorities for the democratic privileges of the majority. Since the "state culture" reflects the preference of the majority – vis-à-vis its languages, holidays, symbols, values, and political institutions – minority groups "are unfairly disadvantaged" (Kymlicka 1995: 109). This inequality needs to be compensated by providing cultural privileges to minority groups.

The democratic privileges of majorities have led courts to assume that majorities need no special legal protection; the majority is considered to be well-off. Canonical texts and leading caselaw claim either that majorities do not exist or need no protection. This philosophy also guides international law. It assumes that individuals need special protection as members of ethnic, religious, or linguistic *minority* groups (ICCPR, art. 27), yet not as members of ethnic, religious, or linguistic *majority* groups. International law offers instead the notion of self-determination of "peoples," which is not identical with the concept of "majorities." In principle, the term "Peoples" can refer to groups that define their identity in an ethno-cultural sense – as in "the Jewish people" or "the Slovak people." However, once a state has been established, international law remains vague on whether self-determination also includes the perpetuation of the majority status of the foundational ethnic group, or enduring privileges for its culture in the public domain. Within the framework of established states, "the people" is defined in international law and in most liberal-democratic constitutions as "the citizenry," regardless of ethnocultural features. Neither democratic constitutional theory nor international law recognizes a concept of "majorities" and, overall, assumes that majority populations are well protected.

What Defines a Cultural Majority?

A major challenge to any theory of majority rights is the claim, advanced by several authors in this volume (e.g., Bauböck and Joppke), that cultural majority groups do not exist, except as an unwarranted and anti-pluralist reification, because they are too internally heterogeneous and not static across time. Sociological and historical variability of group boundaries and the content of their "groupness" is certainly a fact, but it applies equally to majority and minority groups. Therefore, it is an argument that can only be valid if one concludes that group rights are illegitimate or impracticable for majorities and minorities alike. Moreover, the historical change argument disregards that any political decision, including one to grant or deny group rights, is always temporary in a democracy (with the rare exception of some countries whose constitutions contain "eternal" clauses that cannot be amended by a democratic majority). Decisions on majority or minority rights can always be overturned in the future if sociological and electoral realities change. The fact that people may have thought differently in the past, and perhaps will in the future, is not an argument against making democratic decisions now.

The heterogeneity argument cannot be a fundamental, normative argument, either. If the (nominal, potential) cultural majority group is too internally divided on particular recognition, rights or identity claims, it will not be able to translate them into numerical electoral majorities. This would still leave the option to the proponents – as suggested, for instance, by Patten (2020) and Goodhart (this volume) regarding marginalized rural or working-class populations – to couch their demand in terms of minority rights. The notion of majority rights, however, requires that the majority constitutes not only a cultural group but also can garner numeric majority support for its claims. In reality, cultural majority populations are not nearly as fragmented as the critics want us to believe. Limiting immigration, requiring immigrants to assimilate to the dominant language and core values of the society, rejection of expressions of fundamentalist religiosity such as full-face covering – all these can reckon with the support of the vast majority of the population in virtually all liberal democracies. Also, in terms of what characteristics define the majority culture, there is often a broad consensus. In a 2019 representative study, when asked about Dutch national identity, only 6 percent of the Dutch population chose the option "Dutch national identity does not exist" and 11 percent said "I don't know." However, 42 percent agreed fully that Dutch national identity exists, and 41 percent that it exists "in certain respects." Moreover, there was a broad consensus about the content of national identity when respondents were asked in a multiple-response question, "what contributes most to your sense of belonging to the Netherlands?" The answers showed that most respondents defined Dutch national identity as a combination of universalistic values (e.g., freedom of expression, democracy, equality of men and women, and equality of homosexuals and heterosexuals), and more particularistic elements such as the Dutch language, national symbols (e.g., the flag, the anthem, and King's Day), historical experiences (e.g., the Second World War and the Holocaust), and folk traditions (e.g., "Sinterklaas," the Dutch ancestor of Santa Claus). Clear majorities saw all of these as being part of Dutch national identity.

A majority rights debate is emerging because, in an increasing number of cases concerning immigration, cultural, and identity issues, clear numerical majorities do not translate into concomitant political decisions. The core problem majority rights address does not lie, as Ziblatt (this volume; also Bauböck, this volume) mistakenly assumes, in those cases where some "smaller faction of a cultural majority may claim to speak on behalf of a self-perceived cultural majority," but in those cases where there are clear numerical majorities regarding specific cultural claims, yet nonetheless these claims are not implemented.

One cause of this mismatch between political demand and supply is that contemporary political, cultural, and economic elites tend to have views on these issues that strongly diverge from those held by most ordinary citizens (see De Wilde et al. 2019, for extensive empirical evidence from Germany, the United States, and other countries). Elites, while often very affirmative toward minority rights, are much less inclined to endorse majority identities and majority cultural particularism, subscribing instead to a supranational, cosmopolitan ethos (the "Anywhere liberal ethos" of Goodhart, Chapter 11). Dissatisfaction with this elite-mass divide is only very partly expressed in support for populist parties because, for many voters, the price of supporting the latter's chauvinist and illiberal expressions of majority claims is simply too high.

The second reason why numeric majorities regularly do not translate into political decisions is the advance of minority and human rights legal and normative regimes that constrain (often by way of court decisions or their anticipation) not only the realization of particular majority demands, but even the expression and recognition of majority identities. Before the Second World War, national independence and the attendant unlimited national sovereignty rights sufficed to guarantee the cultural rights of national majorities within "their" nation-state. While for minority groups, it has remained – or has since the Second World War become – legitimate to manifest their identities and mobilize on behalf of their interests in ethnic terms, it has increasingly come to be regarded as normatively illegitimate to define "Dutch" or "Danish" as ethnic categories. These national labels are nowadays only regarded as normatively legitimate if they formalistically refer to "everyone who lives in the Netherlands" or "everyone who has the Danish nationality," but the Dutch or the Dane as a member of an ethnic group with its own cultural traditions has disappeared as a normatively legitimate category. Nation-states are now expected to follow universalistic norms and not to make distinctions on the basis of culture, except where the recognition and protection of cultural minorities are concerned. What used to be a normative advantage for cultural majorities – that they had their "own" sovereign nation-states – has turned into a normative burden, namely these nation-states are now expected to implement universalistic norms and no longer to reflect a particular culture. Christian Joppke, in his contribution (this volume), states this position crisply: "'Danes,' 'Dutch,' or 'Italians' are no longer a 'group' in any meaningful sense." Yet most ordinary Danes, Dutch, and Italians – including more than a few with immigrant backgrounds – would wholeheartedly disagree with this proposition.

A Majority–Minority Shift

The assumption that the majority can take care of itself is thus no longer self-evident. This is due to various reasons, among them fundamental changes in the scale, character, and intensity of global migration, the rise of cultural minority rights, and legal limitations that make it relatively more difficult for majorities to demand integration from newcomers and minorities.[4] Majority groups in the West have become smaller in size and their cultural identity has become more vulnerable. The percentage of people with "migrant backgrounds" (defined as being born abroad or having at least one parent born abroad) is between 20 and 25 of the population in several European states, including France, Germany, the Netherlands, and Sweden. In Germany, among children under the age of fifteen, its share amounts to 38 percent. And because immigrants tend to concentrate in metropolitan areas, the majority has become a numeric minority in some cities, for instance, in the largest cities of the Netherlands (Amsterdam, Rotterdam, and The Hague). These demographic changes would be of little concern if people of migrant backgrounds were to integrate into the host society, adopting the political and cultural values that are at the *core* of the majority self-understanding of society. To the extent that this does not happen, the majority may end up feeling culturally like "strangers in their own land." One may argue that this is the way of modernization, in which no one has any special claim to a certain part of the world and, therefore, members of majority groups should accept the inevitable. This may be a possible position, but it cannot be easily combined with a simultaneous defense of only the cultural rights of minorities.

The majority–minority shift is also a function of globalization and technological developments. In a globalizing world, majority cultures face intense assimilation pressures from the outside, just as national minorities and indigenous groups are subjected to assimilation pressures from inside the societies in which they live. Languages, even if they are official state languages, have come under pressure due to the proliferation of English as the dominant language. Master's programs in Europe are predominantly taught in English. Similarly, in the domain of cultural products – such as cinema and popular music – the market share of local products has been declining for decades. Free markets, international media, the Internet, and global transport challenge the notion of cultural exceptionalism. Transcultural diffusion is greater today than in any other period in human history. Even if the state can control the flow of migrants, it cannot control the flow of ideas and cultures. Free movement zones, such as the Schengen area and the ECOWAS, and modern technology – low-cost flights, high-speed trains, and short-term rental platforms – have led to a massive increase in the number of visitors, who change the landscape of cities. "Tourists go home" is a popular slogan in small cities, such as Venice and Dubrovnik. This process is apparent particularly in Europe, where majority populations have become a minority community in the Union, striving to preserve their identity by cultivating a local bond that goes beyond Western European values (Orgad 2015: 85–112).

Two transformative changes have occurred in the intersection between the rapidly changing patterns of migration, the rise of cultural minority rights, and the accumulated effect of globalization and technological developments. First, majorities face an identity crisis. Paradoxically, the expansion of minority rights and the growing number of migrants have paved the way for the revival of cultural majority demands; they have boosted the majority's sense of being culturally distinctive as well as its fears of being under cultural pressure.[5] We are witnessing an interesting phenomenon in which states seek to protect their unique identity (e.g., Britishness), but are normatively constrained to clearly specify what it is, given their commitment to universalism.

Second, cultural conflicts between majority and minority populations have increased. Some of the conflicts relate to liberal values – topics such as freedom of speech and gender equality. Others concern liberal principles and institutions, such as the rule of law and the authority of Western constitutions (rather than the supremacy of God) as the supreme law of the land. These conflicts are not "a mere disagreement on a certain policy," as Tamir (this volume) shows, but concern "the sources of political legitimacy," the basic organizing principles of liberal communities on which a minimum agreement is essential for the operation of government (Jay 1787; Madison 1787). These are not cultural conflicts about the way things are done "here," but about the fundamental backbone of a liberal society (Barry 2001: 284–86). Conflicts have also emerged around the role of religion in public life and sexual openness – topics such as gender segregation, homosexuality, "covering-up," and nudity. Gaps on different values and attitudes are not always becoming smaller in second- and third-generation migrants, and sometimes they are even growing wider. Alongside conflicts around liberal values and principles, there are increasing tensions around local lifestyles and folk traditions – topics such as burial, dress code, food, holidays, national symbols, and ways of doing things in schools, worksites, and public places. Minority demands in these areas often show little sensitivity to local historical and cultural contexts and different systems of meanings and connotations of the host society. Examples are the debates around Zwarte Piet ("Black Pete") in the Netherlands and the tradition of the "Sternsinger" ("Three Kings' Day" on January 6) in Germany and Switzerland. Local practices are often judged by imported, mostly American standards, instead of within the context of their original social meaning. Thus, Kymlicka's (1995: 83) argument that "to understand the meaning of a social practice, therefore, requires understanding … the language and history which constitute that vocabulary" does not always apply where majority cultures are concerned. In a global world in which the Anglo-Saxon culture sets the norm in many domains, the distinction between "dominant" and "minority" cultures no longer exclusively applies within nation-states but can also refer to the unequal balance of power between cultures of nation-states.

The topic of cultural majority rights has become the focus of academic attention. In Canada, under the title of interculturalism, Gerald Bouchard has made a strong case for protecting "the interests of the majority culture, whose desire to perpetuate and maintain itself is perfectly legitimate" (Bouchard 2011: 438–39; see also Eisenberg 2019; Da Silva & Weinstock, this volume). A similar view has been endorsed by Charles Taylor (2012: 420). The concern of Bouchard and Taylor is the cultural identity of the French-speaking majority population in the province of Quebec, an interesting twist since it is a minority in relation to the English-speaking majority in Canada and thus can invoke minority, rather than majority rights. In the United States, support for cultural majority rights comes from liberal circles. Alan Patten, for one, claims that "majorities do have certain rights and permissions with respect to the expression and defense of their culture." He also touches upon the connection between majority rights and minority rights: "It seems arbitrary to restrict theories of multiculturalism to minority cultures if the application of the labels – 'minority' or 'majority' – can flip so easily according to context and baseline ... concepts, terminology, and arguments deployed by multicultural theorists in favor of minority rights sometimes seem relevant and applicable to the situations of majorities" (Patten 2020: 2–4). Patten supports a thin version of cultural majority rights and mentions that this can be done "without opening the floodgates to racist and chauvinist forms of majoritarianism" (Patten 2020: 2–4). In Europe, where the backlash against minority rights has arguably been the fiercest, Tariq Modood is a strong voice for majority rights. "[I]t is fair to say that multiculturalists have not addressed the issue of the majority and do need to do so," he states, and adds, "I confess to being guilty here" (Modood 2014: 307). Modood puts the finger on one of the biggest flaws in the democratic theory: "Multiculturalists normally assume that the majority already has what the minority is seeking" and concludes that "multiculturalists need to show the same sensitivity to change, and identity anxiety in relation to the majority as to the minority" (Modood 2014: 309–10). Modood calls for a "political adjustment," which would be mutually "sensitive to anxieties about threats to identity on the part of the majority as well" (Modood 2014: 310–11; for similar views, see Koopmans 2018).

Back in 1995, in developing a theory of minority rights, Will Kymlicka stated that such a theory is a necessity: "There is little hope that stable peace will be restored, or that basic human rights will be respected, until these minority rights issues are resolved" (Kymlicka 1995: 5). Kymlicka was right then. But the same necessity applies today to the need for a liberal theory of majority rights. Kymlicka (this volume), however, seems to remain in the 1990s: "in a world organized on the logic of nationhood ... majorities are inherently privileged, and minorities are inherently penalized." For Kymlicka, the idea of a needy cultural majority is logically implausible: "there is no credible story of how smaller and typically poorer groups could impose their will on majorities in a democratic system" (Kymlicka 1995: 11). Yet, these presumptions do not reflect contemporary Western reality, where majorities do not feel "inherently privileged" but, instead, feel (and often are) culturally vulnerable, sometimes pushed to adapt themselves to the minority culture (Bouchard 2011: 445).

Whether this is true in a given society is an empirical question, but social perceptions are part of political reality. Claiming that majorities do not exist, or have no legitimate claims, is part of the "problem," not the solution.[6] While Modood suggests a political adjustment to accommodate changes in the past decades, Kymlicka offers none. Perhaps this is why, in their reply to Kymlicka, Da Silva and Weinstock (this volume) remind him that "the issue is political, not philosophical" and, further, that "rebranding" multiculturalism "under a new name [e.g., interculturalism] will not change this," due to "the unpopularity of the multiculturalist 'brand'." Hence, a new theory, based on revised assumptions that consider the changing political reality, is urgently needed.

Talking about majority rights causes uneasiness due to fears of possible abuse of the concept for illiberal agendas. In *Liberalism of Fear: The Second Coming*, Tamir (this volume) shows how fears triggered the discourse of nationalism: "Minorities fear the power of the majority, and nowadays majorities fear the growing influence of minorities. What you fear reflects where you stand. In order to understand political reality in all its depth we must therefore query who is afraid of whom, why and when." Tamir's point is compelling: The challenge of majority nationalism can only be addressed when majority fears are not ignored. Silencing fears leaves a fertile soil for populism. The more liberalism has envisioned a post-national world, the more post-liberal nationalism has become. A liberal theory of majority rights is not only in the interest of those who care about cultural majority rights – it certainly should not be left to right-wing parties – but it is also in the interest of those who care about cultural minority rights.

Classical liberalism positioned individuals at its center, not groups. It recognized neither minority rights nor majority rights. However, in a world where groups exist, de facto if not *de facto and de jure*; assimilation is unwelcome, even condemned; and minority rights are alive, and even over-catered, there are cases in which majorities need protection as well. Such protection should apply when the structural democratic privileges of the majority are insufficient to slow down its cultural dissolution (for "asymmetrical multiculturalism," see, e.g., Kaufmann 2019: 52–54, 516–21).

Vulnerable Majorities

A situation in which majorities need protection for their cultural rights can occur in at least two contexts. The first relates to migration control. The majority culture may become vulnerable in four paradigmatic cases (Orgad 2015: 189–95). (1) *Dwindling majorities*: This relates to a case in which majority groups have reached a point in which a fundamental feature of society faces a significant challenge due to, among other things, migration. This challenge is a function of the scale of migration and the capacity to absorb more migrants without a reasonable likelihood that their admission would radically affect the majority's ability to freely define its "self" in a state-based framework. Polynesian Fijians are an example. They are still a numeric majority but wield less economic power than the large numeric minority of Indo-Fijians, which is of migratory origin. The Kanaks of New Caledonia have already lost their majority status on both counts and, as a result of migration, make up less than 40 percent of the population. (2) *Regional-minority majorities*: This relates to a situation in which there is a considerable gap between the characteristics of the majority within the state and the regional characteristics. A fundamental feature of the majority can be that it is a regional minority.[7] In the Baltic countries or Ukraine, the non-Russian majority lives in countries bordering the Russian Federation. Russian migration, which joins the Russian-speaking minority, is perceived as dangerous by the local regional-minority majorities of Estonians, Latvians, and Lithuanians. This is especially the case of newly independent states, which are generally less secure about their social solidarity and political independence. (3) *Victimized majorities*: This relates to a case in which the majority has a rich history of persecution or colonization; victimization is comprehensively rooted in the group's ethos, and there is a plea not to be dependent on the goodwill of others. The Jewish majority in Israel is an example. Jews in Israel see public conflicts through the lens of the Holocaust, as a metaphor for a long history of an ongoing threat and the narrative of "never again." (4) *Minoritized majorities*: Referring to a situation in which, for historical reasons, a national majority displays the collective "state of mind" of a national minority, acting as if it is weak and living in fear for its future survival. It is a majority with "minority complexes." Examples are the Slovaks and the Hungarian minority in Slovakia, Poles and the German minority in Poland, Romanians and the Hungarian minority in Romania, and the Croats and the Serbian minority in Croatia. In such cases, further migration of people of a minority background is perceived by the majority as a threat to its integrity. The central point is whether migration brings a transformative *normative* change that seeks or leads to a significant departure from a society's basic structure. It is not necessarily about numbers or ethnic and religious backgrounds, but rather about a transformative change to a society's basic character.[8]

The second context in which majorities increasingly feel "needy" is domestic affairs. In Western societies, there are growing demands for the adaptation of the majority culture, in its different expressions, to minority demands and rights. For instance, calls have been made for France to abandon the principle of *laïcité* to accommodate the reality of multiculturalism. In the United Kingdom, there have been voices to revisit the status of the Church of England to fit in with the United Kingdom's changing demographics. Western societies face salient demands on behalf of minorities to conform to *their* way of life in the context of traditions (dress codes, customs), shared histories (core curriculum in schools), and commitment to constitutional values. In most cases, the demand is for accommodation – e.g., exemptions from compulsory mixed swimming lessons – but in other cases, the demand goes beyond that and seeks to compel the majority to adopt the minority way of doing things in the public sphere. A useful distinction (Rubinstein 2017) is between "*illiberal* minorities," which maintain illiberal ways of life but do not seek to change the liberal way of life of the political community (e.g., the Amish), and "*anti-liberal* minorities," which maintain illiberal ways of life yet also seek to use political power to impose their way of life in the public sphere, that is, to change the way of life of others, who are non-members of the group (e.g., ultra-orthodox Jews in Israel). Anti-liberal minorities put at risk not only liberal values but also the very idea of multiculturalism, on the basis of which it is invoked. This is because the existence of multiculturalism depends on the *prerequisite* that the dominant culture is one that recognizes the idea of equality of cultures.

Discussing the topic of vulnerable majorities requires defining a majority (Orgad 2015: 182–89). Providing a definition that fits all cases is theoretically misguided and practically impossible, since the defining characteristics of the collective conscience of the dominant majority differ among societies, as does the dividing line between majorities and minorities. In some nations, the dividing lines are religion or ethnicity, in others, culture or language, and in some, political ideals and institutions. The core of the majority varies: primordial, civic, and cultural (Eisenstadt & Giesen 1995). It is also a function of the political system. One can think of a "constitutional majority," whose values are reflected in the constitution, alongside a "political majority," whose values are reflected in a political body. Constitutional theories also matter (Volkmann 2017: 1650–51). A constitutional majority can refer to a text (constitution as a form), or to basic conventions of the political community that are not written in a formal text (constitution as a substance). For originalists, the key may be the timeless truths of a historical majority, while living constitutionalists may support an approach that accommodates a changing society. Finally, majorities have different conceptions of peoplehood. Some groups are open and wish to expand their power and sovereignty (in this regard, citizenship is seen as a method of national growth and is favorable), while other groups engage with political closure and local preservation (in this regard, new members are not encouraged). Historically, Rome was an example of the first type, while Sparta and Venice of the second.

Talks about the tyranny of the minority may be premature. However, while the idea of minority rights has been baked-in for decades, the notion of majority rights is relatively new. Political theory and human rights law still depart from the presumption that "the majority is omnipotent, and the minority defenceless" (Adams 1787: vol. 6, III, ch. 1). This narrative is predominantly one of multicultural citizenship, under which the majority is assumed to control the state and govern it according to its own conceptions of the good life. This is no longer a full representation of Western reality. A new approach to address minority–majority constellations is thus needed.

An Intergroup Differentiation Approach

The conceptual foundation for theorizing minority rights has mainly been laid down by Will Kymlicka, who distinguishes between three types of ethnocultural minority groups – indigenous peoples, national minorities, and migrant groups – and formulates the rights that ought to be granted to each type. "Indigenous peoples," such as Māori people or Native Americans, are entitled to self-government and land claims; "national minorities," such as the Catalans or Quebecois, are entitled to territorial autonomy and linguistic rights; and "immigrant groups" are entitled to reasonable accommodations and access to citizenship (Kymlicka 1995). In this typology, the legitimacy of minority groups' claims to state institutions varies according to the type of the group. In Kymlicka's analysis, "the state is understood in generic terms as a 'Western liberal democracy'" (Kymlicka 2009: 374), without considering how majority group-differentiation can or should influence the legitimacy of minority claims. Majority groups are categorically undifferentiated. In Kymlicka's words: A theory of "minority rights is virtually destined to take the form of group differentiated rights that are applicable to all (democratic) states. In short, minorities are differentiated, states are undifferentiated ... both in the challenges they face and in the normative evaluations they should adopt in relation to minority claims" (Kymlicka 2009: 376–77). International human rights law follows this path. The scope of minority rights is not affected by the type of the majority groups; majorities are presumed to be the same.

Michael Walzer offers a different approach to theorizing minority rights. For him, the type of protection afforded to minority groups should be a function of the type of state. Walzer distinguishes between four types of states: empires (e.g., the Ottoman empire), federations (e.g., Switzerland), post-ethnic multinational states (e.g., the United States), and nation-states (e.g., Germany). Each type offers a different set of minority rights: liberal tolerance in empires, autonomy in federations, pluralism in multinational states, and access to citizenship in nation-states. In Walzer's analysis, states are differentiated, while minorities are undifferentiated. Hence, minority rights are the same for all types of minority groups (indigenous, national, migrant); the factor that affects them is the state's conception of statehood – "This is the crucial point that follows from acknowledging that there are different sorts of states" (Walzer 1983a: 382).

Neither Kymlicka nor Walzer develops a relational theory of majority–minority relations. Kymlicka's *minority*-differentiation theory and Walzer's *state*-differentiation theory are unfit to deal with the challenge of *majority* groups around the world. Majorities are not one unified category but vary according to historical experiences and surrounding circumstances, which define their type, interests, aspirations, and sense of commonality, and, as a result, shape not only their rules of membership but also the essence of their political membership (Safran 1997). In order to obtain a conceptual grip on different majority–minority constellations, we thus propose applying the distinction between migratory and non-migratory groups to majority groups as well.

Homeland majorities are historically rooted in (and have a special tie to) a particular territory. Their identity rests on a cross-generational cultural and political history, linked to a territory that recalls and symbolizes the past. It includes the burial places of ancestors, real or imagined, the statues of heroes, ancient ruins and historical buildings, and features of the landscape, both natural (such as the Lorelei narrows of the Rhine Valley in Germany) and human-made (such as the onion-shaped church towers dotting Bavarian valleys or the dikes and polders of the Dutch lowlands). Historical places are imbued with positive and negative associations. In Germany, they include Wittenberg (where Luther preached), Frankfurt's Paulskirche (seat of the country's first elected parliament), as well as the Dachau concentration camp and the Berlin Wall. Cultural identity includes shame as well as pride, but the common denominator of both is the desire to transmit them to future generations, often in a particular place. David Miller argues that the majority's attachment to a specific territory is crucial for justifying the protection of its culture: "When a people with a distinctive national culture occupy territory over time and transform it to meet their needs, they acquire the right to preserve and enjoy the value that they have thereby created. Part of that value is material, but another part is symbolic, as the territory comes to bear the imprint of the national culture" (Miller 2016: 12). Culture is reproduced through territory: "members of the national majority come to understand their own historic identity partly through their direct experience of the environment they and their predecessors have created" (Miller 2016: 12). Bouchard (2011: 442, 451) reaches a similar conclusion. In referring to the culture of the "founding majority" – in the sense of the initial act of settlement and nation-building – he asserts that it "can legitimately claim some elements of contextual precedence based on its seniority or history" and, as a result, "preserve the cultural and symbolic heritage that serves as the foundation of its identity."

Migratory majorities cannot make similar claims. In particular, they can make no claims concerning the groups which were already in the territory when the first settlers arrived – Aboriginals, First Nations, or Native Americans. At most, migratory majorities can claim privileges vis-à-vis later generations of migrants who joined an already-established society with regard to elements of the culture of the majority that emerged *after* such migration (Huntington 2014: 39–46).[9] The Thanksgiving tradition and the United States Declaration of Independence are uniquely American cultural features, as are the memories of slavery and the Civil War. However, no equivalent privilege can be accorded to elements of the majority culture that predated migration and originated in the majority's country (or countries) of origin. Migratory majorities have given up their claim to such rights by their voluntary movement to a new land. Thus, they do not have the same right to privilege their cultural identity or religion in the public sphere, as do homeland majority groups. Moreover, because migrants in settler countries come from several cultures of origin (e.g., the English, Dutch, and German roots of the original colonies of the United States, or the French and Anglo-Saxon origins of Canada), the post-migration aspects of the culture of such countries tend to emphasize cultural pluralism as a "nation of immigrants," rather than a specific ethno-culture as the core of national identity.

The combined effect of the type of the majority group (homeland, migratory) and the type of the minority group (indigenous and national, migratory) has never been systematically examined. In such a framework, the type of the majority group should be balanced with the type of minority group to decide the legitimacy of the claims made by each group toward the other group. Table 1.1 presents the four ideal-typical combinations that result from this framework.

Table 1.1 shows that, in addressing minority–majority constellations, it is essential to consider the characteristics of minorities *and* the type of majority they face. An indigenous minority may face majorities that are also indigenous in the sense of being historically rooted in a specific land and having a distinctive cultural identity (e.g., English and Scots, Hindus and Muslims in India, Jews and Palestinians in Israel). In this case, while there is numeric imparity between the majority and the minority, there is normative parity between them. The same holds true for the diagonally opposite constellation in which both minorities and majorities are of migratory origin (e.g., Muslims in the United States). Overall, descendants of earlier migrants have a weak normative basis to claim cultural privileges over other immigrant cultures,

Table 1.1 ***Majority–minority constellations by indigenous or migratory origin***

		Majority is –	
		Indigenous	Migratory
Minority is –	Indigenous	Scots and English in the United Kingdom; Muslims and Hindus in India	First nations in settler countries, e.g., Maori in New Zealand; Kanaks in New Caledonia
	Migratory	Immigrant minorities in Europe (e.g., Turks in Germany, Moroccans in the Netherlands); Indian minorities and Polynesian/ Malay-Muslim majorities in Fiji and Malaysia	Immigrant minorities in settler countries, e.g., Ukrainians in Canada; Muslims in the United States

which happened to arrive later. A different case exists when homeland minorities face a migratory majority (e.g., indigenous Māori and British settlers in New Zealand). This constellation provides the strongest type of *minority* claims. In contrast, the case that provides the strongest ground for *majority* claims exists when homeland majorities face minorities of migratory origin (e.g., immigrant minorities in most European societies). For this reason, there should be no generalizations from analyses of minority–majority constellations in the settler countries of the New World to the countries with indigenous majorities of the Old World. There is a general tendency to extrapolate conclusions drawn from the literature on minority rights, which draws heavily on settler countries (notably, the United States and Canada), to European debates. In the absence of a theoretical consideration of the majority type, attempts to Americanize or Canadianize European states are theoretically misplaced.[10] The legitimacy of minority claims (e.g., territorial autonomy, recognition of religious law, or exemptions from rules) should depend not only on the type of the minority group (indigenous peoples/national minorities vis-à-vis migrant minorities), but *also* on the type of the majority (i.e., homeland or migratory).

Deciding which group is of indigenous or migratory origin is an exercise in classification; there is no one-size-fits-all formula, and the classification is often the core of the debate. The question what it means for a group to be "indigenous" is challenging for majorities as it is for minorities. In referring to indigenous minorities, the Venice Commission at the Council of Europe finds that the "time element is one of the essential criteria when it comes to the definition of the term 'indigenous peoples': the latter are the original inhabitants of the land on which they have lived from time immemorial or at least from before the arrival of later settlers" (Venice Commission 2007: 9). There is no fixed timeframe, and the answer is context-dependent. In Europe, people sometimes advance the claim that "we are all descendants of previous waves of immigrants" and, in that sense, countries such as Germany or Italy are seen as no different from Canada or the United States. There may be some truth in this claim, but it is based on a genealogical (or racial) view of political membership. In our framework, what matters is not genealogy but whether the group members share a distinctive history and cultural identity and define themselves as an ethnic group in a Weberian sense.

A similar challenge applies to the reverse question: what does it mean that a minority group is of "migratory origin"? For first-generation migrants, born in another country, this question is easily answered. For the second and further generations, born in the country of immigration of their ancestors, it is once again crucial to distinguish a genealogical (or racial/racist) view of group membership from the cultural view. To the extent that the offspring of immigrants, or even first-generation immigrants, choose to identify with core aspects of the majority culture, they become part of the majority cultural group, regardless of their skin color or of where their own cradle or that of their ancestors stood. It is a matter of choice. To the extent that they choose to retain the cultural identity of the homeland of their ancestors, they cannot claim the same rights for that culture as apply to those who practice the indigenous majority culture. Blood and place of birth are irrelevant in a liberal approach of cultural group membership; what counts is identification.

By adopting this group-differentiated approach, we deviate from the idea, most eloquently defended by Bauböck (Chapter 2, this volume), that all cultural groups should enjoy equal recognition. By contrast, we argue that even the "same" ethnocultural group should receive different levels of recognition and rights depending on the context. Danes – defined as those who speak the Danish language, identify with Danish history and adhere to other Danish values that a majority of contemporary Danes deems central to Danish identity – should enjoy different levels and types of rights depending on where they find themselves and in relation to whom they stand. In descending order, Danes have their strongest claim to cultural recognition and rights in Denmark, where they constitute the historical majority group; followed by Northern Germany, where they are an indigenous national minority; then the United States, where they live as an immigrant community among descendants of other immigrant groups; and finally Greenland, where they live as a minority of descendants of colonizing settlers among the majority of indigenous Inuit. The world of cultural rights is not "flat": history and territorial links matter.

Practical Examples

At the center of majority–minority constellations are three policy areas: immigration, citizenship, and accommodation in the public sphere. Offering a normative assessment for each area will be the focus of separate essays, yet we seek to demonstrate our claim by providing two examples, one relates to the public sphere and the other focuses on immigration policy.

The first example concerns the legitimacy of religious identities of the majority in the public sphere. When it comes to national and indigenous minorities, human rights law requires states to "protect the existence and the national or ethnic, cultural, *religious* and linguistic identity of minorities," and "encourage conditions for the promotion of that identity" (United Nations Declaration on Minority Rights 1992: art. 1), including taking measures "to create favourable conditions to enable persons belonging to minorities to express their characteristics and to develop their culture, language, *religion*, traditions and customs" (art. 4(2)). The European Framework Convention for the Protection of National Minorities (1998) is even more explicit. It requires states to "promote the conditions necessary for persons belonging to national minorities to maintain and develop their culture, and to *preserve* the essential elements of their identity, namely their *religion*, language, traditions and cultural heritage" (art. 5), and to "establish religious institutions, organisations, and associations" (art. 8). When it comes to persons belonging to the majority, however, they have a right to practice and express their religious practices and identities as part of the human rights to freedom of religion – as individuals, not as groups. In fact, the majority is expected, often required, to remain religiously neutral in the public space. Yet, if minorities have a right to preserve their religious identities, why should majorities, on equal conditions, not have such a right? The idea that majority identities should remain neutral, or be universal, while minority groups are allowed to preserve their religious particularity, creates asymmetric political and normative realities (Kaufmann 2019: 516–21).[11] When both the majority and minority are indigenous, the "state identity" can and should include the religious identity of the two groups. However, when the majority is indigenous and the minority is migratory, the majority has stronger claims for maintaining its religious identity as the state/public identity (e.g., religious public symbols and holidays or publicly funded faith schools[12]), as long as that had been the state identity before the arrival of the migratory minority (as, e.g., is the case of England, Greece, and Denmark) and subject to the exercise of religious freedom for members of minority groups, without indoctrination, on a sub-state level.[13]

A second example concerns immigration. Unlike national minorities, which often cannot choose between different ways of life without special cultural privileges, immigrants can choose, and indeed they do choose by moving to a new country. Voluntary migration is exactly this: a choice to adopt a new way of life. Kymlicka (1995: 96) claimed that "In deciding to uproot themselves, immigrants voluntarily relinquish some of the rights that go along with their original national membership." Likewise, Miller (2016: 13) asserted that immigrants cannot "expect to be able to reproduce the inclusive 'societal culture' … of the place they have left. They have joined a society with an existing public culture, and although they can reasonably expect that the culture will over time adjust in ways that recognize their presence, for the moment they must acknowledge its precedence in some domains." Immigrants are expected to accept not only universal values and principles but also cultural particularity of the new society – political institutions, national holidays, and religious heritages; "the contract of integration they have implicitly signed entails that they must respect the practices and institutions that the public culture of the indigenous majority supports" (Miller 2016: 13). Asking immigrants to respect the cultural particularity of the host country is not based on deontological or paternalistic grounds as to what is good for the immigrants, but on the majority's demand for *recognition* of its way of doing things *here*, the prevailing understating of living together in *this* society, "even if this is not particularly to their [immigrants] liking" (Miller 2016: 13). Immigrants may require special accommodations or changes in the majority way of life as a condition for their move – this can be relevant when the majority encourages migrants to move out of self-interest – and may try to bring about a democratic change in the essence of the dominant culture once they live in a society as citizens. However, the majority can seek respect for its cultural particularity, even if it is not universally justified, just as minorities need not provide universal justifications for their cultural way of life as a prerequisite for it to be respected and protected (Walzer 1983b: 62; Miller 2005: 199–204). Even Carens (1992: 25), a strong advocate of open borders, seems to agree that immigration restrictions are permissible if "they are necessary to preserve a distinct culture or way of life." Carens provides the example of Japan:

> It seems reasonable to suppose that many Japanese cherish their distinctive way of life, that they want to preserve it and pass it on to their children because they find that it gives meaning and depth to their lives ... It also seems reasonable to suppose that this distinctive culture and way of life would be profoundly transformed if a significant number of immigrants came to live in Japan. A multicultural Japan would be a very different place. So, limits on new entrants would be necessary to preserve the culture if any significant number of people wanted to immigrate. (Carens 1992: 40)

Cultural Majority *Rights*?

The greatest majority privilege is a democratic regime, since democracy, by its nature, provides inherent priorities to majorities. Very often, what is needed to protect the majority's culture is not more majority rights but fewer minority rights. A concrete majority right may be required in two cases: when the majority, due to internal and external pressures or structural political limitations, cannot protect its culture merely by democratic decision-making, *and* when members of the majority cannot secure their cultural interests, as individuals, or impose a duty on another party, but *only* on the basis of a group right, as a joint collective. In this sense, a right is the legal expression of the cultural interests of individual members as a collective. It entails that their interests are strong enough to be legally recognized subject to some limitations.

Cultural majority rights have two sides. A negative right entails living according to cultural essentials (public holidays, social mores, religious traditions, national lifestyles) within the state and maintaining them without the interference of others, even if it is not to their liking, provided that they do not cause severe harm to others. A positive right further includes a demand for recognition of a group's cultural essentials and provides it with (financial, educational, institutional) means for continuity through generations. Continuity may require preservation of some elements of this culture, maintaining them over time, and may call for development and change, as reinterpretation and recreation are essential for cultural survival. A legal right should protect a group from changes imposed against its will, that is, a right to avoid certain types of unwanted changes by external forces. It may be related to content – think of a constitutional monarchy, the principle of *laïcité*, and Holocaust classes – or form, namely, the process of bringing about a cultural change. It is for the members of the majority to generally decide the content of their cultural essentials, and the process/pace of the change.

Using Kymlicka's typology, cultural majority rights may include *internal* restrictions – "the right of a group to limit the liberty of its own individual members in the name of group solidarity or cultural purity"; and *external* protections – "the right of a group to limit the economic or political power exercised by the larger society over the group, to ensure that the resources and institutions" on which the group depends are not vulnerable to external decisions (Kymlicka 1995: 7). Kymlicka's typology, which applies to cultural minority rights, holds for majority rights, too. *Internal* restrictions can protect a group from the decisions of its members, which, due to a collective action problem, fail to defend their culture. Patten (2020: 10) gives a useful example:

A related phenomenon is the recent "AirBnB-ization" of certain historic European cities, like Barcelona and Florence. No individual decision to rent out an apartment as an AirBnB makes much of a difference to the historic cultural community. So even people who value their historic culture may find it rational to do so. But when large numbers of people do it, the impact may be substantial.

In such a case, the cultural defense may protect a majority from itself, since its members face a collective action problem and fail to cooperate to protect the Florentine way of life (as long as they value it and generally desire to preserve it). Perhaps more important is that each group member, as an individual, also fails, as the interest in protecting the cultural particularity of Florence cannot be an individual right but only a collective right, even if its fulfillment limits the freedom (and property rights) of individual members.[14]

Alongside internal restrictions, *external* protections can provide a shield from forces of the larger society, which, in the case of a majority population, can be sub-national demands, such as cultural minority rights, supra-national powers, such as the European Union, and transnational forces, such as international migration. External protection implies the consideration of cultural majority interests when balancing inter-group demands. For instance, it may recognize a policy outcome that, in the absence of cultural majority rights, could be considered unjust. It can be a *justification* for a certain policy, or an *excuse* to deviate from a particular legal norm – a form of mitigating circumstances.

While these observations are general (quite obviously, the scope of majority rights should be country-specific), the justifications for cultural majority rights are stronger when the majority culture is vulnerable – in these circumstances, the majority's claim resembles the characteristics of a minority group facing internal and external pressures of cultural dilution; when the majority is a homeland (rather than migratory) group; and when the claim is based on universal (rather than particular) values. To these three factors – the nature of the claim, the type of the group, and the degree of vulnerability – one should add the type of the minority group, the nature of its claim, and its cultural vulnerability in order to properly assess majority–minority constellations. Other considerations are the severity of the threat posed to the group culture, the probability of it occurring, and its consequences; the moral value of the culture, its strength and centrality in defining the group identity (e.g., historically rooted modes of life); and the principle of justice: Is cultural protection bringing a more, or less, just society? The central consideration is the *normative* transformation that the majority culture faces due to internal and external reasons, rather than the numerical ratio between the majority and the society outside. Numbers may become central when the majority's ability to enjoy cultural preservation, development, and continuity is connected not only with interests to protect some cultural essentials but also with interests to protect the dominant *status* of being the majority in a given territory or the institutional framework that enables this (e.g., immigration control, public school curriculum, state-funded organizations, territorial rights, and constitutional amendment procedures). Taking into account the rights of *both* minority and majority groups allows us to go beyond a one-sided assessment and consider the full spectrum of the issue.

Conclusion

The rise of multiculturalism has been a significant development in human rights law. At the outset, multiculturalism was a demand for respect, equality, and justice, which later turned into a language of accommodation, diversity, and recognition, mostly for oppressed and marginalized minority groups and as a compensation for the errors of democracy, which prioritizes majorities. Yet, multiculturalism has taken on a life of its own, swinging too far in one direction. Recent years have witnessed the demand for the majority identity to remain neutral in the public sphere and even for political liberalism, the structure that has allowed multiculturalism to flourish, to compete with other cultures in "the marketplace of cultures."[15] This is not just a battle of laws but a battle of founding stories of how to organize societies and live in political communities.

Political theories must keep pace with the times. A good theory is rooted in reality. In view of the developments discussed in this essay, we contend that the point of equilibrium between majority and minority rights needs to be adjusted. In a rapidly changing political reality, the cultural identity of majorities, too, can fade or even disappear. And no group, majority or minority, wishes that its culture only be preserved in a museum. Taylor (1994: 40) rightly says, "if we are concerned with identity, then what is more legitimate than one's aspiration that it never be lost?" But the aspiration that cultural identity will never be lost cannot last forever, as cultures often cease to exist. "The body politic, as well as the human body, begins to die as soon as it is born," Jean-Jacques Rousseau tells us regarding nations. Yet, the body politic differs from the human body. The death of the human body is a matter of nature, but the death of the body politic is a matter of politics (Rousseau 1762: book III, ch. XI).

While we have argued that a normative recognition of majority rights and identities from a liberal perspective can help undercut support for populist versions of majority narratives, this is an auxiliary, pragmatic and strategic, but not the fundamental, normative reason to support majority rights. Even if Joppke and Ziblatt's claim (this volume) that populism is, in essence, rooted in increased socio-economic inequalities and neoliberal policies is correct, this does not disable the normative arguments for majority rights, which are independent of whether or not cultural majority recognition is helpful in defeating populism.

For decades, the topic of minority rights has been examined primarily through the lens of minorities; the specific type of the minority group (indigenous, national, migratory) defines its rights and entitlements. The type of the majority group (homeland, migratory) has been absent from the equation and has rarely affected law and policy. Against this background, majority groups in Europe and North America (and elsewhere) have rebelled against asymmetric identity politics in the sense of "not being given adequate recognition – either by the outside world, in the case of a nation, or by other members of the same society" (Fukuyama 2018: 9). The liberal left has often ignored the cultural demands of majority groups, labeling them (sometimes justly) as racist and populist. By simply dismissing the cultural sentiments of majority groups, liberal scholars "have failed to address the circumstances that have provoked these sentiments" (Judis 2018: 20).

This essay has advanced a more nuanced group-differentiated approach that takes into account the type of both minority and majority groups in order to decide their relative rights. Only by a mutual consideration, can competing demands of majorities and minorities be fairly evaluated. This mutual consideration (and recognition) is crucial for understanding the changing premises in democratic theory and contemporary world politics.

Notes

1 See also Kymlicka (1997: 62): "national minorities are no different from the members of majority nations ... Anglophones in Ontario (or Illinois) are as deeply attached to their language and culture as Francophones in Quebec or the Flemish in Belgium. If the demographics were reversed, and Anglophones in the United States were outnumbered by Francophones or Hispanics, then they, too, would mobilize to gain official recognition and support for their culture ... were their identity to be threatened, national majorities would mobilize in just the same way as minorities."
2 Most democratic systems are hybrids, yet their common denominator is a majority rule. "The people" rule through a majoritarian decision-making process or, to use de Tocqueville's words, "the majority governs in the name of the people" (1835: vol. II, part 2, ch. 1).
3 The privileges of the majority in a democracy are *structural*; they are built into the system and guaranteed by design. Think of voting rules, public institutions (e.g., public schools and state-owned media), legal interpretation (e.g., what counts as "reasonable" and "proportional," "treason," and "rape"), dissolution of political parties whose actions undermine the majority's values, and constitutional entrenchment, which obstructs a future majority from advancing a change of the values and institutions of a past/present majority by democratic contestations.
4 For a detailed account of ten changes that have given rise to majority nationalism, see Orgad 2015: 19–50, 170–78. These changes occur in the patterns of international migration (number, composition, pace), the Western society (demographic shifts, identity crisis, human rights laws, welfare states), and the world (geopolitics, technology, globalization).
5 Ironically, it is at this point – when the majority sense of being a culturally distinctive group faces external pressure and becomes defensive – that the majority is also blamed for being nationalist. This is asymmetric because, when a core feature of the minority culture becomes defensive, it is mostly seen as a morally justified response, rather than "minority nationalism."
6 It seems that Kymlicka does not object to the concept of majorities, but to the assumption that they are, or can become, culturally needy. This is an empirical rather than normative controversy.
7 A similar spirit appears in the Additional Protocol on the Rights of Minorities to the European Convention on Human Rights, Recommendation 1201 (1993), art. 13: "The exercise of the rights and freedoms listed in this protocol fully applies to the persons belonging to the majority in the whole of the state but who constitute a minority in one

or several of its regions" (Parliamentary Assembly 1993). A regional-minority majority can also exist within states. Bouchard (2015: 11) refers to the situation of Canada where "The francophone majority is a minority nation within Canada and a cultural minority on the continent." Bouchard (2011: 441) mentions that "the francophone majority is itself a precarious minority that needs protection in order to ensure its survival and development in the North American environment and in the context of globalization." This may also be the case of Scotland, Wales, and Catalonia.

8 For instance, the demographic changes in the population of the United States as a result of migration are more radical than in Europe, yet the normative change in Europe is seen as more dramatic than in the United States.

9 Huntington (2004: 39–46) distinguishes between "migratory majority" and "settler majority" to claim that America's founders were not "immigrants" (who moved to an already-existing polity) but "settlers" (who established an entirely *new* polity). For him, only groups who later joined the Anglo-Protestant majority are "immigrants." From this proposition, he derives the "right" of the majority to require assimilation to its Anglo-Saxon culture from newcomers.

10 We agree with Michael Walzer that, "Most liberal nation-states (think of Norway, France, and the Netherlands as examples) are more like Quebec than Canada. Their governments take an interest in the cultural survival of the majority nation; they don't claim to be neutral with reference to the language, history, literature, calendar, or even the minor mores of the majority" (Walzer 1994: 100).

11 Compare to Miller (2016: 13–14): "in many cases public cultures will bear the imprint of the religion that historically has been dominant in the nation in question. This may take institutional form if the country has an established church, or in some other way gives public recognition to one religion at the expense of others. Under these circumstances, the general obligation that immigrants bear to acknowledge and adapt to the public culture of the receiving society must include an obligation to acknowledge, for public purposes, the precedence of that religion. Clearly, this does not mean that they must convert to the national religion, or give up their own beliefs and practices ... they must acknowledge and adapt only in the sense of recognizing that in matters of public culture, one religion may take precedence, for example where the state recognizes an established church."

12 Such privileges may be restricted only to the indigenous majority and minority groups because they have historically arisen from the desire to

preserve and protect these cultures and do not apply in the same way to immigrant minorities. For instance, having Frisian-language instruction in public schools does not imply that Turks should get that right, too; state funding for Catholic schools does not imply that Muslim schools should have that right.

13 One prerequisite for cultural majority rights is the assurance of cultural minority rights within sub-state units.

14 Patten (2020: 9–10) notes that "Government regulations and restrictions in this kind of context will strike many as a reasonable exercise of the majority's right to protect its culture."

15 In Chapter 8, Moodod places multiculturalism and liberalism on an equal footing and concludes that the liberal state should not prioritize liberalism over other cultures. Moodod presupposes that liberalism is a "culture," which should compete with other cultures, yet does not provide justifications for that or explain the normative implications of this approach. If the dominant "culture" is not liberal, would liberalism still be able to be balanced with other cultures? Would it bring a more or less just society? What if the dialogue between a liberal "culture" and a nonliberal culture ends up with no accepted solution; should the majority tolerate female circumcision and polygamy, two examples that Modood uses?

References

Adams, J. (1787). *A Defence of the Constitutions of Government of the United States of America*. London: John Stockdale. vol. III.

Barry, B. (2001). *Culture and Equality: An Egalitarian Critique of Multiculturalism*. Cambridge: Polity Press.

Berlin, I. (1969). Two Concepts of Liberty. In *Four Essays on Liberty*. Oxford: Oxford University Press, 118–72.

Burke, E. (1790). *Reflections on the Revolution in France: And on the Proceedings in Certain Societies in London Relative to That Event*. Cambridge: Cambridge University Press, 2013.

Bouchard, G. (2011). What Is Interculturalism? *McGill Law Journal*, 56/2: 435–68.

(2015). *Interculturalism: A View from Quebec* (Howard Scott trans.). Toronto: University of Toronto Press.

Carens, J. (1992). Migration and Morality: A Liberal Egalitarian Perspective. In Barry, B. and Goodin, R. E. eds., *Free Movement: Ethical Issues in the Transnational Migration of People and Money*. University Park: Penn State University Press, 25–47.

Constant, B. (1815). *Principles of Politics Applicable to All Governments.* Indianapolis: Liberty Fund, 2013.

Eisenberg, A. (2019). The Rights of National Majorities: Toxic Discourse or Democratic Catharsis? *Ethnicities*, 20/2: 312–30.

Eisenstadt, S. N., & Giesen, B. (1995). The Construction of Collective Identity. *European Journal of Sociology*, 36/1: 72–102.

Fukuyama, F. (2018). *Identity: The Demand for Dignity and the Politics of Resentment.* New York: Picador, Farrar, Straus and Giroux.

Huntington, S. P. (2004). *Who Are We? The Challenges to America's National Identity*. New York: Simon & Schuster.

Jay, J. (1787). Concerning Dangers from Foreign Force and Influence. *Federalist No. 2.*

Judis, J. B. (2018). *The Nationalist Revival: Trade, Immigration, and the Revolt against Globalization*. New York, NY: Columbia Global Reports.

Kaufmann, E. (2019). *Whiteshift: Populism, Immigration, and the Future of White Majorities.* New York: Harry N. Abrams Press.

Koopmans, R. (2018). Cultural Rights of Native Majorities between Universalism and Minority Rights. WZB Berlin Social Science Center, *Discussion Paper* SP VI 2018–106.

Kymlicka, W. (1995). *Multicultural Citizenship: A Liberal Theory of Minority Rights*. Oxford: Clarendon Press.

(1997). The Sources of Nationalism: Commentary on Taylor. In McKim, R. and McMahan, J. eds., *The Morality of Nationalism*. Oxford: Oxford University Press, 56–65.

(2008). The Internationalization of Minority Rights. *International Journal of Constitutional Law*, 6/1: 1–32.

(2009). Categorizing Groups, Categorizing States: Theorizing Minority Rights in a World of Deep Diversity. *Ethics and International Affairs*, 23/4: 371–88.

Nationhood, Multiculturalism and the Ethics of Membership. In *Majorities, Minorities, and the Future of Nationhood* (this volume).

Madison, J. (1787). The Union as a Safeguard against Domestic Faction and Insurrection. *Federalist No. 10.*

Margalit, A., & Halbertal, M. (2004). Liberalism and the Right to Culture. *Social Research*, 71/3: 529–48.

Mill, J. S. (1859). *On Liberty*. New York: Dover Publications, 2002.

Miller, D. (2005). Immigration: The Case for Limits. In Cohen, A. I. and Wellman, C. H. eds., *Contemporary Debates in Applied Ethics*. Malden: Blackwell Publishing, 193–206.

(2016). Majorities and Minarets: Religious Freedom and Public Space. *British Journal of Political Science*, 46/2: 437–56.

Modood, T. (2014). Multiculturalism, Interculturalisms and the Majority. *Journal of Moral Education*, 43/3: 302–15.

Multiculturalism without Privileging Liberalism. In *Majorities, Minorities, and the Future of Nationhood* (this volume).

Orgad, L. (2015). *The Cultural Defense of Nations: A Liberal Theory of Majority Rights*. Oxford: Oxford University Press.

Patten, A. (2020). Populist Multiculturalism: Are There Majority Cultural rights?. *Philosophy and Social Criticism*, 46/5: 1–14.

Raz, J. (1996). Multiculturalism: A Liberal Perspective. In *Ethics in the Public Domain: Essays in the Morality of Law and Politics*. Oxford: Clarendon Press, 170–91.

Rousseau, J.-J. (1762). *On the Social Contract* (G. D. H. Cole, trans.). Mineola: Dover Publications, 2003.

Rubinstein, A. (2017). Unashamed Liberalism: Liberal, Illiberal and Anti-Liberal Minorities. *Public Law*, 2: 270–86.

Safran, W. (1997). Citizenship and Nationality in Democratic Systems: Approaches to Defining and Acquiring Membership in the Political Community. *International Political Science Review*, 18/3: 313–35.

Da Silva, M., & Weinstock, D. M. Reconciling the Cultural Claims of Majorities and Minorities. In *Majorities, Minorities, and the Future of Nationhood* (this volume).

Tamir, Y. The Liberalism of Fear: The Second Coming. In *Majorities, Minorities, and the Future of Nationhood* (this volume).

Taylor, C. (1994). The Politics of Recognition. In Gutmann, A. ed., *Multiculturalism: Examining the Politics of Recognition*. Princeton: Princeton University Press, 1994, 25–73.

(2012). Interculturalism or Multiculturalism? *Philosophy and Social Criticism*, 38/4–5: 413–23.

de Tocqueville, A. (1835). Tyranny of the Majority. In *Democracy in America* (Henry Reeve, trans.), New York: George Adlard, 3rd ed., 255–68.

Volkmann, U. (2017). What Does a Constitution Expect from Immigrants? *German Law Journal*, 18/7: 1641–56.

Walzer, M. (1983a). States and Minorities. In Fried, C. ed., *Minorities: Community and Identity*. Berlin: Springer-Verlag, 219–27.

(1983b) *Spheres of Justice: A Defense of Pluralism and Equality*. New York: Basic Books.

(1994). Comment. In Gutmann, A. ed., *Multiculturalism: Examining the Politics of Recognition*. Princeton: Princeton University Press, 99–103.

Additional Protocol on the Rights of Minorities to the European Convention on Human Rights, Recommendation 1201 (1993).
International Covenant on Civil and Political Rights (ICCPR), December 16, 1966, in force 23 March 1976, 999 U.N.T.S. 171.
Parliamentary Assembly of the Council of Europe, "Official Report" (Forty-Fourth Ordinary Session, Twenty-Second Sitting, February 1, 1993, 22nd Sitting) 620.
UN General Assembly Resolution 47/135, December 18, 1992, on the Declaration on the Rights of Persons Belonging to National or Ethnic, Religious and Linguistic Minorities.
Vademecum of Venice Commission: Opinions and Reports Concerning the Protection of Minorities, CDL-MIN(2007)001, Strasbourg, March 6, 2007.

2 *Are There Any Cultural Majority Rights?*

RAINER BAUBÖCK*

Introduction: Multiculturalism Turned Upside Down

Multiculturalism has been turned upside down. Stated in the 1990s as a theory and policy of cultural minority rights by Iris Marion Young, Charles Taylor, Will Kymlicka, and others, its language of cultural victimhood, oppression, and alienation, and corresponding claims for cultural self-determination, recognition, and protection are now being hijacked by politicians and intellectuals claiming to speak on behalf of national majorities. In India, Hindu nationalism is used as a justification for dismantling the secular constitution and depriving Muslims of access to citizenship. In 2018, the Knesset passed a law declaring Israel to be the nation-state of the Jewish people that cast doubts on the country's commitment to treat its twenty percent Arab/Palestinian minority as equal citizens. In Europe and the United States, right-wing populist parties and leaders have used the language of cultural majority rights when attacking LGBTQ rights and whipping up xenophobia directed at Muslim and Hispanic groups of immigrant origin.[1]

In such a highly politicized context, Ruud Koopmans and Liav Orgad deserve praise for their bold defense of cultural majority rights. They provide an analytical approach to a claim that has hitherto been articulated mostly in the language of populist political rhetoric. And they spell out the kinds of justifications and constraints that could

* I am grateful to Peter Koller, Bouke de Vries, and an anonymous reviewer for helpful written comments on a first draft and to the participants at the April 2019 WZB conference in Berlin, a conference at the Bristol Centre for the Study of Ethnicity and Citizenship in November 2019, and a lecture at the Central European University Vienna in February 2021 where I presented different versions of this chapter. Some of the text of this chapter has been used for an article "Cultural majority rights: Has multiculturalism been turned upside down?" published in *Ethnicities* online first in April 2022.

make demands for cultural majority rights compatible with liberalism. Their goal is not to pitch majority against minority rights but to outline a higher-level theory of cultural group rights that applies to both minorities and majorities and allows for assessing the relative strength of their claims depending on their relations to each other and to the state's territory and history.

I will nevertheless argue – within a liberal democratic framework – that the notion of cultural majority rights is empirically implausible, conceptually incoherent, and normatively indefensible on liberal and democratic grounds. My empirical objection is that, in Western societies, the construction of national majorities has been changing over time and these are today too deeply divided with regard to their cultural identities and attitudes to be considered as distinct groups that could be the bearers of collective rights. Conceptually, from the perspective of democratic theory, national majorities must not be equated with democratic ones. In well-functioning liberal democracies, decisions to establish or protect specific aspects of a public culture are not taken on behalf of national majorities but on behalf of all citizens, and majorities supporting such decisions are formed by ever-changing coalitions. Normatively, I will argue that the three sets of justifications used by Koopmans and Orgad – original ownership or prior occupancy of a territory, self-identification and the demand for recognition, and cultural vulnerability – do not provide sufficiently firm grounds for distinct cultural group rights within liberal states. I suggest an alternative approach that relies on the core values of freedom, equality, and self-government. These values serve to justify cultural freedom rights for everybody, cultural rights for minorities, and powers and duties to establish a pluralistic public culture that includes all citizens. I claim that this covers all cultural rights that can be defended on the basis of liberal and democratic principles. There is no space left for special rights of cultural majorities.

Constructing Cultural Majorities

"Cultural majority rights" is a composite concept, each component of which requires clarification. Let me start by asking: What conception of "culture" and "majority" is implied here? In most uses, as in Koopmans and Orgad's chapter in this volume, the reference is to groups whose members share, and identify with, a common culture, which normally includes the same first language and a set of habits and customs, but is sometimes also characterized by a religious tradition and associated with "racial," that is, phenotypical features. Although the term "majority" overtly refers only to a numerical preponderance within a political territory, it is also assumed that these groups have been historically dominant and that their culture is supported by the state through its public institutions and policies. Where the political territory is an independent state, the group is a national majority, but the concept may also apply at regional or local levels within states. Interestingly, it is virtually never used at supranational levels. There is a discourse on shared European values promoted by the institutions of the European Union and a "Christian Europe" is invoked by populist leaders such as Hungary's Viktor Orbán and Poland's Jarosław Kaczyński. Yet these notions are generally not associated with a distinct European majority population; they are instead regarded as a common denominator or shared feature of the member states' distinct national majority cultures.

As this observation already suggests, cultural majorities do not exist naturally but have been created through nation-building efforts by the states that supposedly now have to protect their rights. As Gest (2020: 6) puts it, "the very idea of a majority is subject to state-driven constructions itself." Theories and comparative historical studies of nationalism pioneered in the 1980s have thoroughly analyzed the process of constructing national majorities (Breuilly 1982; Anderson 1983; Gellner 1983; Hobsbawm 1983; Smith 1991). Once it has been completed, the association of states with a particular national culture and majority population tends to be taken for granted and becomes a banal background feature of public life (Billig 1995). This background assumption can become contested again where rapid demographic changes (high immigration and low fertility of native populations) conjure up the specter of majorities becoming minorities. Yet shifts to a majority–minority society cannot be described as a matter of simple demographic facts about immigration, fertility, race, ethnicity, or religion, but depend on how the majority's group boundaries are defined.

Since majorities have been originally constructed through nation-building, their boundary markers vary between countries, change over time, and can also be radically reconstructed. Even where boundary markers are defined in racial terms, there is a difference between constructing majorities through a binary "not one drop of black blood" rule, as in the United States, or a multi-graded social hierarchy associated with racial features, as in Brazil. Ethnicity and religion are much more malleable than race. In the nineteenth century, the national majority whose culture was promoted in the United States was arguably not just white, but Anglo-Protestant (Gest 2020: 11). If we stick to this historic conception of an American majority culture, then the shift to a majority–minority society is no longer a looming scenario for the future but has already happened sometime in the past and without much fanfare. Yet in the United States, national majorities have been successively "reconstructed" (Gest 2020: 11) to include new waves of immigrants, breaking down religious markers first (Catholics and Jews) and now increasingly also ethnic and racial ones (Hispanics and Asians). Language is in one aspect the most sticky boundary marker of national majorities since very few countries have experienced a change of their dominant national language after independence, but it is also the most inclusive one as, in sufficiently open societies, immigrants tend to adopt the majority language over two or three generations. Huntington's (2004) fear that Spanish could become dominant in Florida and the American Southwest and turn these regions into the United States' Quebec has not been vindicated.

Koopmans and Orgad acknowledge variation in the openness of cultural majorities across national contexts but not within these. They assume that inclusive transformations of national majorities depend on historic patterns of nation-building. Immigrant nations like the United States, Canada, Australia, and New Zealand could adapt their collective identity constructions by incorporating newcomers that were initially defined as alien to the nation. However, European nations are, in their view, built around the culture of majority homeland populations who are less capable of adapting in such ways and also have stronger moral claims to protect their culture against transformative impacts of immigration. Migration historians have challenged the perception that contemporary European nations are really composed of ethnically homogenous populations with historic patterns of settlement inside states' current borders (Lucassen and Lucassen 2009). There is, without doubt, a major difference between European settler states in overseas territories that established their own political institutions after conquering and subjugating indigenous peoples, on the one hand, and European nations that emerged from the constant intermingling of groups marked by ethnic, religious, and language differences within territorial boundaries that often changed over time and rarely matched preexisting group identities, on the other hand. Yet the fact that successful nation-building has created a sense of territorial attachment, national culture, and identity in these latter contexts does not mean that these majorities cannot be transformed once again by contemporary immigration. Take the case of my native Austria, a country that is today proud of its multiethnic Habsburg legacy but whose transformation into a major country of immigration since the second half of the twentieth century is still challenged by parties on the right side of the political spectrum. Immigrants from Turkey in particular are widely regarded as a minority that has been neither invited to become part of an Austrian nation nor has been willing to do so. By contrast, guest workers from Yugoslavia in the 1960s and 1970s and their descendants are today considered almost as Austrian as their Czech predecessors who in the late nineteenth century were the construction workers for the palaces lining Vienna's Ringstraße boulevard and the maids who introduced Czech cuisine into bourgeois households. Austrians of Serbian origin have even become a political constituency that the far-right nativist Freedom Party tries to win over.

In contrast with Koopmans and Orgad's hypothesis that homeland majorities are much more resistant to their own transformation through immigration than settler majorities, Gest's comparison of six historic majority–minority transformations finds that inclusive reconstruction of national majorities has been possible where the state equally enfranchises the newcomer population and where the government's subsequent redefinition of the national identity is inclusive (Gest 2020: 3). This supports expectations that democratic states in Europe have as good a chance as settler states in North America or Oceania to manage majority–minority transitions through reconstructing majorities.

My second empirical observation is that throughout "Western" liberal democracies, the construction of national majority cultures has become hotly contested. The notion of majorities permanently settled in their homelands and embracing a homogenous set of cultural values is invoked by nationalist populists. But these constructions are forcefully rejected by large parts of the very same majorities that these populists claim to represent. As observed by political scientists (Kriesi et al. 2008), the traditional left–right axis that has divided political forces into progressives and conservatives since the French Revolution has been complemented by a globalization divide. A new axis representing openness versus closure runs orthogonally to the left–right distinction and creates a two-dimensional space for democratic politics.

Polarization of attitudes toward immigration, cultural diversity, and sexual minorities indicates that national majorities are deeply divided in their views about what they share as a collective identity and which groups ought to be included or excluded from it. Considering national majorities as stable homeland populations who feel threatened by cultural globalization and immigration and need special rights to preserve their identity thus buys too much into strongly contested populist narratives. These new divisions also run through cultural minorities, but they are not as damaging for their claims as they are for majorities. Whereas divided minorities fragment into subgroups, some of which may still have the same old claims to minority rights, in the case of a divided majority, the very rationale for its claims *qua* majority vanishes. There may still be many cases where national majorities are less divided than they are today in North America and Europe, but then such majorities will not feel threatened in their identity and require special protection for it. Quite paradoxically, the call for special majority rights seems to be strongest where traditional majorities are so divided among themselves that majority support for majority rights has eroded.

The upshot of these observations is that we should not build theories of either majority or minority rights on an essentializing ontology of shared collective identities that may already be shifting or crumbling. What matters normatively is whether individuals are disadvantaged and treated unequally because of their perceived belonging to an ascriptive cultural or ethnic group. From this perspective, the case for cultural majority rights is prima facie much weaker than that for minority rights.

Cultural and Democratic Majorities

If the first move in discourses about cultural majority rights is to wrongly essentialize national majority cultures, the second move consists in conflating these with democratic majorities. Koopmans and Orgad put it like this: "The greatest majority privilege is a democratic regime, since democracy, by its nature, provides inherent priorities to majorities" (Chapter 1, p. 24).

At first glance, this seems a promising strategy. Instead of defending cultural majority rights, where "culture" is the defining attribute of a majority, one could defend instead majority cultural rights, in the sense that democratic majorities can claim among other rights also cultural ones.[2] The conceptual error in this argumentative move lies, however, in failing to realize that majority rule is a purely procedural aspect of democracy that is premised on other more substantive features, such as equal and inclusive citizenship, and free, fair, and competitive elections (Dahl 1989). It is a decision rule stating that when votes are counted, the preferences of *all* members of the polity are better represented when the majority prevails over the minority.

Democratic majorities are not predefined as social groups; prior to democratic procedures, they do not even exist as aggregates of individuals sharing certain political ideas and preferences that can be measured by public opinion surveys. A majority becomes a *democratic* one only as the contingent outcome of a process of deliberation, voting, and decision-making that meets democratic conditions. Among the most important of these is that members of cultural majorities and minorities alike are enfranchised and represented as equal citizens in this process.

The justification of democratic majority rule is thus not that it enables a national or cultural majority to rule over minorities but that it allows taking political decisions in a society characterized by a plurality of divergent interests, identities, and ideologies while representing each citizen as an equal member. In a well-functioning democracy with free and competitive elections, there are no permanent majorities that can be characterized in terms of ascriptive features, such as race or ethnicity; the social composition of democratic majorities will include a broad variety of interest and identity groups and these coalitions will frequently intersect and change over time. Inherent privileges for (national) majorities are thus not at all a *natural* feature of democracy.

Orgad is aware of this. In his 2015 book, *The Cultural Defense of Nations,* he requires that the majority that qualifies for cultural rights must be "not a temporary political majority, represented by a political body, but a more permanent majority, reflected by the values of the constitution. It is a constitutional, rather than an electoral, majority" (Orgad 2015: 205). Yet this move does not resolve the issue as the people from which a democratic constitution draws its authority necessarily includes all citizens as equal individual members and cannot be equated with any permanent majority, such as a dominant ethnic or language group. This does not rule out that the constitution of a plurinational democracy could *also* recognize, at a secondary level, distinct nationalities or ethnic groups either as minorities deserving special protection or as equal co-constitutive collectives of a composite (federated) polity.[3] In neither case must a liberal democratic constitution entrench the prerogatives of a permanent national majority, let alone derive its authority from such a majority.

Such legally entrenched privileges are, however, certainly a *historic* feature of many states emerging from the unhappy marriage between democracy and nationalism. The conflation between national and democratic majorities is therefore not merely a conceptual mistake but has all too often been an institutionalized reality. Where national majorities claim ownership of the state and deny minorities equal citizenship, democracy becomes indeed the rule of ethno-cultural majorities over minorities. The name for this degenerated version of democracy is ethnocracy.[4]

My point is not that any defense of cultural majority rights must end up as an apology of ethnocracy; it is that such a defense cannot invoke the democratic majority principle because the legitimacy of this principle is premised on the equality of all citizens rather than the rule of a national majority. As I will argue below, democratic majorities do have legitimate powers to shape the content of a state's public culture, but this culture must be inclusive for all citizens and reflect their cultural differences.

Koopmans and Orgad indirectly acknowledge this constraint on democratic majorities:

> A concrete majority right may be required in two cases: when the majority, due to internal and external pressures or structural political limitations, cannot protect its culture merely by democratic decision-making, *and* when members of the majority cannot secure their cultural interests, as individuals, or impose a duty on another party, but *only* on the basis of a group right, as a joint collective. (Chapter 1, p. 25, original emphases)

In other words, if democratic majorities fail to adopt policies that sufficiently protect a majority culture and if individual freedom to practice that culture is not sufficient to keep it alive, then specific cultural majority rights may have to be legislated. This brings us finally to the question of what might justify special group rights for cultural majorities in democracies if their mere demographic weight and voting power does not.

Territorial Roots and Collective Identity Claims as Justifications for Cultural Rights

A major novel contribution of Koopmans and Orgad's chapter is the idea that the strength of majority and minority rights needs to be assessed in a relational framework and that the crucial variable here is a group's rootedness in the territory where it claims rights. In a shorthand version, we might sum up the idea like this: The weaker a group's territorial rootedness compared to another group, the weaker its claims to rights vis-à-vis that group. Homeland groups are those with strong and long-lasting territorial roots, and migratory groups are those with weaker and more recent roots. The strongest case for majority rights emerges thus in contexts where majorities are homeland groups and minorities are migratory groups; the weakest case in the reverse constellation.

This raises a whole series of important questions that I cannot explore at length. A first question concerns the relational framing. Is it really the relation between cultural groups that matters or rather the relation of each group to the state? It may seem natural for Koopmans and Orgad to think that majorities need to grant rights to minorities, who bear the corresponding obligations, but this is only because they think of majorities as owning the state. If the relation between groups were morally symmetrical, it would follow that the power and duty to grant majority rights lies with minorities, which is certainly not what the authors intend. The relation they have in mind must therefore be an indirect one: Cultural minority and majority rights claims both address the state that represents all group members as equal citizens. Why should it then matter whether cultural groups are, or have historically been, associated with demographic majorities? Should not liberal states aim instead at equal recognition of all cultural groups? (Patten 2014).

Koopmans and Orgad's additional distinction between homeland and migratory groups might provide an answer, since it aims to capture precisely different historic relations of groups to the state and its territory. But what grounds the stronger claims of homeland groups – is it original ownership of a territory or prior arrival there? First occupancy of a previously unpopulated territory is widely regarded as justifying property-like claims to the exclusion of others and exclusive use of resources. However, political philosophers have also invoked the idea of original ownership of the earth by all humans as a counterargument that puts limits on the kind of exclusion that is legitimate or that grounds duties of redistributive justice with regard to natural resources (Kant 1795/1991; Pogge 2002; Blake and Risse 2006).

The notion of prior arrival seems more plausible, given that, at some point in history, nearly all "homeland groups" have themselves emerged from migrations and settled in territories that were already populated by others. This seems to be what Koopmans and Orgad have in mind when they write that "descendants of earlier migrants have a weak normative basis for claiming cultural privileges over other immigrant cultures, which happened to arrive later" (Chapter 1, p. 19). Descendants of Anglo-American settlers would, on this account, have stronger claims to cultural privileges than those of Italo-Americans and these again have stronger claims than Hispanic Americans.

I wonder which liberal justification is available for such a distinction. Individuals born and raised in a country have presumably the same relation to that country as their homeland, no matter how many generations earlier one of their ancestors first arrived there. Their cultural identities are shaped by the first language spoken in their families, the religious beliefs and practices of their parents, and the stories and customs they learned from them. Treating them as equal citizens means paying equal respect to their cultural identities and traditions instead of ranking their relative worth on a scale determined by the time of arrival of their ancestors in the territory.

Koopmans and Orgad eventually move away from a justification based on territorial rootedness when writing that "what matters is not genealogy but whether group members share a distinctive history and cultural identity and define themselves as an ethnic group in a Weberian sense" (Chapter 1, p. 21). Yet, as they also acknowledge, this criterion fails to distinguish between majorities and minorities. "The human need for cultural recognition is not the monopoly of some groups and should not be contingent on whether the group is a 'minority' or a 'majority'." Self-identification and the need or demand for recognition must play an important role in any liberal theory of cultural group rights. However, as this applies equally to all groups, it cannot ground any relational group rights between majorities and minorities or homeland and migratory groups. This approach would instead support again Alan Patten's argument for equal recognition of cultural identities that puts all groups on a par and aims to create a level playing field for them by removing disadvantages faced by minorities (Patten 2014).

The problem is that self-identification and a need for recognition are at best a justification for cultural freedoms but not for special group rights that require state support or a devolution of state power to such groups. Self-identification and recognition needs cannot be sufficient to justify cultural majority rights if these are mostly about an allocation of public resources and privileges, such as the establishment of a religion, the adoption of an official language, or the right to select immigrants by their cultural similarity. They are at most a necessary condition, which, as I have argued above, is no longer met where majorities are deeply divided on cultural matters.

I guess, therefore, that Koopmans and Orgad want to combine the two sources of justification. They could argue that self-identification provides a general basis for identifying not only minorities but also majorities as cultural groups with potential claims to rights, and that territorial roots determine the relative strength of their rights claims, and more specifically their right to resist a transformation of their culture through immigration. Given that the former justification is insufficient and the normative foundations of the latter shaky, I do not think that this argument succeeds.

The Vulnerability of Majorities

A third and final justification refers to vulnerability. Drawing on Orgad's (2015) earlier work, the authors apply here a standard argument for cultural minority rights to majorities who, in their view, can be vulnerable, too. Let me briefly consider each of the four types of "vulnerable majorities" they list.

The first are demographically dwindling majorities, typically those in high-immigration and low-fertility societies. Apart from the problem of defining who the majorities are in such societies, as discussed above, the normative question is: What grounds a claim of cultural groups to preserve a demographic majority? Note that, by definition, minorities could not raise such claims. In their case, a demographic vulnerability would refer to an absolute, not a relative decline, and protective rights would kick in at a point where their numbers become so small that they can no longer maintain their languages or cultural practices. So it seems we are considering here a risk of cultural majorities losing privileges which, on the authors' views, are bestowed on them by democracy. The language of "vulnerability" is thus rather misleading, and the normative argument is question-begging.

The second type are regional minority-majorities, that is, national majorities in small states facing a regionally dominant majority population, such as the Baltic states in relation to Russia. The question here is no longer one of internal relations between majorities and minorities within a state, but of an external threat posed by a powerful and larger neighboring state. Koopmans and Orgad argue that in such a context, immigration from the regionally dominant majority is perceived as a danger to the national majority. But then the example is not well chosen, since immigration from Russia to the Baltic states is lower than from European Union member states, controlled through immigration laws, and at levels that hardly raise alarm.[5] The real question is whether the external threat from Russia justifies blocking access to citizenship for the already present ethnic Russian population, as Estonia and Latvia have done after independence. And here I think the answer must be no. National majorities do not have the right to exclude minorities from citizenship, even if these immigrated during a previous unjust regime – at least not for much longer than a few years after independence. Instead of alienating ethnic Russian minorities through exclusion, which has caused some of them to turn to Russia for external support, the Baltic states must aim to turn them into loyal citizens, which will also require minority rights protecting and recognizing their language. What the state can demand in return is that they do not adopt Russian citizenship or call upon Russia as an external protector (Bauböck 2007). While this context does raise questions about minority rights, it hardly justifies cultural majority rights against the minority.

A third type closely resembles the second.[6] Minoritized majorities are those who once were in a subordinate position but have become dominant with a change of borders. In such contexts of "reversed majorities" (Kymlicka 2001: 158), which are frequent in Central and Eastern Europe, national majorities are often reluctant to grant minorities extensive group rights because of historic resentment against their former oppressors and because they fear interference by an external kin state of the minority. Once again, while we may understand the background for these feelings and fears, it is hard to see how they could provide liberal arguments for special cultural majority rights that go beyond the perfectly normal prevalence of national majority languages and traditions in the wider public culture or that justify downgrading the rights of minorities. On the contrary, minority rights seem essential for integrating such societies, while majority rights claims are likely to destabilize them.

Victimized majorities that have suffered persecution and oppression in the past and now finally gained control over a state represent a fourth type. Koopmans and Orgad illustrate it with the cultural claims of the Jewish majority in Israel. In this particular case, the legitimacy of cultural majority rights is derived from the ubiquity of anti-Semitism and the historic uniqueness of the Shoah. While these are strong arguments for a Jewish homeland, it is not clear how – within Koopmans and Orgad's relational framework – they justify Jewish cultural majority rights in a state that is also the homeland of an autochthonous Palestinian population. Why should Palestinians have lesser claims to cultural rights than Jews, given the fact that they were not themselves involved in the historic crimes against Jews in other parts of the world?

The authors could have chosen other examples of historically victimized majorities, such as post-Apartheid South Africa, where the relations between a victimized majority and a privileged minority were overturned, not in demographic terms, but in terms of political power. In spite of the injustice perpetrated against Blacks in the name of white supremacy, the post-Apartheid constitution adopted the narrative of a rainbow nation rather than of cultural majority rights.[7] This is not meant to gloss over the flaws of South Africa's handling of race relations after the transition to democracy, but to illustrate that a history of victimhood does not by itself justify cultural majority rights in contemporary contexts, a point that applies equally to the second, third and fourth type of "vulnerable majorities."

There is a fifth context of vulnerability that is mentioned separately in Koopmans and Orgad's essay. This is the vulnerability of national majority cultures by reason of the rise of a global Anglo-American culture. It is a fact that English has become the global second language, providing huge undeserved advantages to Anglophone countries, for example in attracting international students and faculty members to their academic institutions and in boosting their global digital and entertainment industries (van Parijs 2011). While most states have taken a relaxed attitude or have even embraced and promoted English as a second language for their citizens in order to improve their opportunities in a globalized world, France has pioneered public policies in defense of the French language by purging it of English words and has heavily subsidized French arthouse films and other products of its cultural industries.

Countries with small numbers of native speakers of their official languages can hardly resist the steamroller of global English as a second language, but they can still secure the survival of their national languages as the first ones in their territory if they are ready to invest in their education systems and cultural institutions. Is this an instance of cultural majority rights or rather of the legitimate power of states to shape their own public culture? The former interpretation would imply, first, that Anglophone majorities have lesser claims to cultural majority rights than Francophones and that these again have much weaker claims than Danes who lack any sizable population of native speakers outside their small state. Second, the former interpretation could be invoked as a reason for downgrading or denying the rights of cultural minorities inside the country because of the external pressures its dominant language or culture is facing, whereas the power of liberal democracies to shape their own public culture must be guided as well as constrained by the goal of securing equal citizenship for all.

An Alternative Approach: Cultural Freedom, Equality, and Self-Government[8]

Let me sketch an alternative view of cultural rights that can do without attributing special rights to majorities while still taking into account legitimate concerns of democratic states to maintain a shared public culture. This approach combines three types of cultural rights that reflect different manifestations of culture as an individual good, a social marker, and a public culture and are grounded in and justified by the core values of freedom, equality, and self-government as they apply to liberal democratic states.

The first type are cultural rights derived from freedom of conscience, speech, and association, which are at the heart of catalogs of universal human rights. People must generally be free to speak their native languages, practice their religion, and pursue their cultural customs and traditions in private and public spaces. The corresponding duties of liberal states and other citizens are minimally those of noninterference, but more broadly also include a moral "duty of civility" (Rawls 1993: 217). Going beyond Rawls' focus on the duty to justify the advocacy of principles and policies on grounds of public reasons acceptable to all, I suggest that there is also a moral duty to accept a diversity of cultures and treat cultural identities of others with respect.

The liberal justification for these cultural rights is straightforward. Culture here is understood as an important element of individuals' conception of the good. On this view, a liberal state must be neutral between reasonable conceptions of the good and thus must not privilege a particular one over others (Rawls 1993: 217). These cultural liberties apply to individuals and their voluntary associations, not to ascriptive groups. If we consider culture only as a matter of individual conceptions of the good, there is no justification for any special favors handed out by the state to either minorities or majorities, nor for any distinctions based on a group's rootedness in a territory.

Yet, as noted by Koopmans and Orgad, the codification of cultural rights in Article 27 of the International Covenant on Civil and Political Rights, refers specifically to "ethnic, religious or linguistic minorities" and proclaims that "persons belonging to such minorities shall not be denied the right, in community with the other members of their group, to enjoy their own culture, to profess and practice their own religion, or to use their own language." The idea behind this is not that persons belonging to majorities do not enjoy the same rights, but that these rights create a special duty of states to refrain from coercive assimilation of minorities and to protect them against similar threats to their cultural freedom emerging from social pressure exercised by members of cultural majorities.[9] Cultural minority rights are therefore not merely Hohfeldian "privileges" (Hohfeld 1919), which correspond to the absence of a right of others that minority members refrain from exercising their culture. Even under the minimalist conception of culture as an individual good, states have special duties to protect the cultural freedom of minorities.[10] However, this conception of cultural minority rights is still a rather weak one. As long as we think of such rights as merely securing the pursuit of particular conceptions of the good, the state has no duty to actively support minority groups in the sense of granting them official recognition or providing them with public resources to assist them in maintaining their cultures.

I have suggested above that the exercise of cultural freedoms also entails a duty of civility in intercultural relations. There is a tension here between duties of civility and rights of free speech. Respect for cultural and religious differences requires, for example, refraining from causing unwarranted offense yet also from taking unwarranted offense. At the same time, cultural liberties include freedom of speech, which entails a right to express contentious views that others may rightly regard as offensive. This tension, which is at the heart of contemporary debates about "political correctness" and the "cancel culture," cannot easily be resolved through general principles, but can be mitigated by institutionalizing local norms for particular institutions and social settings (Elster 1992). What counts as permissible free speech that includes a right to offend will vary in the performing arts, in street demonstrations, public and social media, academic institutions, parliaments, courts, or companies.

Rights of a second type are grounded in the value of equal citizenship. From this perspective, cultural differences are no longer just about a plurality of individual conceptions of the good but also mark social, economic, and political hierarchies. Cultural rights of this second type go beyond universal human rights and aim to overcome structural disadvantages faced by individuals (because of their belonging to certain groups) that undermine the promise of equal citizenship in liberal democratic states. These rights are thus premised on shared membership in the political community (which in the case of recent immigrants may be an expectation of future citizenship), and they protect groups of citizens against pervasive discrimination or compensate for entrenched disadvantages.

This justification for special minority rights does not only apply to cultural groups. People with physical or mental disabilities also suffer disadvantages in exercising their citizenship that warrant special rights. Cultural minorities suffer such systemic disadvantages where they are excluded from, or not fully included in nation-building projects. Cultural majority dominance thus provides the test and justification for claims to special cultural minority rights. The mere existence of a formally established religion or an official national language is not per se problematic for cultural freedom, since this does not entail that minorities cannot practice a different religion or use a different language (Modood 2007). It may not even be a disadvantage in terms of minority citizenship if the religious establishment is a mere matter of public ceremonies or if an immigrant group itself is keen to assimilate linguistically and is assisted in doing so. Yet where a dominant religion is taught in public schools without giving the same right to religious minorities, or where the first languages of minorities are not used for communicating with them in the provision of health care services, by the police or in courts, the value of minority citizenship is diminished.

There are many different types of cultural minorities that can suffer relevant disadvantages, ranging from small and dispersed indigenous and ethnic groups to recently arrived immigrants. Numbers, geographical concentration, cultural links to other states, and historical rootedness in the state territory explain differences in the likelihood of minority claims-making and must also be taken into account when assessing the justification of such claims. However, there are no categorical differences between types of minorities with regard to these rights. What matters is not where they come from and when they arrived, but how the disadvantages they suffer affect their standing as equal citizens and their opportunities to exercise their rights.

Such minority rights may also be institutionalized in a number of different ways. They include religious exemptions from public laws (e.g., from motorcycle helmet requirements for Sikhs who must wear turbans, or from Sunday closing laws for shops run by orthodox Jews who cannot keep open on Saturday), via protective rights (e.g., making physical violence or verbal abuse targeting racial or religious minorities an aggravated offense), to accommodation rights (e.g., by providing translation and interpreter services for recent immigrant groups), public support (e.g., by subsidizing minority language teaching), recognition (e.g., by declaring a country or region as officially bilingual), and representation rights (e.g., by lowering representation thresholds for ethnic minority parties, or ensuring descriptive representation of minorities in high public offices). Each of these ways of realizing minority rights has to face its own test of reasonableness and justifiability in terms of equal citizenship and is premised on the fulfillment of citizenship duties by the minority.[11] Apart from this constraint, which is inherent in the very justification for cultural minority rights, they are also limited by the cultural freedoms of all citizens, including those belonging to national majorities, and by similar rights of minorities within minorities. For example, conservative religious minorities have to respect the rights of sexual minorities within their own communities.

For our concern here, the upshot is that the justification of this second type of cultural rights pertains only to minorities and not to majorities. And when it comes to the limits of these minority rights, "the rights of others" are an important constraint, but cultural majorities do not have any special claim to be collectively regarded as the relevant others.

This does not rule out a scenario where, say, white working-class communities in deindustrialized hinterlands in European or North American democracies might raise claims to some cultural minority rights on grounds that their sedentary lifestyle and lack of economic opportunities diminish the value of their citizenship.[12] Yet, when raising such claims, they would no longer be arguing from the privileged position of belonging to a cultural majority. They cannot invoke minority rights without reinventing their group as a minority. Their claims to have become a new minority would have to be considered on the same grounds as those of immigrant groups whose consolidation as disadvantaged ethnic minorities signals a failure of integration policies to secure their equal citizenship.

While the second type of cultural minority rights are generally Hohfeldian claim rights with corresponding positive duties of states and other citizens that go beyond noninterference, the third type can better be understood as self-government powers to shape a public culture.[13]

The core task of the state is to provide all residents in a territory with public goods that cannot be generated through spontaneous exchange or coordination among individuals. These public goods include, amongst others, security, an infrastructure for the economy and for individual mobility, public health, and education. The last of these items makes it clear that states cannot function well if they have to be strictly neutral between all the various aspects of culture that individuals regard as important elements of their conception of the good.

This is most obvious for language. The first language one learns as a child has great emotional value for individual identity and may even shape, in certain ways, how individuals perceive the world. Yet languages are also instruments for social communication and need to be standardized and spread within a territory to enable all residents of a modern state to communicate with each other. States must therefore promote official languages through their education system and in their political institutions. And states receiving immigrants from many different origins cannot possibly be neutral toward an endless variety of first languages spoken by their populations.

If states thus have to determine which language(s) receive official status and promotion, how should these be selected? Instead of proclaiming a right of national majorities to have their languages established at the expense of linguistic minorities, we should think of this question as a democratic power that is constrained by cultural liberties and minority rights. The languages that historically have been spoken by the majority of the native population will naturally be chosen as those to be standardized and spread throughout the territory by public institutions. We do not have to invoke cultural majority rights to justify this choice. Democratic legislators should also be free to deviate from it. What weight Ireland gives to English and Gaelic as its two official languages in national educational curricula is a matter to be decided by parliamentary majorities. Reviving Gaelic as a public language is neither a duty owed to the small minority of native speakers in the Gaeltacht areas of Western Ireland nor does it violate cultural rights of the majority of monolingual Anglophones. It is simply a democratic power of the Dáil Éireann – the Irish Parliament, which has already adopted a Gaelic name for itself – that it can exercise if there is sufficient political support for such a policy. By contrast, if the Canadian government abolished official bilingualism in its federal institutions, this would violate the minority rights of Francophone Canadians.

In federated and plurinational states, the power to establish an official language is exercised by democratic majorities not only at the federal level, but also within autonomous provinces or regions and is constrained by minority rights in the same way, except that regional governments in linguistic minority regions may be obliged to enable their citizens to also speak the federal majority language and federal governments may have to accept affirmative policies for regional minority languages that compensate for disadvantages. This is roughly the arrangement between the federal institutions and Quebec in Canada. Despite occasional crises triggered by centralizing efforts of federal governments or by secessionists in Quebec, it has been remarkably stable. While minority rights at the federal level as well as within

Quebec are essential for this democratic stability, the language of cultural majority rights used by both Anglo-nationalists and Quebec secessionists is precisely what threatens to upset it. The same point can also be stated in the language of duties. If national majorities have a duty to grant territorial autonomy to national minorities, then these minorities have a reciprocal duty to maintain the territorial integrity of a state that enables them to govern themselves and shape the public culture in their homeland (Bauböck 2000, 2019).

Language is not the only aspect of a shared public culture in liberal states. Such states also have particular histories, and it is important that government institutions do not remain neutral between rival interpretations of the country's history. Slavery and racism in the United States, the Holocaust in Germany and Austria, colonialism in many Southern and Western European states, and ethnic cleansing in the history of nearly all nation-states must be continuously examined and reexamined. It is not the role of liberal governments to write official histories, but they must promote the critical study and awareness of these histories as a crucial aspect of civic education in their countries. This is quite different from teaching the glorious history of a dominant national majority. As moments of national pride, liberal states will instead emphasize acts of civic courage and solidarity that have united the country across majority–minority divides.

I do not have enough space to enter here the rocky terrain of debates about secularism and the extent to which a liberal public culture can also promote specific religious majority traditions. The main conclusion from the above considerations is that the public culture of a liberal state must be pluralistic and inclusive and thus should not be regarded as promoting only or even primarily the values and traditions of a cultural majority.

I conclude by considering a question raised by Koopmans and Orgad that allows me to clarify the difference between grounding the power to shape a public culture in the value of democratic self-government or in cultural majority rights. Does the current majority population have a right to select and limit immigration if inflows threaten to overturn the public culture of a country? Let us consider a scenario where *prima facie* the argument for such a right seems very strong. Imagine two neighboring countries with roughly similar institutions of domestic citizenship, an existing agreement on free movement and easy access to naturalization for each other's citizens. To make matters less abstract, let us call them Norway and Sweden.[14] Imagine that for some reason more than half of Sweden's 9.2 million people decide within a short period of time to settle in Norway, whose current population is 4.7 million. Apart from all the other problems such a massive movement would cause, Norwegians could complain that a majority of Swedish-origin voters might try to establish Swedish as the new dominant language in their country. Does not the Norwegian majority, therefore, have a right to limit the inflow of Swedes before they take over the country?

Of course, it should be in the power of current democratic majorities to prevent such a rapid change in the population's composition. However, we do not need cultural majority rights to justify this. Massive immigration of this kind would destroy the intergenerational continuity of the Norwegian people as a whole, with all its current cultural groups, and some continuity is essential for a democratic people to maintain a sense of and desire for self-government. Norwegians could thus rightly claim that, although they individually retain their rights to democratic participation, they would no longer be collectively self-governing if half of the electorate were formed by newcomers. In such a scenario, Swedes would no longer be like immigrants joining a democratic society, but almost like settlers occupying it to impose their rule on the natives, except that Swedes would do so through capturing existing democratic institutions.

If immigration from Sweden were less massive and stretched over several generations, Norwegian society could still be changed profoundly, but Swedish immigrants would blend into that changing society continuously and their children would become the next generation of native Norwegians. Unless they conceive of themselves as an ethnic nation, Norwegians could at no point in this process complain that immigration undermines their right to democratic self-government. Instead of having been minoritized, Norwegian majorities would have been transformed through immigration.

This rather fanciful scenario should also help to clarify a puzzle that has been at the heart of debates about liberal multicultural theory: How can one justify the difference between the thin and weak cultural rights granted by liberal states to immigrant minorities and the thicker powers enjoyed by indigenous peoples and national minorities? Will Kymlicka famously proposed that the reason is that immigrants have voluntarily waived the right to protect their societal culture of origin by leaving their homelands and cannot expect their host country to let them fully re-establish it there (Kymlicka 1995: 95–100). I think there is a better and more straightforward argument. Immigrant and native minorities do not differ with regard to their cultural freedoms and their cultural minority rights differ only contextually. There is, however, a categorical difference between current territorial populations and newcomers when it comes to claims to establish a public culture. Immigrants cannot claim collective powers to do so, or else they would become settlers that destroy the native population's right to self-government. Instead, they enjoy individual claims to citizenship and rights to participate in shaping the public culture of their new home as its citizens.

Conclusion

In my response to Koopmans and Orgad, I have argued that historic national majorities in current liberal democracies are so divided in their cultural attitudes that the notion of cultural majorities becomes increasingly meaningless. I have also pointed out that – unlike cultural majorities – democratic majorities are the contingent outcome of a democratic process of deliberation and decision-making and that the legitimacy of majority rule is itself premised on inclusive citizenship. If democratic majority decisions represent the interests of ethnonational majorities instead of those of all citizens, democracy degenerates into ethnocracy.

Once we abandon an essentialist notion of cultural groups, we start to realize that applying principles of multiculturalism to majorities comes at a paradoxical price: those claiming cultural rights on behalf of groups historically associated with national majorities cannot ground their case on demographic facts or democratic procedures. They must argue instead that some groups that used to belong to historically dominant majorities have become minorities and this is what justifies their claims to cultural protection and rights.

I have then considered three justifications for cultural majority rights in Koopmans and Orgad's essay: territorial rootedness, collective self-identification, and vulnerability. While each of these aspects is relevant, they do not seem to be necessary and sufficient justifications for majority rights even when combined.

In the concluding section, I have sketched an alternative approach to cultural rights that relies on the liberal and democratic values of

Table 2.1 *Three types of cultural rights*

Culture as	Basic Values	Type of Rights	Rights to	Correlating Constraints and Duties
Individual Good	freedom	human rights	freedom of conscience, speech, association	noninterference no coercive assimilation duty of civility
Social Marker	equality	minority rights	exemption protection accommodation recognition support representation	cultural freedoms internal minority rights goal of equal citizenship
Public Good	self-government	territorial powers	shaping a public culture	cultural freedoms minority rights inclusiveness of public culture

freedom, equality, and self-government. Table 2.1 summarizes this argument. It does not provide an easy formula for justifying and limiting minority rights. The three fundamental values can come into conflict with each other. Similarly, the three conceptions of culture as individual good, social marker, and public good are not alternative but complementary to each other, which makes it sometimes difficult to say what the response of a liberal state to a particular rights claim should be. If my argument succeeds, however, there is no need to invoke cultural majority rights in liberal democracies in order to justify the powers of democracies to shape the public culture in their territories. Politically speaking, liberals should also be wary about buying into populist discourses about cultural majority rights that reject the inclusive diversity that is the hallmark of a liberal public culture.

The approach I have presented departs from most liberal theories of multiculturalism by advocating a "deculturalization" of cultural rights. Instead of grounding them in the value of secure belonging to a societal culture (Kymlicka) or of neutrality and equal recognition of cultural groups by the state (Patten), such rights should be derived from the values of individual liberty, equal citizenship and collective self-government. This should make it easier to defend multicultural policies within liberal democracies and it could also help to avoid becoming drawn into unproductive culture wars over identity claims raised on behalf of minorities or majorities.

Notes

1 Anti-Muslim propaganda is a general feature of right-wing populism, whereas there is a divide on LGBTQ rights, which is defended by, for example, Dutch populists, but attacked by Polish and Hungarian ones.

2 Patten (2020) uses the term "majority cultural rights" but still regards a shared culture as an attribute of majorities that can claim such rights under certain limited and exceptional circumstances.

3 The 1840 Treaty of Waitangi, which has been reinterpreted as New Zealand's de facto constitution and which regulates relations between Maori and Pakeha (white) New Zealanders, illustrates a case where both rationales are simultaneously present.

4 In Oren Yiftachel's definition, "ethnocratic regimes promote the expansion of the dominant group in contested territory and its domination of power structures while maintaining a democratic façade" (Yiftachel 2006: 3). I do not think that territorial expansion in a contested territory is a necessary feature for characterizing a regime as ethnocratic. In a wider sense, we can call regimes ethnocratic if they overtly promote or establish the domination of an ethnically defined group over others.

5 See, for example, Statistics Estonia (2020) and Central Statistical Bureau of Latvia (2020).

6 I have therefore changed the sequence. In Koopmans' and Orgad's chapter, victimized majorities are the third type and minoritized majorities the fourth.

7 Patten (2020: 546) discusses post-Apartheid South Africa as a case of legitimate majority cultural rights, arguing that the persistence of stigma and disadvantage against Blacks may justify special recognition and accommodation of Black majority culture(s) on reparative grounds. In my view, the goal of equal citizenship can justify transitional forms of affirmative action to flatten social hierarchies, but not a special right of majorities to establish their previously oppressed cultures in such a way that they become exclusionary rather than open for all citizens.

8 I have first elaborated this typology of cultural rights in Bauböck (2008). Thanks to Peter Koller, who urged me to clarify that the three conceptions of culture I discuss in this section are complementary and not alternative and that minority rights also entail minority duties.

9 The notion of minorities here is not a numerical one. In nondemocratic states, the majority population may be dominated by a cultural or religious minority, as is, for example, currently the case in Syria where a majority of Sunni Muslims is oppressively ruled by a regime representing a Shia sect.
10 See Office of the High Commissioner for Human Rights (1994).
11 This does not rule out a "partial citizenship" status with exemptions from some duties for some self-insulating minorities, such as the Old Order Amish in the United States, who refrain from claiming and exercising many citizenship rights. It casts, however, doubts on exemptions for ultraorthodox Jews if they simultaneously use their voting power to entrench their privileges (Spinner-Halev 1994).
12 See also Patten (2020: 543).
13 Patten (2020: 547–50) suggests that majority cultural rights may exceptionally be justified if they are required to resolve collective actions problems (such as protecting a majority language in a territory where it is rational for majority speakers to switch to a dominant lingua franca) or if they fall within a range of discretion that democratic majorities have to decide on cultural policies. Both of these grounds can be covered under the notion of self-government powers. My disagreement is that I do not regard them as rights of cultural majorities.
14 I borrow this example and some of the text in this paragraph from Bauböck (2009). A similar scenario has more recently been discussed by Yakobson (2016), although with different conclusions.

References

Anderson, B. (1983). *Imagined Communities. Reflections on the Origins and Spread of Nationalism.* London: Verso Editions and New Left Books.

Bauböck, R. (2000). Why Stay Together? A Pluralist Approach to Secession and Federation. In Kymlicka, W. and Norman, W., eds., *Citizenship in Diverse Societies*. Oxford: Oxford University Press, 366–94.

(2007). The Trade-Off between Transnational Citizenship and Political Autonomy. In Faist, T. and Kivisto, P., eds., *Dual Citizenship in Global Perspective*. London: Palgrave Macmillan, 69–91.

(2008). Beyond Culturalism and Statism. Liberal Responses to Diversity. In *EUROSPHERE Working Paper Series* 6: Eurospheres Project.

(2009). Global Justice, Freedom of Movement and Democratic Citizenship. *European Journal of Sociology/Archives Européennes de Sociologie*, 50/1: 1–31.

(2019). A Multilevel Theory of Democratic Secession. *Ethnopolitics*, 18/3: 227–46.

Billig, M. (1995). *Banal Nationalism*. London: Sage.

Blake, M., & Risse, M. (2006). Is There a Human Right to Free Movement? Immigration and Original Ownership of the Earth. *John F. Kennedy School of Government, Faculty Research Working Paper Series* (RWP06-012).

Breuilly, J. (1982). *Nationalism and the State*. Manchester: Manchester University Press.

Central Statistical Bureau of Latvia. (2020). International Long-Term Migration by Country Group, https://data.csb.gov.lv/pxweb/en/iedz/iedz__migr/IBG020.px

Dahl, R. (1989). *Democracy and Its Critics*. New Haven: Yale University Press.

Elster, J. (1992). *Local Justice: How Institutions Allocate Scarce Goods and Necessary Burdens*. Cambridge: Cambridge University Press.

Gellner, E. (1983). *Nations and Nationalism*. Oxford: Blackwell.

Gest, J. (2020). Majority Minority: A Comparative Historical Analysis of Political Responses to Demographic Transformation. *Journal of Ethnic and Migration Studies*, online first.

Hobsbawm, E., & Ranger, T., eds. (1983). *The Invention of Tradition*. Cambridge: Cambridge University Press.

Hohfeld, W. (1919). *Fundamental Legal Conceptions as Applied in Juridical Reasoning*. New Haven: Yale University Press.

Huntington, S. (2004). *Who Are We? The Challenges to Americas National Identity*. New York: Simon and Schuster.

Kant, I. (1795/1991). Perpetual Peace: A Philosophical Sketch. In Reiss, H. S., ed., *Kant: Political Writings*. Cambridge, UK: Cambridge University Press, 93–130.

Kriesi, H., Grande, E., Lachat, R., et al. (2008). *West European Politics in the Age of Globalization*. Cambridge: Cambridge University Press.

Kymlicka, W. (1995). *Multicultural Citizenship. A Liberal Theory of Minority Rights*. Oxford: Oxford University Press.

(2001). Western Political Theory and Ethnic Relations in Eastern Europe. In Kymlicka, W., and Opalski, M. eds., *Can Liberal Pluralism Be Exported? Western Political Theory and Ethnic Relations in Eastern Europe*. Oxford: Oxford University Press, 13–106.

Lucassen, J., & Lucassen, L. (2009). The Mobility Transition Revisited, 1500–1900: What the Case of Europe Can Offer to Global History. *Journal of Global History* 4: 347–77.

Modood, T. (2007). *Multiculturalism*. London: Polity.

Office of the High Commissioner for Human Rights. (1994). CCPR General Comment No. 23: Article 27 (Rights of Minorities).

Orgad, L. (2015). *The Cultural Defense of Nations*. Oxford: Oxford University Press.

Patten, A. (2014). *Equal Recognition. The Moral Foundations of Minority Rights*. Princeton: Princeton University Press.

(2020). Populist Multiculturalism. Are There Majority Cultural Rights? *Philosophy and Social Criticism*, 46/5: 539–52.

Pogge, T. (2002). *World Poverty and Human Rights*. London: Polity.

Rawls, J. (1993). *Political Liberalism*. New York: Columbia University Press.

Smith, A. (1991). *National Identity*. London: Penguin Books.

Spinner-Halev, J. (1994). *The Boundaries of Citizenship. Race, Ethnicity, and Nationality in the Liberal State*. Baltimore: The Johns Hopkins University Press.

Statistics Estonia. (2020). Migration, www.stat.ee/en/find-statistics/statistics-theme/population/migration

van Parijs, P. (2011). *Linguistic Justice for Europe and for the World*. Oxford: Oxford University Press.

Yakobson, A. (2016). The Prince of Denmark Facing Mass Immigration from Germany. *Verfassungsblog*. Berlin, https://verfassungsblog.de/the-prince-of-denmark-facing-mass-immigration-from-germany/

Yiftachel, O. (2006). *Ethnocracy. Land and Identity Politics in Israel/Palestine*. Philadelphia: University of Pennsylvania Press.

3 *Identity Not Culture*

Where Ethnic Majorities Are Disadvantaged

ERIC KAUFMANN

Introduction

People in the West live in increasingly polarized societies. On the one hand, national populism (Eatwell and Goodwin 2018) is an electoral force in almost all Western democracies; increasing the risk that minorities may be demeaned and feel unwelcome. On the other hand, over the past five decades, the cultural-left ideology I term *left-modernism* (Kaufmann 2004) has become the hegemonic paradigm in elite cultural institutions and, since the 1990s, has made inroads into the wider bureaucracy and corporate world. It is also, as I have already argued, a major catalyst for the rise of national populism because it sets narrow limits to discourse for mainstream parties, opening space for political entrepreneurs (Kaufmann 2018a).

Left modernism starts from a good place, seeking to protect minority welfare. At root, this belief system is underpinned by a broader *liberal identity*, a narrative which produces a reflexive warmth and protectiveness towards minorities and suspicion of the majorities that have traditionally oppressed them. This has its origins in the older liberal concern over the "tyranny of the majority" (Koopmans and Orgad, this volume). The liberal identity was required to mobilize social action on behalf of principles of equal rights for historically disadvantaged groups. However, in my estimation, this has now overreached in the cultural sphere, resulting in unequal treatment of identity groups and discrimination against majorities. In the economic and public-cultural realm, the traditional focus on minority rights remains largely valid but this is not the case when it comes to the politics of recognition.

My contention is that Koopmans and Orgad break important ground by raising the question of majority rights. Moreover, I contend that this, rather than questions of multiculturalism, liberal nationalism, or universalist individualism, will be the central question for the normative theory of multiculturalism in the coming half-century. Koopmans and Orgad draw attention to minoritized, regional-minority, and dwindling majorities, suggesting they derive rights from conditions that are analogous to those mooted for national and ethnocultural minorities. They argue that political theory has not been able to respond to concerns thrown up by the current populist moment. I concur with this assessment. The authors set forth a vital research agenda that, in my view, will only grow more urgent. While I applaud most of the authors' contentions, this exercise is more interesting if I pick up on my disagreements. These are as follows:

(1) In common with others in the political theory literature, the authors fail to distinguish "culture" from identity. For most ethnic majorities, culture is not usually the problem, but identity is. At the same time, minorities are disadvantaged in the politico-economic and cultural spheres albeit advantaged in the sphere of ethnic identity recognition.
(2) Minoritized majorities are a subset of a wider problem concerning what political theorists choose to make salient and what they choose to overlook. When it comes to majorities, the dominant outlook truncates the relevant spatial context to nation-states and, on occasion, to sub-state nations, rather than operating below or above this scale, while collapsing the temporal context for majorities to the present. This highly selective perspective creates the normative universe most theorists are comfortable in, but it is a partial and socially constructed tableau.
(3) Indigenousness is important but should not be defined in terms of the first group to inhabit a territory. Rather, it should be based on what portion of identification with ancestry is based on groups with central origin myths in the native territory. This also allows for the indigenization of former migratory groups. It permits indigenousness to vary depending on scale, from national to local.

I begin by outlining the seismic demographic shifts that are occurring this century, the populist response, and the progressive blind spot that prevents many theorists from empathizing with majority ethnic grievances. I then turn to the aforementioned substantive critiques of Koopmans and Orgad's otherwise laudable essay.

Changing Context: Ethno-Demographic Change in the West

Koopmans and Orgad point out that majority rights carry low normative legitimacy, with those advocating for them derided as "racist," "nativist," or "populist." They add that ethno-demographic shifts have altered the terrain on which these discussions take place and that the balance between the concerns of the majority and minorities has swung too far in the direction of the latter.

This is vital for theorists to appreciate. Ethno-demographic projections suggest that composite white majorities will fall below half the population in the United States, New Zealand, and Canada around mid-century. Western Europe will follow by the end of the century, with high-immigration Australia closer to the North American pattern (Kaufmann 2018a: 266–67). For context, the white share in 1960 was 85 percent in the United States, 93 percent in New Zealand, and 97 percent or more in Canada, Australia, and Western Europe. While the racial majority was not coterminous with the ethnic majority in 1960 (Catholics and Jews were outside the ethnic majority in North America, for instance); and the blurring of ethnic boundaries (i.e., many mixed-race people and white Hispanics identify as white) makes it difficult to divine the precise size of future majorities; Koopmans and Orgad are correct to highlight this development as critical.

We have considerable survey-based regression and experimental evidence that shows that immigration levels are significantly connected to populist right support in the West. Priming American whites to think about their group becoming a minority in 2050 makes them more likely to back conservative policies. Britons who are reminded of the ethno-demographic effect of higher immigration levels increase their support for restrictive immigration policies by 20 points, even when this means lower migrant skill levels (Craig and Richeson 2014; Willer et al. 2016; Kaufmann 2018b). While publics greatly overestimate the share of immigrants and minorities, this is as true of minority respondents as whites and is partially a reflection of concern – since emotive issues tend to lead to analogous response errors for similar issues such as crime or police shootings. It should not be read as meaning that information campaigns and education will reduce innumeracy – indeed, experiments that attempt to correct misperceptions by presenting respondents with the actual numbers have not been able to successfully liberalize attitudes (Alba et al. 2005; Hopkins et al. 2016).

It is also worth noting that opinion is relatively numerate with respect to change over time: Nine of ten West European societies studied by Dennison and Geddes (2018) show a significant connection between immigration levels, the salience of immigration among the public, and populist right support between 2005 and 2016. The 2007–2008 economic crisis had no consistent effect on right-populist support, whereas the 2015 European Migrant Crisis had a marked impact in most West European countries and arguably even contributed to the "Leave" side in Britain's Brexit referendum. This is less true for Eastern Europe, though even there, ascendant national populism is found in countries such as Hungary or Poland, which are inside the European Union, proximal to diverse nations and potentially exposed to inflows, rather than countries such as Ukraine or Serbia which are not.

The mistaken contention that diverse places like London did not vote for Brexit and, therefore, that immigration is not the cause of national populism fails to grapple with the fact that immigrants and minorities, as well as professionals, are less likely to vote for populists. Comparing apples to apples (i.e., white working-class Londoners and white working-class rural English voters), Londoners were as likely to vote "Leave" as anyone else. This is not a moral panic conjured out of thin air but something intimately related to actual migration levels. Should immigration decline to low levels (as obtained in Britain prior to 1997), ethnic change will continue but populism is likely to ebb. Yet, given population aging and the pro-migration advocacy of business groups and human rights organizations, national populism may become an endemic feature of Western politics. This is all the more reason to heed Koopmans and Orgad's call to update our ethical frameworks to respond.

Why the Blind Spot?

Political theory, Koopmans and Orgad remark, must respond to these challenges to remain relevant, but some of its practitioners, like Will Kymlicka (this volume), express a perspective that reflects the period of the 1980s and 1990s – when the study of minority rights emerged in political theory – that perceives majorities as "inherently privileged" while minorities are "inherently penalized." Before outlining the problems with Kymlicka's approach, however, it is vital to ask why it has been so difficult for theory to adapt to our rapidly changing reality.

Those characterized by high levels of the psychological trait of openness, which is related to ideological outlook, choose academic and other creative pursuits. Political discrimination is also a contributing factor, with around four in ten social science and humanities (SSH) academics in the United Kingdom, Canada, and United States willing to discriminate against a known "Leave" or Trump supporter for a job, or against a right-leaning grant application. The result is that, among SSH scholars, supporters of the left outnumber those on the right 9:1 in Britain and approximately 14:1 in the United States and Canada. The share of "Leave" voters among SSH academics in Britain is around 10 percent, compared to 52 percent nationally, and in the United States, the share of SSH academics who voted for Trump is below 5 percent. While six in ten Britons want immigration reduced, the share of SSH academics in the United Kingdom who do is 11 percent. Meanwhile, there has been a significant increase in the share of far-left academics in these disciplines in both the United Kingdom and North America in the past two decades (Langbert 2018; Adekoya et al. 2020; Kaufmann 2021).

It is important to distinguish between liberal *identity*, a myth-symbol complex (i.e., Smith 1986) in which connections between events and symbols are affective, and liberal *principles*. In the former case, the minority carries a positive emotional valence and the majority a negative. For instance, white liberal Americans are the only racial-ideological combination that feels more warmly towards outgroups than their racial ingroup (Goldberg 2019). This emotional DNA explains the apparent seamlessness of significant logical contradictions. Transitioning from advocating for the equal *treatment* and individual rights of minorities (i.e., pre-1965 civil rights movement) to advocating a policy such as affirmative action, which abridges individual liberty in the name of attaining equal *results* for minority groups (i.e., Lyndon Johnson's 1965 Howard University speech), is consistent with a liberal identity, but not with liberal principles. It may be that affirmative action is the right policy but it should not be labeled liberal.

A similar attempt to alter the meaning of liberalism is at work in attempts to use "cultural appropriation" or speech codes to silence forms of expression. There is little reflection on how categories of majority and minority, "advantage" and "disadvantage," are in part socially constructed, nor awareness of how liberal principles have been violated. Conservatives suffer from the same biases, but in an environment where one political viewpoint is highly dominant, research suggests that people nudge each other toward one normative pole. For instance, Sunstein (2019) shows that on three-judge panels where all justices are Republican, decisions are more extreme than when a Democratic judge is present, even though Republican judges have the same majority power to render their verdict in both cases.

Asymmetrical Multiculturalism

The progressive blind spot when it comes to majority rights is rooted in a long tradition of what I (2004) term "asymmetrical multiculturalism." The genesis of the contemporary left-modernist gaze is found in Randolph Bourne's 1916 essay *Trans-National America*, in which he urges his fellow WASP Americans to seek out those of immigrant backgrounds to overcome their parochial upbringings and find the "cosmopolitan note." Anglo-Protestants are characterized by Bourne and his 1920s successors as boring, repressed, and unexpressive compared to European minorities or African-Americans with their jazz and dance culture. Bourne celebrates the "Jew who sticks to his faith," and implores immigrants not to become "cultural half-breeds" who have assimilated into the Anglo society (Bourne 1916 [1964]). Though Bourne was influenced by Horace Kallen, who was more consistent and recognized WASPs as a group, it is Bourne's paradigm, which denigrates the majority while lauding minorities, that has instead come to define the liberal identity.

There is an almost uniform pattern among academic theorists in which many writers from an ethnic majority background gravitate to cosmopolitanism (i.e., Jeremy Waldron and Martha Nussbaum) or towards parts of their background untainted by association with the ethnic majority. Martha Nussbaum's description of her "very sterile" WASP New York background is a case in point. Charles Taylor's attachment to his French-Catholic background and similar (to Nussbaum) repudiation of his WASP heritage is another unremarkable instance of this widespread phenomenon (McLemee 2001; Rogers 2008).[1] I term this stance "asymmetrical multiculturalism" (2004) because it embraces a contradictory positive and negative attitude to ethnicity, depending on whether it is borne by a minority or a majority. It juxtaposes exciting modern multiculturalism against the bland and oppressive monocultural past. This embeds a positive conception of the good ("celebrate diversity") rather than the principled, negative-liberal "tolerate diversity," even if you prefer commonality over difference. Given that our predilection for difference or commonality is half hereditary (Morin 2013), this calls for the eradication of people's deep-rooted tastes that differs little from calling upon those who dislike sardines to pretend they like them.

Having said this, analytic political theory has more intellectual diversity (e.g., Tamir, Walzer, Wellman, Miller, Orgad, Koopmans, Modood, and Joppke) – even as these writers are also almost all politically left or liberal – than post-analytic "critical" theory – which was explicitly conceived as a left-wing project and oriented against majority perspectives on society (i.e., Rojas 2007). Even so, the paucity of conservative voices even in mainstream theory should be considered problematic in that greater political diversity would lead to a deeper questioning of readily accepted progressive claims, forcing proponents of established truths to better defend their claims. Evidence for the limited degree of political diversity can be adduced from the fact that a recent study using matched United States voter registration data for a complete sample of registered academics drawn from 51 leading liberal arts colleges found that of 108 academics in critical "studies" fields (i.e., gender, Africana, and peace), 100 percent were Democrats. Even in mainstream disciplines, such as Philosophy, Republicans were outnumbered 18:1by Democrats (Langbert 2018). I reject the notion from standpoint epistemology that only those who come from a community can study it. However, some representation from the vantage point under study is surely important for checking assumptions and strengthening a discipline's understanding of the normative outlook of conservative members of ethnic majorities, who typically comprise between a third and a half of the electorate in many Western countries (i.e., Benedetto et al. 2020). An important role for analytic theorists, I believe, is to maintain distance from critical theories, whose intellectual roots are more political and anti-foundational.

How Multicultural Theory Has Framed the Problem

Nonetheless, even among analytic theorists, as in the rest of academia, the liberal identity is very dominant. This therefore affects how theorists have framed philosophical problems and how they have defined the relevant units of analysis. Accordingly, the problem most have tried to resolve consists of triangulating between the nation-state (i.e., Canada) and sympathetic groups, including ethnocultural minorities (i.e., Black Canadians), indigenous minorities like the First Nations and minority nations such as Quebec or Catalonia. The "solution" that left-liberals such as Kymlicka or Taylor find involves balancing between the state and the three sympathy-evoking categories, whilst treating ethnic majorities such as the French-Canadians of Quebec or the Anglo-assimilated white Canadians of English Canada as unmentionables whose concerns may be safely ignored. Attention is paid to language rights and political autonomy, which are important questions but arguably growing less so. Concurrently, increasingly pressing issues around immigration-led ethnic change, vernacular cultural protection (i.e., proper names and traditions), the narration of history (i.e., statues and school texts) and majority group recognition are either sidestepped or reflexively shelved as questions that obviously must be resolved against the majority group interest.

Meanwhile, relationships among ethnic minorities (i.e., Hispanic attitudes to Blacks or Muslims, Asian mobility compared to other minority groups) are overlooked in favor of what Sakamoto terms the binary white-nonwhite, "majority-minority paradigm" (Martin 2017). This is so even as surveys suggests that minorities are proportionately more likely than whites to be involved in anti-Black discrimination (Ehsan 2021: 31). Minorities who seek to assimilate also do not fit the narrative, and, since the 1960s, have received limited treatment in the literature, though Richard Alba's empirical work is an important exception (Alba 1990; Brubaker 2001). How many normative theorists, for instance, have grappled with the legitimacy of full voluntary "identificational" assimilation (Gordon 1964) into an ethnic majority as a version of the good life?

In some fora, those who contest dearly held tenets consonant with the liberal identity, as I have, expose themselves to repeated attempts by well-organized extremists to undermine their reputations and careers or simply to make their existence difficult. Sakamoto, for instance, because he has criticized the "majority-minority" paradigm, speaks of sociology panel chairs refusing to make eye contact or uttering hostile remarks, backs turned in corridors, and papers which fail to support the narrative of majority discrimination being repeatedly rejected until the offending sections are excised (Martin 2017).

Now, more than ever, reasonable conservative and classical liberal voices need to be heard, and tolerant traditional leftists who engage with them deserve more attention. This forum presents a paradigm case of this, and I commend Ruud Koopmans and Liav Orgad for bringing this diverse group of thinkers together. Orgad, with his groundbreaking *Cultural Defense of Nations* (2015), is emerging as a pioneer of the political theory that will be required to find a workable ethics for the coming era. In the book, he points out that majorities are not recognized in international law, so nations typically defend their ethnic majorities through telling "white lies" that allow them to practice de facto ethnic favoritism – such as Denmark's rule that only spouses over age 24 can join their husbands in Denmark (a deterrent to brides from non-European societies where early marriage is common).

Why Things Are Different Today

Changing "facts on the ground" call for new normative approaches. For instance, in an era of limited voluntary immigration, endemic minority secessionism and insecure borders in Europe, Kohn's (1944) "ethnic-civic" paradigm of nationalism helped explain differences in the character of national identity across societies – though it was too schematic even for the Europe of 1944. It has proven much less useful for understanding life in a period of large-scale, long-distance immigration, majority ethnic decline, and secure borders. Rather than ethnic or civic nations, we have voting blocs in all nations who want slower ethnic change and a smaller, more highly educated segment of the electorate who are comfortable with rapid change and high heterogeneity. Minorities similarly tend to lean towards a pro-change outlook. The key to a lasting settlement will be reaching an accommodation between these conflicting views rather than trying to bludgeon the former into submission through accusations of racism.

Fewer than 10 percent – in many cases as low as single digits – in many Western countries are ethnic nationalists who want zero immigration, oppose interracial marriage, and believe a minority cannot be equal citizens. Yet, with our ethnic-civic totalizing binary, we have no vocabulary for describing someone who believes a nonwhite person is equally British and fully accepts interracial marriage; but at the same time feels that Britain's ethnic composition forms one component of the nation's distinctiveness from other nations, and that the rate of ethnic change is too fast in relation to the rate of ethnic assimilation. Here I use the term "ethno-traditional" as distinct from ethnonationalist (Kaufmann 2019a). The established left-liberal paradigm currently demonizes such a person as an ethnic nationalist, tantamount to a Nazi or Klansman. The liberal identity collapses the nuance and complexity of public attitudes into a totalizing black and white binary.

Classical political theory, developed in an era of low immigration and high ethnic homogeneity (albeit with a religious difference) in the 1700–1965 period, had to be updated for an era of immigration by Kymlicka, Taylor, Iris Young, and others. What is required is a normative theory appropriate for a period of declining ethnic majorities, populism, and increasing political polarization over questions of majority ethnicity and ethno-traditional nationhood. The as yet few academic advocates of majority rights and pro-assimilation minority voices will play an outsized role here, alongside those of fair-minded left-communitarians such as Modood (2014: 307–10). They can articulate the legitimate sentiments of those unsettled by the current dispensation and yet address reasonable concerns for minority rights.

Koopmans and Orgad's Approach

I now turn to the substance of my critique of the generally laudable position articulated by the authors. Their "dwindling majority" category is by far the most pertinent for the present populist moment, so it will be the center of my discussion.

Culture and Identity

As I note elsewhere (Kaufmann 2000), political theorists seem wedded to using the amorphous term "culture" to mean both observable practices, such as speaking a language, and subjective narratives, like identifying as Yoruba. Koopmans and Orgad adopt this convention. But to understand precisely where majorities are advantaged and disadvantaged, we need to cut this Gordian knot. The French language, for example, is in no danger in France, nor English in the United States. The pull of the media and commerce favors the majority, so children of immigrants all linguistically assimilate. We could say the same about major holidays like Christmas and Halloween, though there are some challenges at the edges, i.e., Columbus Day, and this could be challenged with sufficient growth of non-Christian religious minorities. Kymlicka (1995) is correct that first-mover network effects endow the majority with an insuperable advantage. Just as another search engine is unlikely to challenge Google, foreign languages are unlikely to threaten the majority language. The same holds for mass customs like queuing.

The same cannot be said for majority ethnic identity. This entails a process of subjectively identifying with the myth of ancestry, collective memory, and vernacular traditions of the majority group. In Quebec, for instance, French may hold up well through minority linguistic acquisition, but the share of Quebeckers tracing their origins to the 10,000 *habitant* settlers of the early 1600s has fallen from around 80–85 percent in 1960 to 60 percent today, and will drop below 50 percent by 2050 (Gaudreault 2019). It is likely that Quebec's immigrant-origin population will be attached to the civic Quebec nation. But until enough intermarry with ethnic French-Canadians and their descendants, and identify with their French-Canadian lineage, ethnic assimilation will not take place in sufficient quantity to offset demographic change.

In many Western countries we have a situation where immigrants and their descendants undergo the first stages in Gordon's (1964) multi-step assimilation process, including socioeconomic, linguistic and cultural assimilation, but are not moving swiftly enough towards the marital and "identificational" steps to offset the increased identity diversity brought in by immigration. Thus, the share of those who identify with the narrative and myth of descent of the ethnic majority is falling and projected to become a minority in Western countries between 2050 and 2100. Thus, it is in the realm of majority ethnic *identity* – a subjective narrative encompassing genealogy, not so much the "objective" visible majority *culture*, that there is a majority disadvantage that needs to enter the calculus of communitarian political theorists.

Identity Not Culture: When Are Majorities Disadvantaged?

Majorities are not disadvantaged in many spheres, quite the opposite. Field studies, which submit the same resume to prospective employers and only alter the ethnic provenance of a candidate's name, show almost no examples of minorities being favored over whites. While there is a debate over how much of the effect is to do with racial discrimination, class prejudice (given the use of stylized working-class Black first names) or a perception that a person may have lower cultural compatibility, there is no question that ethnic majorities have at least some employment advantage. Muslims appear to come off worst (Adida et al. 2010; Rich 2014).

On the microsocial level, majorities' greater comfort with their own group could lead to lost opportunities for minorities, even if discrimination is "in favor of" in-groups rather than against outgroups – at least so long as majorities remain numerically dominant and powerful within the organizations that control access to prestigious positions and resources. Likewise, on language, major public holidays, and public mores, as noted, majority groups are advantaged and unlikely to need special protection. Multicultural theory remains relevant for some spheres.

Where the calculus shifts is when we move from language to religion. Religion is much more "counter-entropic" (resistant to assimilation) to use Gellner's (1983) term, and thus the religious composition of society is likely to change through immigration-related processes even as its linguistic composition remains largely unaffected. The growth of non-Christian religion (not merely Islam) in a largely secular or Christian society is one example. The United States, for instance, saw its Catholic share increase from 2 percent in the 1820s to around 35 percent by the 1920s. It is one thing to make room for difference, another for a society's central self-conception to be redefined. In the first case, America is majority Protestant, with Protestantism central to the particularity of its national self-concept, even as there is a Catholic minority. In the second, the entire national identity becomes bi-religious in character. The latter represents a more fundamental transformation. The concern among Protestant Americans of the 1920s that their society could be transformed cannot, in my view, be reduced to simple anti-Catholic bigotry, though this was also present.

It is the identity component of majority rights that needs protection rather than culture per se. The question of religion is important mainly because it governs the prospective assimilability of immigrants into Durkheim's *conscience collective* (shared communal beliefs and ideas) of the ethnic majority. Of course, when the ethnic majority came to be redefined from WASP to "white," including Jews and Catholics, between Kennedy's election in 1960 and the 1980s, the perceived problem of the rising Catholic (and, to a lesser extent, Jewish) share fell away (Kaufmann 2004). Yet we cannot assume, as Rainer Baubock does (this volume), that majorities will seamlessly expand their boundaries and redefine themselves. The existence of deeply polyethnic Hawaii, Guyana, Fiji, or Belize, for instance, shows that polycentric societies can crystallize based on waves of migration.

The fact that majorities are divided between a cosmopolitan-liberal subgroup with low ethnic attachment and a high-identifying plurality or majority is also not pertinent. Baubock (this volume) is correct that minorities have stronger attachments than majorities, but the difference is spectral rather than clear-cut. Jardina (2019: 62–65) finds that 36–42 percent of white Americans in 2016 said their racial identity was "very" or "extremely" important to them, with a further 25–31 percent saying it was "moderately" important. Black and Hispanic respondents reported higher levels of racial attachment, with 49–85 percent saying their racial identity was very or extremely important. Likewise, in a 2019 representative YouGov survey I conducted, 45 percent of white Americans attach importance to their racial group compared to 68 percent of nonwhites. For attachment to narrower ethnic groups such as Irish or Thai, the numbers are 58 and 76 percent, respectively (Kaufmann 2019b). In other words, there is a sufficient mass of identifiers among majorities to back an ethnic rights claim – unless we are to insist on 100 percent identification, in which case minorities would also fail the test.

To wit, the "dwindling majority" problem occurs primarily with identity – subjective myths of origin and collective memory – and only to a lesser degree with culture. With regard to cultural practices, it is typically only vernacular culture, such as NASCAR, rodeo or Christmas decoration, that is affected, and even then, only in terms of maintaining a critical mass necessary for the cultural practice. The freedom to produce and consume it is rarely in danger. The oft-discussed examples of official language or public holidays are generally not the issue.

Much of the anti-majority effect is related to the aggregate balance between subjectively defined identity groups in a society as it changes. Ethno-demographic shifts do not prevent the majority from celebrating its traditions, even if it becomes a minority. The effect instead runs through two pathways. The first is an ethnic group's "association with a specific territory" and with the nation to which it gave rise (Smith 1991). As its perceived territorial ecumene changes character, this could undermine a majority ethnic group's attachments or ontological security. Specific neighborhoods such as Five Points, New York (due to Irish arrival in the 1840s), may be lost with only local impact, but this then moves up to the scale of cities like Leicester in Britain or Los Angeles, which were among the first cities in their respective countries to become "majority-minority." Larger units such as US states (i.e., California and Texas) may follow in this transition. This affects majority attachments and existential anxiety. A meta-analysis of quantitative studies of Western countries I co-authored finds that the rate of ethnic change is almost always associated with higher populist right voting and anti-immigration sentiment (Kaufmann and Goodwin 2018). Meanwhile, national media content, advertising and other communication networks underpinning the national "imagined community" change with the demography of their market. It is understandable that a group may wish to slow such change in the hope that sufficient assimilation will take place to partially reduce ethno-territorial dissonance.

Ethno-Traditionalism Is Not Ethnic Nationalism

This must not become a paranoid quest for purity or freezing of time but rather should make space for a mutually negotiated level of diversity, as well as for a flexible and long-term view that acknowledges the likelihood of assimilation. This "liberal ethnicity," based on a loose-bounded view of ethnic community, contrasts with tight-bounded forms that arise due to religious proscriptions against intermarriage, a history of conflict or patrilineal descent rules (Kaufmann 2000; Wimmer 2008). As the majority share declines without being replenished by assimilation, its claims to ethnic identity protection should gain greater weight, especially if the majority's democratic control over the pace of cultural change is undermined. This is because ethnic majorities typically ground their memories, attachments and narratives in the territory of the nation-state, thus the loss of this correspondence poses a greater detriment to the ontological security of its members than to those of diaspora groups whose ontological security is more rooted in a homeland abroad. Where tight ethnic boundaries exist and assimilation is minimal, such as in Northern Ireland, demographics shifts translate fairly readily into changes in the ethnic balance. Thus, claims based on demographic decline should be accorded greater weight in tight-bounded societies unless boundary tightness is being maintained primarily by the declining majority group.

A second pathway runs through national identity, with which those of all ethnic backgrounds tend to identify. Cohen's (1996) notion of "personal nationalism," and my (2016) concept of complexity and nationhood, suggests that different people attach to different symbolic aspects of the nation. In England, for instance, a BBC survey of 20,000 people shows that 85 percent of ethnic majority respondents see the landscape as important for their Englishness compared to 50 percent for minority Britons (BBC 2018). Partisan affiliation also matters, with American, British, and Canadian conservatives much less attached to "diversity" and immigration as symbols of nationhood than their left or liberal counterparts (Leal and Kaufmann 2019).

While progressives are attached to ethnic diversity and multiculturalism as symbols of nationhood, conservatives tend to be fonder of what I term an *ethno-traditional* "majority-minority" ethnic composition. Note that this is not coterminous with Kohn's ethnic nationalism (1944) – in which only members of the ethnic majority can be fully national and thus foreigners must be excluded – a stance held only by the far-right fringe. Ethno-traditional nationalists are also more invested in "everyday nationalist" symbols like accent, landscape, and history than liberal nationalists (Kaufmann 2019a). This is also true of minority conservatives, such as Hispanic and Asian Trump voters, who appear to be as attached to the country's European-Christian heritage as white Trump voters (Kaufmann 2018a). This attachment, and the concomitant desire on behalf of those of any ethnic background to preserve a critical mass of "everyday" symbols such as accent, religion and ethnic composition, is, in my view, a legitimate position compatible with negative liberty.

Notice the difference: it is wrong to exclude people from national membership on the basis of ethnicity, accent, or religion, but it does not follow that it is illegitimate to seek to protect a critical mass of such characteristics through a reduced pace of immigration. One can believe that someone with any accent can be Irish whilst also believing that there is a characteristic Irish accent whose loss – in terms of critical mass – reduces the distinctiveness of Irish national identity. Collapsing the latter claim into a charge of exclusion by eliding the distinction between collective distinguishing properties and individual membership criteria is to commit the fallacy of composition.

Ethnic Majorities Are Not Recognized

We come to the question of recognition, to which Taylor, Fukuyama, and others have drawn attention. This, too, is an identity rather than a cultural issue. Namely, that minority groups' identities are recognized while ethnic majority identity is, to put it mildly, frowned upon. Wherever Euro-American societies are mooted, they are attacked as white supremacist hate organizations. This has the paradoxical effect of scaring all but white supremacists from espousing ethnic majority identity in a self-fulfilling prophecy. Nowhere does one find a discussion of British-Canadians or "Canadian" (the most popular census ancestry choice) Canadians in Canadian multiculturalism discourse or policy. To insist that such people – whose ancestry may embody a blend of different strains – identify as a more acceptably folkloric category, such as Scottish, is to deny recognition to their actual, lived identities.

In France or Germany, the concept of French or German ethnicity is essentially denied. Partly, this stems from republican tradition in France, and partly because members of the ethnic majority only understand themselves through the idiom of nationhood – albeit one in which an ethnic component is deemed a seamless part of a person's national identity. Yet the French or German communities of shared history and ancestry are not coterminous with the nation-states of the same name, which are increasingly defined in creedal or multicultural terms with a critical approach to their past. Indeed, much effort has rightly gone into detaching nations from their ethnic roots so all can feel included. While the *culture* of such nations, such as language or holidays, is that of the majority, the *identity* is not: the myth of ancestry for these nations is polyethnic. In the previous section, I argued that majority cultural dominance opens up space for minority claims, but identity recognition is only accorded to minorities and not majorities, validating majority grievances. In short, there is no space for the recognition of majority ethnic groups *qua* ethnic groups, i.e., for their collective narrative of peoplehood and myth of origin. The ethnic majority are thus disadvantaged by being unrecognized.

Discrimination in Cultural Representation

On the everyday level of high culture and celebrity pop culture, ethnic majorities also experience identity-based disadvantage. Whether as stock villains in films, the object of jokes, or the targets of open hatred from a radical minority within elite institutions, majorities – especially working-class – in the Western world are treated differently from minorities. It is increasingly unacceptable to target minorities but remains *de rigeur* to disparage the majority. I do not claim that hostile statements about the majority are new: anti-WASP pronouncements were common among iconoclastic radical WASP intellectuals like Randolph Bourne in America from the late 1910s (Bourne 1916 [1964]). Yet the scale of the problem is greater today. In radical quarters of academia, which increasingly influence university policy, writing about "the abolition of the white race" and "white lives don't matter" is permissible and even encouraged, whereas a statement such as America being a "colorblind society" or "land of opportunity" is judged to demean minorities (al-Gharbi 2020).

This discursive double-standard is always wrong but may be overlooked when minorities are small, and there are empirically demonstrable risks of allowing minorities to be castigated in sweeping terms. This outlook may also have material consequences when it bleeds into social policy, as where the underperformance of white working-class children, especially boys, in school, and their under-representation at university, garners little concern compared to racial disparities (Coughlan 2020). As ethnic majorities decline, this contradiction becomes increasingly visible. No wonder the far-right seizes on this cultural inequality as an entry point from which they can indoctrinate people with anti-Semitic conspiracy theories such as "white genocide."

There is a further problem of implicit association. Implicit Association Tests show that respondents associate national symbols with majority ethnic characteristics, spotting American images like the United States flag or bald eagle more quickly when paired with white faces than with minority faces (Devos and Banaji 2005). The same implicit association between ethnic majorities and national symbols holds, I would argue, for a nation's history – especially the pre-1960s past when Western nations were highly ethnically homogeneous. This means that denigrating the national past, or contrasting contemporary diversity favorably against a boring "monocultural" past constitutes a critique of the ethnic majority – even if the majority is not named as such. This does not mean the past should not be approached critically, but a treatment that was sensitive to ethnic majority sentiment would proceed in a much more contextualized manner, taking care to balance negatives with positives. After all, if a public institution rendered a one-sided portrayal of British-Pakistani history (oppression of Bangladeshis, Mughal tyranny over Hindus) or the Chinese-Canadian past (Han culture's oppression of women, the genocide of Dzungar Mongols), this would be rightly viewed as an unfair reading of history which fails to take into account people's collective attachments and sensibilities. Here, we find unequal treatment of Western majority ethnic groups compared to minorities.

Minoritized Majorities

Koopmans and Orgad adroitly draw attention to "minoritized majorities," those such as the Estonians or French-Canadian Quebeckers who perceive themselves to be minorities within a wider region but are the ethnic majority inside a nation. This is, however, an incomplete diagnosis of a wider problem in normative theory caused by the influence of the Western liberal identity: the selective narrowing of time-space horizons.

We might, for example, adjust our scope to alternatively cover the globe, a world region like the Middle East, a nation-state, sub-state nation, or locality. Koreans are a majority in certain sections of New Malden, in Greater London, and Jews in parts of the Upper West Side of New York City. Hispanics are the majority ethnic group in Los Angeles County or Miami. Protestants are a minority in the European Union. Globally, those of European origin are a 10 percent minority. What is the relevant unit of analysis?

One could claim that the nation-state is the relevant administrative geography for normative theory since, in practice, this is often where the relationship between individuals, groups, and democratic authority is established. If so, then proscriptions on expressions of ethnic French-Canadian or Scots-Protestant identity cannot be justified. If we include sub-state nations, these groups are no longer minorities in need of protection. Nevertheless, it then becomes difficult to understand why Hispanics in Los Angeles or Miami, ethnic Austro-Germans in South Tyrol, or Kalenjin in the Kenyan Rift Valley are able to continue to claim the status of minorities, with the identity recognition and attendant benefits this entails. Are they not also majorities in their local units who should lose protection? In deciding who is deserving of special rights, contemporary liberal culturalism tends to exclude global and supranational units, always include nation-state units, and sometimes include sub-state provincial units while ignoring local and municipal ones.

The time dimension is equally important. On the one hand, white Americans are a majority of the United States' population. Taking a "goldfish" perspective, in which the past is instantly forgotten, these majorities are demographically advantaged. This ahistorical vantage point is the dominant view in political theory today. On the other hand, white Americans or ethnic French-Canadians in Quebec are both declining groups, from around 80–85 percent of their unit's population in 1960 to a minority by 2050. Indeed, they are declining in absolute terms. Minority groups are, by contrast, on the increase. From a synchronic perspective, white Americans and ethnic French-Canadians are advantaged. From a diachronic point of view, they are disadvantaged. Grasping that demographic growth produces the psychic privilege of optimism while demographic decline induces the predicament of ontological insecurity is an urgent task for normative theory.

A related form of bias concerns the way domination and oppression are constructed. Shall we exclusively focus on the past century or two, or do we go back 500 years, or a millennium? Only in our country, the wider West, or the globe? Jared Diamond writes that agriculturalists and pastoralists, with their immunity to disease and technological advantages, have conquered and displaced hunter-gatherers almost everywhere on earth. British settlement of North America and Australia is one example of this, taking the form of a conquest of indigenous peoples. Yet no attention is paid to the Bantu conquest of San and pygmy hunter-gatherers in Africa, a process which only ended as Afrikaner settlers moved north in southern Africa (Diamond 1997). What are we to make of the imperialism of the Aztecs and Incas, not to mention the ethnic violence carried out by the Iroquois Confederacy or the empires of the Zulu, Comanche, or Maori (Fynn-Paul 2020)? Why consider European colonialism a distinct moral universe, entailing present-day obligations that do not apply to ethnic groups and nations who committed similar infractions but identify with their achievements, i.e., of the Mughal Empire (1526–1857), Ottoman Empire (ending 1914) or Mongol Horde?

Similar selectivity characterizes the way collective trauma is processed by theory. While the claims of the generation that experienced a trauma like Jim Crow, the Holocaust, or Japanese internment is beyond question, this is less straightforward for subsequent generations. Here remembrance and social construction play important roles in reproducing communal traumas, especially where alternative, less traumatic, narratives are available. Armenian identity can, for instance, opt to emphasize the genocide, or contemporary Armenian achievements and public culture. The Irish can flag the traumatic narrative of Famine and British colonialism, or the Celtic Tiger economic miracle and Irish literature. The risks of granting nobility to traumatic identity narratives also must be factored into theory. Indeed, a focus on competitive trauma fuels ethnic conflicts such as in Israel-Palestine, the former Yugoslavia, or Rwanda. A proper accounting would entail placing all judgments in a world-historical context while applying a consistent set of principles that either hold universally over space-time or justify clear premises for time-space discounting.

Indigenousness

Koopmans and Orgad suggest that group rights claims should apply less to indigenous than migratory ethnic majorities. Indigenousness is recognized in international law. While I concur with the importance of indigenousness for claims, my position is that indigenousness is more of a sliding scale and that indigenization can place the children of settlers or immigrants on an equal ethical footing with older indigenous populations. Here I have some sympathy with Baubock's position (this volume).

Smith notes that one component of the definition of ethnicity is the association with a specific territory, identified as a "homeland" (Smith 1991). Indigenousness is important because part of people's ontological security is connected to holding a majority presence in a "homeland" territory, which helps protect their identity and culture for future generations. This must, of course, be balanced against competing liberal obligations and cannot be permitted to become extreme, cascading into a paranoid quest for ethnic purity. On the other hand, it is also wrong to suggest that the desire for majority presence in a particular homeland is a slippery slope on the way to genocide and ethnic cleansing. This is a favored trope, but cannot be justified by the empirical evidence, where few ethnic "homelands" around the world have degenerated into ethno-puritanism and ethnic chauvinism is no more likely than universalist ideologies to be associated with genocide

(Harff 2003). Only if we select on the dependent variable, arguing from the rare instances of ethnic genocide to a general law, can such a stance be maintained. So far so good for Koopmans and Orgad's claims about indigenous groups.

Where the problem arises is when settlers or immigrant groups begin to bury their dead in a new territory and produce a native-born generation. The new generation may remain wedded to myths of origin elsewhere, and thus function as a diaspora. In this case, the authors' argument that majority rights should apply to indigenes but not migratory groups makes sense. Yet things are rarely so simple. Migratory groups may develop new narratives of settlement origin, which displace diaspora consciousness. In Milton Gordon's terms, they have been "transmuted." This is why it makes little sense to speak of a British-American diaspora. The Anglo-Protestants who made up 80 percent of America's white population in 1776 are now attached to settlement origin myths (Plymouth Rock, Jamestown, Western settlement) rather than the green and pleasant land of England or the Scotch-Irish Presbyterian farming country of County Antrim. The French-Canadians of Quebec, Black Americans, Cajuns of Louisiana, ethnic Taiwanese, Afrikaners, Ulster-Protestants, and other migratory-origin groups are primarily attached to new homelands through settlement origin myths. So too for mixed groups like Cape Coloureds, Mauritian Creoles, Canadian Metis and Mexican Mestizos. One could even make the case for Chinese-American indigenousness in stable, long-established, urban neighborhoods like San Francisco's Chinatown or Mexican-American indigenousness in East Los Angeles.

The risk in neat categorization arises when one group, such as Sinhalese, claims to be original, while those that arrived somewhat later, such as Tamils (perhaps 1000 years ago!), are portrayed as interlopers. To call Ulster Protestants, with their 400-year history, colonial "settlers," as some Irish nationalists have done (to justify territorial claims), is a recipe for conflict and injustice. Better to have a more capacious definition of indigenousness that allows for indigenization and New World origin myths and attachments, placing all on an equal footing. However, there should still be scope for stronger or lesser claims where one group, such as Irish-Americans, has access to a diaspora consciousness and a sense of ontological security derived from a foreign homeland while other groups, such as "American," unhyphenated white, or Black Americans; or Zapotec Mexicans, do not.

Conclusion

I argue that majorities in Western societies are advantaged in some spheres and disadvantaged in others. They have an advantage in the economy, micro-social interactions, language, and public mores. They are disadvantaged when it comes to identity recognition, equal treatment of their ethno-history, and protection from discrimination in elite and pop cultural narratives. The core distinction between *culture*, defined as language and public holidays, and *identity*, in the form of collective memory and myths of ancestry, is central to understanding where majorities are advantaged and disadvantaged. Ethno-demographic change and improvements in minority rights protections over the past half-century have rendered majority concerns more salient in relation to minority ones, and will continue to do so. While there are spheres where attention must continue to prioritize minority protection, demographic change and improved minority protection is exposing a growing blind spot of injustice towards ethnic majorities. The ideal is not to maximize one against the other, but to optimally advance both.

The prominence of what I term "liberal identity" in academia and Western high culture more generally has resulted in a reflexive protectiveness towards minorities and suspicion of majorities. This has proved a useful way of mobilizing against numerous injustices, some of which persist, although it has also led liberals to minimize majority concerns. Yet, this will not make such claims disappear, as the post-2014 populist challenge makes clear. Will normative theory remain relevant outside its academic ecosystem? A big question is whether analytic political theory can successfully update liberal-communitarian theories. Only then can it address the growing majority anxiety whose political expression, national populism, threatens to become a permanent fixture of twenty-first century Western society.

Note

1 Unpublished material from Charles Taylor interview with *Prospect*, in which I participated as one of the interviewers (recording available).

References

Adekoya, R., et al. (2020). *Academic Freedom in the UK*. London: Policy Exchange.

Adida, C. L., et al. (2010). Identifying Barriers to Muslim Integration in France. *Proceedings of the National Academy of Sciences*, 107/52: 22384–90.

Alba, R. (1990). *Ethnic Identity*. New Haven: Yale University Press.

Alba, R., et al. (2005). A Distorted Nation: Perceptions of Racial/Ethnic Group Sizes and Attitudes toward Immigrants and Other Minorities. *Social Forces*, 84/2: 901–19.

al-Gharbi, M. (2020). Who Gets to Define What's "Racist?" *Contexts*, May 15.

BBC. (2018). BBC/YouGov Englishness Survey. March, 9–26.

Benedetto, G., et al. (2020). The Rise and Fall of Social Democracy, 1918–2017. *American Political Science Review*, 114/3: 928–39.

Bourne, R. S. ([1916] 1964). Trans-National America. In Resek, C., ed., *War and the Intellectuals: Collected Essays, 1915–1919*. New York: Harper Torchbooks, 107–23.

Brubaker, R. (2001). The Return of Assimilation? Changing Perspectives on Immigration and its Sequels in France, Germany and the United States. *Ethnic and Racial Studies*, 24/4: 531–48.

Cohen, A. P. (1996). Personal Nationalism: A Scottish View of Some Rites, Rights, and Wrongs. *American Ethnologist*, 23/4: 802–15.

Coughlan, S. (2020). University Entrance: The "Taboo" About Who Doesn't Go. BBC, September 27.

Craig, M. A. & Richeson, J. A. (2014). More Diverse Yet Less Tolerant? How the Increasingly Diverse Racial Landscape Affects White Americans' Racial Attitudes. *Personality and Social Psychology Bulletin*, 40/6: 750–61.

Dennison, J. & Geddes, A. (2018). A Rising Tide? The Salience of Immigration and the Rise of Anti-Immigration Political Parties in Western Europe. *The Political Quarterly*, 90/1: 107–16.

Devos, T., & Banaji, M. R. (2005). American = White? *Journal of Personality and Social Psychology*, 88/3: 447.

Diamond, J. (1997). *Guns, Germs, and Steel: The Fates of Human Societies*. New York, London: W. W. Norton & Co.

Eatwell, R., & Goodwin, M. (2018). *National Populism: The Revolt against Liberal Democracy*. UK: Penguin.

Ehsan, R. (2021). Race, Identity, and BLM: What the UK Really Thinks. *Centre on Social & Political Risk, Henry Jackson Society*, February.

Fynn-Paul, J. (2020). The Myth of the "Stolen Country". *Spectator*, September 26.

Gaudreault, C. (2019). The Impact of Immigration on Local Ethnic Groups' Demographic Representativeness: The Case Study of Ethnic French Canadians in Quebec. *Nations and Nationalism*, 26/4: 923–42.

Gellner, E. (1983). *Nations and Nationalism*. Blackwell: Oxford.

Goldberg, Z. (2019). America's White Saviors. *Tablet Magazine*, June 6. www.tabletmag.com/jewish-news-and-politics/284875/americas-white-saviors

Gordon, M. M. (1964). *Assimilation in American Life: The Role of Race, Religion and National Origins*. New York: Oxford University Press.

Harff, B. (2003). No Lessons Learned from the Holocaust? Assessing Risks of Genocide and Political Mass Murder since 1955. *American Political Science Review*, 97/1: 57–73.

Hopkins, D. J., et al. (2016). *The Muted Consequences of Correct Information About Immigration*. Paper presented at American Political Science Association.

Jardina, A. (2019). *White Identity Politics*. Cambridge: Cambridge University Press.

Kaufmann, E. (2000). Liberal Ethnicity: Beyond Liberal Nationalism and Minority Rights. *Ethnic and Racial Studies*, 23/6: 1086–119.

(2004). *The Rise and Fall of Anglo-America: The Decline of Dominant Ethnicity in the United States*. Cambridge, MA: Harvard University Press.

(2018a). *Whiteshift: Populism, Immigration and the Future of White Majorities*. UK: Penguin.

(2018b). Why Culture Is More Important than Skills: Understanding British Public Opinion on Immigration. *LSE British Politics and Policy Blog*, January 30.

(2019a). Ethno-Traditional Nationalism and the Challenge of Immigration. *Nations and Nationalism*, 25/2: 435–48.

(2019b). White Identity and Ethno-Traditional Nationalism in Trump's America. *The Forum*, 17/3: 385–402.

(2021). *Academic Freedom in Crisis*. Los Angeles, CA: Center for the Study of Partisanship and Ideology.

Kaufmann, E., & Goodwin, M. J. (2018). The Diversity Wave: A Meta-analysis of the Native-Born White Response to Ethnic Diversity. *Social Science Research*, 76: 120–31.

Kohn, H. (1944). *The Idea of Nationalism: A Study in Its Origins and Background*. New York: Macmillan.

Kymlicka, W. (1995). *Multicultural Citizenship: A Liberal Theory of Minority Rights*. Oxford: Clarendon Press.

Langbert, M. (2018). Homogenous: The Political Affiliations of Elite Liberal Arts College Faculty. *Academic Questions*, 31/2: 186–97.

Leal, D., & Kaufmann, E. (2019). Timeless Landscape or Diverse Urbanity: Nationhood in the US and England. Paper presented at American Political Science Association, Washington, DC.

Martin, C. (2017). Arthur Sakamoto, Paradigms in Sociology. *Half Hour of Heterodoxy*, October 10.

McLemee, S. (2001). What Makes Martha Nussbaum Run? *The Chronicle of Higher Education*, October 5.

Modood, T. (2014). Multiculturalism, Interculturalisms and the Majority. *Journal of Moral Education,* 43/3: 302–15.

Morin, R. (2013). Study on Twins Suggests Our Political Beliefs May Be Hard-Wired. *Pew Research Center.*

Orgad, L. (2015). *The Cultural Defense of Nations: A Liberal Theory of Majority Rights.* Oxford: Oxford University Press.

Rich, J. (2014). What Do Field Experiments of Discrimination in Markets Tell Us? A Meta Analysis of Studies Conducted since 2000. *IZA Discussion Paper 8514*, October.

Rogers, B. (2008). Charles Taylor Interviewed. *Prospect*, February 29.

Rojas, F. (2007). *From Black Power to Black Studies: How a Radical Social Movement Became an Academic Discipline.* Baltimore: Johns Hopkins University Press.

Smith, A. D. (1986). *The Ethnic Origins of Nations.* Oxford: Blackwell.

(1991). *National Identity.* UK: Penguin.

Sunstein, C. R. (2019). *Conformity: The Power of Social Influences.* New York, NY: NYU Press.

Willer, R., Feinberg, M., & Wetts, R. (2016). Threats to Racial Status Promote Tea Party Support among White Americans, *SSRN Working Paper*, May 4.

Wimmer, A. (2008). The Making and Unmaking of Ethnic Boundaries: A Multilevel Process Theory. *American Journal of Sociology,* 113/4: 970–1022.

4 *Nationhood, Multiculturalism, and the Ethics of Membership*[*]

WILL KYMLICKA

What does justice require in majority–minority relations? Contemporary political philosophers often work with a two-level theory of justice:

(a) Claims we have on each other as human beings. I will call these the obligations of universal humanitarianism, often expressed in the idea of universal human rights.
(b) Claims we have on each other as members of a shared society. I will call these the obligations of membership in particular bounded societies, often expressed in the idea of citizenship rights.

This is a familiar distinction, but it might help to give a simple illustration. As a visitor to the Wissenschaftszentrum Berlin für Sozialforschung (WZB) in Berlin, I have human rights, which I carry with me as I move around the globe, including the right not to be tortured, experimented on, enslaved or treated in ways that are degrading or dehumanizing. However, I do not have membership rights in Germany, such as the right to vote in German elections or the right to access most social benefits, such as public housing.

As the example shows, membership rights require distinguishing insiders from outsiders, and for this reason, some cosmopolitan theorists are suspicious of membership rights. They would prefer a world in which most or all rights attach solely to our status as human beings, with few if any rights tied to social membership. I have discussed this cosmopolitan position elsewhere, but for the purposes of this chapter, I will simply assert that we need a two-level theory of justice. Both

* Thanks to Liav Orgad and Ruud Koopmans for the invitation to WZB, and to the conference audience for their helpful questions. This chapter draws on research done in collaboration with Keith Banting and Allison Harell, and would not have been possible without their expertise and insights. Thanks also to Liav, Ruud and Sue Donaldson for comments on an earlier draft.

shared humanity and social membership are morally salient, each giving rise to distinct claims of justice (Kymlicka 2015). In any event, the current world order rests on a two-level view, and this is likely to remain our political reality for the foreseeable future.

What does this two-level view imply for the evaluation of majority–minority relations? Controversies can arise at both levels. In terms of universal human rights, there may be disagreements over how to interpret rights to asylum for example, or rights to bodily integrity.[1] These debates over universal human rights are important, but I don't think they are the crux of the current public debate. The most politically charged debates – and the most difficult philosophical questions – are around membership rights. In particular, we confront hard questions about (i) who qualifies for membership rights, and (ii) what are the rights and responsibilities of membership? In any event, this will be the focus of my chapter: what do majorities and minorities owe each other at the level of membership claims, rather than at the level of universal human rights.

My analysis of membership rights will proceed in four steps. First, I will argue that debates about membership in Western democracies are fundamentally debates about national membership. The "shared society" that provides the locus for membership claim is typically understood in national terms (Section 4.1). I will then explore whether this link between nationhood and membership provides grounds for privileging the majority national culture (Section 4.2). I will argue on the contrary that it provides grounds for defending minority rights (Section 4.3). More specifically, the fact that membership claims are filtered through the lens of nationhood creates a series of formidable "membership penalties" for minorities (Sections 4.4 and 4.5). I will conclude with some suggestions about how a robust commitment to multiculturalism and minority rights might remedy these membership penalties as part of a more inclusive ethics of membership (Section 4.6).

4.1 The Centrality of Nationhood to Membership Rights

There is no logical necessity why membership rights should be tied to nationhood. Historically, membership rights have been tied to other types of polities: city-states, empires, monarchies, and theocracies. And citizens today have politically salient feelings of membership in units above the nation (e.g., the EU) or below the nation (e.g., cities). But in the contemporary West, membership claims are primarily tied to membership in the nation-state.

The extent to which contemporary Western states are appropriately described as "national" states is controversial. Some people think that since liberal democracy requires states to treat all its members as equal citizens, regardless of their race or religion, they no longer can be said to be based on nationhood. According to Joppke, for example, when states today attempt to describe what it means to be British, German, or French, they end up restating "nationally anonymous" values of freedom, equality, and democracy (Joppke 2004: 253).

That is misleading. It's true that Western democracies have embraced norms of non-discrimination and have rejected certain kinds of racial exclusions and religious hierarchies. However, they nonetheless remain committed to ideologies of nationhood. One way to make this clear is to ask about the units of liberal democracy. Being British, German, or French is not just about having a commitment to liberal democracy, but also about having a moral commitment to enacting liberal democracy within a particular unit – that is, among a particular group of people on a particular territory.

This is not a trivial point. For peaceful politics to be possible, people must agree, not just on principles of liberal democracy but on the unit of liberal democracy. Think about cases where there is no such agreement. Consider Northern Ireland. Both Irish-Catholic republicans and British-Protestant unionists accept liberal-democratic principles, but republicans think that the relevant unit of liberal democracy is Ireland, that the territory and people of Northern Ireland belong with the rest of Ireland as part of a self-governing Irish people. Conversely, unionists think that the relevant unit of liberal democracy is Britain, that the territory and people of Northern Ireland belong with the rest of Britain as part of a self-governing British people. This disagreement has led to political paralysis, and even to violence, not because of a disagreement on the principles of liberal democracy, but because of disagreement on the unit of liberal democracy.

You might think that Northern Ireland is an exception. But nothing in liberal-democratic theory justifies the assumption or expectation that people will have converging preferences on the unit of liberal democracy. On the contrary, all else being equal, liberal-democratic theory would expect us to predict diverging preferences. After all, the core premise of liberal-democratic theory is that people have diverging political preferences – that's why we need democracy – and there's no reason why that wouldn't equally apply to preferences about units as to preferences about policies. In order to be stable, liberal democracies require citizens to exhibit this unusual combination of divergent preferences about policies and convergent preferences about the units within which policies are decided.[2] Yet nothing in liberal-democratic theory entitles us to that assumption.

So why aren't there more cases like Northern Ireland, where people disagree over the unit? The answer is nationhood: most Western democracies have been successful in inculcating ideas of nationhood amongst their citizens. The vast majority of citizens in the vast majority of Western democracies embrace the belief that they form "a people" (among other people), and that as a people, they belong together in a single polity, have territorial rights over the territory of that polity, and that it is right and proper that they govern themselves and their territory. In Rogers Smith's terms, they embrace a "story of peoplehood" that singles out a particular group and a particular territory as the rightful unit of liberal democracy (Smith 2003). Moreover, this is not a momentary or provisional commitment. Rather, the commitment to nationhood is understood as intergenerational, reaching into the past and extending into the indefinite future. Citizens think of themselves as having historically formed a people with rights to govern themselves and their territory, and believe that they will continue to form a people with those rights. As the American pledge of allegiance and French constitution both emphasize, to be French or American is not just to endorse liberal democracy, it is also to think of the French and American people as "indivisible" – as belonging together and forming an enduring "we." Western states have been very successful in inculcating these stories of peoplehood, and of marginalizing or suppressing any competing claims about which people and which territories belong together.[3]

So nationhood plays a vital role in stabilizing democracy by helping to create this (otherwise puzzling) combination of diverging preferences on policy but converging preferences on units. Nationhood is also arguably at the core of the welfare state. To be sure, the welfare state is a complex package of different policies with different justifications. Some aspects of the welfare state are based on universal humanitarianism to alleviate suffering (e.g., duties of rescue); other parts of the welfare state are based on prudential self-interest (pooling of risks).

But other parts of the welfare state have as their goal the recognition and promotion of social membership. Many of the public goods dimensions of the welfare state (parks, museums, and libraries), as well as its more redistributive aspects, are rooted in an ideal of "social justice," and the term here is instructive. Social justice suggests the idea that we share a society, a society that belongs equally to all its members, and the task of the welfare state is to shape social relationships in accordance with the idea of equal membership. In the famous words of T. H. Marshall, the welfare state rests on "a direct sense of community membership based on loyalty to a civilisation that is a common possession" (Marshall 1950: 96). The task of the welfare state is to provide the kinds of public goods and redistributive policies that help to create a society that will be seen as a "common possession" of all its members.

Note how different this is from the moral logic of humanitarianism. It is not a response to suffering or to the denial of human dignity, but rather seeks to enable members to see society as a "common possession." The assumption is that we form a community, that the function of the welfare state is to ensure that everyone feels equally at home in the community, that everyone can equally partake in its social and cultural life and enjoy its civilization, that everyone can feel that they belong to the community, and that the community belongs to them. In this sense, we can say that one key function of the welfare state is to distribute membership goods or *membership stakes*: the welfare state secures what people need to flourish as members of a shared society. Whereas universal human rights recognize and respect us as human beings with inherent dignity, the welfare state empowers us as members of a particular society to enjoy our shared society as a common possession.

But this conception of social justice only makes sense if people do indeed think of themselves as forming a shared society, and moreover, value their shared society and wish to maintain it into the future. It presupposes that people are oriented towards a shared social world, and that they formulate their claims in relation to it.[4] If they do not see themselves as forming a shared society, or do not wish to continue to do so, then the justification for the distinctive obligations of social justice diminishes, leaving us with just the moral logics of universal humanitarianism and prudential self-interest as grounds for the welfare state.[5]

So here again, the question is how do people imagine the boundaries of this shared society? The answer cannot be physical proximity or actual interpersonal interaction. As someone who lives near the American border, I am physically much closer to Americans who live five miles across the St. Lawrence River than I am to Canadians who live in Newfoundland thousands of miles away. I am also much more likely to meet foreign professional colleagues than I am to meet, say, Canadian loggers. The answer, again, is a story of peoplehood, which nurtures a belief that we belong together in a shared society that is a common possession. In Anderson's famous words, nationhood encourages us to imagine that we form the kind of society that generates a "deep horizontal comradeship" with our co-nationals (Anderson 1983: 7).

In short, the moral purpose of the welfare state is not just to respect universal interests in personhood or dignity, but to give people membership stakes in a particular society, and this in turn presupposes that people identify with and orient themselves towards a shared society. Nationhood underpins that identification and orientation. The same sense of belonging together that underpins a consensus on the units of liberal-democratic governance also helps render intelligible the idea of social justice as membership stakes in a shared society.

In these and other ways, liberal democracy requires that citizens be committed, not just to liberal-democratic principles or to universal humanitarianism, but also to an ethic of membership. It requires people to believe that they belong together and that they form the kind of society that generates obligations of social justice. Stories of peoplehood have filled this need. As Tamir (1993) noted, while liberals may not self-identify as nationalists, and indeed may reject the label, their visions of democracy and the welfare state in fact presuppose the successful inculcation, not just of nationally anonymous liberal-democratic principles but of a story of peoplehood.

4.2 Majority Rights?

To recap the argument so far, I've argued that political justice operates at two main levels: universal humanitarianism and membership claims, and that membership claims are primarily defined by (or filtered through) nationhood.[6] How does this bear on the assessment of majority and minority claims? Interestingly, we can use this diagnosis to support either majority rights or minority rights. I will consider both responses in turn.

How can this diagnosis be used to support majority claims? Here's one line of argument: if it is true that liberal democracy rests on the widespread inculcation of ideas of nationhood, then we need to monitor the health of this national identity and work to strengthen it. Canovan (1996) famously said that nationhood is like a battery that powers politics, and that like any battery, it can be more or less depleted or charged. Many commentators worry that the battery of nationhood has been depleted, due to globalization, new technologies, migration, or political correctness, and that we need to recharge it. We need to make our stories of peoplehood more visible or vocal. We may also need more sticks and carrots to encourage people to embrace the story and better tools to monitor how well it is being inculcated.

This appeal to recuperate and revive nationhood is traditionally associated with the right, but an increasing number of voices on the left are also making this argument (Singh 2018; Tamir 2019; Gidron 2018; Mounk 2018). Indeed many people argue that a crucial failure of the contemporary left is that it abandoned the language of nationhood, leaving the right with a monopoly over the interpretation of these stories of peoplehood. What we need, they argue, is an authentic language of left nationalism that draws on the battery of nationhood to support more truly participatory democracy (as against our current plutocracy) and/or more truly solidaristic welfare states (as against neoliberalism).

This appeal has, at first glance, some plausibility. I agree that it was a mistake for the left to abandon the field of nationhood to the right. I also agree that the state has a legitimate role to play in imparting stories of peoplehood. For example, it is a long-standing feature of civics education (for both children and newcomers) to focus not just on nationally anonymous principles of liberal democracy, but also to include the stories of peoplehood that explain how citizens came together to form a national "we," which asserts rights to govern themselves and their territory. I think that is legitimate and appropriate.[7]

However, proponents of this view typically do not simply want to defend long-standing civics education. Rather, they want to deepen the investment in nationhood: to make nationhood more salient or pervasive. And if so, I think this is potentially a mistake. For one thing, I doubt that the battery of nationhood is depleted and in need of recharging. As I said earlier, most states have been remarkably successful in inculcating stories of peoplehood. I do not believe that either elites or masses have disinvested in the nation,[8] and the identification of immigrants with the nation is often remarkably high. In the United Kingdom, for example, identification as "British" is similar (or even higher) amongst immigrants as amongst native-born whites.[9]

So I don't think the national battery is depleted, and I don't think it needs recharging. But perhaps the problem is that these national identities, while present, are too latent or passive, and that they need to be politically *activated* or triggered if they are to do progressive work. Perhaps we need to make these national identities more *salient* in people's everyday lives, that is, increasing the contexts in which people are consciously told or reminded that they are (or should be) "British," "Dutch," or "Danish."

But then we face a different problem. The evidence about the effects of activating national identities – as opposed to simply having national identities – is quite mixed. To be sure, this may be appropriate in moments of crisis or emergency where invoking national identities may be needed to generate particularly high levels of effort and sacrifice. Appeals to British national identity during World War II are widely seen as promoting voluntary compliance with the burdens and restrictions of wartime shortages, rationing, and curfews.

But defenders of a revivified nationalism are not thinking of these exceptional cases. They are rather proposing that national identity be rendered more salient in everyday life. Social psychologists call this the priming of national identity – bringing it to the front of people's minds. There are now several studies done on the impact of priming national identities and the evidence is very mixed. For example, there are studies on the impact of priming national identity on attitudes towards immigrants. In these studies, some respondents are directly asked for their beliefs about the pros and cons of immigration – for example, whether they agree or disagree that immigrants enrich society or take away jobs. Other respondents, however, are asked these question after first having their national identity primed – for example, the experimenters say: "you're Dutch. Do you agree or disagree that immigrants enrich society or take away jobs?" The evidence is that the priming of national identity typically leads to more xenophobic reactions – people who are primed to think of their national identity express more prejudice against immigrants (Sniderman and Hagendoorn 2007).

Note that the difference here is not in their level of national identity or national pride. Since respondents are randomly distributed into the two groups, they are indistinguishable in their average levels of national identity or national pride. The difference is that in the second group, this identity is primed: that is, national identity is called up from the back of people's minds to the front of people's minds. All of us have many different identities and attachments – occupational, family, hobbies, religious – only some of which are primed or activated in specific situations. And it appears that priming or activating national identities when people think about immigration can generate xenophobic responses.

What explains this finding? One possibility is "prototypicality" effects. Studies show that even those Americans who endorse a racially inclusive "civic" conception of nationhood – that is, who support (and vote for) laws that enable immigrants to become citizens – nonetheless think that white Christians are more "prototypically" American than others (Davos and Banaji 2005; Devos and Heng 2009). So there is a distinction, not just between members and non-members, but also between members and prototypical members. And this matters – the evidence suggests that people, in a purely automatic and unconscious way, accord greater weight to the views of those who are seen as prototypical. Priming national identities may trigger these prototypicality effects.

Findings about the priming of national identities may also be related to what social psychologists call "collective psychological ownership." As I noted earlier, stories of peoplehood are not just about cherished identities or attachments, but also about territorial rights – that is, the right of the people to govern what is perceived as "their" territory. Nationhood thereby implicates the psychology of ownership, and with it, what social psychologists call "gatekeeper rights." Priming national identities may encourage citizens to think of themselves primarily as gatekeepers of something they collectively own, and this may lead to more exclusionary attitudes about immigrants (Verkuyten and Martinovic 2017; Brylka et al. 2015).

In these and other ways, it appears that priming national identities can generate illiberal responses. I do not want to overstate this phenomenon. As I said, the evidence is mixed. In Canada, priming national identities does not seem to exacerbate anti-immigrant attitudes (Breton 2015), and in India, priming national identities does not exacerbate anti-Muslim attitudes (Charnysh et al. 2015). And priming national identities may have more beneficial effects in relation to other issues, such as willingness to pay taxes, vote, show concern for the environment, or other "citizenship behaviors" (Qari et al. 2012). So there is no universal law at work here. We do not in fact have a good account of when priming national identities has progressive or regressive effects, in which contexts, for which issues, for which respondents.

But we have enough evidence to at least raise questions about how quickly we can move from the desirability of *having* national identities to the desirability of *activating* these identities. Liberal-democratic welfare states may depend on the broad inculcation of nationhood, but it does not follow that we should be constantly pumping and priming these identities, particularly in contexts of inter-ethnic relations.

How can we make sense of the idea that having national identities serves liberal-democratic goals but that activating these identities may have illiberal effects? One possibility is that nationhood works best when it is implicit, in the back of people's minds, operating in a habitual, unreflective way, but that it can become dangerous (for certain issues, in certain contexts) when it is pushed to the front of people's minds.[10] Following Bourdieu, we might say that nationhood functions well when it is part of the habitus.

This is speculation on my part, but it fits a long line of nationalism scholarship that emphasizes the importance of "banal" or "everyday" nationalism. Recall Billig's famous example of national weather maps (Billig 1995). People see national weather maps on a daily basis, and take such maps for granted. Yet few if any people stop to consciously think of this in "national" terms. When people see a national weather map, they don't consciously think to themselves: "I'm Danish, and it is therefore right and proper that the weather be presented in national terms."[11] They instead simply think "it's getting cold" or "our picnic will be rained out." Watching a weather forecast does not activate national identity in the sense of bringing it into explicit consciousness. Yet, the fact that the weather is presented in national weather maps does, in an unconscious way, operate to reproduce the idea that the Danish people belong together. National weather maps help to create a national habitus: they operate in an unconscious and habitual way, to reflect and reproduce the idea that Danes belong together and form a shared society. In my view, this sort of banal nationalism – the unconscious reproduction of feelings of peoplehood – is arguably more important – and less dangerous – than the conscious priming of national identities.[12]

In short, even if nationhood plays an essential role in liberal democracies, it doesn't follow that we should be ramping up national identities. I don't think the battery of nationhood is depleted, and pumping national identities may just worsen intergroup relations.

4.3 Minority Rights?

In fact, I draw the opposite conclusion: insofar as liberal democracies are built around stories of peoplehood, we need to strengthen the rights of minorities. The dangers of priming national identities, I would argue, are just one small indicator of a much deeper problem with organizing the world along the lines of nationhood, namely that it inherently privileges majorities and disadvantages certain minorities. Whatever story of peoplehood is told in a particular country – whatever story is told about how we came together as a particular people on this particular territory and of why we belong together into the indefinite future – it will inevitably give centrality to the history, language and culture of the historic founding majority, while viewing the history, language and culture of minorities as at best abnormal, and at worst, as a threat to the cohesion or survival of the people.

This is perhaps clearest in the case of Indigenous peoples and historic minorities who were the casualties in the process of the formation of peoplehood: for example, Indigenous peoples in the New World, or sub-state and kin-state minorities in Europe (e.g., German-speakers in Italy), who often had quite different ideas about which territory belonged to which people. At the origins of any story of peoplehood, there was almost always some competing stories of peoplehood that was suppressed (often violently). And these historic cleavages persist, marking these groups as potentially disloyal, as "marked citizens" (Pandey 2006), subject to either assimilation or exclusion, if not persecution, expulsion, or demographic engineering. Nation-states have been particularly harsh on minority groups seen as carriers of a competing story of peoplehood that might contest the territorial rights of the state (Toft 2005).

Stories of peoplehood also put immigrants under a cloud of suspicion. They are less likely to be seen as challenging the territorial rights of the nation (unless they come from a neighboring power with expansionist histories or ambitions, as with ethnic Russians in the Baltics). But as newcomers, they are literally foreign to the prevailing story of peoplehood. They may share universal liberal-democratic principles, but they do not share the particular language, history, and culture that explains why these people belong together on this territory. And insofar as they maintain any commitment to their "foreign" language, history, and culture, this is seen as prima facie evidence of their failure to embrace the story of peoplehood. There may be a process for immigrants to "naturalize," but this has historically been understood as subtractive or assimilationist, that is, immigrants need to renounce their "foreign" language, culture, and history in order to embrace the national language, culture, and history.

The result is to stigmatize any visible expression of immigrants' cultural difference. Imagine that members of the both the majority and an immigrant minority are engaged in some cultural practice that is consistent with human rights (i.e., with the requirements of universal humanitarianism) – speaking its language, celebrating its religious holidays and national heroes, engaging in its traditional forms of arts and leisure, or its rituals of greeting and mourning, and so on. In the case of the majority, the free enjoyment of its culture is always already seen as consistent with the story of peoplehood. Indeed, this is one of the central purposes of peoplehood. In the words of the United Nations, the whole point of the right to self-determination is so people can "freely pursue their economic, social and cultural development." But when immigrant minorities attempt to freely pursue *their* social and cultural development, they are always already subject to suspicion as a threat to national unity or to social cohesion. And so, historically, immigrants – like indigenous people and national minorities – have been told that the only route to inclusion in the national "we" is to renounce their "foreign" identity and culture.

We can see this in recent studies of dual citizenship. When immigrants naturalize, they make a commitment to their new country of residence, but surveys show that native-born citizens do not credit this commitment unless immigrants simultaneously renounce their prior citizenship. Immigrants who maintain their original citizenship are often seen as potentially disloyal, and this leads to reduced support for their right to make political claims (Jasinskaja-Lahti et al. 2019; Kunst et al. 2019). National membership is seen as subtractive – immigrants must renounce their prior attachments and affiliations to be fully accepted.

I won't belabor the point: we all know the long history of exclusionary and assimilationist policies adopted by nation-states towards both new and old minorities. Many commentators argue that the era of nationalism has been uniquely hostile to minorities, and that the shift from empires to nation-states has rendered the status of minorities radically precarious.[13] Indeed, this risk of mistreatment is so severe that many commentators have argued that nationhood cannot be redeemed. They believe that a world structured on the logic of nationhood can never truly accommodate minorities, and that we need to find some post-national alternative to the current world order.

However, for the reasons discussed earlier, I don't see any alternative to the nation-state for the foreseeable future.[14] Moreover, we shouldn't minimize the benefits that nationhood has secured for many people(s), including democratic stability, the welfare state, and indeed self-determination, including the right to "freely pursue their social and cultural development."

However, this long history of mistreatment does have a clear implication for our moral priorities in relation to majority and minority rights. The fundamental priority in terms of justice cannot be to ramp up nation-building, but on the contrary to *constrain* nation-building by minority rights. As I have discussed elsewhere (Kymlicka 1995), these minority rights will take a different form depending on the nature of the minority and the majority. In relation to historic minorities, it may take the form of acknowledging rather than suppressing their alternative stories of peoplehood: e.g., through according territorial rights and self-government rights to Indigenous people and sub-state nations. In relation to immigrants, it may take the form of a package of policies that (i) affirm basic rights to enjoy one's culture and religion in association with other members of the group; (ii) repudiate older subtractive/assimilationist models of integration/naturalization; (iii) strengthen anti-discrimination provisions, including (iv) policies of recognition and accommodation that enable members of minorities to see themselves in the institutions of the larger society and to participate in them without having to hide or deny their identity and cultural difference.[15] All of these are fundamentally protective or defensive rights, that is, they protect minorities from predictable threats of injustice that arise from the state's commitment to nationhood. And as such they are a fundamental requirement of justice in a world of nation-states.

4.4 Asymmetric Multiculturalism?

So far, I've argued that we continue to live in a world organized on the logic of nationhood, and that in such a world, majorities are inherently privileged and minorities are inherently penalized, and hence there is a moral imperative for minority rights. Nothing I've said is particularly new: versions of this dialectic of nation-building and minority rights have been a staple of the multiculturalism literature for several decades.[16]

What is perhaps new in the literature is the claim that we have entered an era of "asymmetric multiculturalism" (Kaufmann 2018). According to some commentators, while minorities may indeed have been treated unjustly in the heyday of majoritarian nationalism, Western societies have embraced multiculturalism so zealously that they have overcompensated for this unfairness, and are now being unfair to majorities. The expression of minority cultural identities is accepted as legitimate and valorized, but the expression of majority cultural identities is seen as illegitimate. There is a recurring rumor, for example, that public schools in Canada are required to celebrate minority religious holidays but are prohibited from celebrating Christmas.[17] And to avoid this sort of asymmetric multiculturalism, the appropriate remedy is to more explicitly assert the cultural rights of the majority (e.g., Koopmans 2018).[18]

There are two different versions of this asymmetric multiculturalism argument that are worth distinguishing. The first argues that while majorities may be privileged with respect to minorities within the state, they may nonetheless be vulnerable in relation to external forces of globalization. For example, they be under pressure to adopt English as the language of higher education, or may be unable to sustain a domestic film industry given the global power of Hollywood. So, both minorities and majorities may face cultural vulnerability. But, it is argued, there is an asymmetry in how international law responds to these threats. International law has enshrined a set of minority rights to protect minority cultural interests from majority nationalism, but international law has not recognized the rights of majorities to protect their cultural interests from globalization.[19]

I agree with the premise of this argument: namely, that globalization can pose a threat to majority cultural interests just as nation-building poses a threat to minority cultural interests. But it is not clear to me that international law does exhibit the alleged asymmetry. States maintain wide latitude to adopt cultural protectionist policies, such as quotas requiring a certain percentage of media be locally produced, or that Hollywood movies be dubbed in the local language. Canada has a long history of adopting such "Canadian content" rules regarding television, radio and cinema, and while American governments have periodically expressed displeasure about this, there is nothing in international law that prohibits them. The protection of domestic languages and cultures against the forces of globalization is accepted as a legitimate aim of states in the exercise of their sovereignty. This may not be formulated in the language of "majority rights," but giving states the right to "freely pursue their economic, social and cultural development" is in effect giving majorities the right to adopt cultural protectionist policies to mitigate the forces of globalization. We may think that states require more latitude to adopt such policies: for example, perhaps we need a stronger or more explicit exemption of domestic cultural industries from certain WTO rules.[20] But it's not clear that the language of "majority rights" is necessary or helpful in making that case. Here, as elsewhere, the more familiar concepts of state sovereignty grounded in the self-determination of peoples can provide the tools needed to protect majority cultural interests. In any event, it is important to emphasize that the right to exempt cultural industries from international trade law are directed against the international community, not against internal minorities. It is international bodies who are the bearers of the duty to respect the right of states to adopt such cultural protection measures.[21]

However, there is a second version of the claim about asymmetric multiculturalism. When Kaufmann coined the term asymmetric multiculturalism, he was not arguing that majorities need the same protection against globalization that minorities have against nation-building. His claim, rather, was that the protection of minority cultures has gone too far. States have over-compensated for any historical injustice done to minorities, and now minority cultures are privileged over the majority culture in public spaces and public institutions. Hence the eternally recurring meme that public schools are required to celebrate minority religious holidays but are prohibited from celebrating Christmas.[22]

In my view, the idea that we have moved to an era of asymmetric multiculturalism is implausible. One reason for skepticism is that some of the alleged examples – including the claim about Canadian public schools being prohibited from celebrating Christmas – turn out to be fabricated by the media.[23] A rigorous review of actual cases in the Quebec context showed that these rumors are often inventions, abetted by sensationalistic media reports,[24] and the same "phoney war" has been documented in the US and UK media.[25]

But there are deeper reasons for being skeptical about Kaufmann's theory of asymmetric multiculturalism. As a matter of basic political science, democracy requires putting together "minimum winning coalitions," and it is difficult to see how any government could be elected on a program of asymmetric multiculturalism. And there is a conceptual reason why minority rights cannot reverse the inequality. Recall the problem: states are grounded in stories of peoplehood. As a result, members of the founding dominant group are always already seen as members of the people, and hence always already authorized to tell the story of peoplehood. Moreover, even when minorities are acknowledged as members, it is still individuals from the dominant group who are seen as "prototypical" members, and hence accorded greater weight. Immigrants, by contrast, have to prove that they are no longer "foreign" and have properly "integrated," and national minorities have to prove they are no longer disloyal carriers of competing projects of nationhood, in order to have any authority in relation to the story of peoplehood. Minority rights can counteract some of this pressure, and create legal space for the safe expression of difference, but they cannot reverse the basic inequality in groups' relationship to the legitimizing power of nationhood. Even in those countries that have taken significant steps towards protecting minorities from the worst excesses of nation-building, expressions of the majority's history, language, religion and culture are still systematically normalized, valorized and supported, while expressions of the minority's culture are systematically questioned and burdened. And if so, then invoking majority rights will not operate to counterbalance an excessive commitment to minority rights, but rather will operate to uphold and exacerbate the built-in privileging of majorities.

So I do not find Kaufmann's version of asymmetric multiculturalism compelling. But this is clearly a matter on which people have diverging perceptions, perhaps rooted in their own local debates. People on all sides of this debate are prone to cherry-picking a single example where minority claims are either ignored by the majority or exalted over the majority, and then building entire theories of minority oppression or asymmetric multiculturalism around them. To make progress it would help if we had some more systematic way of measuring the relative privileging or burdening of majorities and minorities.

4.5 Measuring Membership Penalties

How could we test the claim that minority cultural practices are valorized while majority cultural practices are penalized, or vice-versa? One difficulty we face here is that we lack any clear or well-established indicators or metrics of the legitimacy of majority and minority identities and practices. I suggest that one (partial) route into this question is to look at the deservingness literature. Martin Gilens famously said that

> Politics is often viewed, by elites at least, as a process centered on the question "who gets what." For ordinary Americans, however, politics is more often about "who *deserves* what." (Gilens 1999: 2)

These deservingness judgments are, I believe, a natural place to look to see who is privileged and who is penalized by the prevailing ethics of membership. If I'm right that stories of peoplehood create membership penalties for minority groups, then we should expect these penalties to show up in people's judgments of "who deserves what." Exploring deservingness judgments provides a potential window to see membership penalties in action.

And indeed the literature shows that minorities are often subject to harsh deservingness judgments, although as will see, the explanation for this is contested. Perhaps the most common finding in studies of deservingness judgments is that immigrants are at the bottom of the "deservingness ladder" across the Western democracies in relation to welfare state benefits. When asked about a range of possible beneficiaries of the welfare state – the elderly, single mothers, people who are sick or unemployed, people with disabilities, immigrants – immigrants are ranked last. This is so ubiquitous that van Oorschot calls this "a truly universal element in the popular welfare culture of present Western welfare states" (2006: 25).

Why are immigrants seen as less deserving? The usual explanation draws on a comparison with the case of Blacks in the United States. Studies show that whites view Blacks as less deserving because they are seen as lazy (and hence responsible for their own disadvantage) or as cheating (and hence not truly in need) (Gilens 1999). These are two of the core dimensions of deservingness: lazy versus hard-working; genuine need versus misrepresentation. Since immigrants seem to suffer the same harsh deservingness judgments as Blacks, it has widely been assumed that they too must suffer from stereotypes about laziness or dishonesty.

For a variety of reasons, I have never found this convincing, at least for Canada. Canadians have their share of stereotypes about immigrants, but laziness is not one of them. On the contrary, surveys have consistently shown that most Canadians "agree with the statement that immigrants tend to work harder than people born in Canada" (Environics 2019: 5).

But if the usual explanation focused on need or responsibility is incorrect, why then are immigrants seen as less deserving? My hunch is that deservingness judgments are intimately linked to ideas of membership, and prevailing stories of membership disadvantage minorities. Recall that social justice, including redistributive solidarity, unlike universal humanitarianism, is tied to the idea of a moral commitment to a shared society. And as we've seen, this idea of a "shared society" is typically understood in national terms, in a way that puts members of the dominant group at the prototypical center of this shared society, while putting the burden of proof on minorities to show that they belong at all. If this analysis is correct, then we should expect that members of minority groups, *even if they are not seen as lazy or dishonest*, would still be seen as less deserving because they are seen as less morally committed to the shared society. Moreover, these membership penalties should apply not only to newly arrived immigrant groups, but also to "old" historic minorities – such as Indigenous peoples or the Quebecois – who are seen as carriers of some alternative or competing story of peoplehood.

Surprisingly, this hypothesis has never been tested. The deservingness literature is so focused on perceptions of responsibility and need that the impact of membership perceptions has never been directly tested. So,

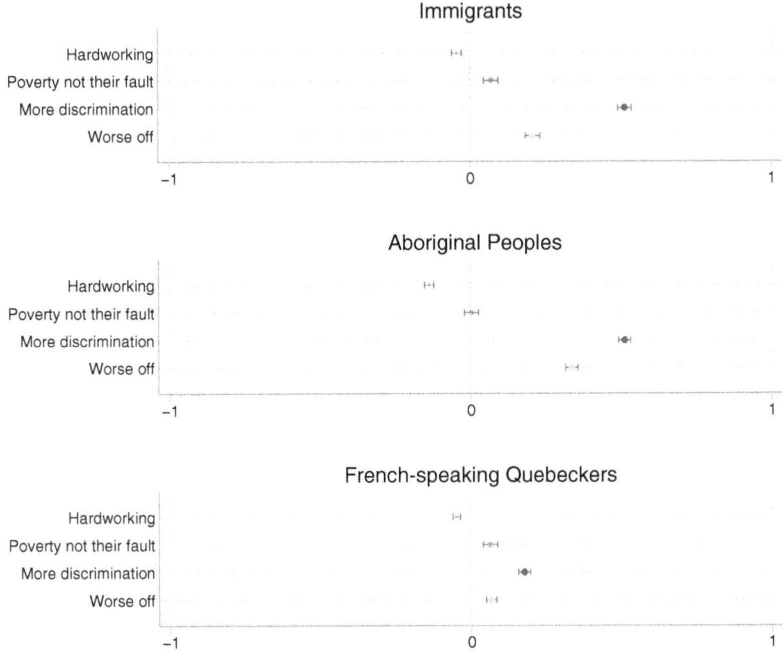

Figure 4.1 Minorities not seen as at fault or cheating

together with a few colleagues, we tested this hypothesis in a recent survey of Canadians, and here are some interesting if preliminary results.[26]

First, as I expected, minorities in Canada score reasonably well in terms of the standard criteria of responsibility ("not their fault") and need ("worse off"). Canadians generally accept that minorities are in genuine need, and that this is not their fault (Figure 4.1).[27]

However, as I feared, Canadians do penalize minorities for their alleged lack of commitment to the larger society. We devised a battery of eight questions to capture different dimensions of this idea of a moral commitment to a shared society. For example, one of our questions – which proved to be highly informative – is a simple "Cares" question: "How much do you think [immigrants] care about the concerns and needs of other Canadians?" Another question was "Sacrifice": How willing do you think [immigrants] are to make sacrifices for other Canadians." (See Appendix for full wording of questions). On all eight criteria, minorities are judged to be significantly less committed (Figure 4.2).

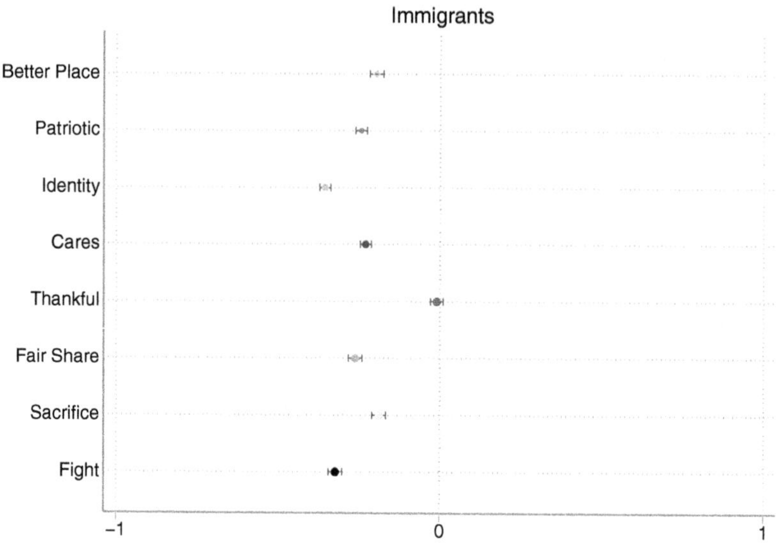

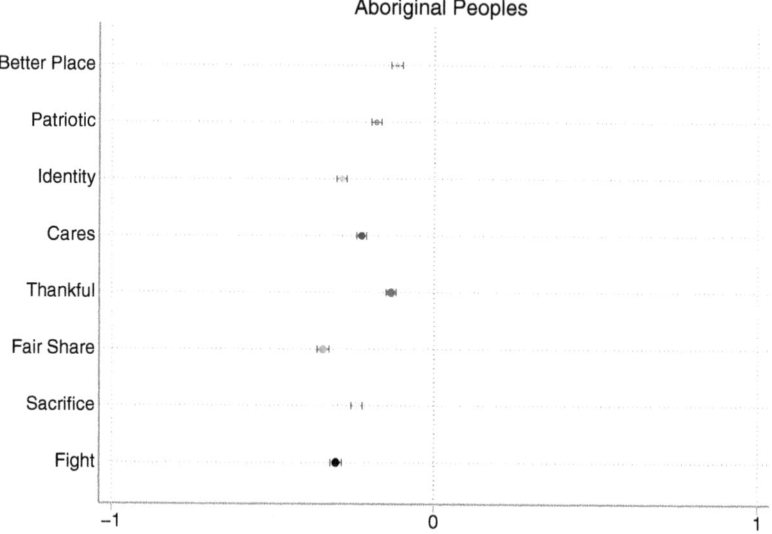

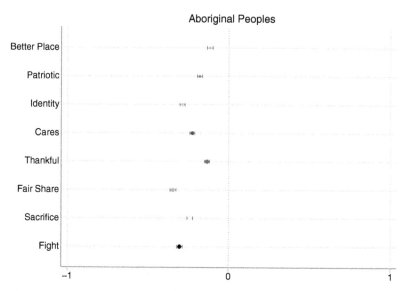

Figure 4.2 Minorities are seen as less committed to society

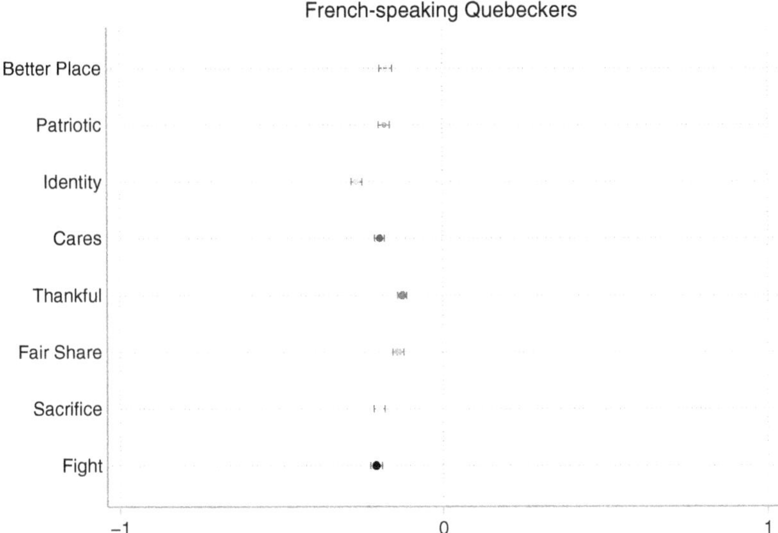

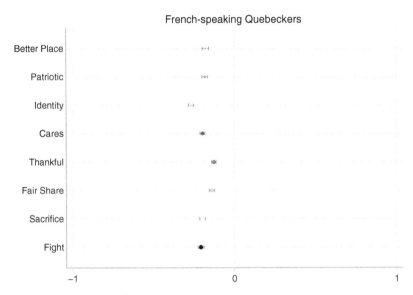

Figure 4.2 (continued)

This is a strikingly consistent result. Across all eight dimensions of perceived membership commitment, all three minority groups suffer from what we call a "membership penalty."

And this "membership penalty" matters: it drives down support for redistribution to minorities. We measured this in two different ways. First, we measured how perceptions of membership commitment affect support for "inclusive redistribution" – that is, whether members of minority groups should have access to general welfare programs. (For example, whether immigrants should have access to general unemployment or health care benefits). Second, we measured how perceptions of membership commitment affect support for "targeted redistribution" – that is, spending programs targeted at particular needs of minority groups, such as immigrant multiculturalism, the protection of Quebecois culture, or reconciliation with Indigenous peoples. Membership perceptions have a clear effect on support for both inclusive and targeted redistribution (Figures 4.3 and 4.4). Indeed, strikingly, perceptions of membership commitment matter more than beliefs about laziness or need (Figure 4.5).

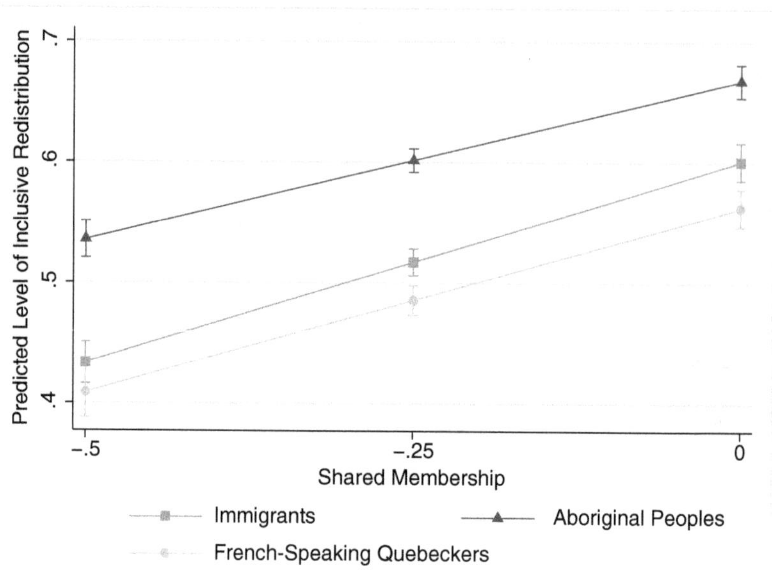

Figure 4.3 Impact of membership perceptions on support for inclusive redistribution

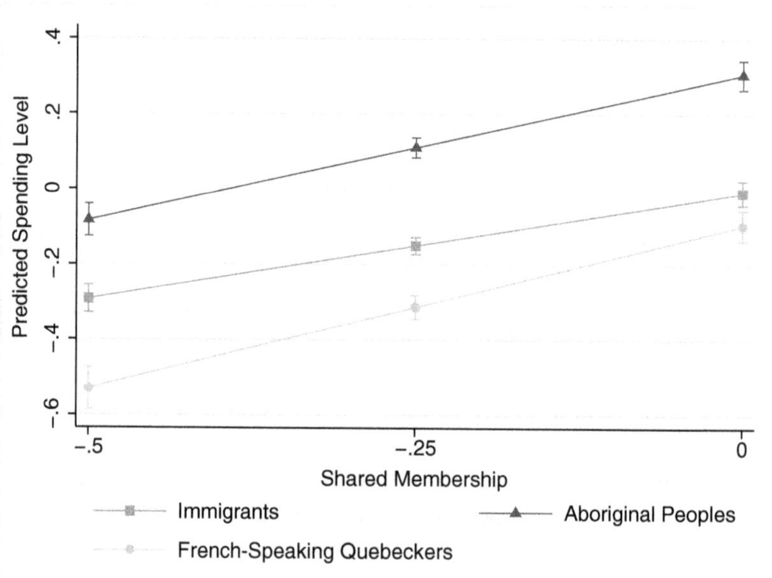

Figure 4.4 Impact of membership perceptions on support for targeted redistribution

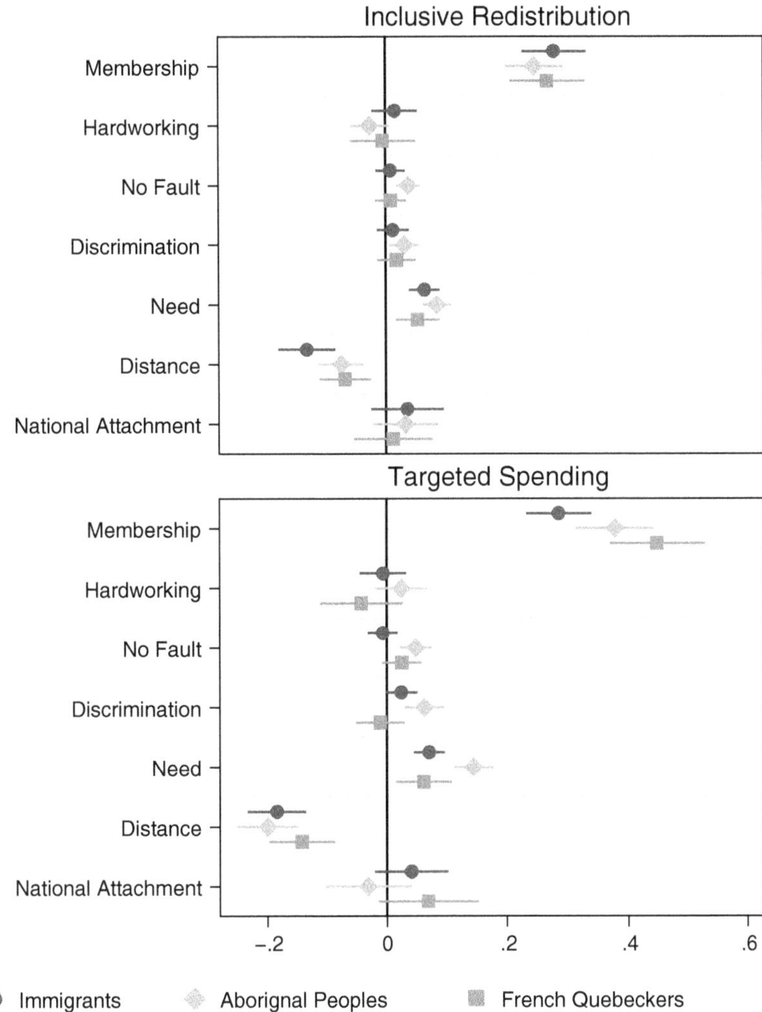

Figure 4.5 Relative impact of membership perceptions compared to other deservingness factors

So here is evidence that minorities suffer an important disadvantage within a world of nation-states built around stories of peoplehood. They are seen as less committed to the national project, and as a result are seen as less deserving of welfare state benefits, regardless of their need, work ethic or honesty. In related work, we have found similar membership penalties in people's assessment of the legitimacy of minorities' political mobilization and claims-making – for example, the legitimacy of engaging in street blockades. Minorities are seen as having less of a right to engage in such mobilization, and the size of this penalty is tied directly to perceptions of their membership commitment. The less respondents see minorities as committed to the larger society, the less they view minority political mobilization as legitimate. Membership penalties apply not only to the social solidarity of the welfare state, but also to what we call democratic solidarity (Harell et al. 2022).

4.6 Addressing Membership Penalties

This suggests that membership penalties are an important dimension of justice in contemporary nation-states. A just society needs to find a way to eliminate or at least reduce these penalties in perceptions of membership-based deservingness. How might we go about addressing membership penalties? These survey findings are just one snapshot of public attitudes, at one moment in time, in one country. As a result, it is premature to jump to conclusions about the causes or remedies of these membership penalties. For example, we do not know how these membership penalties have changed over time in Canada: are they larger or smaller today than, say, 10 years or 25 years ago? Nor do we know how these membership penalties differ across countries: for example, are these penalties larger in pro-multiculturalist countries like Canada and Sweden or in more assimilationist countries like France and Germany? Without data about how membership penalties change over time or vary across different societies and different policy regimes, it is impossible to draw conclusions about their likely causes or remedies.

However, as a first step, it is worth noting that, in the Canadian case at least, these membership penalties are found across all three types of minorities: Indigenous peoples, Quebecois and immigrant groups. And so they cut across the many of the standard divides used to explain outgroup attitudes. For example, hostility to immigrants and Indigenous peoples in Canada is often explained in terms of racism, and indeed there is much evidence for racist attitudes in Canada (Harell, Soroka, and Ladner 2014), but this cannot explain membership penalties for the (white) Quebecois.[28] Similarly, hostility to immigrants in Europe is often explained in terms of Islamophobia, and there is indeed evidence for Islamophobic attitudes in Canada (Triadafilopoulos and Rasheed 2020), but this cannot explain membership penalties for (predominantly Christian) Indigenous peoples and Quebecois.[29] Yet others explain hostility to out-groups as a result of fears that poor minorities will depress working-class wages or will burden the welfare state. And indeed there is evidence that economic insecurity affects attitudes to immigrants in Canada (Banting and Soroka 2020). But these materialist/economic anxieties cannot explain why membership penalties arise not just for poor Indigenous peoples but also for well-off Quebecois.[30] Yet others explain hostility to immigrants as an inevitable response to rapid demographic change: people adapt to high levels of diversity if they are stable, but feel threatened by rapid increases in levels of diversity (Kaufmann 2018; Goodhart 2017). And here too there is evidence that Canadians are uncomfortable with rapid changes in levels of neighborhood diversity (Soroka et al. 2007b). But this cannot explain hostility to long-settled and sedentary Indigenous and Quebecois groups.

In short, membership penalties in Canada do not simply track race, religion, class, or rapid demographic change. All of these matter, and they all need to be addressed on their own terms, but the pattern of membership penalties is wider, and cuts across these divides. There appears to be something more going on, something more structural, affecting all types of minorities, new or old, rich or poor, white or non-white. And this is what we would expect if, as I've argued, membership claims are filtered through stories of peoplehood. This pattern of membership penalties is the predictable result of the interconnections between social justice, an ethics of membership, nationhood and deservingness. Put schematically:

- Social justice, including redistributive solidarity, is tied to an ethics of membership (not to universal humanitarianism).
- An ethics of membership involves a moral commitment to a shared society.
- In our world, this idea of a shared society is tied to national stories of peoplehood.
- National stories of peoplehood put members of the dominant group at the prototypical center of this shared society, while putting the burden of proof on minorities to show that they belong at all.
- All minorities (new or old, rich or poor, white or racialized, Christian or non-Christian) are therefore likely to be penalized in terms of their perceived deservingness for membership-based claims.

At any rate, this is one plausible interpretation of the Canadian data, although we need more evidence to confirm it.

If so, then the next question is what societies can do about these membership-based deservingness judgments. The prospects for justice in diverse societies depends on having effective strategies to counteract these predictable membership penalties.

Here we can imagine different possibilities. One possibility would be to try to break the link between "deservingness" and social justice claims. After all, the very language of "deserving" and "undeserving" sounds regressive and archaic, a retreat to Victorian-era moralism. Priming people to think about "deservingness" often seems to lead people to revert not only to xenophobic and racist tropes about who really belongs, but also to classist, ableist, and sexist tropes about responsibility and contribution. Indeed, some commentators suggest that the prevalence of deservingness judgments reflects the triumph of neoliberal tropes about self-reliance and "responsibilization" at the expense of bounded solidarities (Somers 2008). On this view, solidarity and deservingness are incompatible frameworks: the more solidaristic we are, the less we would engage in deservingness judgments. Progressives have therefore been very wary of "deservingness" talk, and many have sought to develop a conception of bounded solidarity that avoids or pre-empts questions of deservingness.[31]

But this neglects the diverse sources of deservingness judgments, and in particular the distinction between responsibility-based and membership-based deservingness judgments. It is entirely plausible that neoliberalism has led to harsher assessments of whether individuals are responsible for their disadvantage, and whether they could succeed if they just worked harder. But as I noted earlier, this is not the basis on which minorities are judged less deserving in Canada. On the contrary, they are seen as less responsible for their disadvantage than members of the majority, in part because of the widespread recognition that they face discrimination, and in part because they are seen as hard-working. In that sense, neoliberal responsibilization judgments are as likely to target the majority as the minority, particularly native-born white poor, including the unemployed, or single mothers, or people with disabilities. The rise of these increasingly harsh responsibility-based deservingness judgments is a profound problem, and we need to think about how to challenge and disrupt these neoliberal tropes about individual responsibility.

It is less clear, however, that membership-based deservingness judgments are tied to neoliberalism, or that they are incompatible with robust solidarity. Certainly, there are some contexts where the legitimacy of people's claims should not depend on perceptions of membership. The right not to be tortured, for example, is not something one "deserves" or "earns" through fulfilling an ethic of membership. It is owed to us simply as human beings. However, as I noted earlier, this sort of universal humanitarianism cannot support the robust and routinized redistributive demands of a progressive welfare state, which rest instead on membership claims. And once claims are tied to an ethic of membership, then we are likely to see membership-based deservingness judgments. When making membership-based claims, it is not enough to say that one is human or has urgent interests–that is the logic of humanitarianism. Rather, membership-based claims require individuals *to have certain types of social relationships and affiliations*. Someone is part of the national "we" because she has made a life here, complies with its social norms, shares in the burdens of social cooperation, participates in its institutionalized forms of reciprocity and risk-pooling, shows concern for its collective well-being and collective future, and contributes in ways that suit her capacities. It is these membership-based attitudes and behaviors that justify distinguishing solidaristic obligations to co-members from humanitarian obligations to tourists or foreigners. And if so, then bounded solidarity generates its own logic of deservingness. Our solidaristic obligations to co-members depend on the assumption that they have a depth of commitment to and engagement in our society that non-members do not have. And this, arguably, is what membership-based deservingness judgments track.

While the historical evidence is limited, I think it supports this claim that deservingness judgments are not unique to the era of neoliberalism, nor to liberal market societies as opposed to social-democratic or corporatist welfare states.[32] Contrary to some nostalgic commentators, even in the golden age of postwar social democracy, before the onset of neoliberalism, polls reveal a constant public assessment of (and anxiety about) the deservingness of recipients.[33] Deservingness judgments may simply be the unavoidable flip side of an ethic of membership. If, as Marshall argued, the welfare state is rooted in a "sense of community membership," then citizens are likely to ask whether others display the attitudes and behaviors that distinguish members from non-members (or conversely, whether someone has renounced the responsibilities of membership, shown no commitment to society and its future).

This suggests that the question is not *whether* citizens make deservingness judgments – this may be characteristic of any ethic of membership – but *how* they make them. How do citizens evaluate the affiliation and commitment of others? The worry here is that dominant groups are likely to make deservingness judgments in biased ways. All too often, citizens privilege those who belong and contribute in the same way that they do. Inherited conceptions of membership have been defined by and for historically dominant groups, in ways that valorize their specific modes of being and belonging, while discounting the cooperation and affiliation of those who differ from them.

I think we can see this asymmetry in the survey results. Recall the data: members of the majority in Canada perceive members of all three minorities as less likely to care about the larger society, less likely to make sacrifices for the larger society, and less willing to do their fair share to protect and promote the general good of the larger society. Where do these ideas come from?

There may well be times and places where these perceptions are well-grounded. Think of the Sudeten German minority who practically invited the Nazis to invade Czechoslovakia. Far from cooperating with the Czech majority to defend the country, they collaborated with its conquest and dismemberment. We can find many other examples of minorities who are at best indifferent to the larger society, and at worst, collaborate with neighboring enemies.

But this is not the situation in Canada (or in most Western democracies). Minorities in Canada have been allies of the majority, not enemies, in the great struggles of the twentieth century, whether it was the two world wars, or the Cold War against communism. All three minorities have fought bravely alongside other Canadians, and no one today fears that any of these groups would collaborate with Canada's enemies. Minorities in Canada are not seen as fifth-columns for enemy powers.

So what then explains this perception of a lack of commitment or loyalty? The answer, I suggest, lies in the way stories of peoplehood differentially locate majorities and minorities. Whenever majorities engage in political mobilization and make political claims – for or against increased taxes, say, or for or against building pipelines – this is taken as evidence of their concern for and commitment to the country and its future. They are seen as carrying forward the story of peoplehood, for which they are the natural (prototypical) bearers. By contrast, when minorities engage in political mobilization for the recognition of their differences, they are seen, not as expressing a commitment to the larger society, but as engaging in selfish behavior, as a form of group egoism. Majorities see themselves as acting from a commitment to the collective "we," whereas minorities are seen as more likely to be acting upon group egoism rather than concern for others.

As a result, the regime of minority rights in Canada creates a potential trap. While Canada provides safe legal space for minorities to politically assert their identities, any attempt to actually exercise these rights is perceived as evidence of group egoism rather than concern for the larger society.[34]

If this is indeed what is happening – and I emphasize this is a speculative interpretation of preliminary data – then it is a particularly perverse perception of Canadian realities. There is a healthy dose of group self-interest on all sides of inter-group relations in Canada, but if there is one group that has distinguished itself historically by its level of group egoism, it is surely the English-settler majority. The settler-state was built on the conquest and dispossession of Indigenous peoples, through the imposition of British law, language and culture, and though what has arguably been the most self-interested immigration policy in the world. And the majority has had no hesitation in imposing burdens and sacrifices on minorities to pursue its aims, from the recruitment of Chinese workers to build the national railway to the ongoing recruitment of Mexican farm workers to harvest our food. And yet the story of peoplehood magically turns these instances of majority group egoism into "nation building," seen as evidence of a moral commitment to a wider collectivity.

By contrast, throughout history, minorities in Canada – unlike the Sudeten Germans – have often reached out the hand of civic friendship to the English majority, seeking to establish relationship of trust and cooperation. To be sure, minorities have often challenged the particular role that the national story of peoplehood assigns to them – as, say, "vanished races" or "grateful refugees" [35] – and argued for a relationship that is more responsive to their interests and identities. But this is indeed the pursuit of a *relationship* with the larger society, and there's ample evidence that minorities care about this relationship, and are willing to make sacrifices to protect that relationship and see it flourish into the future. There are important elements of concern, commitment and sacrifice built into the political claims of minorities.[36] And yet, when viewed through the lens of the story of peoplehood, these political aspirations start to look like group egoism.

In short, stories of peoplehood operate to cloak majority political mobilization in the veneer of moral commitment, while casting minority political mobilization in the veneer of group egoism, leading to pervasive and systematic membership penalties.

If so, the question is what can be done to shift the majority perceptions of minority claims-making out of the box of group egoism and into the box of moral commitment? Sadly, some commentators argue that the clearest cases on record of such shifts are from the experience of war – nothing seems to highlight the membership and contribution of minorities more than their wartime military service (Saldin 2011). Military service even in peacetime may help; willingness to fight for one's country is a familiar indicator of shared membership, and the evidence suggests it still matters for perceptions of minority's commitment to the larger "we."

But military service is hardly a satisfactory strategy for promoting inclusive solidarity. So what are the alternative routes by which excluded/stigmatized groups gain recognition of their membership/contribution? And here I want to return to ideas of multiculturalism. We can think of multiculturalism as having two faces or dimensions. On the one hand, as noted earlier, it has a purely protective or defensive function, to protect minorities from the excesses of nation-building. On the other hand, multiculturalism also has a more reconstructive or transformative function, not just to protect minorities from majoritarian nationalism, but to transform majority attitudes, and in particular to transform majority conceptions of membership and belonging to create a more inclusive solidarity. The task here is to think about minority rights, not just as a set of defensive constraints on nation-building, but as positive contributions to a shared project, and hence as embodying an ethic of membership. This transformative function is important, I believe, in addressing membership penalties.

How might multiculturalism transform these membership-based deservingness judgments? Let me start with the case of immigration. In some countries – particularly in Europe – immigrant multiculturalism is seen as an invitation to ethnic groups to segregate themselves from the mainstream, and to exist in "parallel societies." Understood in this way, it seems to reproduce, or indeed exacerbate, the perception of a lack of commitment to the "we." But this is not the only way to understand multiculturalism. In the Canadian context, multiculturalism has always had the opposite intention: multiculturalism was designed to recognize immigrants as vital contributors to the larger society, and to invite their further contributions.[37] And the evidence suggests that multiculturalism in Canada has helped to reduce the membership penalty for immigrant-origin ethnic groups (Bloemraad 2011), in part because it is framed in a way that highlights immigrants' participation in an ethic of membership. Where multiculturalism is understood as simply an apolitical celebration of diversity, or as an encouragement to isolation, it is unlikely to have a beneficial impact on membership-based deservingness perceptions. But where multiculturalism is tied to ideas of participation and contribution – a kind of "multicultural nationalism," if you like – it may help to reduce the membership penalty, acting as a counterweight to recurring efforts to re-inscribe Britishness as the core of Canadian nationhood (Abu-Laban 2014).

The case of historic national minorities and Indigenous peoples is more complicated, since in some respects they do indeed involve maintaining "parallel societies," or at any rate, maintaining parallel stories of peoplehood. Nonetheless, we can think of the task of reconciling these competing stories of peoplehood as something "we" (majority and minorities) do together. For example, perhaps both settler Canadians and Indigenous Canadians could take pride in together facing up to the challenge of reconciling their competing stories of peoplehood. And if so, we could then show that minorities are in fact fully and equally committed to this morally valuable project and to this valued relationship, and that in this respect, they fully embody an ethic of membership, including the willingness to make sacrifices for this shared project. Negotiating minority rights for sub-state national groups would no longer be seen as minority group egoism against a moral commitment to the "we," but rather building a new "we" that minorities and majority alike are committed to and willing to make sacrifices for.

These suggestions about how multiculturalism might address membership penalties are, at this stage, speculative. In the absence of comparative data on membership penalties in different countries or over time, it is difficult to predict the impact of adopting or rejecting multiculturalism policies on these penalties. So we will have to await the results of further research. But my hunch is that multiculturalism policies will turn out to have beneficial effects in reducing membership penalties, and that this will be particularly true if and when multiculturalism is designed with transformative as well as protective functions in mind. That is just speculation at this point, although several recent studies of the impact of multiculturalism on intergroup attitudes would seem to support this (Guimond et al. 2013; Igarashi 2019; Kongshøj 2019). A recent pilot of our membership perceptions questions in an eight-country European survey also suggests that membership penalties in relation to immigrants are lower in countries with stronger multiculturalism policies (Harell et al. 2022b).

This is a potential path to reducing membership penalties without abandoning either stories of peoplehood or minority rights, both of which I believe are essential to a decent and just liberal democracy. This may sound vague and not without its own dangers. But if the findings from our Canadian survey are sound, then the challenge is clear. Support for social justice depends on citizens seeing each other as expressing an ethic of membership, as having a moral commitment to the wellbeing and future of a morally salient "we." If so, then we need to show how struggles for minority rights, and the active exercise of these rights, are not just forms of group egoism, but rather are ways of making a commitment to a "we."

In my view, it is one of the perverse injustices of a world of nation-states that minorities continually face the burden of proving this moral commitment, whereas the naked group egoism of the majority goes unremarked, or indeed celebrated as nation-building. But that is the world we live in, and so we need to find ways of addressing the membership penalties that minorities face, without resorting to assimilationist/subtractive models of nationalism that are neither politically feasible nor morally legitimate.

Notes

1 For example, the recent debate in Germany about whether male circumcision should be seen as a violation of children's basic human rights (Triadafilopoulos 2019).

2 For example, polls show that the policy preferences of Americans in New England are closer to eastern/central Canadians than to southern Americans (Grabb and Curtis 2005). Joining Canada would make it more likely

that their policy preferences are adopted, while still upholding liberal-democratic principles. So why does no one in New England propose seceding and joining Canada? Because they are not just nationally-anonymous liberal-democrats, but think of themselves as belonging with other Americans.

3 Northern Ireland is the exception that proves the rule: British efforts to suppress competing Irish republican views have failed and the result is political instability.

4 This orientation to a shared society plays a double role in the welfare state: it shapes the *content* of people's claims (i.e., as membership stakes), and the *motivation* to comply with the claims of others (i.e., citizens are willing to forego advantages in order to support the membership claims of others because of a shared sense of "we"-ness, a joint desire to live together and belong together in a shared society). Unlike either prudential self-interest or universal humanitarianism, compliance with membership-based claims goes through our shared commitment to a "we."

5 In his chapter in this volume, Joppke argues that neoliberalism is eroding this distinction between bounded solidarity and universal humanitarianism, and that "citizens rights are being 'levelled down' to migrant rights, while the joint yardstick for both are increasingly universal human rights." This may be an accurate description of (one version of) the neoliberal agenda, but countries vary enormously in the extent to which they have followed this agenda, and even where policies have moved in this direction, public opinion remains stubbornly committed to bounded solidarity based on an ethic of membership. I return to the role of neoliberalism in Section 4.6.

6 These two levels do not exhaust the moral space. There are other moral logics at work in politics, such as compensatory justice claims for past injustice (e.g., towards ex-colonies), as well as special obligations arising from transnational agreements and alliances (e.g., towards other EU states), both of which generate claims which fall somewhere in-between universal humanitarianism and full membership claims. However, I believe these additional moral logics are more contingent, whereas the moral logics of humanitarianism and of membership are structural features of all liberal democracies. One possible explanation for the weakness of pan-EU solidarity is that it is not the natural locus for either universal humanitarianism (which would prioritize the truly poor countries outside the EU) or bounded solidarity (which would prioritize the claims of co-nationals). Indeed, recent survey evidence shows not only that citizens have a stronger sense of solidarity towards co-nationals than other EU members (Kuhn and Kamm 2019), but also, strikingly, that "solidarity with fellow Europeans is lower than the support for people

outside the EU" (Lahusen and Grasso 2018: 256). Lahusen and Grasso suggest that this "seems to reflect the attachment of citizens to the various reference groups, because citizens feel most attached to their own country and to humankind, while fewer respondents feel European" (Lahusen and Grasso 2018: 256). This language of "attachment" suggests that all three targets – co-nationals, fellow EU members, global poor – are being ranked on a single scale of closeness of attachment. I would suggest instead that we see two different moral logics at work: universal humanitarianism (which prioritizes the global poor regardless of attachment) and social membership (which prioritizes co-nationals).

7 Although children and newcomers should also learn about the ways these stories have been contested: for example, learning why republicans in Northern Ireland do not accept the story of British peoplehood, or why Indigenous peoples in Canada do not accept the story of Canadian peoplehood (Kymlicka 2011). As I discuss below, this sort of dialectic of nation-building and minority rights is the crux of my position.

8 Tamir (2019) argues that while the masses retain high levels of national identification, elites have disinvested from the nation and embraced cosmopolitan loyalties instead. But as Sandelind notes in her chapter in this volume, there is little evidence for this: national attachment does not vary across class. See also Teney and Helbling (2017) for an empirical test showing that globalized elites in Germany have not disinvested in the nation.

9 When the 2003 UK Home Office Citizenship Survey asked "how strongly you belong to Britain," 85.95 percent of Indians, 86.38 percent of Pakistanis, and 86.85 percent of Bangladeshis said that they belong either "fairly" or "very" strongly to Britain – numbers that are essentially identical to the 86.7 percent of whites who said they either fairly or very strongly belong. As Maxwell says, these results "encourage skepticism towards the notion of a national identification crisis among Muslims and South Asians in Britain" (Maxwell 2006). By contrast, only 8.5 percent of Catholics in Northern Ireland identify as British (Coakley 2007). A similar story applies in Canada: immigrants have much higher levels of national identification than either the Quebecois or Indigenous peoples (Soroka, Johnston and Banting 2007a: 586). If there's a problem with national identity, it is often with "old" minorities not "new" immigrants.

10 George Bernard Shaw once said "A healthy nation is as unconscious of its nationality as a healthy man of his bones. But if you break a nation's nationality it will think of nothing else but getting it set again." The first

sentence is broadly correct, but we might amend the second sentence. To generate assertive nationalist responses, it is not necessary to "break" a nation's nationality: it might be enough to "prime" it.

11 Unless we are in a context of contested nationalisms, where weather maps are indeed consciously debated. On the fascinating Basque case, see https://johnpostill.wordpress.com/2009/03/21/banal-nationalism-and-weather-maps-in-the-basque-country/.

12 Interestingly, the Indian study cited earlier showing that priming national identity encouraged pro-social behavior towards Muslims involved an unconscious prime – the presence of an Indian flag in the background (Charnysh et al. 2015).

13 For example, centuries-long practices of tolerance and co-existence amongst ethnic and religious groups in the multinational Ottoman and Habsburg empires were swept away in the transition to nation-states. On the unmixing of peoples in the transition from empires to nation-states see Brubaker (1995).

14 In her chapter in this volume, Sandelind suggests a commitment to the republican value of "non-domination" can replace nationhood as the basis for political community, and thereby avoid the tendencies of nationhood towards exclusion. As she puts it, "citizens' prior allegiance to the ideal of nondomination" provides a normative ideal which is "privileged before attachment to the community." But we have no reason to assume that people who share a commitment to nondomination will agree on the *units* within which this ideal should operate. Just as nothing in the theory of liberal-democracy guarantees that people who share liberal-democratic values will agree on the units of liberal-democracy, so too nothing in republican theory guarantees that people who share a commitment to non-domination will agree on the units of republican non-domination. Some independent "attachment to the community" is needed to generate converging preferences on the appropriate units of republican self-government.

15 In some countries, these are called "multiculturalism" policies, but since that term means different things in different countries, I focus on the content of the policies, not their label.

16 I discuss how this basic analysis is shared amongst the different schools of multiculturalism in Kymlicka (2019).

17 Kaufmann (2019) argues that this sort of asymmetric multiculturalism explains the rise of nativist populism.

18 So here majority rights re-enter the picture, not to recharge the battery of liberal-democratic nationhood (as discussed in Section 4.2), but as remedies for asymmetric multiculturalism.

19 Versions of this argument are made in both Koopmans and Orgad (2021) and Da Silva and Weinstock (2021) in this volume. The original version of my paper did not discuss this first version of the asymmetric multiculturalism argument – an omission that Da Silva and Weinstock rightly criticize in their commentary. My formulation here is indebted to their commentary.

20 For the complicated history of Canada's fight for cultural exemptions in international trade agreements, see Lemieux and Jackson (1999).

21 Da Silva and Weinstock (this volume) emphasize this point: if there are majority rights, they should be seen as directed at international bodies.

22 See Tamir's chapter in this volume for discussion of this perception that multiculturalism has gone beyond protecting minorities from injustice and is now being used to "enhance a cultural and religious takeover."

23 For the sad story of how fabricated rumours about a war on Christmas created a toxic environment for students and teachers in a Canadian school, see Mo (2019).

24 See the scathing review of media inaccuracies in the reporting of minority requests for "reasonable accommodation" in Quebec in the report of the Bouchard-Taylor Commission. In 15 of 21 cases examined by the Commission, it found that the media distorted facts in its coverage for sensationalism (Bouchard and Taylor 2008: 69).

25 www.theguardian.com/world/2006/dec/08/religion.communities; www.inquisitr.com/3648019/fact-check-did-sweden-just-ban-christmas-lights-to-appease-muslim-immigrants/.

26 The following data is drawn from Banting, Kymlicka, Harell and Wallace (2019), and Harell, Banting, Kymlicka and Wallace (2021). The (speculative) interpretation of the data I give later is my own, for which my co-authors are not responsible, and with which they might not agree.

27 In the following figures, the center line indicates that majority respondents do not view members of minority groups as either more or less deserving than members of the majority. If the marker is the right, this indicates that majority respondents view minorities as more deserving; if the marker is to the left, majority respondents view minorities as less deserving.

28 Moreover, it is worth noting that we included a standard measure of outgroup animosity – a social distance thermometer – as a control. Membership perceptions have a profound effect even when controlling for social distance (Harell et al. 2021a).

29 Or indeed for most immigrant groups: Muslims only form around 10 percent of the immigrant intake in Canada, and so when Canadians hear the term "immigrant" they do not generally equate this with "Muslim."

30 In the Canadian context, immigrants are not automatically perceived as poor. Because of Canada's selective immigration system, immigrants often are highly educated, and their children do better-than-average in

school, so that immigrants are not in general seen as economically disadvantaged or dependent on welfare benefits. On the contrary, it is widely believed in Canada that immigration is essential for keeping the public pension scheme afloat.

31 In this respect, progressives have often adopted the same attitude toward deservingness that they have taken to nationhood. Because it is seen as potentially toxic, they have tried to avoid it entirely, leaving the field entirely to the right. This then becomes a self-fulfilling prophecy. Having failed to develop their own progressive account of either nationhood or deservingness, the left has ensured that the public discourses around nationhood and deservingness are indeed predominantly regressive.

32 Van Oorschot (2006) finds that Europeans share a common "deservingness culture," regardless of welfare state regime.

33 Hudson et al. (2016a; 2016b) cite surveys showing that British citizens made these deservingness judgements from the 1940s to the 1970s.

34 See Amarasingam et al. (2016) and Thurairajah (2017) for two of many recent examples where the public expression of minority identities is interpreted as lack of concern for the country.

35 On the discourse of Indigenous peoples as "vanishing races," and its role in establishing stories of peoplehood in settler states, see Brantlinger (2003). On its enduring consequences, see Orr et al. (2018). On the discourse of "grateful refugees," and its role in upholding settler stories of peoplehood, see Nguyen (2013) and Ngo (2016).

36 The perception that the English majority have rebuffed "gambits" by the Quebecois and Indigenous peoples to establish (or re-establish) valued relations of trust and consent is a familiar refrain in the literature. See Tully (1994); Karmis and Rocher (2018).

37 For a comparison of European and Canadian understandings of multiculturalism, see Miller (2019).

References

Abu-Laban, Y. (2014). Reform by Stealth: The Harper Conservatives and Canadian Multiculturalism. In Jedwab, J. (ed.), *The Multiculturalism Question: Debating Identity in 21st-Century Canada*. McGill-Queen's University Press, 149–72.

Amarasingam, A., Naganathan, G., & Hyndman, J. (2016). Canadian Multiculturalism as Banal Nationalism: Understanding Everyday Meanings among Sri Lankan Tamils in Toronto, *Canadian Ethnic Studies*, 48/2: 119–41.

Anderson, B. (1983). *Imagined Communities: Reflections on the Origin and Spread of Nationalism*. Verso Books.

Banting, K., & Soroka, S. (2020). A Distinctive Culture? The Sources of Public Support for Immigration in Canada, 1980–2019, *Canadian Journal of Political Science*, 53/4: 821–38.

Banting, K., Kymlicka, W., Harell, A., & Wallace, R. (2019). Beyond National Identity: Liberal Nationalism, Shared Membership and Solidarity. In Gustavsson, G. and Miller, D. (eds.), *Liberal Nationalism and Its Critics*. Oxford University Press.

Billig, M. (1995). *Banal Nationalism*. Sage.

Bloemraad, I. (2011). *The Debate over Multiculturalism: Philosophy, Politics, and Policy*. Migration Policy Institute www.migrationpolicy.org/article/debate-over-multiculturalism-philosophy-politics-and-policy

Bouchard, G., & Taylor, C. (2008). *Building the Future: A Time for Reconciliation: Report of the Consultation Commission on Accommodation Practices Related to Cultural Differences* (Gouvernement du Québec).

Brantlinger, P. (2003). *Dark Vanishings: Discourse on the Extinction of Primitive Races*. Cornell University Press.

Breton, C. (2015). Making National Identity Salient: Impact on Attitudes Toward Immigration and Multiculturalism, *Canadian Journal of Political Science*, 48/2: 357–81.

Brubaker, R. (1995). Aftermaths of Empire and the Unmixing of Peoples, *Ethnic and Racial Studies*, 18/2: 189–218.

Brylka, A., Mähönen, T. A., & Jasinskaja-Lahti, I. (2015). National Identification and Intergroup Attitudes among Members of the National Majority and Immigrants: Preliminary Evidence for the Mediational Role of Psychological Ownership of a Country. *Journal of Social and Political Psychology*, 3/1: 24–45.

Canovan, M. (1996). *Nationhood and Political Theory*. Edward Elgar.

Charnysh, V., Lucas, C., & Singh, P. (2015). The Ties That Bind: National Identity Salience and Pro-Social Behavior toward the Ethnic Other, *Comparative Political Studies*, 48/3: 267–300.

Coakley, J. (2007). National Identity in Northern Ireland: Stability or Change?, *Nations and Nationalism*, 13/4: 573–97.

Devos, T., & Banaji, M. (2005). American = White? *Journal of Personality and Social Psychology*, 88/3: 447–66.

Devos, T., & Heng, L. (2009). Whites Are Granted the American Identity More Swiftly Than Asians, *Social Psychology*, 40/4: 192–201.

Environics Institute for Social Research. (2019). *Focus Canada: Canadian Public Opinion about Immigration and Refugees*. Toronto. www.environicsinstitute.org/docs/default-source/project-documents/focus-canada-spring-2019/environics-institute---focus-canada-spring-2019-survey-on-immigration-and-refugees---final-report.pdf

Gidron, Noam. (2018). The Left Shouldn't Fear Nationalism: It Should Embrace It, *Vox*, February 8, 2018. www.vox.com/the-big-idea/2018/2/8/16982036/nationalism-patriotism-left-right-trump-democrats-solidarity

Gilens, Martin. (1999). *Why Americans Hate Welfare*. University of Chicago Press.

Goodhart, D. (2017). *The Road to Somewhere*. Oxford University Press.

Grabb, E., & Curtis, J. (2005). *Regions Apart: The Four Societies of Canada and the United States*. Oxford University Press.

Guimond, S. et al. (2013). Diversity Policy, Social Dominance, and Intergroup Relations: Predicting Prejudice in Changing Social and Political Contexts, *Journal of Personality and Social Psychology*, 104/6: 941–58.

Harell, A., Banting, K., & Kymlicka, W. (2022a). Nationalism, Membership and the Politics of Minority Claims-Making, *Canadian Journal of Political Science*, forthcoming.

(2022b). The Boundaries of Generosity: Membership, Inclusion and Redistribution. In Crepaz, M. (ed.), *The Edward Elgar Handbook on Migration and Welfare* (Elgar), 102–17.

Harell, A., Banting, K., Kymlicka, W., & Wallace, R. (2021). Shared Membership beyond National Identity: Deservingness and Solidarity in Diverse Societies, *Political Studies*, forthcoming.

Harell, A., Soroka, S., & Ladner, K. (2014). Public Opinion, Prejudice and the Racialization of Welfare in Canada, *Ethnic and Racial Studies*, 37/14: 2580–97.

Hudson, J. et al. (2016a). Nostalgia Narratives? Pejorative Attitudes to Welfare in Historical Perspective, *Journal of Poverty and Social Justice*, 24/3: 227–43.

(2016b). Exploring public attitudes to welfare over the Longue Durée, *Social Policy & Administration*, 50/6: 691–711.

Igarashi, A. (2019). Till Multiculturalism Do Us Part: Multicultural Policies and the National Identification of Immigrants in European Countries, *Social Science Research*, 77: 88–100.

Jasinskaja-Lahti, I. et al. (2020). Dual Citizenship and the Perceived Loyalty of Immigrants. *Group Processes & Intergroup Relations*, 23/7: 996–1013.

Joppke, C. (2004). The Retreat of Multiculturalism in the Liberal State: Theory and Policy, *British Journal of Sociology*, 55/2: 237–57.

Karmis, D., & Rocher, F. eds. (2018). *Trust, Distrust, and Mistrust in Multinational Democracies*. McGill-Queen's University Press.

Kaufmann, E. (2018). *Whiteshift: Populism, Immigration and the Future of White Majorities*. Penguin.

Kaufmann, E. (2019). How "Asymmetrical Multiculturalism" Generates Populist Blowback, *National Review*, February 6, 2019. www.nationalreview.com/2019/02/populism-identity-politics-why-they-rise-in-tandem/

Kongshøj, K. (2019). Trusting Diversity: Nationalist and Multiculturalist Orientations Affect Generalised Trust through Ethnic In-Group and Out-Group Trust. *Nations and Nationalism*, 25/3: 822–46.

Koopmans, R. (2018). Cultural Rights of Native Majorities between Universalism and Minority Rights (WZB Discussion Paper SP VI 2018–106).

Kuhn, T., & Kamm, A. (2019). The National Boundaries of Solidarity: A Survey Experiment on Public Support for National and European Unemployment Policies, *European Political Science Review*, 11/2: 179–95.

Kunst, Jonas R., Lotte T., & Dovidio, John F. (2019). Divided Loyalties: Perceptions of Disloyalty Underpin Bias toward Dually Identified Minority-Group Members. *Journal of Personality and Social Psychology*, 117/4: 807.

Kymlicka, Will. (1995). *Multicultural Citizenship*. Oxford University Press.

(2011). Multicultural Citizenship within Multination States, *Ethnicities*, 11/3: 281–302.

(2015). Solidarity in Diverse Societies: Beyond Neoliberal Multiculturalism and Welfare Chauvinism, *Comparative Migration Studies*, 3/1: 1–19.

(2019). Deschooling Multiculturalism, *Ethnicities*, 19/6: 971–82.

Lahusen, C., & Grasso, M. (2018). Solidarity in Europe: A Comparative Assessment and Discussion. In Lahusen, C. and Grasso, M. (eds) *Solidarity in Europe*. Springer, pp. 253–81.

Marshall, T. H. (1950). *Sociology at the Crossroads*. London: Heinemann.

Maxwell, R. (2006). Muslims, South Asians, and the British Mainstream: A National Identity Crisis?, *West European Politics*, 29/4: 736–56.

Miller, D. (2019). The Life and Death of Multiculturalism. In Goodyear-Grant, E. et al. (eds.), *Federalism and the Welfare State in a Multicultural World*. McGill-Queen's University Press, pp. 319–39.

Mo, H. (2019). A Christmas Crisis: Lessons from a Canadian Public School's Seasonal Crisis. In Klassen, P. and Scheer, M. (eds.) *The Public Work of Christmas: Difference and Belonging in Multicultural Societies*. McGill-Queen's University Press, pp. 188–211.

Mounk, Y. (2018). *The People vs. Democracy*. Harvard University Press.

Ngo, A. (2016). "Journey to Freedom Day Act": The Making of the Vietnamese Subject in Canada and the Erasure of the Vietnam War, *Canadian Review of Social Policy*, 75: 59–86.

Nguyen, V. (2013). Refugee Gratitude: Narrating Success and Intersubjectivity in Kim Thúy's Ru. *Canadian Literature*, 219: 17–36.

Orr, R., Sharratt, K., & Iqbal, M. (2018). American Indian Erasure and the Logic of Elimination: An Experimental Study of Depiction and Support for Resources and Rights for Tribes. *Journal of Ethnic and Migration Studies*, 45/11: 2078–99.

Pandey, G. (2006). *Routine Violence: Nations, Fragments, Histories*. Stanford University Press.

Qari, S., Konrad, K., & Geys, B. (2012). Patriotism, Taxation and International Mobility, *Public Choice*, 151/3: 695–717.

Rene, L., & Jackson, J. (1999). *Cultural Exemptions in Canada's Major International Trade Agreements and Investment Relationships*. Parliamentary Research Branch, Government of Canada, PRB 99-25E.

Saldin, R. (2011). Strange Bedfellows: War and Minority Rights, *World Affairs*, 173: 57–66.

Singh, P. (2018). Nationalism Can Have Its Good Points. Really, *Washington Post*, January 26, 2018. www.washingtonpost.com/news/monkey-cage/wp/2018/01/26/nationalism-can-have-its-good-points-really/

Smith, R. (2003). *Stories of Peoplehood*. Cambridge University Press.

Sniderman, P., & Hagendoorn, L. (2007). *When Ways of Life Collide: Multiculturalism and Its Discontents in the Netherland*. Princeton University Press.

Somers, M. (2008). *Genealogies of Citizenship*. Cambridge University Press.

Soroka, S., Johnston R., & Banting, K. (2007a). Ties That Bind: Social Cohesion and Diversity in Canada. In Banting, K., Courchene, T., and Seidle, F. (eds.), *Belonging? Diversity, Recognition and Shared Citizenship in Canada*. Montreal: Institute for Research in Public Policy, pp. 561–600.

(2007b). Diversity and Trust, paper presented at conference on "Diversity and Social Cohesion: US and Canadian Perspectives" (Princeton University, March 2007).

Tamir, Y. (1993). *Liberal Nationalism*. Princeton University Press.

(2019). *Why Nationalism*. Princeton University Press.

Taylor, C. (1991). Shared and Divergent Values. In Watts, Ronald and Brown, D. (eds.), *Options for a New Canada*. Toronto: University of Toronto Press, pp. 53–76.

Teney, C., & Helbling, M. (2017). Solidarity between the Elites and the Masses in Germany. In Banting, K. and Kymlicka, W. (eds.), *The Strains of Commitment*. Oxford University Press, 127–51.

Thurairajah, K. (2017). The Jagged Edges of Multiculturalism in Canada and the Suspect Canadian, *Journal of Multicultural Discourses*, 12/2: 134–48.

Toft, Monica D. (2005). *The Geography of Ethnic Violence*. Princeton University Press.

Triadafilopoulos, T. (2019). Religious Groups, Liberal-Democratic States and Competitive Boundary Making: The Debate over Ritual Male Circumcision in Germany. *Ethnicities*, 19/4: 654–73.

Triadafilopoulos, T. & Rasheed, J. (2020). A Religion Like No Other: Islam and the Limits of Multiculturalism in Canada (Working Paper No. 2020/14, Ryerson Centre for Immigration and Settlement, October 2020).

Tully, J. (1994). Diversity's Gambit Declined. In Cook, C. (ed.), *Constitutional Predicament: Canada after the Referendum of 1992*. McGill-Queen's University Press, pp. 149–98.

Van Oorschot, W. (2006). Making the Difference in Social Europe: Deservingness Perceptions among Citizens of European Welfare States, *Journal of European Social Policy*, 16/1: 23–42.

Verkuyten, M., & Martinovic, B. (2017). Collective Psychological Ownership and Intergroup Relations, *Perspectives on Psychological Science*, 12/6: 1021–39.

Appendix: Membership Commitment Questions

BETTER PLACE	Do demands made by each of the following groups makes Canada a better place to live or a worse place to live?
PATRIOTIC	Where would you rate [group] on the following dimensions: Unpatriotic-Patriotic
IDENTITY	How much do you think each of the following groups identifies with Canada?
CARES	How much do you think each group cares about the concerns and needs of other Canadians?
THANKFUL	The government provides various programs and benefits that seek to help various communities in Canada. How thankful do you think each group is to receive these benefits?
SACRIFICE	How willing do you think the following groups are to make sacrifices for other Canadians?
FAIR SHARE	One way citizens contribute to society is by working and paying taxes. Given the resources available in each community, do you think the following groups are contributing their fair share, or more or less than their fair share?
FIGHT	If Canada was involved in a war, how willing do you think people from each of the following groups would be to volunteer to fight for Canada?

5 Reconciling the Cultural Claims of Majorities and Minorities

MICHAEL DA SILVA AND DANIEL M. WEINSTOCK

Introduction

"Liberal nationalists" of the 1990s/2000s (e.g., Tamir 1993, Kymlicka 2000) sought to pair the motivational force of national identity with basic egalitarian commitments to building a liberal "nation" with which all persons in a jurisdiction could identify. By contrast, a new strand of "majority nationalists" unabashedly claim that majority culture should be at the core of national identity and should determine policy such that several policy domains be conditioned by national "values" and the promotion of majority cultures be an object of public policy (Orgad 2015, Goodhart 2017, Eatwell and Goodwin 2018). The case for this "majority nationalism" takes multiple forms. Some believe that practical and theoretical "pendula" have swung too far toward protecting minority rights and correspondingly culturally neutered conceptions of the nation. Others suggest that it stems from the sense (factually based or not) that majorities are themselves vulnerable; forces over which they exercise no control have (or at least appear to have) placed them in a position of vulnerability akin to that of minorities (e.g., Orgad 2015). Both accounts purport to ground majority cultural rights in a manner akin to those recognized for minorities.

Will Kymlicka's chapter "Nationhood, Multiculturalism, and the Ethics of Membership" develops two arguments for resisting majority rights recognition. First, accepting majoritarian claims as valid bases for cultural rights would inevitably have deleterious effects on minority rights, leading to a questioning and, potentially, rolling back of existing minority protections and fueling those who oppose them in countries that have not yet recognized them. Second, emphasizing majority cultures more would exacerbate "membership penalties" paid by minorities that are key to the nationalist project. Kymlicka concludes that problems raised by majority nationalism deserving theorists' attention should lead people to work toward "nationalizing" the multiculturalist project.

The problem raised by majority nationalism is, we argue, likely more difficult than Kymlicka suggests. Kymlicka's arguments for nationalizing multiculturalism and against majority rights rest on assumptions with which one can reasonably disagree, namely, that there is nothing to majority rights claims, and that the main challenge that it raises has to do with "repackaging" multiculturalism so as to make it more palatable to members of majorities. But the grounds on which Kymlicka himself defends minority rights may require recognizing at least some majority rights. As we outline below, Kymlickean liberals appear bound by parity of reasoning to countenance some majority nationalists' claims and seek ways to institutionally accommodate them. Some of these claims must be *addressed*, not just neutralized. A plausible Kymlickean variant of the vulnerability-based argument for majority rights does not mean that liberal-democrats must address *all* majoritarian cultural claims. But it may be the case that some should, subject to their satisfying basic liberal-democratic constraints.

Kymlicka's Argument

A reconstruction of Kymlicka's argument helps explain why we think the majority rights issue is more complicated for a Kymlickean liberal than it may initially seem. That argument revolves around a number of main claims. Some will be familiar to readers of Kymlicka's previous work. Others constitute important new developments. We re-order them for simplicity of presentation. The first claim lays the groundwork for much of the argument. It holds that nationalism is an empirically essential condition for achieving many progressive political objectives. Creating a sense of shared membership is particularly essential for stabilizing support for the welfare state, which is grounded not in universal feelings of humanitarian justice or self-interest, but in the sense that "we" constitute a unit that is joined by a common transgenerational identity for which it makes sense to make the sacrifices involved in the welfare state. When making social policy, we do not ask ourselves for whom we are making social policy. The fact that we have a shared identity forecloses that question. On Kymlicka's view (shared by other progressives, like Philippe Van Parijs), a shared national identity is an important historical achievement largely because it provides a motivational base for the welfare state and creates a rampart against the kind of sectarianism found in places, like Northern Ireland, where the "who" of politics remains indeterminate.

The second claim is that minority rights must remedy problems raised by this needed national solidarity. Even benign nationalisms emphasize the culture of a historically rooted majority (Kymlicka, Chapter 4, in this volume). Nationalism's advantages as a support for the welfare state and break on possible sectarian violence makes accepting its risks worthwhile, but the risks must themselves be offset by minority rights guarantees: "The fundamental priority in terms of justice cannot be to ramp up nation-building, but … to *constrain* nation-building by minority rights" (p. 99).

The third claim denies the legitimacy of majority rights. Kymlicka worries about the impact that acceding to some majoritarian claims might have on the hard-won minority rights. He also argues that the claims lack empirical grounding. Majorities claim that the "battery" of national identity (to use Margaret Canovan's image) has been depleted and can no longer "power" the progressive causes to which it has historically been put. Kymlicka denies this is so. Though nationalism and national identity may not be "front of mind" for many people today, it powerfully grounds identities, all the more so, perhaps, for being imperceptible and, to use Michael Billig's expression, "banal." Kymlicka further claims that foregrounding national identity to a greater degree than we do already by default, risks tipping the subtle balance between majorities and minorities crucial to nationalism doing its progressive work without lapsing into discrimination and exclusion.

The fourth claim is that the cultural distance of minorities from the "paradigmatic" member of the nation raises problems of justice. This perceived distance tends to breed suspicion of minorities' commitments to the nation and corresponding deservingness of full membership benefits. This suspicion is exacerbated by the kind of mobilization minority groups engage in to secure their rights. Whereas, political mobilization by majority members is interpreted by other majority members as a normal manifestation of membership in the polity, minority mobilization is viewed as betokening distance. Minorities thus face a "penalty" for protecting their cultures. We return to this argument, which is severable from the others, in more detail below.

We thus arrive at an unwelcome tension, bordering on contradiction. On the one hand, multicultural policies of the kind that Kymlicka has long advocated are necessary components of the liberal nationalist picture given the antecedent likelihood that even the most seemingly inclusive nationalisms tend to emphasize majority cultures. On the other hand, the policies required to address this fact are likely to exacerbate sentiments that minorities are not really part of "us." The search for a liberal nationalism capable of fulfilling its intended role remains elusive.

The solution to this seeming dilemma cannot be to negate either minority rights or majority nationalism. Rather, Kymlicka proposes a kind of Hegelian *aufhebung* of its horns. Rather than thinking of multicultural policies as ones in which minorities oppose the steamroller of majoritarianism and defend against their predations, people should think of multiculturalism as a national project, something that "we" do together. "Nationalizing multiculturalism" can re-describe the claimed dilemma's horns to reveal their potential compatibility and complementarity.

Rethinking Multiculturalism

The idea of a national multiculturalist project is intriguing. Indeed, even minorities who use constitutional rights to secure judicial protections of their cultures could be described as reflecting a form of patriotism. They use one of society's central institutions to protect values that have been formally recognized as central to the polity's identity. Yet legal rights claims formally present themselves as oppositional. A majority expresses its will through its majoritarian institutions, and a minority attempts to thwart it by recourse to the judiciary. What's more, to revert to a hoary political-philosophical distinction, minorities advocate on the basis of the "right," eschewing talk of the "good." One can interpret Kymlicka as calling for a different "framing" of multiculturalism according to which it should be redescribed in a way that brings out the aspects of it that conduce to the good of a whole society that are not sufficiently highlighted when the focus is placed on its oppositional dimensions. All members of society might be more likely to get on the multiculturalist "bandwagon" if multiculturalism is something "we" do together. The idea of a society in which all stand in defense of each other's legitimate differences is on the face of it far from an unattractive conception of the good. National multiculturalism has clear appeal.

Kymlicka's proposal nonetheless faces formidable obstacles. The first is political. Multiculturalism's political fate has been at best, mixed. Whatever multiculturalism's theoretical merits and whatever its success as a model of immigrant integration in countries that implemented multiculturalist theory-inspired integration, attempts to "nationalize" multiculturalism will be hampered by the unpopularity of the multiculturalist "brand." Moreover, support for multiculturalism is weakest precisely where the call for an affirmation of majority nationalism is the strongest – and thus where rhetorical reimagining of multiculturalism seems most needed on Kymlicka's account (Alexander 2013). "Rebranding" under a new name will not change this. For instance, while "interculturalism" has been adopted in some societies that reject multiculturalism as a model of integration, it is unclear whether substantive differences exist between the models (Weinstock 2013), as Kymlicka himself notes (Kymlicka 2016). Opponents of multiculturalism are generally unconvinced by claims that interculturalism is a true alternative (Bock-Côté 2016).

As a result, one may question the empirical case for nationalizing multiculturalism as a solution to this problem. One can reasonably worry about whether nationalizing multiculturalism will have the predicted effects. Critiques of earlier "liberal nationalisms" might also apply to "nationalist multiculturalism." For instance, one could, again, be dubious about the idea that majority nationalists who are skeptical of liberalism would be willing to accept a liberal view just because it is repackaged in a nationalist form (see Da Silva 2020, on "moderate nationalism"). One may further wonder whether the "best of both worlds" would actually be realized in a joint nationalist-multicultural project or if protections for national and multicultural goods present a "zero-sum" game like the one applied to alternatives as suggested by Kymlicka. Moreover, even if "nationalist multiculturalism" is a genuine alternative to traditional nationalism and traditional liberalism or multiculturalism that reflects the best of both worlds, one may wonder whether the moral psychology of proponents of traditional views will lead them to respond to this fact by adopting the amalgamation (Da Silva 2020). Clara Sandelind's contribution to this volume raises more questions about national multiculturalism's ability to change majority views – and still others about its ability to secure other intended benefits, like bolstering the kind of support for solidarity that is valuable for maintaining a thriving welfare state (Sandelind, Chapter 6, in this volume). The balance of (clearly limited) existing evidence could support a prediction to the contrary as much as it does Kymlicka's proposal.

Finally, and most importantly, the rhetorical strategy that "nationalizing multiculturalism" represents is premised on the assumption that the "battery" of majority nationalism is fully powered in all places in which calls for a greater recognition of majority culture have been heard. It supposes that giving greater pride of place to these claims will imperil minority rights without yielding corresponding benefits to do with the satisfaction of possibly national majorities' legitimate moral claims. Yet both assumptions can be reasonably questioned. Kymlicka's proposal that multiculturalism should be rendered more attractive to members of national majorities by being "nationalized" actually belongs to a family of proposals made by those who are sensitive to the destabilizing effect that majorities can have when they wrongly believe that they are victims of injustice. While Kymlicka's strategy is to bring majorities on board by framing policies justifiable on non-nationalist grounds in ways that at least rhetorically resonate with national majorities (a strategy similar to that of fellow liberal nationalist Yael Tamir (2019)), others propose more robust, oppositional political strategies, like "militant democracy" (Kirshner 2014). All these otherwise different political proposals are united in the belief that there is normatively nothing to the claims made on behalf of national majorities and the claims simply have to be confronted or channeled into more benign directions to avoid their potential political costs. So, the issue is political, not philosophical. Sandelind's "cosmopolitan patriotism"– based approach too, likely fits along this continuum insofar as it denies the value of majority nationalist claims and promotes an alternative political position that would require majority nationalists to abandon central concerns. Among these views, we are open to the possibility that Kymlicka's strategy might be best if there is nothing to national majorities' claims. To the degree that the polities to which they belong fully satisfy their legitimate claims, further claims majorities make for greater recognition or accommodation are to be neutralized or rendered benign, rather than addressed.

However, the most fundamental point to be made against the "nationalizing multiculturalism" solution is that it is premised on the assumption that there is nothing normatively significant to the claims of national majorities, and that all that needs to be done about them is to neutralize them or channel them in a politically benign way. There is, in short, reason to question whether all majority rights claims are indeed invalid. In what follows, we argue that there is at least a set of cases in which the claims of national majorities should be addressed, rather than neutralized or combatted. What's more, these are cases to which Kymlicka himself should be sensitive.

In a nutshell, there are at least some cases in which some national majorities are rendered vulnerable by political and socioeconomic forces that, all things being equal, are morally analogous to the kinds of forces that make minorities vulnerable, and that have historically underpinned the arguments in Kymlicka's work for group-differentiated rights. At least some national majorities are today rendered culturally vulnerable by forces that are in at least certain crucial respects morally analogous to those that afflict some minorities. In the main, they result not from the ill intent of others, but from the operation of political forces that are, aside from their effects, in and of themselves morally neutral. What's more, protections afforded to individuals in what Alan Patten (2014) calls the "standard liberal package" (individual rights protections in the case of members of minority groups, control over democratic majoritarian institutions in the case of members of national majorities) are insufficient to offset the vulnerability created by these forces (Armstrong 2019). By parity of reasoning, theorists who are convinced by Kymlicka's arguments for minority rights should be prepared to consider that some cultural majorities have at least prima facie rights.

Our point is not that majorities and minorities are both groups and should thus have the same kinds of groups' rights (Newman 2018). Rather, we argue that the same normative reasons that are said to ground minority cultural rights can ground at least some majority cultural rights. These facts suffice to make majority rights claims the kinds of things that must be addressed in normative theorizing. While one could build a parity of reasoning argument on several grounds (e.g., Patten 2020), we focus in what follows on a vulnerability-based argument inspired by Kymlicka's work. Further facts are then necessary to explain how and when the rights claimed require institutional responses. But we should not assume that protecting rights is a zero-sum game absent strong evidence therefor. Accordingly, one cannot deny the possibilities that morality will sometimes require institutional protections for majority rights consistent with minority rights protections and that those institutional demands can be justly instantiated consistent with minority rights.

A Parity of Reasoning Argument[1]

People are often skeptical about majority claims for cultural protection due to two implicit assumptions: (1) cultural protection is a remedy for vulnerability and (2) vulnerability tracks minority status. Yet majority cultures could be vulnerable by virtue of a number of political processes for which the fact of possessing control of nation-state-based majoritarian institutions does not represent a sufficient safeguard. For example, such vulnerability can stem from membership in a larger group with more powerful members (e.g., the Baltic states in the European Union), geographic proximity with countries the languages of which exercise significant sociolinguistic pressures, and the like (Weinstock 2020). As Orgad (2015) notes in another parity of reasoning argument, globalization, mass immigration, and minority rights claims could make majority groups more vulnerable still. Many of these pressures surely correspond to requirements of justice. For instance, refugee rights "trump" concerns about majority cultures (Weinstock 2020). But even then, the recognition that the vulnerability-based claims made by majorities are not as weighty as other justified claims might be does not mean that they have no weight. Even outweighed moral claims leave moral remainders. What's more, as we will now suggest, some of the pressures that contribute to the vulnerability of some national majorities are not requirements of justice. The second assumption is thus only even contingently true if modified into a claim about the groups' relative vulnerability. Yet relative vulnerability should matter if we care about cultural diversity and use it to justify minority rights. The first assumption then appears persuasive only when grounded in earlier assumptions about the value of cultures and cultural diversity. Those should apply equally to majorities and minorities.

Cultural vulnerability, in other words, is not conceptually connected to minority status (Armstrong 2019). If we value culture as the justification for existing minority rights protections, we should care about threats to culture regardless of whether the group culture is a majority or minority one. Some majority cultures can be and likely are currently vulnerable. So, some majority claims for cultural protections should have at least prima facie weight even if these claims are outweighed by other, weightier moral considerations.

Now, one may object that there is no reason to protect any culture simpliciter. Cultural protections can "freeze" (Borrows 2016) and/or folklorize (Patten 2014) culture, inhibiting the very self-determination of people that is meant to ground cultural protections. We agree, but this purported objection applies equally to minority protection rights and so does not undermine our parity of reasoning argument. While one may suggest that there is a form of domination in the minority rights case that makes it differ from the majority rights case, it is not clear whether domination is missing in the case of some majority cultures in smaller states. This objection thus does not undermine majority cultural rights alone but unduly inflexible cultural rights of all kinds.

Linguistic globalization is a plausible instantiation of the phenomenon we seek to identify. This phenomenon has rendered majority languages vulnerable in a way that makes them plausible candidates for rights by parity of the same reasoning Kymlicka applies in earlier work. Consider what one of us recently termed "mere numbers cases" in which linguistic groups of different sizes co-exist and interact across national borders in the absence of obvious injustice (Weinstock 2015, 2020). Linguistic globalization makes it the case that languages are no longer necessarily well protected by the fact of having, to use Van Parijs' (2011) phrase, "grabbed a territory." Indeed, linguistic globalization, placing as it does languages of radically different sizes in contact, and thus competition, with one another based on "Laponce's (1994) law," renders the languages of national majorities, heretofore thought to be unassailable because of their control of a territory, in a condition comparable to that of minority languages within nation-states. Where language is central to any plausible conceptualization of "culture," it follows that at least some cultures are subject to forces that should concern theorists concerned with the political protection of culture. This is so regardless of whether the language is, on the national level, a majority or minority language.

This is not simply a theoretical worry. There is increasing evidence that majority languages (and cultures) face threats that could require protection in "mere numbers" cases, that is, cases in which languages of quite different sizes interact across national boundaries without the pressure exercised by the larger language betokening injustice. Consider the incentives to study and use English to gain access to elite practices in Sweden (e.g., Berg et al. 2001), as just one example. The survival of Baltic languages is also a matter of constant concern, given the pressures imposed upon them by a regionally dominant language (Russian), by the "bigger" languages spoken by citizens of Baltic states' trading partners in the European Union, and by the global lingua franca, English. The Internet, of course, magnifies the threat posed by "bigger" languages, in Sweden, the Baltics, and elsewhere.[2] While some might argue that language drift and extinction is simply a fact that, when it does not arise from injustice, is regrettable, rather than a matter of justice, this reaction is not obviously available to Kymlicka. On the Kymlickean argument, failures to protect vulnerable cultures against foreseeable threats to their being able to function as "contexts of choice" for their members *constitutes* an injustice, whether that threat emanates from ill intent or from more morally neutral causes. Mere number cases in which no (narrowly construed) injustice is present but threats to majorities remain raise (broadly construed) justice issues that on Kymlicka's analysis appear bound to be viewed as morally significant on pain of inconsistency.

To see how deeply a concern for vulnerable majority cultures should, by parity of reasoning, be rooted in Kymlicka's theory, it is worth considering both his earlier and more recently developed views. His original case for minority rights noted that minorities are subjects to threats to their culture through overt state action or benign neglect, and that some protections are necessary to protect minority cultures central to minority members' self-understanding and basic conception of the good (recall Kymlicka 1989, 1995). This view actually consists of several lines of argument. Two lines of argument are particularly important for the present inquiry: on what one of us once called the "autonomy argument," minority rights are necessary because minority groups provide necessary contexts for exercising individual autonomy and those groups will not be able to fulfill that role absent "group-differentiated" rights protections, while on what one of us called the "equality argument," minority rights protections are necessary to provide members with equal opportunity for the goods of cultural membership (Weinstock 1998 summarizing Kymlicka 1989, 1995). Whether the latter argument can be divorced from the former is debatable, though some non-autonomy-based set of cultural goods plausibly must be identified to complete a severable equality argument. Whether all minority groups to whom Kymlicka sought to provide rights furthered autonomy and/or required minority rights protections to provide a fair range of opportunity remains debatable. Yet the basic idea that minority rights protections were meant to protect against threats against valuable cultures, whichever they might be, is compelling and remains the classic position on minority rights.

In his more recent work, including his contribution to this volume, Kymlicka claims that minority rights are necessary to offset distributional "penalties" faced by those who belong to minority cultures in which minorities are forced to prove their membership in the broader community – and thus entitlement to welfare benefits – by explaining how their identities are consistent with the national one. This appears to be a version of the "equality argument" that is not supposed to rely on appeals to threats to autonomy alone. Majority cultures are viewed as identical to national cultures such that members of majorities never have to defend their membership rights. Minorities are viewed with suspicion and are forced to lobby for their membership rights. They can be denied basic welfare benefits accorded to others when they fail to do so. This creates a distributive justice problem – minorities receive fewer goods than majorities or penalties for receiving the same goods due to the brute luck of their cultural position in a way that violates basic liberal-democratic norms. Minority rights are necessary to remedy this distributional injustice, not to protect "inherently" valuable cultures.

Kymlicka believes that his arguments favor minority rights protections alone, at least when deciding what to do within nation-states. Both early and more recent Kymlickean arguments ground minority rights protections in threats that Kymlicka views as uniquely applying to minority groups and cultures. On both accounts, minorities alone face unjust threats that arise from the state's commitment to nationhood. In the more recent version, the threats take the form of "penalties" faced by minority groups when seeking to protect their cultural interests and/or (it is unclear as stated) secure access to welfare benefits. This view responds to majoritarian concerns that his earlier account valorized minority rights to the detriment of majority cultures. In light of a potential parity of reasoning argument from "threats" simpliciter, Kymlicka's present contribution seeks to identify a unique set of threats, now described as penalties, that apply to minorities alone.

Majorities may face threats to their culture, this piece seems to suggest, but they can act against those threats in manners consistent with furthering the national culture. Those promoting minority cultures, by contrast, are perceived as furthering a non-state identity and as less trustworthy and less deserving of rights and social benefits. Minority rights protections alone are necessary to offset distributional errors in terms of the efforts needed to promote the protection of identities and/or pre-empt welfare benefit distributional injustices.

Contrary to Kymlicka's understanding of his work, the moral considerations justifying minority rights on both accounts now plausibly justify at least some majority claims. Kymlicka's original formulation in terms of threats should be agnostic with respect to whether the threatened culture is majoritarian or minoritarian. Like Kymlicka, we do not view any culture as having inherent value. But the *source* of value of each culture is the same. Majority cultures can be crucial contexts for exercising autonomy. The threats to each culture are now parallel too. This alone should justify some majority cultural protections. While the source of the threats may differ, threats to the goods of cultural community – be they the autonomy central to (at least early) Kymlicka or another good one can import into his view – now apply to an Estonian in Estonia and a Quebecker in Canada. Pointing to the different sources of the threats to justify differential treatment appears ad hoc absent further argument not found in the literature. Where distribution is indexed to these goods, the threats should create distributional problems for all groups to whom they apply.

Even if, in turn, the equality argument can be divorced from the autonomy argument, the assumption that threats to minority groups alone produce distributional errors no longer seems justified. Estonians' opportunities for the goods of cultural membership within an Estonian group that Estonians view as central to their identities are now fewer than an Englishman's opportunities for the same within an English group. Still greater distributional issues arise with respect to the other goods of societal membership writ large when one compares an Estonian's opportunities with those of a cosmopolitan in the same state. Though that particular concern may be more pressing for the more recent penalty-based account than the classic one, it also seems capable of grounding majority rights claims in at least some cases. Focus on distributional justice simpliciter still seems to generate at least some valid majority rights claims. Incentives to be cosmopolitans within states can, in turn, threaten the majority culture within it. Elite English language programs in universities in Sweden take up resources within the state that could be used to foster Swedish language programs, constraining institutional opportunities to grow the Swedish identity that is key to many persons' self-identity – and again raising the general distributional issues in which English language graduates receive greater benefits.

There is then reason to question whether the more recent penalty-based approach uniquely picks out minority cultures for protection as claimed. Let us grant here that this argument is unique – and not "parasitic" on the autonomy argument like an earlier equality argument (Weinstock 1998: 292) – and speaks to different concerns. The cultural good that minority groups face a penalty for furthering (and that majorities do not face) remains undefined. To the extent that we accept a proxy for that good, the case for minority rights protections still may not go through. Kymlicka's more recent account takes for granted that (a) the case for majority rights protections stems from concerns that overly expansive minority rights protections are the source of threats to majorities, (b) desert-based considerations are relevant to assessing the truth of (a) in a way that can lead one to identify the relevant moral considerations for assessing threats and/or penalties, and (c) the framework in (b) identifies how minorities alone face penalties in terms of the efforts one must take to promote protection of one's identity and/or pre-empt welfare benefit distributional injustices. It is not clear that any of these assumptions are warranted or justify minority rights alone as claimed. Contrary to (a), the case for majority rights protections need not rest on concerns about overly expansive minority rights claims in a way that pits the interests of one against the other. As noted above, majority cultures are subject to threats from other sources that are analogous to those facing minority cultures and now ground valid claims for similar protections. The claim that they are necessarily opposed appears unmotivated.

Even if, in turn, we grant that the majority and minority interests and/or rights need to be weighed against each other, whether the deservingness literature provides the best framework for doing so is questionable. Even if we accept *that*, the move from "minorities are viewed as less deserving" to "they alone face penalties for motivating their interests," let alone "so they will need to do more to get welfare benefits," takes work. The last claim is empirically contestable, and this is not the place for empirical debate. But even the idea that minorities alone face penalties in motivating their interests in domestic politics, let alone at the global level, may no longer survive scrutiny. One central insight of the political movements contingently related to majoritarian claims is that access to "elite" institutions within states is now primarily constrained to those who fit a demographic profile that includes mastery of foreign languages, most notably English. This is an identified cause of some forms of modern nationalism (Eatwell and Goodwin 2018). Those who seek to speak in a majority national language that is not in global use do face a penalty in their attempt to further their political, cultural, or economic ends. Where protecting a majority culture through domestic politics increasingly requires also learning another language to prove one's international and elite bona fides, the penalties for promoting one's own language should be clear and serve as at least one source of threats to even majority languages. This may not mean that majorities face the same threats to accessing welfare benefits as minorities, but the source of those difficulties may not be attributable to penalties for furthering one's interests in domestic politics and similar penalties now accrue to all groups. These points also undermine (b) and (c) above.

Moreover, even if Kymlicka is right that minorities uniquely face these penalties within states, and that these penalties alone are relevant for assessing the need for legal protections within states, this would not suffice to establish that there are no reasons to recognize majority rights as morally valuable and incorporate majoritarian claims into a broader account of justice. The parity of reasoning argument for majority rights would still go through at a more global level. Kymlicka's distributional argument would then be compelling in the narrow boundaries in which it is made in his important contribution to this volume, but we would still need an explanation of why that narrow domestic sphere alone is morally important for assessing majority rights claims. The same kinds of considerations that led Kymlicka to focus in the case of national minorities on external protections – that is, on protections that might be written into the broader state's constitution, rather than on internal restrictions – might lead in the case of vulnerable majority cultures to focusing on protections available in global institutional settings, rather than domestically, where the control by majorities of majoritarian institutions might lead them to adopting measures aimed at protecting their cultures that unjustifiably limit minority rights protections.

In order to meet this challenge, one might be tempted to reach back into Kymlicka's original argument for minority rights, grounded in the notion of "contexts of choice." The counter-argument would be to the effect that Kymlicka's argument cannot extend to majority rights claims because majorities do not face threats to their contexts for choice and the plausibility of Kymlicka's case for minority rights protections stemmed from the way in which minorities were deprived of a context of choice in liberal-democratic states, not threats to their culture simpliciter. On this view, the value of minority rights lies in their ability to protect against threats to group members' contexts of choice. Majority rights, it might be claimed, never protect against *those* threats. According to this line of argument, the majority's context of choice always remains in place even in the case of vulnerable cultures, because majorities ex hypothesi have a state that paradigmatically makes their likely choices the default outcome of the operation of majoritarian institutions. Insofar as culture is valuable as a context for choice, its value always remains in majority states because the majority and state culture are identical. Something like this argument could explain Kymlicka's claims in this volume that majorities are not subject to penalties because their culture and the state culture are largely coextensive. The relevant interests are, on this criticism, simply dis-analogous.

Yet while majority cultures are often (albeit, it is worth noting, not always) coextensive with national ones, this does limit the scope of relevant moral interests as claimed. The issue of whether focusing on the importance of contexts for choice actually justifies applying Kymlicka's arguments to paradigmatic cases of necessary minority rights protections was once a subject of lively debate (Weinstock 1998: 288–92). To the extent that limiting application of his argument to circumstances where there is a threat to the context of choice rules out majority cultures from the protective ambit of group-differentiated rights, it may also rule out minority cultures that have a reasonable amount of political independence within an encompassing state. This move would thus prove too much. At minimum, it would not suffice to establish that there is no parity of reasoning argument for majority cultural rights. Those who believe that minority cultures are subject to threats qua contexts of choice need to establish why the threats discussed here do not qualify as analogous threats. If languages really are core components of societal cultures, and thus, of contexts of choice, and locally majority languages are under pressure, it follows that some majoritarian contexts of choice are under threat and in need of protection. Minorities may face *greater* threats, but this simply establishes that they are in greater need of protection. Absent evidence that rights protection is a zero-sum game, this does not undermine our arguments. One can be privileged with respect to X and vulnerable with respect to Y or overall. Vulnerability to Y should be able to ground valid claims for all groups to which it applies.

Alternatively, one could say that the cases differ because the sources of vulnerability differ across them. Minorities are threatened by the operation of majoritarian democratic institutions, whereas majority cultures are threatened by more diffuse global forces. However, on Kymlicka's account, the source of threats should not be central in determining whether they can form the basis of a moral claim that liberal-democrats must address. The point of minority rights is to address threats to moral goods that we value, rather than focusing on certain *kinds* of threats (threats that emerge from injustice or ill intent, for example). Indeed, international law's particular concern with minority rights is best rendered legible in recognition of the fact that domestic protections alone cannot protect minority cultures subject to multivariant threats, not all of which can be easily attributed to any specific actor. Analogous majoritarian protections are now warranted in political morality, if not law. While some other explanation of why different kinds of vulnerability that only apply to minority cases could justify a disanalogy claim, it is presently unclear what that might be.

This fact also helps address the concern that the preceding argument misses Kymlicka's point because at least Kymlicka's present contribution is explicitly concerned with justice *within* nation-states. Majority cultures are the beneficiaries of the nation-state-based world order. Minority cultures are not. Minority cultural rights remedy that distributional issue alone. Expanding the argument to address further concerns simply misunderstands the scope of Kymlicka's argument on this objection. However, the above point about majoritarian difficulties in domestic politics remains. Moreover, even if that line of argument fails, it is unclear why injustices within states should be the sole source of moral concern here. As we hinted above, one could plausibly state that equality of opportunity for the goods of cultural membership within states always favors the majority group. Estonians are always better able to enjoy the social benefits of cultural membership *in Estonia* than non-Estonians. Yet, even if we grant this empirical claim, it is still not clear that Estonians are equally able to enjoy the benefits of social membership when compared with other national groups, nor is it clear that this form of inequality is morally unimportant and/or should not be addressed in liberal-democratic politics. Again, even stating that minority rights alone are justified within states does not entail that they alone are justified all-things-considered. *Global* justice concerns remain important. Indeed, whereas Kymlicka takes the division of the world into nation-states for granted and seeks to analyze its distributional impacts, it would appear ad hoc to ignore the broader context of distribution of powers. The goods of cultural belonging cannot be analyzed at the state level alone. If this is so, the concerns underlying Kymlicka's argument do not suffice to show that there are no valid majority rights claims that liberal-democrats must address in at least some political spheres. As we will detail in future work, attending to the broader relevant context provides a clear case for expanding the scope of concern to the international level.

There is, then, at least one domain in which claims about threats to majorities have to be addressed by liberal-democratic theory. This leaves several questions open. For instance, is linguistic globalization, and the attendant linguistic insecurity to which it gives rise in some national majorities, the only case that fits the various requirements we have set forth in order to identify cases of majority cultural insecurity to which liberals ought to pay some heed if they are to be consistent with their defense of certain minority rights? Would the defense of other aspects of culture breach the principle according to which liberals should only concern themselves with protecting the aspect of culture that has to do with cultural "structure," rather than its "content" (Kymlicka 1995)? Attending to which other aspects of culture can justifiably be protected and when requires its own work. Yet even a limited sense of parallel application is potentially important. Indeed, a finding that Kymlicka's arguments might apply to majority groups remains notable even if parity of reasoning would only require majority linguistic rights.

Constraints on Majority Rights Claims

Having to some extent opened the conceptual window for the legitimacy of some majority nationalist cultural claims, we will conclude our arguments by placing a filter on it. Ours is a liberal-democratic account of majority claims, and so, in a manner that extends its parity of reasoning nature, we want (as Kymlicka does with minority rights claims) to define constraints that any claim (judged by us to be legitimate) must satisfy. This seems particularly important in the present context where the kinds of claims we are considering have been put forward by decidedly non-liberal-democratic movements and parties. Indeed, one motivation of the present project is to find a way of giving liberal-democratic expression to some majority rights claims in a manner that at least partly blocks what has often been the almost automatic association of majority nationalism with populist, conservative, and nationalist political movements. Regardless of whether addressing majoritarian claims in liberal-democratic politics will best "neutralize" the more problematic views contingently related to them, it strikes us as worth evaluating those claims independently of those views. But incorporation may have political benefits tied to not assuming that only right-wing populism can be a vehicle for some cultural majorities' concerns.

The first constraint that we propose requires some indication that the people in the state in question actually value the majority culture and wish to protect it. We do not, again, believe that any culture is intrinsically valuable and so must be protected absent any interest in doing so. We do not wish to "freeze"/folklorize cultures. The point of our parity of reasoning argument is that some cultures provide important moral goods to members of the culture and we should be concerned with threats to the cultures because they also threaten individual goods. If people no longer value a culture and explicitly wish to change it, the case for protection no longer applies. Our concern is cases where people wish to maintain a reasonably justly-formed majority culture that is threatened by factors that lead even those who value the culture to act in ways that may run contrary to even minimally sufficient protection of the relevant majority culture.

The second constraint is that of factual plausibility. The *perception* and the *reality* of vulnerability are different things. The former can be generated, absent any plausible empirical basis, by a number of factors. Two seem particularly important to specify here. First, some national majorities may experience a sense of loss because they have been compelled by various political forces to give up a prior position of unjustified and unjust superiority. For example, the requirement (imposed, e.g., as a condition of joining a group like the European

Union) that majorities respect minority rights where they previously had not done so may give rise to a sense of loss and vulnerability. We will not countenance or accommodate any claims grounded in perceptions of loss of unjust privilege. Second, perceptions of vulnerability are often the result of political entrepreneurship undertaken by political parties, movements, and media that strategically induce false perceptions of vulnerability in the majority population to position themselves as best capable of responding to the sense of threat that they themselves created without empirical basis. Again, liberal-democrats should not be in the business of accommodating the political expression of such perceptions or the activities that generate them. The liberal-democrat concerned with vulnerability should only be concerned, as a theoretical matter, with real majority vulnerabilities (Eisenberg 2019).

The final constraint we will discuss here is that political measures adopted to address vulnerabilities cannot deny or abridge minority rights. This reflects a more general constraint implicit in our approach under which no measure can violate basic liberal-democratic norms. Just as Kymlicka was insistent on distinguishing between external protections and internal restrictions, we take as parametric that addressing the global problem of cultural vulnerability involves the hard-wiring of minority rights into the basic architecture of pluralist liberal-democracies. Unlike Kymlicka, we see no reason to assume that majority and minority rights protections cannot co-exist, at least absent further argument. Minority rights protections are sometimes presented by conservative nationalists as a cause of majority culture erosion. Their limitation is then presented as part of the solution to that problematic erosion. But we cannot simply assume that protections for both sets of rights cannot co-exist, at least in the linguistic case. While Laponce's law makes the co-existence of languages difficult, *protections* for multiple sets of languages challenged by that law may co-exist. In contrast, the solutions that we envisage to address justified majority nationalist claims view minority rights protections as non-negotiable. In further work related to the present inquiry, we look toward international law and institutions as the spaces within which to articulate solutions to the claims made on behalf of majorities that do not end up being in a zero-sum relation to minority rights protections. But we cannot assume the zero-sum nature even here.

Conclusion

There is, then, at least one family of majority rights claims that must be addressed in liberal-democratic theory by parity of reasoning used to require addressing minority rights. This case and reasonable questions about assumptions underlying Kymlicka's proposal for voiding majority rights claims suggest that some majority rights claims complicate the moral landscape more than some liberal-democrats suppose. Of course, institutional responses to even potentially valid majority rights claims are themselves only acceptable when liberal-democratic constraints apply. But we cannot assume that no institutional response is capable of existing subject to those constraints or that majority and minority rights protection is a zero-sum game. Further work should attempt to examine if and when institutional responses to majority rights claims can be justifiable subject to these constraints. It should also, as we have suggested in this comment and will argue in further detail elsewhere, look to the area of international law and politics as the appropriate conceptual and institutional space within which to attempt to effect this reconciliation.

Notes

1 In the final version of his piece in this volume, Kymlicka now acknowledges the force of this parity of reasoning argument. What flows from this is a question for further investigation. It is at least possible that recognition of state sovereignty will not provide adequate protections as claimed. Indeed, they appear unable to do so in the cases at issue here. The precise forms of international actions that may be required must be the subject of further work, which we plan to produce. The question of whether these issues are best dealt with in terms of "rights" is, in turn, largely a semantic issue.

2 On the Baltics, see, e.g., the essays on Latvian and Estonian collected in Vila Moreno (2012). For insight into the Internet's role as the vehicle of linguistic globalization, see e.g., <www.theguardian.com/education/2014/mar/26/digital-extinction-europe-languages-fight-survive>.

References

Alexander, J. C. (2013). Struggling over the Mode of Incorporation: Backlash against Multiculturalism in Europe. *Ethnic and Racial Studies*, 36/4: 531–56.

Armstrong, F. (2019). *Minoritization and Vulnerability: New Foundations of a Non-Ideal Theory of Multiculturalism.* PhD thesis, Department of Philosophy, McGill University.

Berg, E. C. et al. (2001). Shaping the Climate for Language Shift? English in Sweden's Elite Domains. *World Englishes*, 20/3: 305–19.

Bock-Côté, M. (2016). *Le Multiculturalisme Comme Religion Politique.* Éditions du Cerf.

Borrows, J. (2016). *Freedom and Indigenous Constitutionalism.* Toronto: University of Toronto Press.

Da Silva, M. (2020). Review Essay: The Case for "Moderate" Nationalism. *Res Publica*, 26/4: 597–605.

Eatwell, R. and Goodwin, M. (2018). *National Populism: The Revolt against Liberal Democracy*. UK: Penguin Books.

Eisenberg, A. (2019). The Rights of National Majorities: Toxic Discourse or Democratic Catharsis? *Ethnicities*, 20/2: 312–30.

Goodhart, D. (2017). *The Road to Somewhere: The Populist Revolt and the Future of Politics.* London: C. Hurst & Co.

Kirshner, A. S. (2014). *A Theory of Militant Democracy: The Ethics of Combatting Political Extremism.* New Haven: Yale University Press.

Kymlicka, W. (1989). *Liberalism, Community, and Culture.* Oxford: Oxford University Press.

(1995). *Multicultural Citizenship*. Oxford: Oxford University Press.

(2000). *Politics in the Vernacular: Nationalism, Multiculturalism, Citizenship*. Oxford: Oxford University Press.

(2016). Defending Diversity in an Era of Populism: Multiculturalism and Interculturalism Compared. In Nasar, M. et al. eds., *Multiculturalism and Interculturalism: Debating the Dividing Lines.* Edinburgh: Edinburgh University Press, 158–77.

(this volume). Nationhood, Multiculturalism, and the Ethics of Membership.

Laponce, J. (1994). *Langues et Territoire.* Québec: Presses de l'Université Laval.

Newman, D. (2018). Why Majority Rights Matter in the Context of Ethno-Cultural Diversity: The Interlinkage of Minority Rights, Indigenous Rights, and Majority Rights. In Pentassuglia, G., ed., *Ethno-Cultural Diversity and Human Rights: Challenges and Critiques.* Leiden: Brill Nijhoff, 59–89.

Orgad, L. (2015). *The Cultural Defense of Nations: A Liberal Theory of Majority Rights.* Oxford: Oxford University Press.

Patten, A. (2014). *Equal Recognition: The Moral Foundations of Minority Rights.* Princeton: Princeton University Press.

(2020). Populist Multiculturalism: Are There Majority Cultural Rights? *Social Philosophy & Criticism*, 46/5: 539–552.

Sandelind, C. (this volume). Linking Minority Rights and Majority Attitudes: Multicultural Patriotism.

Tamir, Y. (1993). *Liberal Nationalism*. Princeton: Princeton University Press.

(2019). *Why Nationalism?* Princeton: Princeton University Press.

Van Parijs, P. (2011). *Linguistic Justice for Europe and for the World*. Oxford: Oxford University Press.

Vila Moreno, X., ed., (2012). *Survival and Development of Language Communities. Prospects and Challenges*. North York: Multilingual Matters.

Weinstock, D. (1998). How Can Collective Rights and Liberalism Be Reconciled? In Bauböck, R. and Rundell, J. eds., *Blurred Boundaries: Migration, Ethnicity, Citizenship*. Ashgate: Aldershot, 281–304.

(2013). Interculturalism and Multiculturalism in Canada and Quebec: Situating the Debate. In Balint, P. and Guérard de la Tour, S. eds., *Liberal Multiculturalism and the Fair Terms of Integration*. London: Palgrave, 91–108.

(2015). Can Parity of Self-Esteem Serve as the Basis of the Principle of Linguistic Territoriality? *Critical Review of International Social and Political Philosophy*, 18/2: 199–211.

(2020). Liberalism and Language Policy in "Mere Number Cases". In Tamir, Y. and Weinstock, D. eds., *Language Ethics*. Montreal, McGill: Queens Press, 178–201.

6 *Linking Minority Rights and Majority Attitudes*

Multicultural Patriotism

CLARA SANDELIND

A central critique of nationalism is that, at best, it marginalizes and renders invisible or, at worst, persecutes and kills those minorities which are not viewed as part of the nation. Proponents of nationalism therefore painstakingly describe how their preferred form of national identity would be inclusive. By limiting the notion of a national culture to the public sphere and removing notions of race and ethnicity, liberal nationalism has been portrayed in such inclusive ways (e.g., Gustavsson 2019a; Miller 2020). To critics, however, these efforts are not enough. In their view, the exclusionary elements of nationalism make it fundamentally incompatible with liberal progressive values. Yet a key claim of liberal nationalism is that, historically and conceptually, nationalism is a *prerequisite* of such values. To liberal nationalists, the benefits of nationalism are not regrettable. Instead, nationalism is to be celebrated for its achievements in securing and stabilizing liberal, democratic welfare states (Tamir 2019).

Kymlicka is also concerned with the question of how nationalism can be made more inclusive, although his defense of nationalism is more reserved. While he believes that nationalism has brought "democratic stability, the welfare state and [...] self-determination" for "many people(s)," he also states that "I don't see any alternative to the nation-state for the foreseeable future" (Chapter 4, in this volume, p. 99. I agree with Kymlicka's diagnosis of one problem with nationalism; that it privileges stories of peoplehood which disadvantages and penalizes minorities. Moreover, his solution, for multiculturalism to "transform majority conceptions of membership and belonging to create a more inclusive solidarity" (p. 116), is promising. However, there is insufficient clarity on how *minority* rights will translate into a change in *majority* attitudes, particularly as Kymlicka (p. 97) favors "banal nationalism" as a way of maintaining the function of nationhood.[1] Instead, I apply a recent account on cosmopolitan patriotism developed by Lior Erez and Cécile Laborde (2019) to suggest that a form of *multicultural patriotism* would be more successful in engendering inclusive solidarity. I also suggest that such multicultural patriotism aligns well with Kymlicka's argument. First, let me briefly outline how Kymlicka diagnoses nationalism's problem in generating inclusive solidarity, and his preferred solution.

Minority Rights and Inclusive Solidarity

The main benefit of nationalism, according to Kymlicka, is that it constructs an "ethic of membership," which can form the basis of bounded solidarity; social justice among members as opposed to all human beings, thereby engendering support for redistribution. Yet this bounded solidarity relies on stories of peoplehood that often exclude or stigmatize minorities. When minorities pursue their culture, they are likely to be mistreated in various ways (p. 97). Nation-building, therefore, needs to be constrained by minority rights, to protect minorities against these predictable injustices (p. 97). Yet, such rights will not be able to overcome all inequalities arising from nationalist stories of peoplehood. The Canadian survey data presented by Kymlicka lends empirical evidence to his idea that nationalism penalizes minorities. He argues that when members of the majority judge how "deserving" minorities are as recipients of redistributive rights, they suffer "membership penalties." They are judged to be less deserving of such rights because they are not perceived as part of the community. This exclusionary logic of nationalism, Kymlicka suggests, cuts across racism, Islamophobia and perceived threats to in-group economic interests (p. 110). It is based on an imaginary of the "prototypical" member of the nation, in which minorities are not included. Thus, while the (instrumental) defense of nationalism is based on its supposed function of sustaining progressive values, Kymlicka shows how it can instead drive down support for redistribution, at least for minorities. It also causes inequality in the ability to make claims against the state. Some people are viewed as less entitled to redistributive rights because they do not fit the story of peoplehood understood to authorize the state.

Whether or not nationalism can really undergird social solidarity (e.g., Breidahl et al. 2018), this data suggests that inclusive forms of nationalism are more amenable to progressive ends than exclusive forms. The latter may indeed have the opposite effect, driving down support for inclusive and targeted redistribution. *If*, then, it is the case that nationalism supports progressive values, it is *only* insofar as it is inclusive. This makes the challenge to construct an inclusive nationalism even more pertinent to those defending it on progressive grounds. Kymlicka does not think that we should abandon membership-based deservingness judgments, because they underpin our "solidaristic obligations to co-members" of the redistributive community (p. 113). Instead, the solution he offers is "multicultural nationalism" (p. 117 see also Kymlicka 2015). Minority rights, in addition to their protective function, should be framed in such a way as to transform membership based deservingness judgements. Kymlicka thus maintains the centrality of nationhood, and stories of peoplehood, in creating an "ethic of membership" that underpins the welfare state (p. 92). Multiculturalism on this account enhances the "ethic of membership," as minority rights should be designed in ways that portray minorities as participating and contributing to the community; as "ways of making a commitment to a 'we'" (p. 118). In this way, minority rights transform ideas about who is the "prototypical" member of the nation and, in turn, who is entitled to make claims to redistributive rights.

Majority Nationalism

The survey data presented by Kymlicka is a welcome contribution to the empirical research literature in this area, as it unusually focuses on majority perceptions of minority belonging. Research on majorities' national identity tends to look primarily at how it is defined; whether, for example, it is "civic" or "ethnic" (Wright and Reeskens 2013). On the other hand, research on integration and social cohesion tends to focus on immigrants' and minorities' sense of belonging to their country of residence (Ersanili & Saharso, 2011). Yet, the claim that the democratic welfare state requires an "ethic of membership," or some other form of bounded solidarity, is premised on the existence of a collective imaginary of community. What matters is therefore not how either majorities or minorities perceive *their own* identification with the nation, i.e., how strongly they identify as, for example, Swedish, Canadian, or British, but whether they perceive that they are part of a nation or community where *others* also identify and/or display an ethic of membership. What matters, in other words, is not how members perceive their own identity, but how they perceive others' identity. Indeed, what matters is whether they see others as members at all.

In this regard, some of the research trying to test the liberal nationalist argument has been somewhat misplaced when it has focused on whether identification with the nation generates attitudes of trust and solidarity. What is at stake, rather, is whether the perception of *being part* of a nation generates such attitudes; the notion of "shared membership." This depends just as much, if not more, on evaluations of others' belonging, as of one's own identity. As Kymlicka points out, minorities often feel a strong(er) sense of belonging to the country in question, but this does not help in generating (bounded) solidarity if members of the majority do not perceive them to be full members.

Indeed, evidence makes it clear that progressive welfare attitudes can be harmed by perceptions that welfare recipients are different from oneself. Several studies have shown that when people are primed to view welfare recipients as racialized or cultural "others," such as aboriginals (Harell et al. 2014) or ethnic and immigrant minorities (Ford 2016), are less in favour of redistribution. The worry is that this kind of prejudice will eventually also drive down support for generalized redistribution, as citizens increasingly view recipients as people who do not belong (e.g. Eger 2010). Reducing membership penalties is therefore important to secure support for the welfare state in diverse societies. To this end, research must seek to understand how majorities can come to view minorities as part of the community. The end goal might even be to dispense with the dichotomy of minority/majority culture as a relevant political categorization.

As Kymlicka is careful to stress, this is not the same as asking how minorities can come to identify with the majority. To a seemingly large extent, this is irrelevant for the perceptions of majorities. The problem at hand is that majorities do not view minorities as full, or sometimes even as partial, members of the community. Solutions to this problem tend to focus on the identity of immigrants and minorities. They are asked to "integrate" better and to embrace values and cultural norms of the majority. Sometimes the solution is simply to limit immigration to facilitate integration (e.g., Miller 2016). Take for example recent public debates in Sweden about introducing a citizenship test. One political commentator argued that citizenship needs a higher status, achieved through the introduction of tests, in order for "all new Swedes to truly be viewed as Swedes and an obvious part of the community" (Expressen 2019, *my translation*). The basic assumption is that social cohesion will only come about once immigrants can prove that they have "integrated." Kymlicka rightly shifts the focus onto the attitudes of majorities and their ideas of membership.

I do not want to suggest that demonstrating one's commitment to the wider redistributive community, whether one belongs to the minority or majority, is entirely irrelevant or an unreasonable demand by any liberal standards.[2] Nor do I think that there can never be any friction between the dominant values of a society and those of some of its newest members (cf. Sandelind 2017). Yet the attitudes of minorities are not sufficient to change the perceptions of the majority about minority belonging. A look at the European Social Survey (2020) demonstrates that immigrants feel almost as attached to the country in which they live as natives do; 7.4 on average for immigrants compared to 7.9 for non-immigrants on a 0–10 scale. Moreover, though the research in this area is limited, there is evidence suggesting that immigrants' feelings of belonging to the new country are affected by majority views of the nation. When majorities value "attainable," as opposed to "ascriptive" criteria of belonging to the nation, immigrants are more likely to feel a sense of belonging (Simonsen 2016). In short, even if it is important to study minorities' sense of belonging to the nation the attitudes of majorities should be in focus if the aim is to establish inclusive solidarity. This is because majorities' ideas about membership affect both immigrants' sense of belonging to the country and how majorities perceive minorities' sense of belonging. To this end, Kymlicka suggests that what is required is to transform how the majority "[evaluates] the affiliation and commitment of others" via multiculturalism (p. 114).

This argument entails an important rebuttal of claims that (majority) nationalism is in decline and that multiculturalism has gone too far, which some claim to have resulted in the revolts of the "left behind" demonstrated in various successes of populist parties (e.g., Tamir 2019; Goodhart 2019). Survey data consistently show how national attachment is strong across class divides (Gustavsson and Miller 2020: 8), rather than being preserved for the "left behind," the "somewheres" or the "immobile" (e.g., Goodhart 2017; Tamir 2019). It is a mistake to think that national attachments do not matter for a large, privileged, segment of society.[3] In the European Social Survey (2020) there is no difference in the level of attachment to the country between those with or without a university degree.[4] But as Kymlicka discusses, nation-building or majority rights are increasingly called on to rectify what is seen as the lost or threatened status of majority identity.

In the wake of so-called populist moments, such as Brexit and the election of Donald Trump as President of the United States, scholars and political commentators have been particularly concerned with the predicament of the "white working class" that has supposedly been disadvantaged by a combination of multiculturalism, globalism, and capitalism – "The nationalism of the vulnerable is a revolt against the betrayal of the global elite" (Tamir 2019: 9). One account of populism claims that most of those voting for nationalist populists are not primarily interested in egalitarianism, but in "fairness," interpreted as the national group being "prioritized over immigrants in fields like employment and welfare" (Eatwell and Goodwin 2018: 276). But from the perspective of redistributive and political justice, these accounts overlook that minorities are and have been on average even less advantaged (Bhambra 2017). Yet their "vulnerability" is not suggested to legitimize minority group rights. As Gurminder Bhambra (2017: 217) asks: "Why was their precarity, and the different political choices they made in relation to that precarity (not voting for Brexit or Trump), not of concern within the debates?"

Indeed, Kymlicka's concern that minority claims are interpreted as group egoism echoes Bhambra's (2017: 217) critique of studies claiming that these populist moments were preceded by a "privileging of *identity politics* over concerns with *socio-economic inequality*":

> Campaigns in the UK in the post-war period to address issues of racial inequality and the US civil rights movements are reinterpreted as movements of racial identity that enabled ethnic minorities to gain advantages over others in similar positions (emphasis in original).

What we seem to be witnessing, not as a response to the *actual* privileging of identity politics, or "asymmetric multiculturalism" or minority "group egoism," but rather as a consequence of accounts *claiming* those causes, is the assertion of majority identity politics. While some scholars pay heed to the fact that some minority voters supported Brexit and Trump, their main concern is nonetheless "hyper ethnic change," threats to "settled communities" and national identity, concerns around "racial self-interest," or resentment toward redistribution targeted at immigrants or minorities (Eatwell and Goodwin 2018; Kaufmann 2017). Their solution is majority nationalism and, just as Kymlicka notes, this is not seen as group egoism but as the legitimate claims of national partiality (Eatwell and Goodwin 2018). These diverging analyses of minority and majority claims demonstrate the asymmetry in majorities' and minorities' standing vis-à-vis the state, grounded in exclusionary stories of peoplehood.

Such exclusionary stories of peoplehood are reproduced by methodologically nationalist or uncritical understandings of the relationship between minorities and majorities. For example, David Miller (2018: 335) argues that multiculturalism in the form advocated by Kymlicka and partially implemented in Canada is not suited to European states that have an "indigenous majority with deep historical roots." Immigrant integration must, Miller maintains, match the historical trajectory of the state. This, he argues, renders multiculturalism problematic in Europe as there are majority national cultures who can claim a "privileged status, by virtue of historical primacy" (Miller 2018: 335). Yet, as Bhambra (2017: 220) points out, in the United Kingdom case, there was never a British nation, only an empire. The relation between majority and minority in at least this postimperial state is not one of a privileged majority versus "new" minorities. Rather, many minorities and recent immigrants from former colonies also have deep historical roots to the state. Those who are thus portrayed as occupying a less privileged status, "came as *citizens*" and "were gradually turned into *immigrants*" (Bhambra 2017: 221, emphasis in original see also Amighetti and Nuti 2016).[5]

Another example is Eric Kaufmann's (2017: 520) argument that multiculturalism is acceptable if "whites could be viewed as a group like any other with their own parochial interests," rather than "denigrating" white majority identity. Majority and minority group claims should, on his account, be recognized as equal. Majorities may of course be strongly attached to and care about their culture. But the idea that "whites" constitute such a cultural group, and that they have a "shared interest" in slowing "ethnic change", merely reproduces a story of peoplehood built on a history of oppression. Kaufmann's proposal thus stands in stark contrast to Kymlicka's notion that multiculturalism can transform ideas of membership that privileges the majority identity. Discussing the American case, Kaufmann (2017: 63–64) does indeed provide evidence for how whites are implicitly regarded as "prototypically" American, as is the English language and Anglo surnames. Kaufmann (2017: 61–62) interprets this to mean that "the struggle to defend the Anglo-Protestant tradition of the American national identity" has a cultural explanation, reflecting that the "memes of whiteness and Americanness have come to be inextricably linked." On this basis, majority "white" cultural claims can be placed on par with minority ones. Despite describing how people of color were disenfranchized at the time of independence (though there is little to no discussion of the legacies of slavery), and subsequent racist immigration policies, Kaufmann depicts the link between whiteness and Americanness in cultural terms, rather than with reference to power or oppression. Yet the link between American nationhood and whiteness has clearly emerged from violent oppression of minorities and the unequal political relations of power that this has entailed.

These examples illustrate the importance of challenging stories of peoplehood that portray the prototypical member as from the majority. These stories tend to exclude the relations that exist between the state and certain minorities due to histories of colonialism, and neglect the oppressive regimes that have excluded minorities. For this reason it is problematic to be neutral between minority and majority rights, as proposed by Michael Da Silva and Daniel Weinstock in their comment, and, although via quite a different route, by Kaufmann. For Bhambra (2017: 220), the difference between minority and majority group claims (or "sentiments") is that "the former arise in the context of a wish for *inclusion* and *equality*, while those of the latter are a consequence of a wish to *exclude* and to *dominate*" (emphasis in original). Her claim is too stark; Da Silva and Weinstock's focus on cultural vulnerabilities that may arise from transnational pressures are helpful in understanding why. The desire to maintain certain cultural practices does not always or necessarily equate with a desire to exclude and dominate. Yet as pointed out above, cultural vulnerabilities do not tell the whole story. Portraying majority claims as primarily cultural masks their political origins and effects. Majority nationalisms have excluded and dominated, and as a result contemporary stories of peoplehood are, more often than not, based on histories of oppression. The claims by Miller and Kaufmann overlook this. Instead, they reproduce these histories.

The distinctive vulnerabilities facing minorities outlined by Kymlicka are therefore central. The first vulnerability, against stigmatization, mistreatment and assimilation, may indeed be conceptually neutral between majorities and minorities in the way Da Silva and Weinstock describe. The second vulnerability, however, is primarily about the relationship between different groups and the state. Who is viewed as the prototypical member who legitimizes the state? If the function of minority rights in this second sense is to challenge exclusionary stories of peoplehood, they cannot be neutral between majorities and minorities. Instead, the result of majority rights will be to reinforce the patterns of prejudice described by Kymlicka. He shows how minorities continue to be perceived as less deserving, based on majority nationalist ideas of the "prototypical" member of the community. At least insofar as the aim is to generate inclusive solidarity, more active majority nation-building or strengthened majority cultural rights will exacerbate the problem of forging social solidarity in diverse societies. And such efforts may further lead to redistributive inequalities between majorities and majorities, as the latter's claims are undermined by their exclusion from the dominant story of peoplehood that legitimizes such claims.

In sum, Kymlicka's core claim, that multiculturalism should be implemented to transform views of the "prototypical" member of the community so as not to penalize minorities, is an important corrective to narratives promoting or privileging majority identity. I believe this also offers an important political defense of multiculturalism, as opposed or in addition to the one based on cultural rights. For the purpose of multiculturalism here is to challenge the unequal relations of power between minorities and majorities that are embedded in dominant stories of peoplehood that usually mask histories of oppression and exclusion, as well as transnational interconnection. However, such transformation only seems possible if multiculturalism can enable critical engagement with stories of peoplehood that reproduce these inequalities between majorities and minorities. The focus on the perception and judgments of majorities is a helpful and necessary starting point in thinking about inclusive solidarity. Yet, of course, minority rights target minorities, not majorities. What is the link between minority rights and majority attitudes? How can the kind of inequalities flowing from majority nationalism, which (re)produce the idea of the "prototypical member" in the image of the majority culture, be transformed?

Minority Rights and Majority Attitudes

On Kymlicka's account, then, the aim of minority rights is twofold. On the one hand, it is restorative, redressing the assimilationist force of majority nationalism. On the other hand, it is constructive, aiming to transform the attitudes of majorities, to overcome membership penalties suffered by minorities and which undermine inclusive solidarity. The latter aim of minority rights does not stand in opposition to nationalism, but is way of reconstructing the image of the nation, or the "we," in more inclusive ways. This aim of minority rights can therefore be conceptualized as a form of "multicultural nationalism," which Kymlicka (2015) has also argued for elsewhere. It is not just rights to protect minorities, but a means of changing ideas about membership among the majority. The purpose is to "show how struggles for minority rights, and the active exercise of these rights, are not just forms of group egoism, but rather are ways of making a commitment to a 'we'" (p. 118), and the desired outcome is to transform ideas of membership held by majorities:

> But where multiculturalism is tied to ideas of participation and contribution – a kind of "multicultural nationalism," if you like – it may help to reduce the membership penalty, acting as a counterweight to recurring efforts to re-inscribe Britishness as the core of Canadian nationhood (p. 117).

Kymlicka hypothesizes, plausibly, that the key driver of membership penalties is that the "prototypical member" is viewed in the majority's image. Therefore, it is right to focus on ideas of membership held by majorities. It is less clear, however, precisely how minority rights would translate to a change in majority attitudes. As noted, minority rights are targeted at minorities, yet one of the desired outcomes is a transformation of majority attitudes. What is required to make this causal link?

The link between minority rights and majority attitudes on Kymlicka's account seems to be made at the level of political discourse: in the framing and political rhetoric of policies. Such framing, rather or in addition to specific policies themselves, might determine whether minority rights will be viewed as group egoism or as an "ethic of membership." For immigrant minorities, minority rights are to be framed "in a way that highlights immigrants' participation in an ethic of membership" (p. 117), rather than in a way that creates parallel societies. Here we could imagine, for example, exemptions for religious clothing or practices. A controversial issue in some Western countries has been the practice of some religious minorities to avoid shaking hands with people from the opposite sex, leading Denmark to introduce handshaking as a requirement for citizenship.[6] The opposite attitude, that of exemptions, may instead allow minorities to participate more easily in the daily life of the community and thereby demonstrate an "ethic of membership." Another obvious example is the much-debated issue of a ban on various forms of veiling. Such ban results in the exclusion of some Muslim (and Jewish) women from public life, thus preventing them from contributing to the community. For national and indigenous minorities, Kymlicka suggests that negotiating minority rights can be part of a process of "reconciling their competing stories of peoplehood" (p. 117). By framing these rights as a way of overcoming and reconciling the difficult historical relationship between the majority and minorities, rather than as only a mechanism of corrective or remedial justice, the outcome could be a new imaginary shared membership.

However, framing minority rights in such ways does not seem like an easy feat. At least not in contemporary European states where minority rights, such as faith schools or the introduction of halal or kosher food in schools, are often viewed as ways of separating communities from each other and/or threats to "European" ways of life. Kymlicka himself seems to express some skepticism as to the effectiveness of minority rights. Rebutting claims about "asymmetrical multiculturalism," he writes that "[minority rights] can counteract some of this pressure [for immigrants to prove that they have 'integrated'], and create legal space for the safe expression of difference, but they cannot reverse the basic inequality in groups' relationship to the legitimizing power of nationhood" (p. 102). Yet, is it not precisely this privileged "relationship to the legitimizing power of nationhood" that needs to be challenged for inclusive solidarity to emerge? It is hard to see how minority rights could have the desired function of demonstrating minorities' ethic of membership if the identity of the majority remains at the forefront of imaginaries of membership, which in turn legitimizes political claims.

To clarify. The objective is to change the image of the prototypical member; to transform ideas of membership among majorities. The suggested tool is minority rights that allow minorities to contribute to and demonstrate a commitment to the community. For the tool to work, minority rights need to not only allow minorities to contribute, but also to be framed in such a way that majorities perceive them as such. Since Kymlicka does not want to abandon the overall framework of nationalism such framings must work within the confines of a nationalist discourse. This might prove difficult, in particular if challenging majorities' claim to the "legitimizing power of nationhood" is one key way in which minority rights can prove effective in transforming majority attitudes and reducing membership penalties.

Before discussing the problems that attach to nationalism in this regard, I want to raise a worry about "banal nationalism," which Kymlicka favors over nation-building as a way of retaining the alleged positive effects of nationhood (p. 96). Kymlicka warns that priming or activating national identities via nation-building policies has the potential of worsening intergroup relations. Instead, nationalism works best when it is banal, a part of the "habitus" (p. 97). I am not convinced that nationalism is less likely to damage intergroup relations if it is banal – "implicit," "unconscious," or "unreflective" (p. 97). Nation-building is an exercise of state power and it is partly so forceful precisely because it goes unnoticed. As Billig (1995: 6) himself stressed, "banal does not imply benign." On the contrary, it may be that it is precisely because nationalism goes unnoticed that stories of nationhood that contain the violent oppression of minorities can be reproduced relatively uncontested, as the "natural order of things." It may be that majorities come to view minorities as different, or "other," because of this naturalization of the majority culture, and the exoticization of minority cultures (cf. Phillips 2007: 108). Viewing the majority culture as "neutral" or "natural" is part of what allows the construction of the image of the "prototypical" member as belonging to the majority culture. Arguably, it is nationalism in the implicit that allows people to view their own culture as the norm, perhaps not even as culture at all (perhaps merely as 'civilization'). Tamir (2019: 72), for example, argues that banal nationalism works because "power is invisible," as nationalist actions "seem natural." Rather than being a benefit of nationalism, I maintain that this banality of nationalist ideology makes it more difficult to challenge exclusionary stories of peoplehood.

Nevertheless, it might still be problematic to promote nation-building policies because of a more general skepticism that nationalism can be married with inclusive solidarity. While some narratives around a shared "we" or community may be beneficial for various reasons, including those mentioned by Kymlicka, I do not think nationalism is the answer. The next section discusses the limits of nationalism in providing the link between minority rights and majority attitudes.

Nationalism and Transforming Stories of Peoplehood

The framing required to fill the "gap" between minority rights and majority attitudes must enable a change of majorities' ideas of membership that can truly transform the privileging of majority culture in legitimizing political claims-making toward the state.[7] I will suggest two reasons why we may wish to frame minority rights around a wider discourse of patriotism, rather than nationalism, if we want to engender inclusive solidarity.

First, the framing required to make the link between minority rights and majority attitudes might be hampered by the potential Eurocentrism of nationalism. The link frequently made between the nation-state and liberal progressive values, or modernity, is both historical and conceptual (e.g. Tamir 2019). Because the nation-state is seen as a largely European invention, emanating from the French Revolution, nationalism can easily become Eurocentric in the sense that European cultures/nations are viewed as a necessary requirement for the realization of liberal progressive values (cf. Bhambra 2007). In other words, not only is nationalism seen as conceptually linked to the realization of liberal progressive values, but because nationalism is viewed as a European invention, it is European nations that are historically linked to the realization of such values. The amalgamation of historical and conceptual accounts of the nationalism/liberal values relation appears ubiquitous in contemporary nationalist discourse in many Western states. It can be traced to the ways in which "civic" nations nonetheless draw such historical *and* conceptual links between the national culture and liberal progressive values (Rostbøll 2010: 408; Lægaard 2007). The upshot is that minorities' cultures, insofar as they are non-Western, are viewed as incompatible with liberal values (or modernity). Viewed in this light, (non-Western) minority rights are highly problematic, challenging the progressive function of the nation-state.

This is evident in several debates and policies in Western states regarding minority practices. The Danish handshake requirement is one example. Justifying the policy, the Danish Integration Minister said: "If you don't shake hands, you don't understand what it means to be Danish, because in Denmark we have equality and that is something generations before us fought to achieve" (Reuters 2019). The progressive value of equality is linked not only to Danish identity, but also to Danish history. Other policies directed at minorities, such as bans on veiling or the construction of minarets, have been justified on similar grounds; that they are protecting the majority national culture as a way of safeguarding (universal) liberal progressive values. For this reason, I believe we should be very cautious in thinking that nationalism – even of the multicultural kind – can provide the necessary transformative link between minority rights and majority attitudes. If the (presumed) progressiveness of nationalism is premised on the privileging of European/Western cultures, then it is hard to see how any nationalism could engender inclusive solidarity.

Second, to reduce membership penalties, minority rights should contribute to a reconstruction of majority ideas of belonging that challenges the privileging of majority culture as legitimizing the state. Such privileging, as discussed and exemplified in the first section, is often rooted in stories of peoplehood that exclude minorities, also noted by Kymlicka. Of course, it is sometimes the case that there are genuinely "new" minorities who have recently immigrated, and who therefore initially may be legitimately excluded from the historical narrative of the community. But, it is also often the case that minorities, including immigrants, already have a prior political (and cultural) relation with the state due, for example, to colonialism or other forms of state interdependence. And even in the case of new minorities, their history ought to be retrospectively included in that of the political community as a whole, to be fully inclusive.[8]

For minority rights to transform majority attitudes, they must therefore be framed in a way that facilitates challenges to or reconstructions of exclusionary stories of peoplehood. This is in line with Kymlicka's argument of how minority rights of at least national minorities should be framed but I believe that it is too optimistic to think that this can be achieved within the framework of the nation-state. This is because stories of peoplehood, such as those described above that render invisible certain minorities' deep-rooted connections to a state, may need to be transformed in ways that unsettle nationalism's basic assumption of congruence between a territorially circumscribed nation and the state. Such transformation needs to be both inclusive and expansive. It is inclusive when it incorporates existing minority members in the historical narrative of the community. It is expansive when it includes very new or even prospective members of the community, who may have a political standing vis-à-vis the state resulting from colonialism or various foreign policy interventions but who are not present on the territory of the state (cf. Achiume 2019).[9]

These inclusions and expansions of the ideas of membership could help provide the necessary framing that links minority rights to majority attitudes. As I argued in the first section, the privileging of majority stories of peoplehood, which often distorts historical political relations between minorities and the state, or emerges from histories of oppression, enables imaginaries of the prototypical members as being from the majority. They need to be reconstructed. But it is hard to see how such reconstructions of stories of peoplehood are compatible within a political discourse of nationalism. Expanding the story of peoplehood beyond the boundaries of the state, including transnational political relations, connections, and interdependencies, is not easily reconcilable with nationhood and the nationalist principle of congruence between state and nation. Instead, moving toward a form of "multicultural patriotism" may offer clearer transformations of membership.

Multicultural Patriotism

In a recent piece on the compatibility of patriotism and cosmopolitanism, Erez and Laborde (2019: 3) argue that a central trait of a *cosmopolitan* patriotic identity ought to be critical engagement with the country's past and present. The hope is that such engagement will allow citizens to turn criticism of their country's actions into a desire to bring about change. Critical engagement, they maintain, necessarily entails identification with a political collective, as otherwise collective responsibility would be precluded. If identification is too strong, they claim, people are more likely to rationalize injustices perpetrated by their state ("blind allegiance"), yet if it is too weak, it is too easy to distance oneself from the state and not facilitate change ("alienated disdain") (Erez and Laborde 2019: 3). They submit that collective identification is important so that members can feel shame toward their nation, in order to mobilize around cosmopolitan values (cf. Laborde 2002: 602), but nationalist identification is too strong. Their account is useful, I believe, in highlighting the importance of critical engagement with one's political community, in particular its history, to make it more inclusive. While their focus is on engendering cosmopolitan values toward outsiders, the account may also usefully be applied to minority insiders.

They are mistaken, however, in arguing that the main difference between various forms of collective identity lies in the *strength* of identification by members. As at times they also acknowledge, it is the *kind* of community attachment that matters for whether someone will be able to critically engage or express "blind allegiance," not the strength of attachment (Erez and Laborde 2019: 5–6). As I have pointed out, most people have high levels of attachment to their country. The question is if nationalism can sufficiently enable critical engagement with the political community, in particular stories of peoplehood, given the kind of community attachment it constructs. Erez and Laborde (2019: 5) suggest that there is a causal link between attachment being based on social identity, rather than normative ideals, and the strength of identification. Yet it is not clear why an identity based on ideals could not be equally strong, only directed toward a different community value. What we need is an account of how cosmopolitan patriotism can, more effectively than nationalism, facilitate critical engagement with stories of peoplehood that privilege majorities on the basis of histories of exclusion.

Gina Gustavsson (2019: 703) provides a useful distinction between conservative nationalism, liberal nationalism, and constitutional patriotism. She suggests that while conservative nationalism regards the national history with reverence, liberal nationalism takes a "cookbook" approach to history, by which it "lays out the existing principles of cuisine and provides a base from which experimentation and innovation are possible" (Miller cited in Gustavsson 2019: 703). Constitutional patriotism, on the other hand,

> does not portray historical legacies as a natural starting point for the national identity, but rather as something towards which the national identity must actively take a "scrutinizing attitude," and which should only be endorsed when specific cultural traditions can be said to be "consonant" with abstract universalist principles (Gustavsson 2019: 703).

I think Gustavsson's characterization of Habermas's constitutional patriotism is somewhat misleading, as the starting point for any critique of national identity must be its historical legacy (Laborde 2002: 594). Thus, I do not think the difference is so much the starting point as the end point. Constitutional patriotism may end up getting rid of the cookbook altogether if it is not consistent with liberal values – it has the potential of being more subversive than liberal nationalism. For this reason, constitutional patriotism lends itself to a critical and potentially radical reinterpretation of national history (Laborde 2002: 595). Yet, as Laborde (2002: 595–6) cautions, this critical interpretation of constitutional patriotism risks going too far, potentially getting rid of both universals and the possibility of collective identification, and thereby critical engagement as opposed to critical distance.

Thus, none of the three ideas of membership discussed by Gustavsson are ideally placed to critically engage with a country's past and present to the extent that it can provide the transformative link between minority rights and majority attitudes. Specifically, liberal nationalism's cookbook metaphor implies that the history of the nation still enjoys a certain level of authority or privilege, even if not to the extent of conservative nationalism. This is problematic in cases where dominant interpretations of history must be radically transformed to move away from current exclusionary ideas of membership and solidarity. The cosmopolitan patriotism favored by Erez and Laborde (2019: 7), based on a republican ideal of citizenship, is therefore attractive, focusing on citizens' prior allegiance to the ideal of non-domination and where "[critique] is understood not as a rejection of patriotism, but as a constitutive part of it." It is similar to constitutional patriotism, and different from nationalism, in its privileging of normative ideals before attachment to the community, but different from "radical constitutional patriotism" in the emphasis on "virtuous citizenship" and the "importance of identification with one's political community, including willingness to take responsibility for the freedom of one's state" (Erez and Laborde 2019: 6). Such an ideal, if coupled with multiculturalism, may be better placed than nationalism to critically engage with ideas of membership that penalizes minorities. I think it would also fit Kymlicka's description of what an ethic of membership entails.

Kymlicka maintains that nationhood is at the core of the welfare state, as people must see themselves as members of a community; "our solidaristic obligations to co-members depend on the assumption that they have a depth of commitment to and engagement in our society that non-members do not have (p. 113)." As noted, I do not want to take issue with the idea that some deservingness judgments in relation to others' *commitment* to a shared society is helpful in creating social solidarity. Yet, the kind of commitment described by Kymlicka does not necessarily include any attachment to the culture or history of the nation, but rather individual participation and forward-looking contribution:

> Someone is part of the national "we" because she has made a life here, complies with its social norms, shares in the burdens of social cooperation, participates in its institutionalized forms of reciprocity and risk-pooling, shows concern for its collective well-being and collective future, and contributes in ways that suit her capacities (p. 113).

This kind of commitment is equally compatible with more political forms of identity,[10] such as Erez and Laborde's republican notion of patriotism, which focuses on the state rather than a pre-political community. Indeed, the idea of an "ethic of membership" is similar to the republican notion of civic virtues, requiring citizens to demonstrate a certain commitment to the community, albeit the latter emphasizes that the commitment must be premised on allegiance to the value of non-domination. Such a commitment sits well with the idea that minority rights are to transform majority ideas of membership in ways that can equalize minorities' and majorities' claim to the state via stories of peoplehood.

As I suggested in the first section, one benefit of Kymlicka's account is that it can rebalance the political relations between minority and majority in relation to the state, and not only their respective cultural claims. This is better understood as *multicultural patriotism*, which holds the value of non-domination at the core of virtuous citizenship, or an ethic of membership, rather than multicultural nationalism. While there is evidence that people who are committed to multiculturalist "community values" are more positive both to generalized and inclusive solidarity compared to other ideas of membership (Breidahl et al. 2018), the Canadian-style multiculturalism advocated by Kymlicka has not been sufficient or successful in eradicating membership penalties in Canada, as demonstrated by the data Kymlicka presents. Thus, rather than ordering more of the same, multiculturalism coupled with a more, critical and transformative patriotism, rather than liberal nationalism, could be more successful in engendering inclusive solidarity.

Returning to Kymlicka's suggestion that minority rights ought to be framed as an ethic of membership, rather than group egoism, the patriotic ideal of a virtuous citizen would be particularly helpful. Kymlicka stresses that minority rights struggle to transform majority attitudes when they are seen as an "apolitical celebration of diversity" (p. 117). Instead, he suggests, minority rights must be viewed as a way for minorities to participate in and contribute to the community. The patriotic ideal can enable this by providing the framing that links minority rights to majority attitudes in the desired transformative way, which in turn can reduce membership penalties and engender inclusive solidarity. This is because minority rights framed around a patriotic ideal as sketched by Erez and Laborde would focus on how minority rights could enable both minorities and majorities to critically engage with histories of domination and advance the value of freedom as defining of the community.

In practical terms, moving toward a multicultural patriotism may not drastically change the framing of minority rights from that suggested by Kymlicka, as it fits well with his idea of allowing minorities to demonstrate an ethic of membership. Indeed, I argue that it fits better than a multicultural nationalism, as the latter dampens the ability of minority rights to truly transform ideas of membership and reduce membership penalties.[11] To truly generate inclusive solidarity, nationalist stories of peoplehood, which sanitizes, naturalizes and depoliticizes the privileged position of the majority culture, need to be radically challenged. The interconnections between minorities, immigrants, and potential immigrants to the state in question must be brought into the public imaginary of membership. Such challenges must illuminate that legitimate claims to the state may not result from stories of nationhood alone or at all, and indeed that myths of the nation as a territorially circumscribed entity with sole claim to the state are just that – myths. I expressed some doubt above as to how easy it would be to transform public discourse in the direction of multicultural nationalism. Multicultural patriotism, insofar as it more radically challenges the legitimacy of the nation-state, seems even more difficult to implement. I do not dispute this. However, the difficulties of multicultural nationalism are partly that it is not radical or critical enough. While it is counterintuitive that an even more radical would be more successful, at least a multicultural patriotism dodges the pitfalls of nationalism that ultimately make the transformative link between minority rights and majority attitudes difficult to make.

Conclusion

The new data presented by Kymlicka makes a very important contribution to contemporary debates around the relationship between ideas of membership, diversity, and solidarity. It highlights that, despite claims that multiculturalism has gone too far, minorities are still not viewed as full members of the nation-state, even in multicultural Canada. Perhaps more importantly, it shows that those advocating nationalism as a way of securing liberal progressive ends must ensure that what is being promoted are inclusive ideas of membership. Otherwise, nationalism has the opposite effect, undermining progressive values. Kymlicka's plan for ensuring such inclusive solidarity is for minority rights to be implemented and framed in ways that transform majority ideas of membership. I have attempted to draw out a bit further how it is possible to make this link between policies targeted at minorities and the desired outcomes aimed at majorities. In particular, I have focused on the limitations of nationalism in providing such a link and thereby cautioned against Kymlicka's acceptance of nationalism. Applying Erez's and Laborde's cosmopolitan patriotism, which emphasizes critical engagement with the country's past and present to engender solidarity with outsiders, I suggest that a multicultural patriotism could serve this function toward minority insiders.

Notes

1 I will not discuss or take issue with the idea that shared identity is necessary to achieve progressive ends. For such a discussion, see Sandelind (2019).

2 Although this requirement, as well as the existence of social solidarity, should not be exaggerated compared to other variables in relation to the function of the welfare state (cf. Meer 2016).

3 It probably matters more to some people than they are willing to admit.

4 The average for both groups was 7.8 on a 0–10 scale. Indeed, because an overwhelming majority of survey respondents tend to say that they are very attached to their country, it is difficult to conduct research where the level of national attachment is used as a meaningful variable, as I have recently discovered when collecting new survey data on this topic.

5 Tendayi Achiume (2019) goes as far as to argue that due to the failure of de-colonialization in establishing equal political relations between First and Third World states, resulting in neo-imperialism, prospective migrants from the Third World to the First World are not, as suggested by liberal nationalist theory, *political strangers*. Rather, they still exist within a (coerced) political relationship of "co-sovereignty," which entails that First World states have no right to exclude them (Achiume 2019: 1547).
6 A requirement to shake hands for employment by a local council was deemed unlawful in Sweden (SVT 2021).
7 To an extent, such privileging is unavoidable and not problematic, if merely reflective of the fact that there are more people belonging to the majority culture, rather than of a privileged political status. In this regard, as Kymlicka argues, minority rights function as corrective or compensatory.
8 Gina Gustavsson (2019b) has made this point in relation to immigrants in Sweden and their history, arguing that liberal nationalism requires their stories to be included in the national narrative. I think this is a very important point, but do not see in what ways it is a nationalist, rather than a patriotic, position.
9 To be sure, many nations already have such expansive narratives of the nation, but they tend to be limited to ethnic affinities with "members" residing outside of the state territory (cf. Hobbs and Souter 2020). Such ethnic affinities are usually not embraced by liberal nationalists, as they are based on too exclusive criteria of membership.
10 I do think it is a mistake to describe these identities as "thinner," or "weaker," than national (cultural) identities. Laborde's (2002) civic patriotism, for example, includes quite extensive political values (social-democracy) and inclusive attitudes, which arguably makes it quite "thick." Just as Abizadeh (2004) has argued that liberal values are no less "concrete" than "culture" or "nation," neither are identities that put such values before commitment to the nation (such as constitutional and civic patriotism) thinner in the sense of having less content than a national identity built around commitment to a specific culture. It is better to describe the differences in terms of their content, for example "political" versus "cultural" identities.
11 One potential additional benefit of moving away from nationalism is that we can eschew the assimilationist implications of nationalism's insistence that state and nation are congruent. Though I do not think Kymlicka is wrong that there needs to be widespread agreement about the unit of democracy, I do wonder if we can afford to live with an ounce of disagreement even about this. Kymlicka's example of Northern Ireland

is important, but both the United Kingdom and Canada are nonetheless well-functioning democracies despite recent (and perhaps future) independence referendums of national minorities. Another example is the reactions to a controversial statement made by a politician from the far-right Sweden Democrats. He argued that Swedish national minorities, including the Sami and Jews, are Swedish citizens, but not part of the Swedish nation. Rightly, this caused outrage from these groups, and it is clearly a racist statement, defining the Swedish nation as exclusively ethnically and culturally Swedish. Yet some also agreed. One Jewish commentator insisted that the Sweden Democrat was not wrong: "I am not Swedish, I'm Jewish. I am a part of the Jewish people who happens to be a citizen of Sweden." While not in response to the Sweden Democrat, an elected representative of the Sami parliament expressed in a documentary the same sentiment; that he has Swedish citizenship, but is not a Swedish national. These sentiments among minority groups do not seem to threaten the integrity of the Swedish state, nor result in violence. The above-cited Sami MP argued that he does not seek an independent state, merely more self-determination rights. And the part of the Jewish diaspora who embrace these versions of Zionist ideals may, at most, emigrate to Israel, but they do not undermine the territorial or democratic integrity of Sweden.

The point is that, perhaps, we should not exaggerate the need for everyone to feel like part of the nation. For some, political identity is sufficient to reaching agreement on the unit of democracy, despite viewing their homeland as either a subsection of the state territory or a different territory altogether. These people need minority rights in Kymlicka's first sense, as protective against majority nation-building, but may not be interested in rights that are framed as part of a shared national project. A multicultural patriotism may be more amenable to allowing such differences to exist without undermining the shared democratic project.

References

Abizadeh, A. (2004). Liberal Nationalist versus Postnational Social Integration: On the Nation's Ethno-Cultural Particularity and "Concreteness," *Nations and Nationalism*, 10/3: 231–50.

Achiume, E. T. (2019). Migration as Decolonialization. *Stanford Law Review*, 71/6: 1574–90.

Alesina, A., & Glaeser, E. (2004). Fighting Poverty in the US and Europe: *A World of Difference*. Oxford: Oxford University Press.

Amighetti, S. and Nuti, A. (2016), A Nation's Right to Exclude and the Colonies. Political Theory, 44/4: 541–566.

Bhambra, G. (2007). *Rethinking Modernity: Postcolonialism and the Sociological Imagination*. Basingstoke: Palgrave MacMillan.

(2017). Brexit, Trump, and "Methodological Whiteness": On the Misrecognition of Race and Class. *The British Journal of Sociology*, 68/3: 214–32.

Billig, M. (1995). *Banal Nationalism*. London: Sage.

Breidahl, K., Holtug, N., & Kongshoj, K. (2018). Do Shared Values Promote Social Cohesion? If So, Which? Evidence from Denmark. *European Political Science Review*, 10/1: 118–987.

Eatwell, R., & Goodwin, M. (2018). *National Populism: The Revolt against Liberal Democracy*. London: Penguin Books.

Eger, M. (2010). Even in Sweden: The Effect of Immigration on Support for Welfare State Spending, *European Sociological Review*, 26/2: 203–17.

Erez, L., & Laborde, C. (2019). Cosmopolitan Patriotism as a Civic Ideal. *American Journal of Political Science*, https://doi.org/10.1111/ajps.12483

Ersanili, E., & Saharso, S. (2011). The Settlement Country and Ethnic Identification of Children of Turkish Immigrants in Germany, France, and the Netherlands: What Role Do National Integration Policies Play? *International Migration Review*, 45/4: 907–37.

European Social Survey. (2020). ESS9-2018 Edition 1.2.

Expressen. (2019). Ställ högre krav för att bli svensk medborgare, October 29, last accessed February 27, 2020 www.expressen.se/ledare/stall-hogre-krav-for-att-bli-svensk-medborgare/.

Ford, R. (2016). Who Should We Help? An Experimental Test of Discrimination in the British Welfare State. *Political Studies*, 64/3: 630–50.

Goodhart, D. (2017). *The Road to Somewhere: The Populist Revolt and the Future of Politics*. London: Hurst and Company.

(2019). Wishful Thinking and Unresolved Tensions. *Ethnicities*, 19/6: 983–90.

Gustavsson, G. (2019a). Liberal National Identity: Thinner than Conservative, Thicker than Civic? *Ethnicities*, 19/4: 693–711.

(2019b). Det Nationella Bortglömt I Debatten om Handke, Uppsala Nya Tidning, December 19.

Gustavsson, G., & Miller, D. (2020). Introduction: Why Liberal Nationalism Today? In Gustavsson, G. and Miller, D., eds., *Liberal Nationalism and Its Critics*. Oxford: Oxford University Press, 1–22.

Harell, A., Soroka, S., & Ladner, K. (2014). Public Opinion, Prejudice and the Racialization of Welfare in Canada. *Ethnic and Racial Studies*, 37/14: 2580–97.

Hobbs, J., & Souter, J. (2020). Asylum, Affinity, and Cosmopolitan Solidarity with Refugees. *Journal of Social Philosophy*, doi: 10.1111/josp.12313

Kaufmann, E. (2018). *Whiteshift: Populism, Immigration and the Future of White Majorities*. Penguin Books (e-book).

Kymlicka, W. (2015). Solidarity in Diverse Societies: Beyond Neoliberal Multiculturalism and Welfare Chauvinism. *Comparative Migration Studies*, 3/17.

Laborde, C. (2002). From Constitutional to Civic Patriotism. *British Journal of Political Science*, 32/4: 591–612.

Lægaard, S. (2007). Liberal Nationalism and the Nationalisation of Liberal Values. *Nations and Nationalism*, 13/1: 37–55.

Meer, N. (2016). The Ties That Blind Us – The Hidden Assumptions in the "New Progressive's Dilemma": Comment on Will Kymlicka's Article: "Solidarity in Diverse Societies." *Comparative Migration Studies*, 4/7: 1–6.

Miller, D. (2016). *Strangers in Our Midst: The Political Philosophy of Immigration*. Cambridge: Harvard University Press.

(2018). The Life and Death of Multiculturalism. In Goodyear-Grant, E., Johnston, R. Kymlicka, W. and Myles, J. eds., *Federalism and the Welfare State in a Multicultural World.* Montréal and Kingston: McGill-Queen's University Press, 319–40.

Miller, D. (2020). The Coherence of Liberal Nationalism. In Gustavsson, G. and Miller, D. (eds.), *Liberal Nationalism and Its Critics*, Oxford: Oxford University Press, pp. 23–37.

Phillips, A. (2007). *Multiculturalism without Culture*. Princeton: Princeton University Press.

Reuters. (2019). Want to be Danish? You'd Better Shake Hands. January 17, lastaccessed27/02/20www.reuters.com/article/us-denmark-immigration/want-to-be-danish-youd-better-shake-hands-idUSKCN1PB29Q

Rostbøll, C. F. (2010). The Use and Abuse of "Universal Values" in the Danish Cartoon Controversy. *European Political Science Review*, 2/3: 401–22.

Sandelind, C. (2017). Costs of Refugee Admission and the Ethics of Extra-territorial Protection. *European Journal of Political Theory,* https://doi.org/10.1177/1474885117738118

(2019). Can the Welfare State Justify Restrictive Asylum Policies? *Ethical Theory and Moral Practice*, 22/2: 331–46.

Simonsen, K. (2016). How the host nation's boundary drawing affects immigrants' belonging, *Journal of Ethnic and Migration Studies*, 42/7: 1153–76.

SVT. (2021). Rätten Stoppas Trelleborgs Krav på Handskakning. SVT 22 Mars 2021, last accessed March 31, 2021: www.svt.se/nyheter/lokalt/skane/ratten-stoppar-trelleborgs-krav-pa-handskakning.

Tamir, Y. (2019). *Why Nationalism?* Oxfordshire: Princeton University Press.

Wright, M., & Reeskens, T. (2013). Of What Cloth Are the Ties That Bind? National Identity and Support for the Welfare State across 29 European Countries. *Journal of European Public Policy*, 20/10: 1443–63.

7 The Liberalism of Fear
The Second Coming

YAEL TAMIR

We are children of our age,
it's a political age.

All day long, all through the night,
all affairs—yours, ours, theirs—
are political affairs.

[...]

Whatever you say reverberates,
whatever you don't say speaks for itself.
So either way you're talking politics.
A tribute to Judith N. Shklar

We are Children of our Age
– Wislawa Szymborska

Pre-Introduction

I am writing this chapter during the COVID-19 pandemic. No one could be indifferent to the changes it has bought about. The social distancing alongside some of the means used to tackle those infected will certainly change our perception of human rights and the way personal freedom and public safety are balanced.

It is unclear how the pandemic and the social and economic crisis that has followed will influence social structures in general and, in particular, the relationships between minorities and majorities. Some of the changes will certainly force us to rethink our social norms. Here is an example. The title of the first version of this chapter, written in 2019, was *Please Don't Shake My Hand*. It was inspired by the debate over the social role of handshaking, which was then considered an essential part of the Western civilization.

Then came the Corona. Now that we are all avoiding physical contact and handshaking is no longer an option, we find other gestures with which to greet each other. The same is true of face coverings; an act taken to be antisocial has turned into an example of social responsivity. Not covering one's face has become threatening rather than unifying.

This change of heart has exposed a simple truth. It is the reason, not the act itself, which ought to be discussed. What is essential to being able to live together is the ability to converse and explain our actions rather than the actions themselves. This is an important lesson both theoreticians and political activists should carry with them. Developing a language that allows us to converse across cultures and religions is more important than ever.

Many believe that the "rights language" is such a language. This is indeed true in cases of *thin multiculturalism*, when liberal cultures meet. It is not so in cases of *thick multiculturalism* when the liberal world meets the illiberal (nonliberal) one. The search for a common language thus continues.

The Tortellini of Hospitality: An Introduction

In 2019, at the height of the summer, the Catholic Church of Bologna decided to go multicultural, instructing the ring-shaped pasta typical of Bologna, a major component of religious ceremonies, to be filled with chicken rather than pork. "The tortellini of hospitality" were meant to allow the many Muslims living in Bologna to participate in church-organized celebrations. This, Archbishop Matteo Zuppa said, is how we can all sit around the same table.

His good intentions were met with harsh criticism. The Nationalist League party leader, Matteo Salvini, criticized the move: "I'm reading that there are those who are asking for tortellini without meat. It's like proposing wine without grapes … The problem is some Italians forgetting their roots, denying our history." Today, we compromise on our tortellini, and tomorrow we shall compromise on our culture. "If an Italian went to an Arab country to teach them how to eat, drink and pray, how would they react? Denying our history in the name of a misunderstood respect is insanity" (McKenna 2019).

The tortellini of hospitality is a metaphor of our times, encompassing the long and intricate way in which the idea of multiculturalism has evolved from infancy to social acceptance, moments of glorification, and premature obituaries, via a rebuttal in the form of majority rights, until it has degenerated from a unifying ideal into a divisive one.

Reducing half a century of ideological debates into a dispute regarding the proper fillings of a tortellini may seem pretentious, yet it is one of those rare moments when a simple matter illuminates a complex set of affairs. The tortellini of hospitality embodies it all: tensions between reformists and traditionalists, secularists and religious believers, those who want to sit around the same table and those who want to have the table all to themselves.

When the tortellini were served, members of the Nationalist League protested outside, highlighting the fact that it is misleading to reduce multicultural debates to a religious war between the Judeo-Christian civilization and Islam. As the Archbishop demonstrated, the right kind of leadership can induce a desire for religious coexistence. Being a man of faith, the Archbishop was better equipped to converse with other believers and offer a viable compromise. Moreover, he had the authority to make a decision; this allowed him to be generous. Inviting others to join his table was a sign of ownership. In this time and age, open-minded ownership is in high demand.

The present debate over multicultural rights emphasizes the fact that we suffer from a lack of moral and political leadership that can converse across the lines, offering and legitimizing viable compromises. Rigidity is the sad consequence of this state of affairs. Those threatened by the very idea of change wave the banner of tradition, refusing to allow for even minor modifications in what they claim is a sacred way of life, while those ready to compromise fear surrender, alienation, and humiliation. Both search for leaders like the Archbishop who, from his vantage point of self-confidence, could breed tolerance by entering into a cross-communal dialogue. Until such leadership emerges, extremists will govern the debate.

Who Is Afraid of Whom and Why?

This chapter covers the way the debate over multiculturalism has evolved over the past fifty years (1970–2020) revealing the interface between theory and practice; offering an opportunity to understand the way beliefs motivate social and political actions, as much as social and political actions shape beliefs. We think about theory as being motivated by reason – but theoretical reasoning is grounded in actual life experiences. There is no view from nowhere – we judge the morality and utility of our actions in light of their outcomes, and these are determined by the context within which we act.

Understanding the general facts about our society, says the American philosopher John Rawls, is necessary for defining the principles of justice that govern it. What are these facts? There is no simple answer. Much of the present moral and political debate concerns different interpretations of the present political reality. Who is winning and who is losing? Who has justified concerns and who cynically abuses fear?

The past fifty years of social and political theory were shaped by the World Wars that preceded them. A reaction to the horrors of these wars dictated the principles that were to govern a world recovering from the trauma of totalitarianism: Nazism, Fascism, and Communism. The story of this half century thus begins with a deep aversion to the extensive power of the state. Judith Shklar, a Jewish refugee from Europe, describes it in her *Liberalism of Fear* (Shklar 1989: 29).

Liberalism, she argues, is not grounded in "a *summum bonum* towards which all political agents should strive, but it certainly does begin with a *summum malum*, which all of us should avoid if only we could. That evil is cruelty and the fear it inspires is the very fear of fear itself. To that extent the liberalism of fear makes a universal and especially a cosmopolitan claim, as it historically always has done." Fear, Shklar argues, lies close to the core of the human essence, maybe even to the core of individuals as sentient beings; hence, it can be considered as "universal as it is physiological. It is a mental as well as a physical reaction, and it is common to animals as well as to human beings" (Shklar 1989).

Fear, then, is where our journey starts. Not just any fear but a universal one that could be the basis of a theory not grounded in a *summum bonum*; a theory that transcends social and ideological conflicts and has a unifying power, supporting the emergence of a neutral political sphere, governed by agreed-upon principles of justice.

This is an attractive vision, yet it turns a blind eye to individual, cultural, and religious differences. Reading *The Liberalism of Fear*, the words of a tune popular among the Jewish religious right echo in my mind: "This world is a narrow bridge (to the next one), and the essential thing is not to fear at all." The fervent singers are not fearless yet they believe they should fear nothing but God's judgment and their place in the world to come. Suicide bombers make similar assumptions: they die smiling. Hell is the realm of their fears; heaven reached by killing the infidels, the realm of their hopes (Tamir 1997).

Fear, then, is as contextual as any other human feeling. Those who have a state of their own, fear the brutality of the state. Stateless people fear having no state, being defenseless, depending on the protection of others. Minorities fear the power of the majority, and nowadays majorities fear the growing influence of minorities. What you fear reflects where you stand. In order to understand political reality in all its depth, we must therefore question who is afraid of whom, why, and when. The answers are neither trivial nor universal. They are contextual and particular all the way down.

The Illusion of Universalism

The political theory of the second half of the last century turned its back on diversity. Universalization was to pave the way for liberalism's extraordinary success. It was no longer seen as an ideological position but as a representation of the nature of things – its principles grounded in the state of nature, reflecting human nature, defending natural rights. It could have no rivals; it had reached its zenith. What we are witnessing in the twentieth century, Fukuyama argued (1989):

> is not just the end of the Cold War, or the passing of a particular period of post-war history, but the end of history as such: that is, the end-point of mankind's ideological evolution and the universalization of Western liberal democracy as the final form of human government.

Confident in their reign, liberals searched for a set of governing principles that would cement its prominence. John Rawls' groundbreaking *Theory of Justice* (1971) and *Political Liberalism* (1993) sketched these principles and changed the theoretical landscape of the twentieth century.

The essence of political liberalism is a search for an overlapping consensus allowing individuals who hold different comprehensive conceptions of the good to share a political framework. While it seeks common ground and is neutral in its aims, political liberalism "affirms the superiority of certain forms of moral character and encourages certain moral features" (Rawls 1993: 194). It includes an account of political virtues, such as civility and tolerance, or reasonableness and a sense of fairness. Admitting these virtues, Rawls claimed, does not "lead to the perfectionist state of comprehensive doctrine" (Geertz 1973: 311).

Principles of justice were to be drawn behind a veil of ignorance that nullified the effects of specific contingencies "which put men at odds and tempt them to exploit social and natural circumstances to their own advantage" (Rawls 1993: 136). The restrictions imposed on the parties in the original position were meant to balance the influence of particularities on moral judgment, thus avoiding the temptation to inflict injustice upon others.

At the time there seemed to be no better moral protest against past atrocities than adhering to non-biased, blind-to-difference, inclusive principles of justice. Principles that made room for all those previously excluded. National and ethnic minorities, individuals of all races, colors, and genders, members of victimized groups – Jews, homosexuals, and people with disabilities – all were welcomed and treated with equal concern and respect.

To attain this, the public sphere had to change and become equally accessible to all. In an imperfect, neutral public space, everybody was supposed to feel at home. "Home," however, is never neutral. Political sociologists understood the incongruity of the idea of neutrality and the inevitability of cultural, religious, national bias long before political theorists. One thing everyone knows but no one can quite demonstrate, Clifford Geertz wrote in the early 1970s is that "a country's politics reflect the design of its culture" (Geertz 1973) or, more precisely, the culture of the ruling groups. The cultural essence of the state comes to the fore in its political institutions and official language, and also in the symbolic sphere, in the selection of rituals, national heroes, and the like. Cultural, religious, and ideological attitudes toward the political system, interpretations of history, and psychological orientations are unavoidably reflected in the political system. The liberal vision of a neutral public sphere turned out to be an illusion.

Liberalism and Its Critics

In the late 1960s, a solitary voice among mainstream Anglo-Saxon philosophers, Sir Isaiah Berlin, offered an early and little acknowledged theory of the contextual self. Claiming that the individualist definition of self is grounded in a shallow human psychology that overemphasizes the role of rationality, he highlighted the importance of communal membership. In reality, he wrote, our most personal features are "shaped by, and cannot be understood apart from those of the group, defined in terms of common territory, customs, laws, memories, beliefs, language, artistic and religious expression ... factors which shape human beings, their purposes and their values" (Berlin 1980: 341).

Berlin added a communal twist to the Kantian doctrine: Kant's free man, he argued, needs no public recognition for his inner freedom, Berlin's free person, is constituted by his relations with others. I am nothing if I am unrecognized, he wrote, "I am in my own eyes as others see me. I identify myself with the point of view of my milieu: I feel myself to be somebody or nobody in terms of my position and function in the social whole; this is the most 'heteronomous' condition imaginable" (Berlin 1980: 341).

There is a short distance between awareness of our human rootedness and support for the politics of identity, and support for the politics of recognition that Berlin covered in his celebrated *Two Concepts of Liberty* (1969). The lack of freedom about which men or groups complain, he wrote, amounts, "as often as not, to a lack of proper recognition. Individuals desire not only to secure for themselves a set of Millian liberties, but also a recognition of them being members of particular groups, and an affirmation of the uniqueness and worthiness of these groups" (Berlin 1969: 156–57).

Not only do individuals see their freedom as dependent on their group's ability to be self-governing, they also see their own self-esteem as closely linked to the status of their group. Hence, they regard offenses and humiliations of their group as a personal injury and take pride and satisfaction in their group's success and prosperity. Long before the politics of identity and recognition was launched by feminists, Black activists, and members of the LGB community, Berlin wrote the following prophetic words: "At the heart of modern politics lies a great cry for recognition on the part of both individuals and groups and in our own day, of professions and classes, nations and races" (Berlin 1969: 157). The desire for recognition, he concluded, "is surely one of the greatest forces that moves human history" (Berlin 1997: 252).

In the late 1970s Berlin was joined by another philosopher, Charles Taylor, a Quebecois, who brought to the discussion his own life experience and a very special French-Canadian understanding of identity. He, too, was convinced that individuals could define their identity only against the background of things that mattered to them. "To bracket out history, nature, society, the demands of solidarity, everything but what I find in myself, would be to eliminate all candidates for what matters.... Authenticity is not the enemy of demands that emanate from beyond the self; it supposes such demands" (Taylor 1991: 40–41).

By the beginning of the 1980s, an intellectual rebellion against the idea of neutrality was brewing. Feminists, human rights activists, and communitarians united to reintroduce the concept of identity. Michael Sandel's *Liberalism and the Limits of Justice* opened the door to communitarianism. Criticizing Rawls' conception of human agency, Sandel raised the "sociological objection"; liberalism, he argued, "is wrong because neutrality is impossible, and neutrality is impossible because, try as we might, we can never wholly escape the effects of our conditioning. The vaunted independence of the deontological subject is a liberal illusion. It misunderstands the fundamentally 'social' nature of men, the fact that we are conditioned beings 'all the way down'" (Sandel 1982: 11). All political orders embody *some* values; the question is *whose* values prevail, and who gains and losses as a result. The hegemony of the idea of neutrality was fractured; the time was ripe for change.

The liberal self looked about to discover that one was part of a social whole that structured one's values, preferences, hopes and fears, one's understanding of the past, as well as one's hopes for the future. This context gave meaning to individual choices and placed freedom within a cultural web, without which no one could be free.

The Age of Recognition

A new question surfaced: "Is a democracy letting citizens down, excluding or discriminating against us in some morally troubling way when major institutions fail to take account of our particular identities?" (Gutmann 1992: 3). Yes, was the answer of those who for centuries had been silenced, pushed to the back rooms, and deprived of recognition and self-esteem. The remedy they demanded seemed simple: to be granted an entry card to walk through the main door, proudly wearing their identity.

Recognition was now seen not as an act of empathy but as an entitlement. The thesis, Taylor argued, "is that our identity is partly shaped by recognition or its absence, often by the misrecognition of others, and so a person or group of people can suffer real damage, real distortion, if the people or society around them mirror back to them a confining or demeaning or contemptible picture of themselves. Non-recognition or misrecognition can inflict harm, can be a form of oppression, imprisoning someone in a false, distorted, and reduced mode of being" (Taylor 1992: 25).

Cultural biases are transparent to those who legislate, occupy key political positions, and run state bureaucracy, but they are consequential to those who do not belong and are therefore forced to adjust. Individuals taking off their turban, veil, or yarmulke; Black women going through great pains to straighten their hair; businesswomen dressed in men's suits; immigrants changing their names and repressing their accent; homosexuals hiding in the closet – all of whom are compelled to exert great efforts to fit in at the cost of compromising their identity.

In their struggle for social acceptance, members of minority groups endured their pain silently. Yet, once granted a set of legal rights and feeling more secure, they started to voice their objections; soon neutrality was reinterpreted, turning from a liberating to an oppressive concept. Neutrality, it was argued, forced minorities to choose between two evils: retaining their identity while remaining estranged and marginalized, or integrating at the price of self-effacement. The liberal vision was no longer seen as a key to equality – on the contrary it was taken to be a means of perpetuating the existing power relations and leaving all others at a point of social, cultural, and economic disadvantage. Equality demanded a shift in rights language and practice – turning from difference neutrality to difference sensitive.

Special Rights

The politics of identity, characteristic of the late 1980s and 1990s, turned liberal attention to the needs of those alienated from the "neutral" public sphere; people who were permanently disadvantaged and outvoted on a range of issues crucial to their individual and communal well-being. In order to amend this inherent injustice, the influential Canadian philosopher Will Kymlicka argued that liberal states should compensate members of minority groups for the fact that "they have to spend their resources on securing the cultural membership which makes sense for their lives, while members of the majority culture get theirs for free" (Kymlicka 1995: 187).

Kymlicka had three specific minorities in mind: the Quebecois, Canada's indigenous people, and legal immigrants. The first two groups were losers in the age of self-determination, who aspired to secure for themselves a certain degree of political autonomy to make their cultures less vulnerable to majority decisions. A federative kind of multiculturalism, very different from the one that stands at the heart of the present-day political debate, was the preferred solution for these kinds of groups, namely, a "bird's eye" kind of diversity that allowed different communities to live side by side in the same political framework, inwardly preserving cultural and lingual homogeneity.

When it came to immigrants, the third minority group, Kymlicka was much more cautious. Resenting the idea of open borders, he defended the right of majorities to decide who and how many immigrants would join the political union. Those granted entry had to abide by moral and political principles. Rights granted to groups "should not allow one group to dominate other groups; and they should not enable a group to oppress its own members. In other words, liberals should seek to ensure that there is equality between groups, and freedom and equality within groups" (Kymlicka 1995: 194). In order to enjoy the protection that liberalism offered, cultures had to liberalize themselves, allowing their members the same rights they demanded as a group.

Had multiculturalism stopped there, the next sections would have been redundant, but that was not the case. Building on the achievements of the first generation of struggles that strived to secure "equal concern and respect" for all, the second generation added a commitment to respect and protect cultural diversity (at least those cultures that met Kymlicka's liberal principles). Soon Kymlicka's moral constraints were to be removed. Accused of defending only "their own kind" and being paternalistic, liberals were asked to accept a much wider and deeper range of diversity.

Individuals, it was argued, would like to protect the way of life rather than the way prescribed by liberals. Bearers of such claims were mostly second- and third-generation immigrants. Established in their new homelands, well versed in the language of rights, they demanded equal concern and respect for their individuality rather than for the kind of people the liberal majority would like them to be. In a self-secured liberal world, where diversity seemed no more than a source of enrichment – these claims resonated well. Bored with their routine, empowered by a sense of victory, liberals were ready to season their public sphere in order to make it richer, more interesting and intriguing for all.

We Are All Multiculturalists Now

Multiculturalism changed the way American and other Western societies defined themselves. For some conservatives, like Alan Bloom, that meant no less than a moral and cultural surrender. The very idea of majority, he wrote, "now understood to be selfish interest – is done away with in order to protect minorities. This broke the delicate balance between majority and minority in Constitutional thought. In such a perspective, where there is no common good, minorities are no longer problematic, and the protection of them emerges as the central function of government" (Bloom 1987: 31–32). This, according to Bloom, led to cultural relativism, and in turn to the closing of the American mind. Students, he argued, were unified only in their relativism and their allegiance to equality. Without an agreed-upon set of moral principles – societies collapsed. Bloom's conservatism was greeted with harsh criticism and skepticism. I share much of the criticism – though I would have preferred the response to have been more open to the challenge he presented. But times were overoptimistic – it was all for the better, diversity was taken to be the way to refresh, enrich, and diversify our societies.

For its advocates, multiculturalism became "the image of a better America without prejudice and discrimination, in which no cultural theme linked to any racial or ethnic group, has priority, and in which American culture is seen as the product of a complex intermingling of themes from every minority, ethnic and racial group, and from indeed the whole world" (Glazer 1997: 11).

Emphasizing the positive aspects of a newly emerging state of affairs is characteristic of moments of birth as is celebrating anticipated achievements while failing to appreciate the scope of unexpected, unwarranted consequences. Unaware of the anxieties to come, liberals expected multiculturalism to produce a magnificent rainbow coalition, affirming the presence and supporting the rights of members of each and every group that constituted the social fabric.

The most common image of this period was the "Colors of Benetton" – people of different races, ethnic origins, and genders, dressed in colorful "Benetton" T shirts, smiling to the camera, displaying a sense of togetherness and mutual social comfort that sparked happiness.

The combination of individual and group rights was expected to allow human flourishing in the fullest, most satisfying way. Each and every person could express himself, and no one would be obliged to change her/his way of life in order to fit in; a captivating vision – a win–win situation.

Unfortunately, the enthusiasm was short lived. Struggles within and between groups began to surface. Group rights highlighted the importance of in-group unity. This, in turn, produced internal pressures to conform. Having no political structures allowing members to voice their preferences, weak members were silenced and marginalized. Feminists, who were among the first carriers of the politics of recognition, soon found that many of them had become victims of their own success. The inherent tensions between group and individual (especially women's) rights moved out into the open. Finally, Susan Muller Okin dared raise the question: "Is Multiculturalism Bad for Women?" (Okin 1999).

In a clear and decisive way, she claimed that very few cultures defended weaker members from internal pressures. This was especially true of those cultures that oppressed women and subordinated them to the strict control of their families. The vast majority of deviations from liberal principles, Okin argued, "concern gender inequalities: child marriages, forced marriages, divorce systems biased against women, polygamy, and clitoridectomy" (Okin 1999: 17). Honor murders, sexual abuse, and rape could also be added to the list. Group rights, it became obvious, had an oppressive dimension that restricted the rights and liberties of vulnerable members.

Discussions over the status of women in traditional societies forced an acknowledgment that special rights strengthened dominant subgroups and privileged conservative interpretations of culture over reformative and innovative ones. When internal disputes erupted, orthodoxy had the advantage. It presented its followers as loyal to the group's tradition, portraying agents of reform as faithless, frail-minded individuals tempted by the material affluence of the surrounding society, ready to exchange authentic practices for some glittering beads. This was presented not merely as a matter of personal weakness. Reformers, it was argued, risked the very survival of the group. The term "survival" often used in these debates obscured a distinction between two kinds of social processes: surrendering to external pressures and internal desire for change.

Despite the profound moral difference between these two kinds of cases, defenders of special rights blurred the boundaries allowing one to collapse into the other. Under the banner of survival, the rights of dissenters were restricted. Defending the right of the Quebec legislature to enact "language laws" that forced the usage of French in the public sphere, Charles Taylor wrote the following: "It is axiomatic for Quebec government that the survival and flourishing of French culture in Quebec is a good ... It is not just a matter of having the French language available for those who might choose it ... Policies aimed at survival actively seek to create members of the community, for instance, in their assuring that future generations continue to identify as French speakers" (Taylor 1994: 58–59).

Taylor was not alone. When discussing the right of Indians in Canada to defend their way of life, Kymlicka also sided with those who aspired to defend traditional ways of life not only from external but also from internal pressures. This became clear in his discussion of mixed marriages. When Indians living in reserves marry non-Indians a problem of overcrowding emerges. Kymlicka described two traditional solutions to this problem: the first adopted *the blood criteria* according to which "only those with certain proportion of Indian blood can be full members of the band, so non-Indian spouses never acquire membership, nor do children if they have less than the required proportion [of Indian ancestry]" (Kymlicka 1989: 149). The second endorsed criteria based on *kinship*, according to which Indian women who entered into mixed marriage lost their land rights. Both solutions disadvantaged members who deviated from the norm of marrying within the tribe, the kinship approach specifically discriminating against women.[1]

It thus became clear that special rights were particularly damaging for those who could improve their social status only by challenging traditional norms. Freeing traditionalists from external oppression and exclusion, special rights placed additional pressure on the weakest members of the group. Fear, thus, shifted its reign from the public to the private sphere where it often went unnoticed.

The realization that special rights protected a wide range of undesirable social phenomena made supporters of multiculturalism lose their appetite for diversity. Conflicts between those who remained true to the notion of individual rights and those struggling for special group rights deepened and by the end of the 1990s the radiance of the rainbow coalition faded, creating an opening for new political solutions.

Two Concepts of Multiculturalism

In order to understand the rise and fall of multiculturalism, one should distinguish between two concepts of multiculturalism – thin and thick – (Tamir 1995) and follow the way in which the debate unintentionally slips from the first to the second.

Thin Multiculturalism

In cases of *thin multiculturalism* a society consists of different cultural groups, all of which endorse basic liberal principles. Awareness of the importance of identity, recognition, and representation issues induces such societies to add cultural goods to the list of goods distributed, forming a culturally diverse public sphere where members of all the different (liberal) groups feel protected and respected.

This is no small matter. Thin multiculturalism demands considerable adjustments. In a wide range of cases (that are not identity-bound), democratic procedures secure the right of members of the different groups to enjoy equal access to decision-making processes. Once access and participation are secured, the fact that some preferences are outvoted does not imply that their bearers were unjustly treated or that their rights were violated.

When a community is pluralistic and heterogeneous, losing the vote on a variety of issues is unavoidable. Those who hold uncommon preferences are often unable to influence, let alone imprint, political institutions with their choices. Nevertheless, thin multiculturalism suggests that the inability to protect and promote cultural choices – even when resulting from a just political process – is unfair due to two reasons. First, by definition, the cultural-communal interests of a minority are unlikely to gain support. Its members thus become permanent losers. Second, cultural interests are of special importance and being unable to gather support for such interests can cause considerable harm.

Thin multiculturalism thus requires special attention to cultural interests. Suppose the parties in Rawls' original position are aware that their state encompasses various national, ethnic, and cultural groups, yet unaware to which of the particular groups they belong and whether they are members of the majority or the minority. Under such conditions, they are likely to endorse Iris Young's demand for institutionalized means of ensuring the recognition and representation of oppressed or disadvantaged groups.

Adhering to such principles would allow for the development of a society that affirms:

> the presence and supports the claims of each of the oppressed groups or political movements constituting it, and arrives at a political program not by voicing some "principle of unity" that hides differences but rather by allowing each constituent to analyze economic and social issues from the perspective of its experience (Young 1989: 265).

As thin multiculturalism is grounded in a shared commitment to human rights, it does not commit itself to protect the rights of groups that are unable or unwilling to respect these values (Kymlicka 2012: 2). Consequently, "thin multiculturalism" offers a defense of a particular kind of diversity that does not challenge the basic liberal principles that govern society, and hence it does not amount to a real normative threat. This is not the case of "thick multiculturalism" that aspires to change the normative rules of the game.

Thick Multiculturalism

In cases of *thick multiculturalism,* a society is composed of both liberal and illiberal cultures.[2] To complicate things even further, these cases often result from a meeting between religious and nonreligious communities that hold different sets of beliefs concerning the source of political legitimacy. In such cases, there is no shared moral language. Hence, conflicts are much more difficult to manage.

Take for example debates concerning the right of girls to wear a hijab in schools. According to the French civic tradition, schools are public institutions and should therefore be culturally and religiously neutral. Before entering such public spaces, individuals should shed all distinguishing, visible religious symbols, be they a hijab, skullcap, or turban. These may be worn in the private sphere where particular identities are revered and protected.

For religious Muslims, Jews, and some Christians, religious tenets apply to both the public and the private sphere. This leads to an unavoidable conflict of values, and more importantly a disagreement about sources of authority. Those believers who take religious commands to be superior to state law are likely to be frequently facing dilemmas of disobedience Here is one of the earliest examples: in 1995, the French education minister, Francois Bayrou, ordered secondary school principals to ban "ostentatious signs" of religion. If Muslims wanted to impose their traditions and wear their costumes and veil, he argued, that would generate a backlash. "Muslims born in France who don't want to become French are fanatics or invaders" (Kamm 1995).

What French officials saw as moves necessary to create a neutral civic environment, Muslims perceived as a campaign against Islam. Our only ambition, replied Abdallah Ben Mansour, President of the Union of Islamic Organizations in France, "is to become at the same time good Muslims and good French citizens. But as long as people wage campaigns at the peril of Islam, as long as we let rancor and frustrations accumulate, we will encounter all forms of radicalization" (Kamm 1995).

The conflict that started in the 1990s continues today when in response to Muslim terrorism (including the beheading of a French teacher suspected of mocking the Prophet Muhammad) French President Emmanuel Macron declared that he would not allow a Muslim republic to be developed within France and insisted on protecting the secular nature of the public sphere in general and schools in particular.

This is not a mere disagreement on a certain policy; it reflects the fact that members of both groups hold conflicting sets of beliefs. The idea that religion or culture can remain strictly private sits well with post-reformation Christian beliefs but is foreign to the Muslim or Jewish way of thinking. No orthodox Jew would agree to take off his skullcap at school, at court, or in parliament, or eat pork at public events – God's commandments apply everywhere and cannot be overridden by state law.

Why should we change Islam? Muslims ask: "The second a Muslim makes reconciliation he's disobeying Allah. Divine law goes ahead of any other law" (Kamm 1995). One could portray this debate as a conflict between French civic liberalism and Muslim illiberalism, or between French civic (Republicanism) illiberalism and a legitimate

Muslim way of life, or between two illiberal cultures. Be that as it may, it represents cases of *thick multiculturalism* involving conflicts of values as well as a clash between democratic and religious authority that cannot be solved by referring to a set of shared principles, or legal procedures. Social discourse thus reaches a deadlock. Lacking discursive tools to solve the problem an attempt is made to turn the clock backward.

Premature Obituaries

The unplanned and unexpected results of *thick multiculturalism* intensify social conflicts. Majorities feel that diversification has gone too far, turning them into strangers in their own land. Minorities feel disillusioned, frustrated, and isolated. In the public eye, diversity is transformed from a source of social flourishing into a burden.

The first decade of the twenty-first century carried the marks of such unsolved conflicts. Fearful of the unexpected results of cultural and religious diversity, many supporters switched sides. The former British Prime Minister David Cameron was one of the first to mount an attack on multiculturalism:

> Under the doctrine of state multiculturalism, we have encouraged different cultures to live separate lives, apart from each other and the mainstream. We have failed to provide a vision of society to which they feel they want to belong .... We have even tolerated these segregated communities behaving in ways that run counter to our values. When a white person holds objectionable views—racism, for example—we rightly condemn them, but when equally unacceptable views or practices have come from someone who isn't white, we've been too cautious, frankly even fearful, to stand up to them (Burns 2011).

Public opinion turned suspicious and denunciations kept pouring in. The German Chancellor Angela Merkel lamented the fragmentation and destabilization of German society. Greeted with a standing ovation by members of her party, she declared that multiculturalism had "utterly failed." France's former President Nicolas Sarkozy espoused the same tone, arguing that French public policies were too concentrated on the culture of those who had arrived and not enough on the host culture, recommending balancing the rights of immigrants against the common good (Torres 2001). The former Spanish Prime

Minister Jose Maria expressed concern regarding the growing dangers embodied in the refusal of immigrants to integrate into the host society.

The quick shift from seeing multiculturalism as a source of social empowerment to a cause for crisis – has taken liberal multiculturalists by surprise. Within less than twenty years, the challenges of multiculturalism seemed to have overshadowed its virtues. One reason for the sudden change of heart has already been mentioned: under the banner of multiculturalism two very different social processes developed.

In its early days, the image of multiculturalism was inspired by the Canadian experience. Kymlicka's work had an astounding influence on the way people around the world approached issues of diversity. Yet Canadian diversity is exceptional, organized around five principles:

a) Immigrants are not perceived as a security threat.
b) They adhere to a shared commitment to human rights.
c) They enter the country via a controlled and selective process of immigration.
d) Immigrants come from many different countries of origins.
e) Immigrants are chosen by their skills and make efforts to integrate and contribute to the host society.

When these facilitating conditions are present, multiculturalism is a low-risk option and works well. "Multiculturalism tends to lose support in high-risk situations where immigrants are seen as predominantly illegal, as potential carriers of illiberal practices or movements, or as net burdens on the welfare state. However … it is precisely when immigrants are perceived as illegitimate, illiberal and burdensome that multiculturalism may be most needed" (Kymlicka 2012: 2).

Due to its immigration and accommodation policy, Canadian multiculturalism is thin; hence, all is quiet on the Canadian front. Conflicts erupt in those societies that encounter thicker kinds of multiculturalism – where most "others" are guest workers brought in to supply provisional cheap labor; illegal immigrants and refuge seekers. Members of these groups constitute a vital part of the workforce, yet they were never expected to become fully fledged citizens. As a result, no long-term systematic effort of integration were made and newcomers are left to fend for themselves.

Lacking language and professional skills, searching for cheap housing and a sense of community, they cluster in poor neighborhoods.

Property prices and school levels drop, pushing the locals out; ethnic and racial ghettos are formed with enclaves of poverty that slow the integration of both first and second, and even third-generation immigrants.

Moreover, lacking the Canadian or Australian ethos of immigrant societies, nation-states such as Germany, France, Denmark, and the Netherlands have found diversity difficult to stomach. Their nationhood being cultural, historical, and lingual has been threatened by the inflow of newcomers.

Collapsing the two concepts of multiculturalism into one, offering a "one-size-fits-all" set of solutions, creates social, ideological, and political confusion. Both immigrants and their host societies enter the conflict zone holding a concept of rights that protects their interests, but when rights clash power games become more relevant than ever.

The Revolt of the Majority

The present crisis, Will Kymlicka rightly argues, is grounded in an "uncritical celebration of diversity at the expense of addressing grave societal problems such as unemployment and social isolation" (Kymlicka 2012: 1). The present economic crisis, made worse by the COVID-19 pandemic, leaves members of majorities anxious about their ability to cash their cultural capital into a set of securities and opportunities. Fearing the loss of status, exposed to greater internal and external competition, vulnerable members of the majority long to revive the traditional social structures upon which they used to rely (Tamir 2019). Accordingly, they wish to "stop beating about the bush and directly tackle the question of majority rights" (Orgad 2015: 9).

The majorities Orgad defends are those who see themselves as being under threat: Diminishing majorities, regional minority-majorities, and victimized majorities. Yet even sound, well-secured majorities nowadays wish to use majority rights as a means of protection. The example of the minaret debate in Switzerland is enlightening. In a referendum in October 2009, over 50 percent of Swiss voters approved a move to ban the building of minarets. At the time, there were only four minarets in Switzerland. The main reasons for voting yes, according to Jean François Mayer, were: "The conviction that minarets do not belong to the Swiss landscape or culture; the belief that Islam is intolerant and hampers the building of Churches in the country; fear of

Islam's excessive influence and expansion and the idea that Muslims should adapt and integrate" (Orgad 2021).

The results of the referendum teach us that for the majority of Swiss voters church steeples are an integral part of the landscape while minarets are disruptive. The right of the minority, embodied in freedom of religion, to build houses of prayer structured in accordance with their tradition, thus conflict with the right of the majority to preserve the traditional cultural appearance of the public sphere. A clash between minority and majority rights sends us back to the pre-minority rights state of affairs where majoritarianism governed the day.

The rebellion against minority rights emerged due to a growing suspicion that such rights could be used to enhance a cultural and religious takeover. The growing immigration from Muslim countries; a high birth rate in these communities in comparison to native Europeans; declarations of extreme Muslim preachers concerning aspirations "to take over Europe"; alongside recent declarations of Turkish Prime Minister Tayyip Erdogan that Turkey would "flood" Europe with over three million Muslim immigrants, spread the unrealistic fear that Europe was about to fall into Islamic hands.

Michel Houellebecq's dystopic novel *Submission* (coincidently released on the day of the murderous attack on Charlie Hebdo) is an embodiment of such fears. It draws a profile of a France gone Muslim, the Sorbonne governed by religious fundamentalists, female students forced to cover their heads and males compelled to grow beards and participate in public prayers. The new President of the Republic, Ben-Abbes, wins the election and launches a campaign to include North Africa in the European Union with the aim of establishing a new Roman Empire with a Muslim France as its head. The novel ends with its hero, François, exhausted by his solitary resistance, poised to convert to Islam and learning to love his new religion and the benefits it bestows upon him.[3] The book that became an instant best seller reflects the dread of its readers. Though less than 10 percent of French citizens are Muslims (many of whom have adopted the French language and culture and are well integrated in France), the fear that the majority would lose reign is spreading fast.

It is interesting to note that while the twentieth century was marked by fear felt by minorities, the twenty-first century is marked by growing fears felt by majorities. The panic hovering over Europe is not concentrated on the political arrangements of the present, but on a deep concern for the future of liberal civilization (Brubaker 2017). This perception of the future turns social and cultural relationships into a zero-sum game. It is "us" or "them."

Do majorities have a right to take action to prevent a future takeover even if it is carried out in a peaceful manner? Do minority rights depend on a commitment to avoid undermining the power of the majority? As long as these questions remain open, minority rights, more often than not, are seen as a threat.

Moderates who offer a compromise between rights-based demands are caught in the cross fire. Moderate Muslims who would like to practice their religion in both the private and the public sphere – cover their heads, pray, eat halal food, avoid shaking hands, while fulfilling their civic duties, be loyal citizens and trustworthy compatriots – are exposed to both internal and external pressures. The outer world sees them as a threat, while the inner world sees them as traitors. Moderate French, Swiss, or Danish citizens who would like to respect multiculturalism also face dual criticism: The inner world portrays them as weak and naïve, disrespectful of their own culture, while the outer world suspects they are duplicitous, using accommodation as a means of conversion.

The notion of group rights is contested by liberals and illiberals alike. Liberals fear it undermines their way of life, while illiberals suspect it is an instrument of transformation. Both, in a way, are right. Illiberal enclaves spread all over the liberal world. Using the liberal conception of rights, illiberal cultures strive to protect systems of belief that do not respect the very same rights which are the source of their protection.[4] In order to shelter their members from ideas ingrained in liberalism, they ridicule the idea of self-reflection, contrasting it with truth proclaimed through revelation or the handing down of wisdom from one generation to another.

Schools become a conflict zone. Zealots wish to create separate religious/communal schools where future citizens of liberal-democratic states are educated to disrespect the foundations of the liberal way of life. Demands to preserve the liberal Western character of schools by banning ostentatious religious symbols, forcing hand-shaking, and mixed swimming lessons provide leaders of illiberal culture with the perfect excuse for educational segregation. When restrictions on appearance and behavior in the public sphere, meant to promote integration, lead to segregation, those who seek modes of accommodation face a painful dilemma.

Is there a way out? In order to show equal concern and respect and avoid paternalism liberals must acknowledge that in the eyes of many individuals (male and female alike), abiding by commandments and traditions such as covering one's head or wearing a Burkini are not a symbol of oppression or extremism, nor are they an expression of disrespect or unwillingness to integrate (Orgad 2021).

Differentiating between following one's tradition and disrespecting the hosting culture is of utmost importance. A clear distinction must also be drawn between practices that do not violate the rights of others (either members or nonmembers) and those that embody a threat (Tamir 2000). Identity rights as well as freedom of religion and culture should not shelter in-group oppression and discrimination, hate speech, or inflammatory teachings.

Feminism has taught us that individuals should be protected from fear and anxiety in both the public and private sphere. This means that less attention ought to be given to public appearance and conduct and more to safeguarding personal autonomy and well-being in the private sphere. Autonomy-restricting practices such as child marriages, bigamy, sexual abuse, as well as the oppression of women should not be tolerated in either the public or the private sphere. Appearance, on the other hand, should be a private matter. Unless proven otherwise, it should be seen as an expression of devotion rather than extremism, and therefore tolerated. Protecting "freedom of appearance" is an important aspect of present-day multiculturalism.

In Judaism, Islam, and some Christian denominations, religious commandments regarding behavior and appearance cross the public/private line. The "tortellini of hospitality" is therefore a good closing for our story as they are an example of how to make *thick multiculturalism* possible. Filling tortellini with chicken rather than pork is a sign of good will, but also an expression of a deep understanding of the importance of following religious commandments in both the public and private sphere. It is also an expression of the desire to sit around the same table, celebrating together a true spirit of equal partnership. Such acts draw people into the circle of membership. Excluding acts, like stripping women wearing a Burkini or forcing mothers escorting their children to school to remove their veil, push minorities to the social and cultural periphery. It is unnecessary to explain why the first strategy is to be preferred and celebrated.

Liberal societies are searching for ways to accommodate both *thick* and *thin multiculturalism*. When there is no common moral ground, one can reach no more than an uneven compromise that liberals endorse for principled reasons and illiberals endure out of necessity. Such a compromise is likely to leave both sides dissatisfied. But it is the most one can achieve. Perhaps the most important lesson of the last fifty years of rights-talk is that the expansion of the notion of rights offers a tool of social discourse but cannot offer a receipt for how societies should handle themselves.

Notes

1 A great deal of paternalism is embedded in the assumption that while we can survive change and innovation and endure the tensions created by modernity, Indian women cannot; we can reinvent ourselves, our culture, our tradition time and again while "they" must adhere to known cultural patterns. A non-discriminatory solution to the problem of overcrowding will have to surrender the reactionary assumption that in order to retain their identity, all members of the tribe must adopt traditional kinds of occupations that are land-consuming. Why not encourage some Indians to acquire new types of occupations. Why is it assumed that the only way Indians can retain their identity and tradition is by adhering to the same kinds of occupations their forefathers were engaged in? Why is it that Canadians from Toronto can retain their identity despite the fact that they live very different cultural, social, and professional lives from their predecessors while Indian men and women can retain their identity only if they preserve the traditional way of life?

2 I use the term *illiberal* to denote cultures that do not affiliate themselves with the liberal school of thought with an emphasis on three main points: (a) They do not celebrate personal autonomy, self-reflection, and critical thinking but expect their followers to succumb to a higher, external authority. (b) They do not place human rights at their core. (c) They do not celebrate moral and cultural plurality as a source of inspiration and self-reflection. Obviously different illiberal belief systems respond differently to these issues. Yet, for the purpose of this debate, I join them in one category.

3 Much like Winston in George Orwell's ending of 1948: "He gazed up at the enormous face. Forty years it had taken him to learn what kind of smile was hidden beneath the dark moustache. O cruel, needless misunderstanding! O stubborn, self-willed exile from the loving breast! Two gin-scented tears trickled down the sides of his nose. But it was all right, everything was all right, the struggle was finished. He had won the victory over himself.... He loved Big Brother" (1949).

4 *The Mozert case* (1987), in which fundamentalist and evangelical families demanded that their children be excluded from participating in a reading program which they claimed interfered with the free exercise of their religion by "exposing the children to a variety of religious points of view in an even-handed manner, thus denigrating the truth of their particular religion" (*Mozert* v. *Hawkins*, 827 F.2d 1058 (6th Cir. *1987*)) is an example of this inherent asymmetry.

References

Berlin, I. (1969). *Two Concepts of Liberty*. Oxford: Oxford University Press.

(1980). Nationalism. In *Against the Current*. London: The Hogarth Press.

(1997). *The Sense of Reality: Studies in Ideas and Their History*. New York: Farrar, Straus and Giroux.

Bloom, A. (1987). *The Closing of the American Mind*. New York: Simon Schuster.

Burns, J. F. (2011). Cameron Criticizes "Multiculturalism in Britain." *New York Times*, February 5, 2011, A:6.

Brubaker, R. (2017). The New Language of European Populism: Why "Civilization Is Replacing the Nation." *Foreign Affairs*.

Fukuyama, F. (1989). The End of History? *The National Interest,* 16:3–18.

Geertz, C. (1973). *The Interpretation of Cultures: Selected Essays*. New York: Basic Books, 311.

Glazer, N. (1997). *We Are All Multiculturalist Now*. Cambridge: Harvard University Press.

Gutmann, A. (1992). *Introduction to Charles Taylor, Multiculturalism and the Politics of Recognition*. Princeton, NJ: Princeton University Press, 3.

Kamm, T. (1995). The Clash of Cultures: Rise of Islam in France Rattles the Populace and Stirs a Backlash. *Wall Street Journal*, May 1, 1995.

Kymlicka, W. (1989). *Liberalism, Community and Culture*. Oxford: Oxford University Press.

(1995). *Liberalism, Community and Culture*. Oxford: Oxford University Press.

(2012). Multiculturalism: Success, Failure and the Future. Report to the *Immigration Policy Institute*.

Mckenna, J. (2019). Culture War over Crucifixes and Tortellini Sparked by Calls for Italy to Be More Inclusive. *Telegraph*, January 10, 2019.

Mozert v. *Hawkins*, 827 F.2d 1058 (6th Cir. 1987).

Okin, S. M. (1999). *Is Multiculturalism Bad for Women?* Princeton, NJ: Princeton University Press.

Orgad, L. (2015). *Cultural Defense of Nations: A Liberal Theory of Majority Rights*. Oxford: Oxford University Press.

(2021). Forced to Be Free: The Limits of European Tolerance. *Harvard Human Rights Journal,* 34: 1–35.

Rawls, J. (1971). *Theory of Justice*. Cambridge, MA: Belknap Press.

(1993). *Political Liberalism*. New York: Columbia University Press.

Sandel, M. (1982). *Liberalism and the Limits of Justice*. Cambridge: Cambridge University Press.

Shklar, J. (1989). The Liberalism of Fear. First published in Rosenblum, N. ed., Liberalism and the Moral Life. Cambridge: Harvard University Press, 21–38.

Tamir, Y. (1995). Two Concepts of Multiculturalism. *Journal of Philosophy of Education, Special Issue: Democratic Education in a Multicultural State*, 29/2: 161–72.

(1997). The Land of the Fearful and the Free. *Constellations*, 3/3: 296–314.

(2019). *Why Nationalism*. Princeton, NJ: Princeton University Press.

(2000). Remember Amalek: Religious Hate Speech. In Rosenblum, N. ed., *Obligations of Citizenship and Demands of Faith*. Princeton, NJ: Princeton University Press, 321–35.

Taylor, C. (1991). *The Ethics of Authenticity*. Cambridge: Harvard University Press.

(1992). *Multiculturalism and the Politics of Recognition*. Princeton, NJ: Princeton University Press.

(1994). Politics of Recognition. In Gutmann, A. ed., *Multiculturalism*. Princeton, NJ: Princeton University Press.

Torres, C. A. (2001). Is Multiculturalism Dead? *Huffington Post*, August 2, 2001.

Young, I. (1989). Polity and Group Difference; a Critique of the Ideal of Universal Citizenship. *Ethics, 99*: 250–274.

8 *Multiculturalism without Privileging Liberalism*[*]

TARIQ MODOOD

Yuli Tamir's chapter (Chapter 7) consists of three main sections. She identifies the different "waves" of political thinking on multiculturalism and tracks their development over a 50 year period (1970–2020). She then points out where developments became problematic and led to division among liberal supporters. Subsequently, she describes "the revolt of the majority." I would like to elaborate upon her brief history of the rise and fall of multiculturalism and in so doing, offer an alternative account of this phenomenon. This is multiculturalism that is not simply about trends in academic liberalism but refers to claims to national citizenship and national identity by those seeking inclusion in a new sense of the national identity. Moreover, unlike the national pioneer of multiculturalism, Canada, it focuses on post-immigration, ethno-racial, and ethno-religious formations.

A Brief History of Multiculturalism

Tamir offers a characterization of the debate on multiculturalism and its current status. The initial backdrop consists of the horrors of World War II, the inhumanity, the danger of totalitarian ideologies, and the power of the state. These led to a universalism of human rights and John Rawls' theory of justice (Chapter 4, in this volume, pp. 180–181), and we might add, to the humanistic anti-racism of Martin Luther King and the Civil Rights Movement. The initial movement toward universalism was heavily qualified by thinkers such as Isaiah Berlin and Charles Taylor who historicized the pretensions of universalism and emphasized how free individuals were always embedded in specific cultures, which varied

* I am grateful to the book editors as well as a number of friends and colleagues: Clayton Chin, Pier-Luc Dupont, Sune Laegaard, Geoff Levey, Bhikhu Parekh, Thomas Sealy, and Varun Uberoi, for their helpful comments on a previous draft.

across time and place. This second wave was centered on dignity and respect for culturally oppressed and marginalized minorities, whether in the form of an inclusive liberal cultural-nationalism (Berlin) or as "recognition" of the identities of minorities and their accommodation in the shared culture (Taylor). The commitment to diversity naturally led to the third wave in the 1990s, the centerpiece of which was the demand for special rights for vulnerable minorities, a position Tamir associates with Will Kymlicka. She believes that the promise of special rights led to a crisis within multiculturalism. I will however come to that in the next section. In this section, I would like to comment on the extent to which her presentation of the "waves" is a cross-national pattern.

Kymlicka's theory of multiculturalism as "special rights" is liberal egalitarian in a Rawlsian way but we cannot really understand it without knowing that it is a response to Canadian problems. This is important because the experience of other countries is quite different. Canadian multiculturalism was a response to three different sources of political agitation: Quebecker francophone territorial nationalism, indigenous Canadians consisting of many tribes such as the Cree and the Iroquois, dispersed across the vast expanse of rural Canada, and white urban European migrants, such as Ukrainians and their descendants (Uberoi 2009). At first glance these groups seem to have nothing in common. Kymlicka offered a theory of multiculturalism uniting the three groups (Kymlicka 1995). He argued that individuals in minority groups with a "societal culture" distinct from mainstream society, as was the case in Canada, had developed into the individuals they were through accessing and exploring their societal culture. The latter was therefore a "context of choice," consisting of a language, history and way of thinking, that was a prerequisite for the development of individuals who expressed themselves through their choices. The liberal state, the goal of which was to maximize individual freedom and autonomy, had a duty to protect these societal cultures by granting them self-government and separate representation (Kymlicka 1995). While this theory may have been apt in relation to territorial groups such as Quebeckers and native Canadians, it is difficult to see why Kymlicka included immigrants, naturalized citizens, and the "second generation" in his theory, given that he rightly stressed that this latter category of people did not enjoy a separate societal culture in their host country. For instance, in settling in Canada they had left behind their societal culture in their land of origin and now became part of the societal culture of Canada (Kymlicka 1995; see also Levey 1997, Carens 1997 and Modood 2013 [2007]).

This difficulty is deepened by the fact that while Kymlicka included immigrants and their descendants in his theory of multiculturalism, he did not think that they were entitled to the rights at the center of his theory. While Quebeckers and indigenous Canadians were entitled to self-government and special political representation, post-immigration groups were not. The latter's special rights were limited to rights that facilitated respectful integration and prevented exclusion from the mainstream populace as well as the formation of separate communities. While it is fair to say that Kymlicka is the most cited political theorist on multiculturalism and also has attracted the most political interest internationally (Kymlicka 2007/8), most of this interest does not revolve around his full theory, nor indeed the politics ensuing from his full theory. Instead, this interest relates to the issue of immigration and post-immigration integration or settlement; phenomena that have become increasingly prominent over the past fifty years. Thus, the focus is on politics with which his theory of special rights (as opposed to his writings in general) least connects. Of course, Kymlicka has been a prolific writer on issues of post-immigration integration and equal citizenship, and has many acute and compelling comments to make. However, all these fall within Tamir's "second wave" which focuses on diversity within a newly shared culture, and not Kymlicka's theory of special rights. Let me illustrate by reference to the United Kingdom.

In Britain, multiculturalism emerged quite differently to the process in Canada. In Britain there were no indigenous people. There were incipient – and soon to become quite strong – territorial minority nationalisms that could be compared to the case of Quebec, namely in Scotland, Wales, and – albeit differently – Northern Ireland. Such politics, however, were understood in terms of "home rule," devolution, nationalism, or multi-nationalism, never multiculturalism. Hence, what was called "multiculturalism" in Britain fell outside, and was much smaller in scope than the main special rights of Kymlicka's theory. Moreover, in relation to immigrants, the British example had three important characteristics missing in the Canadian case. First, the immigrants were not random individuals who were requesting permission to enter a country with which they had no prior connection (such as the Ukrainians). Originating from countries such as India, Pakistan, and the West Indies, they were part of the British Empire or those parts of it that had very recently become part of the British Commonwealth – they were part of "the British story." This was not merely symbolic. During 1948–1962 their legal status, "subjects of the Crown," was the same as that of Britons, and they had the same right of access into the United Kingdom (Modood 1996 and 2017).

Second, while the Canadian Multiculturalism Policy of 1971 sought to offer integration to immigrants who were white Europeans, while still respecting their cultural distinction, in the United Kingdom the immigrants were not white but marked by "race." Indeed, for decades "immigrant" in Britain meant "colored" or "not white." Even now, "ethnic minority" is a synonym for "not white" and is rarely used to include Jews, the Irish, or recently settled European citizens.[1] Compared to European-origin immigrants in Canada, this racialization in Britain created a much stronger form of exclusion and second-class status – a legacy of the same Empire that now gave them rights equal to those of indigenous British nationals. It also meant that British multiculturalism emerged after a period in which the first political priority was not cultural identity but racial equality and anti-color racism. The result is that anti-racism runs through British multiculturalism which is understood ideationally and as a political action in a way that is not comparable to the position in Canada or possibly anywhere else.[2] These two originating features – British membership and racism – no less than the multinational character of Britain, paved the way for the view that all subjects/citizens were British but that not all were the same kind of British or indeed British in the same way. It took some decades to mature but the seeds of the idea of a plural Britishness have this historical depth, perhaps ultimately one of imperial legacy, and not just on the part of the white British but also of those, for example, from the West Indians, who brought with them concepts such as Britain as the "Mother Country" (Carter 1986). In Britain, the politics of post-immigration began not with issues about naturalization and assimilation – as seems to have been the case in much of continental Europe – but with racial equality and challenging racialized narrow, islander definitions of Britishness (Modood 2017).

The third feature that distinguishes British from Canadian multiculturalism, and Kymlicka's theorizing of it, is religion. As the diversity and distinctive character of different minority groups began to gain recognition in Britain, racial equality was extended to cover ethnicity and religion. The latter characteristics were not easily separated;

illustrated, for example, by the House of Lords' decision whereby banning the wearing of the religious turban by Sikh men actually amounted to a form of ethnic discrimination and therefore racial discrimination in law (*Mandala* v. *Lee*, 1982).[3] As ethnic-group pride and assertiveness became an accepted feature of and indeed the vehicle for promoting equal citizenship, South Asian identities began to increasingly take on an ethno-religious character. Non-whiteness remained a social divide but racism began to be thought of in terms of racisms and in compound forms such as cultural racism, anti-Muslim racism, and so on. From the time of *The Satanic Verses* affair in the late 1980s, Muslim political activism began to loom large in the emergent multiculturalism; furthermore, after 9/11 in the United States and 7/7 suicide-bombings in London, it became central to a multiculturalism that was being overwhelmed by security concerns and, according to some observers, had died (Kepel, 2005). This centrality of religion was reflected in British theorizing (Parekh 2006 [2000], Modood 2005), while Kymlicka made it clear that his theory of special rights and state support was not extendable to religious groups, which had to be content with religious freedom, toleration, and a neutral state rather than expect third wave recognition and accommodation (Kymlicka 2001a, Modood 2013[2007]).[4] Finally, I should add that the story of Canadian multiculturalism – and by that I mean what is popularly and indeed universally understood as multiculturalism (i.e., nothing to do with Quebec-type nationalism nor the rights of indigenous people) – looks like a top-down politicians' policy program. In contrast, the features of British membership, anti-racism, Black pride, and religious-identity assertiveness are very much a reflection of the political priorities of the ethnic minority communities and the campaigns they have mounted (Modood, 1992 and 2005; Sivanandan, 1982). This bottom-up feature in Britain has meant that a politics that begins with the integration of racialized groups expands and complexifies the idea of race beyond its original meaning, yet continues to press for the critical aspect of "race" within multiculturalism (Modood 2005).

This excursus about Britain should make it clear that while Kymlicka created a liberal theory of special rights, most of this theory and its rights addressed Canadian non-immigration issues. Moreover, insofar as Kymlicka's liberalism addressed the rights of post-immigration groups, the nature of these groups in Britain in terms of national history, "race," and religion was quite different from that in Canada. As Kymlicka is central to Tamir's story of multiculturalism as liberalism veering off in the direction of problematic "special rights," my discussion questions the relevance of this story in the case of Britain. My suggestion is not that Britain is typical of other countries; in one sense, all countries are distinctive. My claim is that a Canadianized academic liberalism focused on a secessionist francophone nationalism and indigenous people does not capture the multiculturalist struggles centered on post-immigration ethno-religious groups. The implication is that this lack of fit will apply to other countries for which the challenge of integration and multiculturalism originates in immigration and settlement rather than sub-nationalism and indigeneity.

Where Things Went Wrong: Illiberal Minorities and Thick Multiculturalism

Turning to Tamir's normative analysis, she argues that the third wave of multiculturalism – embodied in Kymlicka's theory of special rights – soon came to create a crisis of multiculturalism. Kymlicka's is an explicitly liberal theory that is meant to protect minority societal cultures from the pressures of the dominant group; it therefore offers "external protections." It prohibits state support for any special rights, referred to by Kymlicka as "internal restrictions," such as those that subordinate women to men in a minority culture (Kymlicka 1995: 35–44). This means that special rights may only be given to those minorities that are internally liberal or can be liberalized. "Yet," Tamir argues, "soon Kymlicka's moral constraints were to be removed. Accused of defending only 'their own kind' and being paternalistic, liberals were asked to accept a much wider range of diversity" (p. 185). The result was that the "realization that special rights protect a wide range of undesirable social phenomena, made supporters of multiculturalism lose their appetite for diversity" (p. 189). Not only did this lead to a loss of support for multiculturalism but it divided multiculturalism into two, a thin and a thick version. Thin multiculturalism "offers a defense of a particular kind of diversity that does not challenge the basic liberal principles that govern society, and hence it does not amount to a real normative threat" (p. 190). "Thick multiculturalism," on the other hand, results from a meeting between liberal and illiberal cultures where the conflicting parties do not share a common set of norms and "values." Tamir adds, "[to] complicate things even further, these cases often result from a meeting between religious and non-religious communities that hold different beliefs concerning the source of political legitimacy. In such cases, there is no shared moral language. Hence, conflicts become much more difficult to manage" (p. 190).[5] Unlike many liberals, however, she believes that liberal societies must search "for ways of accommodating both thick and thin multiculturalism" p. 198.

I recognize Tamir's characterization of the problem here. I believe she approaches it with sensitivity and care but also overstates it ("no shared moral language"?). In any case, I do not share her way of framing the matter; albeit it is fair to say that it is where one ends up if one begins with liberalism or at least Rawlsian individualism. In a contemporary multicultural society one is then forced to choose between giving up on multiculturalism and embracing a liberal individualism; or, holding the Kymlickan line that only liberal minorities deserve to be included within multiculturalism (and the illiberal ones have to be contained or made liberal, perhaps through some form of "muscular liberalism," to borrow a phrase from former Prime Minister David Cameron). An alternative is something like Tamir's sympathetic, liberal pragmatism. These three choices are, however, not the only ones. They seem to be the only ones if one confines oneself to thinking within liberalism. I do not begin with liberalism or give the latter absolute powers over multiculturalism or vice versa. On many occasions, the normative force of liberalism will be compelling but we must not begin with the assumption that it must always be so. At any rate, this is the approach that I have followed, leaning heavily on Bhikhu Parekh on some points, and what has recently been identified as a feature of "the Bristol School of Multiculturalism" (Levey 2019, Modood, Uberoi and Thompson, 2022). I would like to offer a two-part response to Tamir's problem of how to cope with "thick multiculturalism" and "illiberal minorities." The first part draws on an appreciation of the significance of identity and some sociological research. The second part concerns the normative role of dialogue in a context of cultural and value conflicts and is based on my reading of Parekh.

The Role of Identities

Liberalism's primary medium is that of values, principles, and laws. One of the ways to de-absolutize liberalism in relation to multiculturalism and the respectful inclusion of minorities is to recognize the sociological and normative significance of other features of social life. The one I principally have in mind here is the sense of identity. In the 1990s, I was the principal researcher of The Fourth National Survey of Ethnic Minorities, a large, nationally representative survey in England and Wales, comprising over 5,000 respondents, that operated in the field in 1993–1994 (Modood et al 1997). The survey covered many different topics. It included an innovative section on ethnic identity and cultural practices, probing aspects of minority identities that no survey (except to some extent in the United States) had ever carried out with such a large and nationally representative sample. I was particularly struck by four findings.[6] First, different minorities prioritized different kinds of identities. While skin-color (Black) was prominent in the self-descriptions of Caribbeans, it barely featured in the self-descriptions of South Asians, for whom, including for those born in Britain, the country of origin (India, Pakistan, Bangladesh) was more important. One significant aspect of this was that the public discourse in which "Black" was presumed to be the public identity of all who were not white, a concept endorsed by the Commission for Racial Equality, had not displaced the self-chosen ethnic identity of the South Asians (Modood 1988 and 1994).

Second, for South Asians, the religion of one's family was just as important a source of self-identity, and for Muslims a more important one, than national origins (Modood et al 1997). This owed as much to a sense of community as to personal faith, but the identification and prioritization of religion was far from being merely nominal. This was to grow over time, especially for Muslims. A Channel 4 GfK NOP survey carried out in Spring 2006 found that 79 percent of 16–34-year-old Muslims said that religion was very important to the way they lived their life, slightly more than their elders; while on a number of questions, the young tended to be more "Islamic" or more "radical" than their elders (GfK NOP, 2006; see also Mirza et al, 2007, where this generational contrast was even stronger). Moreover, such religious identities could not be characterized as belonging to private life and irrelevant to public policies and resources. For example, half of the Muslims interviewed in the Fourth Survey said that there should be state funding for Muslim schools.

The third striking feature was that these religious and ethnic identities were not simply an expression of behavior or of participation in distinctive cultural practices. For, across the generations and in relation to time spent in Britain, there was a noticeable decline in participation in the cultural practices (language, dress, attendance at places of worship, and so on) that go with a particular identity. Yet, the decrease in self-identification with a group label (Black, Muslim etc.) was relatively small. That is to say, it was not anomalous, for example, for people self-identifying as Sikh or Muslim to not be religious at all. So, if there is a sense in which "race" and ethnicity was "religionized," it was also the case that for some, religion had been ethnicized. These new ethno-religious "associational identities" (Modood et al 1997: 332–38) are not to be thought of as passive or fading identities. That would be to overlook the pride with which they may be asserted, the intensity with which they may be debated, and their capacity to generate community activism and political campaigns.

The fourth important feature was that these minority identities, diverse as they were, did not necessarily compete with a sense of Britishness. Half of the Chinese as well as more than two-thirds of those in the other minority groups also said they felt British, and these proportions were, as one might expect, higher among young people and those born in Britain. The majority of respondents had no difficulty with the idea of hyphenated nationality or multiple identities (Hutnik 1991, Modood et al 1997), which has become a commonplace idea since then.[7] Interestingly, later studies have consistently found that national identification and patriotism among ethnic minorities, including Muslims in Britain are higher than among the population as a whole. An analysis of two Citizenship Surveys concluded, "We found no evidence that Muslims or people of Pakistani heritage were in general less attached to Britain than were other religions or ethnic groups" (Heath and Roberts 2008). A later survey report concluded that, "British Muslims are more likely to be both patriotic and optimistic about Britain than are the white British community" (Wind-Cowie and Gregory 2011: 41–42).

My conclusion from such research is that minority communities and their relations with mainstream society are not just about (differential) values. People have identities, which are adaptable and sometimes can change even over short periods of time. They can be very important to them and not just for purposes of conformity to community norms and cultural practices. The sources of identity can be a sense of self, a collective inter-subjectivity, partly produced by origins and the past but also by one's current location in society, how one is perceived and treated by others, and hopes and struggles to change these perceptions. Moreover, such minority identities are not monistic or "essentialist"[8] but can vary across the group, not least generationally, and are open not just to change but also to fusing or combining with other identities. An important meld is with a national identity such as British or growing and grafting one's minority identity into the national identity. Most ethnic minority persons think of themselves as British, wish to be British, and want to be accepted as such. It seemed to me then, as it does now, that this identity data is fundamental to thinking about multiculturalism. I felt that together with the equal citizenship and racism that I have already referred to, it is a better place to start thinking about and building a multiculturalist society and polity than to begin with the clash of values or the requirements of liberalism. That societies and polities hold together and function because there is a desire to belong; that this is not monistic but multilayered and cross-cutting, including minority identities and the national identity (or identities, in multinational Britain, and with multiple perspectives on Britain: CMEB 2000), and ought to be nurtured as a ground for multiculturalism. Societies hang together or fall apart because of the power of identities and the desire to belong, not just because of values, principles, and laws – the stuff of liberalism. This is a perspective to which Tamir has certainly been sensitive (Tamir 1995, especially in relation to national identity) but it is not present in the section under discussion.

The emergence, nurturing, development, and sustaining of multiculturalism, including necessary forms of commonality, must be carried out at the level of identity and not just in terms of rights and values. Of course, multiculturalism is not value-free. For a start, as Tamir's account of the development of multiculturalism makes plain, the aspiration and movement for multiculturalism depends on concepts of nondiscrimination and concepts of equal concern and respect. However, having established the principle of recognition or equal respect as part of equal citizenship, we should not then decide all questions, all ethical-political dilemmas, by asking: "What would a liberal do here?" In many ways, this would be to go backward into a pre-multiculturalist, abstract universalism. We should ask: "what would a multiculturalist who is part of this society (not just an abstract individual or an unembedded universalist, which Tamir too wants to go beyond) do here?"[9] For example, when we ask if one or more religions should be taught, or organized worship should to be allowed in public schools; or, if turbans can be worn by judges in court; or, whether Holocaust deniers should be imprisoned, and if so, up to what length of time, we know that these questions are answered differently in the United States, Britain, and France. In each case, there will be some deployment of liberal arguments but they will be interpreted in ways that fit the public culture in each country and its own sense of how to balance personal freedom, equality, the public good, religious conscience, free speech, incitement to hatred, and so on. This is the beginning of the second part of my reply to Tamir's crisis of multiculturalism induced by "thick multiculturalism."

Operative Public Values as a Basis for Multicultural Dialogue

In his masterpiece, *Rethinking Multiculturalism* (2000), Parekh argues that if we are to take value diversity – of the kind argued for by Isaiah Berlin – seriously then we must recognize that liberalism is one of a number of value traditions and positions, each of which has something to say about what makes a good life, how society should be organized, what goals should be pursued, and so on. If so, it means that liberalism is one of the players and therefore cannot at the same time be the umpire. It cannot be the exclusive frame in which questions of value are pursued or through which other positions are evaluated. That would be an unjustified privileging of liberalism and such an aspiration must be given up in favor of an umpire-less dialogue between the various moral traditions and forms of life (see also his latest book, Parekh 2019; cf. Oakeshott's idea of a "conversation of mankind": Oakeshott 1962). Liberalism has a lot to offer; it is a persuasive moral philosophy but it must also be prepared to learn from other moral perspectives. Yet, most practical dilemmas to do with policy, institutional rules, and law cannot be addressed by such lofty dialogue. Considering practical and policy questions, Parekh argues that every society must appeal to some values to regulate its public spaces and he calls these "operative public values" (OPVs), and these will vary by society, though there are bound to be some overlaps across societies (Parekh 2000: 267–71).

The OPVs are not all derived from a single principle, indeed, while "interrelated, they do not form a coherent whole and sometimes pull in different directions" (269)[10]. Nevertheless, a practical dialogue concerning such issues as whether female circumcision or polygamy should be allowed must start here. The OPVs are embodied in the constitution, the laws and norms governing civic relations of the society in question. They reflect a particular historical and moral legacy and so in that sense are not universal and may indeed be said to be biased against newly settled minorities and others. It means that every society "needs to periodically reassess its operative public values, and the fact that a minority practice offends against some of them provides it with a welcome opportunity to do so" (270). In a society like Britain, the OPVs have a strongly liberal character, but the country has its own take on the nature of the liberal values which will not be identical to the way they are interpreted elsewhere (cf., how liberty and equality are quite differently interpreted in Britain and France: Modood and Thompson 2018). Moreover, while Britain is a liberal society it is not merely liberal. It is also conservative, Christian, collectivist, and nationalist in various ways and this is reflected in its OPVs. Consider the case of marriage: pure liberalism might leave the drafting of a contract to whatever two (or more) individuals choose for themselves (as J S Mill argued) but that is not what we have in Britain. Britain is liberal in some ways and in recent decades has become more liberalized though few argue that this liberalization should be taken to its nth, Millian degree. It is this distinctly contextualized and qualified liberalism, which is neither pure nor the same as anywhere else, that sets the terms of dialogue in relation to minority practices that are queried as being, prima facie, unacceptable.

It may be thought that this is not real dialogue as the terms are loaded in favor of the majority and the status quo. The important point to note is that there should be the possibility of a dialogue rather than merely status quo (liberal) enforcement, and where else could a practical dialogue begin? An "illiberal" minority is likely to feel that it has less room for maneuver and that it is being coerced if told that its practices must be subjected to liberalism, because it will perceive the latter as the majoritarian rather than an independent standard. The honest description of what faces a minority here is that to defend its practices it will need to "appeal to values the wider society itself subscribes to or can be persuaded to share" (272), or, I would add, with which it can co-exist.

Parekh illustrates this formula for a dialogue in relation to controversies such as female circumcision and polygamy. An example of a successful dialogue that I have witnessed over the years relates to the protection of Muslims against aggressive words in Britain. When Muslims in Britain first expressed their anger against Salman Rushdie's novel, *The Satanic Verses*, many voiced their outrage by designating it as "apostasy." When that was met with incomprehension by the media and public commentators and particularly when that charge was mixed up with Ayatollah Khomeini's *fatwa* calling for the death of the author, most Muslims asked to be protected by the laws of blasphemy. When it became clear that there was little support for the existing law of blasphemy among politicians, let alone extending these laws to Muslims, the same activists and organizations started framing their demands in terms of legislation against incitement to religious hatred to complement the racism laws. Initially, the main body of informed opinion thought that this too was inappropriate for religion and a threat to free speech; though in due course it became law. Moreover, at the time of the Danish Cartoons Affair, several major European newspapers republished the cartoon out of a sense of solidarity. British papers did not do so on the grounds that such publications would give gratuitous offence (Modood 2019a: 66). This is the kind of dialogue and two-way learning that is described here as a multiculturalist use of OPVs and exemplifies Parekh's point that "[s]ince moral values cannot be debated and defended in an objective way and conclusive manner, and since it is difficult to be wholly detached and open-minded about one's moral values, the dialogues involves passages of incomprehension, intransigence, irreconcilable differences" (272). He concludes "while a society has an obligation to accommodate the minority way of life, it has no obligation to so at the cost of its own, especially if it remains genuinely unconvinced by the minority's defence of its practice" (273). This neatly leads us to the third part of Tamir's chapter (Chapter 7).

"The Revolt of the Majority"

As the argument concerning OPVs and the above quoted passage from Parekh shows, at least some multiculturalists have always been mindful of the normative and other power of the majority society and sought to qualify it in certain ways though they have not dismissed it as illegitimate (cf. Eisenberg 2020: 3). Rather, the majority society is the normative context within which claims of minority accommodation are made, even when it is clear that a minority is not being treated fairly or respectfully or is not being heard in the way co-citizens deserve to be dialogically heard. In Kymlicka's terms, when it comes to the integration of immigrants and their progeny (but not in relation to indigenous people and minority nations), the normative context is the societal culture of the majority, including its political and legal system and practice of citizenship. However, in the past few years I have come to think that to treat the normative significance of the majority in these terms only is not enough.

As seen from the above quote, Parekh, unlike Kymlicka and Tamir, does not argue that minority rights are compensatory, and neither do I. Every society has a right to create a public culture, to which the "recognition argument" adds that minorities too have a collective character and identity needs and that these should be included in the public culture. How this is accomplished will vary from minority to minority, but it should be, to use a Taylorian term, additive, whether by way of an exemption, a parallel provision, inclusion of hybridity, non-coercive assimilation or by broadening, pluralizing and synthesizing the shared culture and should be a matter of working dialogically with OPVs to meet minority identity needs. "Additive" means that it is not about "deconstructing," displacing, privatizing, or eliminating the majoritarian character of the public culture. Rather, it is about multiculturalizing the public culture by adding minority cultural needs and identities and their interpretations of the public culture and how it can be made more inclusive and enable their participation within and sense of belonging to it.

It has been said that this "additive" approach may work with cultural practices but what can be done when there is a clash between a universal principle such as gender equality and a cultural practice such as polygamy (especially, polygyny)?[11] First, we have to recognize that the contemporary Western objection to polygamy is not merely about liberal principles but is mixed up with a preference for certain sexual relations and family formations that clearly have a cultural form. Otherwise, the objection would be to polygyny only, whereas no liberal public discusses the possible inclusion of polygamy. In relation to monogamy, consider how far Western society has moved away from the norm of life-term heterosexual marriages to co-habitation, divorces, and re-marriages (which could be described as serial monogamy or staggered polygamy), step families, and multiple partnering (as long as they are without legal responsibilities). While Muslims in the main discourage and regret these trends, they tolerate those that can be institutionalized into a marital system. The idea that the West believes in monogamy and Muslims in polygamy and that there is a fundamental clash of values and practices here is quite simplistic and overlooks the fact that conservative monogamy is practiced more in Muslim-majority countries (and the South generally) than it is in western Europe (for a multiculturalist discussion of the merits of monogamy and polygamy, see Parekh 2000/2006: 282–92).

So, how can such a form of multiculturalism respond to "the revolt of the majority" as described by Tamir? There is a "rebellion" (also known as "backlash") and it has created a worrying polarization. However, we have to capture accurately the nature of the polarization. It is not majority versus minorities polarization, but rather one between persons advocating pro-diversity and diversity skeptics. Electoral analyses of the Brexit referendum and the support for Trump and Boris Johnson's victory at the end of 2019 show that the polarization cannot be captured by the traditional class divide, nor simply by adherence to the left or right in terms of economics, nor white and non-white, but by people's views on immigration and diversity and whether they live in more or less diverse areas (Cutts et al 2020, Sobolewska and Ford 2020). While multiculturalism is one of the poles and part of the dynamic resulting in the other pole (hence the aptness of revolt/backlash), it can be adapted to be part of the solution. Depolarization involves being able to reach out toward the other pole, and multiculturalism can do this; indeed, it can do so better than most other alternatives.[12]

I suggest that multiculturalism can make three positive contributions to depolarization.

1. *Immigration*: Multiculturalism is a national identity re-making project, which may in some circumstances lead to legitimate concerns about the identity effects of immigration, including its effects on existing citizens and minority groups. Multiculturalists are not and have not been against a reasonable and non-discriminatory immigration policy (Parekh 2008, Kymlicka 2017, Levey 2017, Modood 2017). It is clear that countries that have pursued multiculturalism in significant ways, such as Canada, Australia, and the United Kingdom have exercised immigration controls across all three of Tamir's "waves." Multiculturalism has to engage with

migration at three levels. First, identifying and opposing negative/racist/othering discourses, actions, and policies against migrants, no less than against citizens (while recognizing that some citizenship-constituting rights and opportunities, such as of residence or access to full welfare benefits, will not be available to migrants). Second, protecting and promoting the policies, forms of governance, and understandings that constitute the core of post-immigration multiculturalism, especially in relation to accommodation and civic recognition of ethnic minority citizens and accommodation of ethno-religious groups. Third, protecting and promoting the multicultural nation-building project. Yet, insofar as anxiety about the pace and accumulative scale of immigration is a source of majoritarian anxiety, it is something that multiculturalists can sympathetically address and about which they may be able to find some level of practical agreement, or at least show those who tend to oppose multiculturalism that differences on immigration are not a ground for their opposition, and that some of their concerns are shared by minority co-citizens and multiculturalists.

2. *Identity Anxiety:* In some cases, perhaps even in many cases, majoritarian opposition to public recognition and institutional accommodation of minority cultures and identities will have mixed motives, and the mixture may include xenophobia, Islamophobia, racial prejudice, and so on. The concern in question, however, is not reducible to these; it can and does exist without racism, and so has to be considered in its own right: it may be accepted even where the racism has to be opposed (Katwala et al 2014). Moreover, while it is known that the media, especially the tabloid press, can exacerbate public anxieties in deplorable ways through sensationalist coverage, that does not mean that the anxieties do not have to be addressed. Some perceptions about the scale and effects of multiculturalist recognition are likely to be mistaken and so while they cannot be regarded as self-validating, they also cannot be ignored. The situation is similar to when we take perceptions of racial discrimination as indication but not proof that discrimination is taking place; an indication that there may be a problem that should not be dismissed but requires investigation and discussion. The point I want to make here is that multiculturalism understands identity anxiety; it is built on appreciating why minorities can experience identity anxieties and so this appreciation can be extended to majority identities. Majoritarianism that seeks to privatize or

individualize minority identities while demanding public assimilation is problematic, but this does not mean that multiculturalism cannot see the narratives of the historically evolved and evolving majority as central in the national identity. Similarly, the project to multiculturalize national identities can recognize the composite nature of majorities. Given that project's sensitivity to the normative and political importance of identities and to the plural nature of identities, it is well placed to appreciate why majorities can come to feel anxious about identity change and that this anxiety has to be taken into account in working for inclusive national identities.

3. *National Identity:* Multiculturalism is built on national citizenship and national identity, though this has to be an inclusive national identity, which recognizes minority identities and offers both institutional accommodation to minority ethno-religious needs and remakes the public space and the symbols of national identity so that all can have a sense of belonging (CMEB 2000). That is the core of the multiculturalism for which I have argued over three decades (my first book was entitled "Not Easy Being British" (Modood 1992)) and which I have latterly come to call "multicultural nationalism" (Modood 2019b). Such multicultural nationalism unites the concerns of some of those currently sympathetic to majoritarian nationalism and those who are pro-diversity and minority accommodationist. My suggestion is that it is both pro-diversity and a bridge to the more nationalist diversity-skeptic end of the nationalist pole. Given Tamir's trail blazing work on pro-diversity nationalism (Tamir 1995) we may not be far apart here – except that she now seems to think, without I should say any evidence, that liberal autonomy offers a more optimistic basis for creating consensual majorities, including majorities for multiculturalism.

If we take these three contributions together, we have a serious basis for depolarization, for bringing together enough people from each pole to create a majority consensus on diversity; I shall elaborate on the idea of multicultural nationalism in the following section.

Multicultural Nationalism

Multiculturalism, as I understand it, is the idea that equality in the context of "difference" cannot be achieved by individual rights or equality as sameness but has to be extended to include the positive inclusion of marginalized groups marked by race and their own sense of ethno-cultural identities. It is not opposed to integration but emphasizes the importance of respecting diverse identities. It should be understood as a mode of integration, just as assimilation is another mode of integration.

I agree with Tamir that no state, including liberal democracies, is culturally neutral – all states support a certain language or languages, a religious calendar in respect of national holidays, the teaching of religion in schools and/or the funding of faith schools, certain arts, sports and leisure activities, and so on. Naturally enough, this language, religion, arts, or sport will be that of the majority population. This is true even if no malign domination is at work. Hence, it is important to distinguish when the institutional domination of the majority culture is or is not present. Moreover, when it has or may legitimately have normative value. For example, the English language has a de facto dominant position in Britain that is manifested in so many ways. Yet, one can also recognize that the position of English is of normative value, given the meaning that it has historically and today for the people of Britain. This normative primacy can be explained without having to bring in any domination concepts such as whiteness, or at the very least, without reducing it to questions of whiteness. For multiculturalism, however, it is a matter of extending this valued condition – of creating a society based on one's cultural identity – to include minorities. At minimum, the predominance that the cultural majority enjoys in shaping the national culture, symbols, and institutions should not be exercised in a non-minority accommodating way. The distinctive goal of multicultural nationalism is to allow people to hold, adapt, hyphenate, fuse, and create identities important to them in the context of their being not just unique individuals but members of sociocultural, ethno-racial, and ethno-religious groups, as well as national co-citizens. National co-citizens care about their country, which is not just another place on the map or workplace opportunity – it is where they belong, it is their country. So, on the version of multiculturalism I am now presenting, people can have group identities and attachments to specific countries – they are not just individuals for whom the achievement of autonomy is the highest purpose of government, nor are they citizens of the world.

But of course that country – say, Britain – may not allow all its citizens to feel British, to be accepted as British; some may be treated as foreigners, or as being of the wrong color; second-class citizens.

Multiculturalism is about changing that – it is, among other things, about "rethinking the national story." This was the most important – yet the most misunderstood message of the report of the Commission on Multi-Ethnic Britain in 2000. Chaired by Bhikhu Parekh, it argued that the post-immigration challenge was not simply eliminating racial discrimination or alleviating racial disadvantage, important as these were to an equality strategy, rather, the deeper challenge was to find inspiring visions of Britain, which showed us from where we came and where we were going, how history had brought us together, and what we could make of our shared future. No one was to be rejected as culturally alien and not sufficiently British because of their ethnicity or religion but rather we had to reimagine Britain, so that, for example, Muslims could see that Islam was part of Britain; and equally important, so that non-Muslims, especially secularists and Christians could see that Muslims were part of the new, evolving Britishness (CMEB 2000).

So, the multiculturalism I am arguing for is not based on positioning autonomy as the highest and unrestricted value, it also takes a different normative approach to the idea of a national culture compared to most liberals. The general liberal and civic nationalist approach is to say that diversity requires a "thinning" of the national culture so that minorities may feel included and not feel that a thick majoritarian culture is being imposed on them. This is also the approach of liberal multicultural nationalists. Kymlicka argues that "liberal states exhibit a much thinner conception of national identity. In order to make it possible for people from different ethno-cultural backgrounds to become full and equal members of the nation ... In so far as liberal nation-building involves diffusing a common national culture throughout the territory of the state, it is a very thin form of culture" (Kymlicka 2001b: 55–56). Whilst thinning may indeed be what is sometimes necessary or part of what is necessary, this is to turn a means to an end into a principle. As I have stated above, mine is an additive approach to national culture, including the place of Muslims, a group, which clearly is at the center of "thick multiculturalism." Let me illustrate with frequently used examples of mine. I have often argued that multiculturalism does not require disestablishing a national church (such as the Church of England) but entails bringing other faiths like Islam and Judaism into a relationship with it; nor does it require taking religious instruction and worship out of state schools (on a voluntary basis, for those religious groups who want it, knowing that not all groups will want it) in addition to religious education as a straight-forward school subject. These are two brief examples of not thinning the presence of religion in the constitution or state ceremonies or the presence of religion in state schools; they are a *pluralistic thickening*, an addition to the national public culture. In general, a multicultural society requires more state action not just to respect diversity but to bring it together in a common sense of national belonging. In many instances that means adding to a sense of national culture and not hollowing it out. Bringing minority faith communities to play a role in aspects of the national or public culture alongside Christians and humanists, requires us to think differently about the country and may require an appropriate public narrative about the type of country we are, as well as the state promotion of a composite national culture (Chandra and Mahajan 2007). My approach thus clarifies that a national identity or a national public culture has a plural or composite character without connecting this to a presumption of national "thinness" (Soutphommasane 2012, Chin 2019 and 2020).

This multiculturalism does not begin with liberal principles and seeks to go beyond liberalism but it does exist within a liberal-democratic framework of individual rights and a culture of civility and dialogue as well as protest and radical activism. It presupposes a robust framework of rights that it seeks to multiculturalize through continually arguing about rights and reforms and policy measures to assist disadvantaged groups as well as eliminate abuse of individuals within groups. Some of these arguments may be recognizably liberal; others will focus on how to dismantle "othering," offer positive recognition and meet the distinctive needs of minorities without assimilating their needs and preferences to those of the majority.

I concede that there is, as Tamir says, a limit to the flexibility of identities. Multiculturalizing the national identity, however, is important for bringing people together across ethno-cultural differences, which itself is essential to multiculturalism (Uberoi 2007 and 2018). So, while a focus on identity, both in terms of recognition and in terms of fostering commonality and societal unity is not sufficient, it is a necessary dimension that political theorists who frame things in terms of liberalism miss, and thereby miss both what needs to be addressed and what is needed to secure liberal among other values (Chin 2020, Dikici 2021). Nor do socialists, human rights champions, cosmopolitans, or localists give minority identities and national belonging the same centrality as is conferred by multiculturalism. Multicultural nationalism therefore may represent the political idea and tendency most likely to offer a feasible alternative rallying point to monocultural nationalism, the form that diversity skepticism will continue to take unless sympathetic bridges from the pro-diversity camp can offer an alternative to some currently inclined in that direction.

Notes

1 An ambiguous case relates to the Turks, Iranians, and Arabs, who mark themselves as white in the Census and other forms but are popularly understood to be members of ethnic minorities, i.e., non-white.
2 This anti-racism was greatly influenced by the African-American struggle and is not on the same scale as in the United States, but I am assuming that the United States does not count as an instance of state multiculturalism (Alexander 2006).
3 Interestingly, Jews, an ethno-religious group similar to the Sikhs, have always been regarded as a "race" within the meaning of the law. This is due to the biologized version of antisemitism of the Nazis and others.
4 However, he is not consistent as many of the examples in the book relate to religious minorities such as the Amish, Christians, Muslims, Jews, Sabbatarians, etc. (Levey 2008). Latterly, Kymlicka has come to the view that 'all of the arguments for adopting multiculturalism as a way of tackling the legacies of ethnic and racial hierarchies apply to religion as well' (2015: 28).
5 In a footnote, she explains that she uses "the term illiberal to denote cultures that do not affiliate themselves with the liberal school of thought with an emphasis on three main points: 1. They do not celebrate personal autonomy, self-reflection, and critical thinking but expect their followers to succumb to an higher, external authority. 2. They do not place human rights at their core. 3. They do not celebrate moral and cultural plurality as a source of inspiration and self-reflection. Obviously different illiberal belief systems correspond differently to these issues. Yet for the purpose of this debate, I cluster them into one category."
6 I discussed the political theory implications of the survey in Modood (1998).
7 There was also evidence of alienation from or a rejection of Britishness in the PSI survey. For example, over a quarter of British-born Caribbeans did not think of themselves as being British (Modood et al. 1997: 328–331).
8 See Modood 2013 [2007]: ch. 5.

9 I distinguish between liberal, democratic, citizenship-based, and other forms of political multiculturalism. While clearly I work only with the former – to the neglect of the latter – I am not arguing that there is an essential link between liberalism and multiculturalism (Modood 2013 [2007]: 8).
10 Cf. Oakeshott on traditions: 'neither fixed nor finished', with 'no changeless centre', and with no part 'immune from change' (1962, p. 128).
11 I am grateful to Ruud Koopman for pressing this point to me.
12 I distinguish multiculturalism from human rights cosmopolitanism (with which it is often confused or which is a different kind of multiculturalism).

References

Alexander, J. C. (2006). *The Civil Sphere.* Oxford: Oxford University Press.

Carens, J. H. (1997). Liberalism and Culture. *Constellations*, 4/1: 35–47.

Carter, T. (1986). *Shattering Illusions: West Indians in British Politics*. London: Lawrence and Wishhart.

Chandra, B., & Mahajan, S. (eds). (2007). *Composite Culture in a Multicultural Society*, Longman.

Chin, C. (2019). The Concept of Belonging: Critical, Normative and Multicultural. *Ethnicities*. Advance Online.

(2020). Multiculturalism and Nationalism: Models of Belonging to Diverse Political Community. *Nations and Nationalism,* 27/1: 112–29.

Commission on the Future of Multi-Ethnic Britain (CMEB). (2000). *The Future of Multiethnic Britain*. London: Profile Books.

Cutts, D., Goodwin, M., Heath, O., & Surridge, P. (2020). Brexit, the 2019 General Election and the Realignment of British Politics. *The Political Quarterly*, 91/1: 7–23.

Dikici, E. (2021). Nationalism Is Dead, Long Live Nationalism! In Pursuit of Pluralistic Nationalism: A Critical Overview. *Ethnicities*, 14687968211063694.

Eisenberg, A. (2020). The Rights of National Majorities: Toxic Discourse or Democratic Catharsis? *Ethnicities*, 20/2: 312–30.

GfK NOP. (2006). Attitudes to Living in Britain – A Survey of Muslim Opinion, A Survey for Channel 4 Dispatches. London.

Heath, A., & Roberts, J. (2008). *British Identity, Its Sources and Possible Implications for Civic Attitudes and Behaviour*. London: Department of Justice, HMSO.

Hutnik, N. (1991). *Ethnic Minority Identity: A Social Psychological Perspective*. Oxford: Clarendon Press.

Katwala, S., Ballinger, S., & Rhodes, M. (2014). *How to Talk about Immigration*. London: British Future.

Kepel, G. (2005). www.opendemocracy.net/en/londonistan_2775jsp/

Kymlicka, W. (1995). *Multicultural Citizenship: A Liberal Theory of Minority Rights*. Oxford: Clarendon Press.

(2001a). *Politics in the Vernacular: Nationalism, Multiculturalism and Citizenship*. Oxford: Oxford University Press.

(2001b). Western Political Theory and Ethnic Relations in Eastern Europe. In Kymlicka, W. & Opalski, M., eds., *Can Liberal Pluralism Be Exported?* Oxford: Oxford University Press, 13–105.

(2007/8). *Multicultural Odysseys: Navigating the New International Politics of Diversity*, Oxford: Oxford University Press.

(2015) 'The Three Lives of Multiculturalism' in S. Guo and L. Wong (eds) *Revisiting Multiculturalism in Canada: Theories, Policies, Debates. Sense Publishers.*

(2017). Multiculturalism without Citizenship? In Triandafyllidou, A., ed., *Multicultural Governance in a Mobile World*. Edinburgh: Edinburgh University Press.

Levey, G. B. (1997). Equality, Autonomy, and Cultural Rights. *Political Theory*, 25/2: 215–48.

(2008). Secularism and Religion in a Multicultural Age. In Levey, G. B. & Modood, T., eds., *Secularism, Religion and Multicultural Citizenship*. Cambridge: Cambridge University Press, 1–24.

(2017). Multiculturalism on the Move. In Triandafyllidou, A., ed., *Multicultural Governance in a Mobile World*. Edinburgh: Edinburgh University Press, 183–202.

(2019). The Bristol School of Multiculturalism. *Ethnicities*, 19/1: 200–26.

Mirza, M., Senthilkumaran, A., & Ja'far, Z. (2007). *Living Together Apart: British Muslims and the Paradox of Multiculturalism*. London: Policy Exchange. www.policyexchange.org.uk/wp-content/uploads/2016/09/living-apart-together-jan-07.pdf

Modood, T. (1988). "'Black,' Racial Equality and Asian Identity," *New Community*, 14/3.

(1992). *Not Easy Being British: Colour, Culture and Citizenship*. London: Runnymede Trust/Trentham Books.

(1994). Political Blackness and British Asians. *Sociology*, 28/4.

(1996). Book Review of *Multicultural Citizenship: A Liberal Theory of Minority Rights*, by Will Kymlicka. *The Political Quarterly* 67C.

(1998). Anti-Essentialism, Multiculturalism and the "Recognition" of Religious Minorities'. *Journal of Political Philosophy*, 6/4: 378–99.

(2005). *Multicultural Politics: Racism, Ethnicity and Muslims in Britain*. Minneapolis and Edinburgh: University of Minnesota Press and University of Edinburgh Press.

(2013 [2007]). *Multiculturalism: A Civic Idea*, Second Edition, Cambridge: Polity Press.

(2017). Multicultural Citizenship and New Migrations. In Triandafyllidou, A., ed., *Multicultural Governance in a Mobile World*. Edinburgh: Edinburgh University Press, 183–202.

(2019a). *Essays on Secularism and Multiculturalism*. London: ECPR Press.

(2019b). A Multicultural Nationalism? *Brown Journal of World Affairs*, 25/2: 233–46.

Modood, T., Berthoud, R., Lakey, J., et al. *Ethnic Minorities in Britain: Diversity and Disadvantage: The Fourth National Survey of Ethnic Minorities*. Policy Studies Institute.

Modood, T., Uberoi, V., & Thompson, S. (2022). The Centre for the Study of Ethnicity and Citizenship: Multiculturalism, Racialisation, Religion and National Identity Twenty Years On. *Ethnicities*, https://doi.org/10.1177/14687968221085093

Modood, T., & Thompson, S. (2018). Revisiting Contextualism in Political Theory: Putting Principles into Context. *Res Publica*, 24/3: 339–57.

Oakeshott, M. (1962). *Rationalism in Politics and Other Essays*. Methuen.

Parekh, B. C. (2006 [2000]). *Rethinking Multiculturalism: Cultural Diversity and Political Theory*. Basingstoke: Macmillan.

(2006). Finding a Proper Place for Human Rights. In Tunstall, K. E., ed., *Displacement, Asylum, Migration: The Oxford Amnesty Lectures 2004*. Oxford: Oxford University Press.

(2008). *A New Politics of Identity: Political Principles for an Interdependent World*. Macmillan International Higher Education.

(2019). *Ethnocentric* Political Theory*: The* Pursuit *of* Flawed Universals. Springer.

Sivanandan, A. (1982). *A Different Kind of Hunger: Writing on Black Resistance*. London: Pluto Press.

Sobolewska, M., & Ford, R. (2020). *Brexitland: Identity, Diversity and the Reshaping of British Politics*. Cambridge: Cambridge University Press.

Soutphommasane, T. (2012). *The Virtuous Citizen: Patriotism in a Multicultural Society*. Cambridge: Cambridge University Press.

Tamir, Y. (1995). Liberal Nationalism. In *Liberal Nationalism*. Princeton University Press.

Uberoi, V. (2007). Social Unity in Britain. *Journal of Ethnic and Migration Studies*, 33/1: 141–57.

(2009). Multiculturalism and the Canadian Charter of Rights and Freedoms. *Political Studies*, 57/4: 805–27.

(2018). National Identity: A Multiculturalist's Approach. *Critical Review of International Social and Political Philosophy*, 21/1: 46–64.

Wind-Cowie, M., & Gregory, T. (2011). *A Place for Pride*. London: Demos.

9 *Why Every Nation Should Nurture (a Thick and Inclusive) Nationalism*

MAYA TUDOR

Any essay interrogating conflicts over identity, culture, and rights – and the peaceful resolution of such conflicts within a democracy – must start by underscoring that the need to belong and seek group status is a definitive attribute of human societies. Essays herein cite Isaiah Berlin's elegant formulation of this need – "the great cry for recognition on the part of both individuals and groups" – as one of the, if not the most important force moving human history. Humans ability to cooperate in large, wholly imagined groupings is perhaps most responsible for the success of human societies. Our distinct ability to imagine group belonging through elaborate and cogent systems of beliefs has served an important evolutionary function and is written into our very psychological makeup: "The cooperative imperatives produced by rudimentary culturally transmitted institutions may well have shaped our innate social psychology." (Richerson et al. 2016: 16). Preference for and prioritization of "people like us" is a core psychological attribute that evolutionary pressures have selected for over tens of thousands of years. Consequently, it is unlikely to be overcome. It should instead be effectively harnessed.

Any successful account of how to manage group conflict must thus start by recognizing the universal human desire to seek group belonging and its centrality to politics. This is the starting point of my response to Yuli Tamir's wide-ranging essay tracing evolving understandings of multiculturalism and their compatibility with liberalism. If a hard-wired preference for group belonging is part of our genetic code, then any account of distribution between bigger groups (majorities) and smaller groups (minorities) must take seriously the power and worth of such identities as part of a thriving society that meets the needs of its members. If our social communities create our very sense of self and in doing so, form our values, meanings, and purpose, then our individual identities are both deeply embedded within and in substantial part achieved through our social groupings.

A Fine Balance: Prioritizing Both Individual Autonomy and Group Belonging

Tamir writes that liberal societies can accommodate a "thin multiculturalism" that respects individual autonomy but will struggle to accommodate "thick multiculturalism" in which communities possess fundamentally conflicting beliefs about the source of political legitimacy (typically religion versus the state). Under thick multiculturalism, not all parties to the debate share liberal values which they can invoke to resolve conflict. Different "thick multicultural" perspectives thus pose serious problems for liberalism.

If the centrality of group identity poses problems for theories of liberalism, then perhaps liberalism should not be the North Star by which we judge multiculturalism debates. We should remember that liberalism is itself a normatively compelling principle *because* of its presumption of respect for individual autonomy. But if group identities importantly define individual identities, then we should not approach all questions, all ethical-political dilemmas, by asking: "What would a liberal [focused foremost on individual autonomy] do here?" Modood instead suggests that we should ask "what would a multiculturalist who is part of this society (not just an abstract individual or an unembedded universalist, which Tamir too wants to go beyond) do here?" (Modood: 6). I would similarly ask, what would someone do who takes seriously the centrality of group identities and the moral equality of individuals, with its practical manifestation in equal citizenship laws? In other words, what would someone do to simultaneously promote equal citizenship *and* the dignity of group belonging in the context of a democracy? This is a key question to ask when considering the inclusion of majorities and minorities in the nation. And I argue that the celebration of thick, multiple, and inclusive national narratives must be part of the answer.

Majority Revolts in the Global South Too

Tamir sketches how a "revolt of the majority" in many Western societies arises from myriad structural causes, including unemployment or unstable employment, greater economic competition in a globalized world, the hollowing out of traditional social structures and accompanying social isolation. Worsening economic circumstances importantly combine with an erosion of historical cultural privileges leaving "members of majorities anxious about their ability to cash their cultural capital into a set of securities and opportunities." Greater economic precarity for majorities is combined with greater perceived social precarity as the cultural centrality of majorities in the national imagination is challenged by the assertion of rights that, from the perspective of the majority, favors both subordinate social groups and immigrants.

Majorities in pluralizing countries experience this more critical examination of their historical centrality in the national narrative as a psychological loss. Ground-breaking work in the Behavioral science has shown that most humans possess a consistent bias toward the status quo and experience pronounced psychological costs associated with and that losses loom psychologically larger relative to gains (Kahneman and Tversky 1979, Samuelson and Zeckhauser 1988). These biases have direct political implications, with empirical studies showing that the combined loss of social status *and* loss in economic status together form an especially potent predictor of support for far-right parties that electorally instantiate majority revolt (Gidron and Hall 2017).

A sense of social precarity fuelling majority revolts is not unique to Europe and the United States however. Similar forces are driving the revolt of the Indian majority that has significantly weakened the world's unlikeliest democracy – India. By the standards of any postcolonial country in the world, India's national movement articulated a highly inclusive national narrative with respect to its major social cleavages – caste and religion. India's inclusive founding national narrative visibly incorporated the political equality of castes and religions in the decades before the country's independence in 1947. Notably, the Indian national flag featured a Buddhist wheel and its most celebrated monument was the Islamic Taj Mahal. This inclusive and plural national identity was, when compared to other postcolonial neighbors of Pakistan, Bangladesh, Sri Lanka, and Myanmar, the single most important factor setting India on the unusual path of democracy amidst bewildering diversity after independence (Tudor 2013).

Yet this narrative is being changed under the Modi government through a kind of majority revolt. Modi's emphasis on the centrality of Hinduism in defining the nation has been disseminated through its control of state levers, combined with its rich party coffers and the effective grassroots reach and resources of Modi's BJP party and the affiliated Hindu organizations known as the *Sangh Parivar*. By projecting a majoritarian national narrative that situates religious minorities as second-class citizens, Modi has enabled such a substantive decline in that country's pluralism that democracy watchdog institutes such as Freedom House no longer designate India a democracy. The anvil of India's democratic decline has been a marked rise in violence and targeting of minorities.

India's contemporary democratic decline is also caused by a majority revolt that stems from status loss, albeit led more by aspirational (rather than deindustrializing) classes. India's liberalizing economic reforms delivered decades of strong growth during the 1990s and 2000s at the same time that state protections were growing, poverty was declining, and employment was accelerating. The broader growth of the economy and decline in poverty gave rise to what many called a rising expectations revolution. After four decades of slow growth, rapid improvements in economic circumstances were not only possible but realized for substantial portions of the population. Beginning in 2010 however, economic growth stagnated while inequality and inflation rose. Heightened *economic* precarity relative to previous decades, especially set against growing expectations of prosperity, was accompanied by greater *social* precarity for the higher castes. Expanded affirmative action – called reservations in the Indian context – provided for lower caste quotas in both government jobs and India's elite educational institutions.

In India as in Europe and the United States then, the combination of social and economic loss has driven the rise of an ethno-religious nationalism among the ethnic majority – in this case Hindus who form over three-quarters of India's population. Modi's championing of Hindu nationalism is broadly popular, with his BJP party forming the first single-party majority in 2014 and 2019 after almost three decades of coalition governments, on the basis of 31 percent and 37 percent vote shares respectively (which translate into majorities through first-past-the-post electoral systems). Class patterns (albeit different patterns from the West) are apparent, with the well-to-do generally voting for the conservative nationalist movement in larger numbers. In a class pyramid that is approximately 1/3 poor, 1/3 lower class, and 1/3 middle-class/rich, the middle class and rich vote for the BJP in higher numbers (38 percent and 44 percent, respectively) than do the poor or lower classes (each at 36 percent).

But status matters more, with vote share spreads between castes being significantly greater than between classes. In a religiously sanctioned caste structure that traditionally accords the greatest status to upper castes, followed by other backward classes (OBCs), Scheduled Castes (SCs), Scheduled Tribes (STs), and Muslims, 52 percent of the upper castes voted for the BJP while only 8 percent of Muslims did so. Combining class and status categories creates yawning gaps in Modi's support, even among Hindus. For example, the upper-caste rich voted for the BJP at an average of 58 percent while the middle-class Scheduled Castes voted for the BJP at an average of 30 percent.[1] Modi's support was thus drawn disproportionately from upper castes who were angered by both the rise of lower castes–or the "undeserving men and women who have risen above their station because of reservations rather than talent and merit" (Hansen 2015) – as well as a broad sense that secularism in India has become a byword for the prioritization of minority interests over the interests of the majority. Status anxiety on the part of the middle class/rich and upper castes – who have experienced the twin assaults of economic stagnation and a relative decline in cultural status following the expansion of reservations to lower castes – has fuelled Modi's rise to power and the decline of India's historically remarkable democracy, specifically in the form of sanctioning significantly disproportionate violence against minorities and a range of discriminatory citizenship practices (Human Rights Watch 2019).

Status anxiety similarly contributed to the rise of a conservative Brazilian nationalism under Bolsonaro. Like India's nationalism under Modi, the threatened loss of a newfound economic prosperity that had been hard won in previous decades drove the embrace of an outsider touting conservative nationalist credentials. "The inclusion of the poor into the market economy brought about individual empowerment and a sense of self-worth in the PT era – a process that was threatened by economic recession and unleashed an existential crisis, especially among men. Bolsonaro, as a male figure and his campaign gave order to a changing world, resulting in a reconciliation of personhood and political belonging" (Pinheiro-Machado and Mury Salco 2020: 21).

Grappling with the anxiety of majority groups feeling the twin losses of status and the stagnation of expected prosperity is thus a central matter for stabilizing diversifying democracies around the world, and not just in Europe and the United States. Allaying majority concerns over a loss of social and economic status is difficult amidst the growing recognition that majority cultural identities have in many ways privileged cultural majorities. This is why Tamir's "tortellini of hospitality" is indeed a metaphor for our times – when attempts to enable cross-religious participation was met with protests positioned by some politicians as protecting national tradition. As almost every society is diversifying through immigration as well as religious, ethnic, and racial intermarriage, almost every society is also facing debates over how to create inclusive public narratives and rituals that reflect multicultural societies without alienating majorities.

The Impossibility of Neutral Narratives

Promoting the diversification of public culture is difficult, and not just because minority cultural gains are often perceived as majority cultural losses. It is also because majority cultural privileges are often simultaneously invisible to majorities – whose members feel aggrieved at what appear to be handouts to or appeasements of minorities. Tamir's assertion that a neutral public sphere is impossible is an important baseline for those reflecting upon how to pluralize national culture in ways that make both majorities and minorities secure. "To attain [equal concern and equal respect], the public sphere had to change and become equally accessible to all. In an imperfect, neutral public space, everybody was supposed to feel at home. 'Home', however, is never neutral .... The liberal version of a neutral public sphere turned out to be an illusion." Historians and sociologists have long recognized that public spheres as well as stories of national belonging are not neutral. *Geschichtspolitik,* the German word combining politics and history, reflects that country's pervasive understanding that all collective memory is intimately tied to the legitimation of state power (Halbwachs 1992).

Yet the impossibility of a neutral public sphere should not lead us to conclude that a thinning of national narratives to a lowest common denominator of belonging is desirable. This is another problem arising from using liberalism as a first principle for adjudicating multiculturalism's debates. Liberalism in a multicultural society only allows a "very thin form of culture" that contributes to individual autonomy (Kymlicka 2001: 55–56). For example, Jurgen Habermas argues that the link between the majority culture and the general political culture must be uncoupled and encourages allegiance only to the constitution and its laws (Habermas: 118).

Yet, such an uncoupling of majority culture from the national culture poses its own distinct problems because the strength of group attachment is typically strongest when it invokes emotional salience. This is why statues celebrating *national* heroes, music and myths celebrating *national* moments of significance, literature celebrating the glory of *national* languages, and festivals celebrating *national* foods (such as the tortellini festival of Bologna) assume such importance to public conceptions of who "we" are. Sites, places, and stories of national commemoration often form critical spaces for attachment to a national collective consciousness. And, since individuals with more salient group identities are more likely to participate in collective action on behalf of that group (Ellemers 1993, Kelly 1993, and Klandermans 1997), the salience of attachment to the national identity translates directly into the ability of the state to address collective action problems and provide public goods.

Addressing the most urgent policy challenges of our time – whether these be rising inequality in over two-thirds of the world's countries, the coronavirus pandemic or climate change – necessitates harnessing a society's trust in government and citizens' attachment to each other in order to motivate individual sacrifices in pursuit of the common good. Every successful society must actively invest in a sense of belonging that can power collective action to solve these immense challenges. Allegiance to a set of legal principles such as the constitution, important though it may be on its own terms, may not be sufficiently robust to withstand the onslaught of new forces undermining social solidarities, particularly when these pressures include social media's polarizing algorithms, the rise of China – a global superpower whose own political legitimation is tied to challenging democratic norms, and the growing gaps between skilled and unskilled labor across the global economy. In such times, the ideational glue holding together societies is a threatened resource. Citizens may disagree upon policies or even principles, but they do need shared values and attachments which can be called upon to both mitigate polarizing debates and spur on needed political action on urgent challenges such as climate change and global inequality.

State-sponsored investment in a shared and inclusive but evolving national identity is one of the most important ways of creating this shared public culture. Most human cooperation happens within the context of the nation-state, the most widely accepted political institution of our time. Though addressing policy challenges also requires the global cooperation states remain the single most influential site of policymaking. And these states are legitimated by the nations they represent – which is why the hybrid term nation-state is often invoked in a single word. Nations are, in turn, imagined communities (Anderson 1991) – *imagined* because we will never meet most of our conationals. But they are also *communities* because the national ties are celebrated and frequently invoked to compel social sacrifice – ranging from paying taxes to wearing covid masks and occasionally, giving one's life in the protection of national borders or principles.

The Ahistorical Objections to Nationalism

Two objections are routinely made to calls for the celebration of national communities, or nationalism. The first, a typically Eurocentric historical view paints all nationalisms as equally problematic – xenophobic, discriminatory, and aggressive. This dim view of nationalism is a legacy of the catastrophic twentieth-century world wars of Europe, when nationalism was invoked to initiate one of deadliest wars of modern history. Little wonder that many Western progressives arrived at the consensus that nationalism was the "starkest political shame of the twentieth century" (Dunn 1979: 57).

Yet, this historical view is biased by the salience of World War II rather than a clear-headed assessment of nationalism's effects across space and time. Nationalism has been a force for the creation of democracy at least as often as it has been a force for its destruction. When mass nationalism first diffused across Europe, it was invoked to grasp power from monarchs in the name of self-rule by "the people." Nationalism spurred on the American and French revolutions which directly led to the establishment of nation-states that were, at least in principle, responsible for mandating governments that represented "we the people." Germany emerged when the interests of elites aligned with grassroots movements celebrating an ethno-linguistic German nation that repudiated the power of local princely states. And across former colonial countries as diverse as Morocco, India, Indonesia, and Ghana, nationalism was marshalled by indigenous elite during the twentieth century to found nation-states which freed these societies from deeply exploitative economic and social relations (Lawrence 2013, Kohli 2020).

The invocation of nationalism has *sometimes* contributed to the creation of democratically accountable regimes, as well as a range of other normatively desirable outcomes such as the prevention of genocide, egalitarian economic growth, and the provision of greater public goods (for an overview, see Mylonas and Tudor 2021). One of nationalism's most celebrated scholars, studying nationalism across a range of contexts, understood its potential to promote the public good when he wrote: "In an age when it is so common for progressive, cosmopolitan intellectuals to insist on the near-pathological character of nationalism, its roots in fear and hatred of the Other, and its affinities with racism, it is useful to remind ourselves that nations inspire love, and often profoundly self-sacrificing love. The cultural products of nationalism – poetry, prose fiction, music, plastic arts – show this love very clearly in thousands of different forms and styles. On the other hand, how truly rare it is to find *analogous* nationalist products expressing fear and loathing?" (Anderson 1991: 141–142, emphasis in original). To be sure, all nationalisms, like all meaningful social categories, harness the potential for exclusion, since all groups define themselves, at least in part, relative to "out-groups." Michael Walzer writes that "admission and exclusion are at the core of communal independence. They suggest the deepest meaning of self-determination. Without them, there could not be communities of character, historically stable, ongoing associations of men and women with some special commitment to one another and some special sense of their common life" (Walzer 1983: 62).

But while all nations possess the ability to denigrate other nations, social psychologists have long argued that in-group love does not always imply out-group hate (Allport 1954, Brewer 2007). This important point bears repeating. Social psychology research has consistently found that even in situations when groups are in conflict with one another, individuals *strongly prefer* to engage in in-group cooperation rather than out-group competition (Halevy et al. 2012, Amira, Wright, and Goya-Tocchetto 2021). Moreover, it is worth remembering that a love of nation is a "symbolic public good" that is central to understanding the ability of societies to act collectively to create public goods (Miguel 2005, Straus 2015).

History also demonstrates that nationalism can *sometimes* fuel discrimination, war, and genocide. Beyond Germany's national socialism,

Serbian nationalism was used to incite systematic killings of Bosnian Muslims and the disintegration of Yugoslavia while a historically racialized Rwandan nationalism underlay the 1994 genocide that witnessed ethnic Hutus murdering their Tutsi conationals. If nationalism can lead to democracy and the creation of progressive policy reforms but also aggression and war, the question becomes how to distinguish morally progressive forms of nationalism. In other words, how to separate good from bad nationalism? Or how best to create a world in which citizens are deeply attached to their own particular homelands and still celebrate the importance of other citizens belonging to their own distinctive homelands?

A second, related objection is that nationalism is always xenophobic but can be meaningfully distinguished from its politer cousin, patriotism. Publics and academics alike are prone to make this distinction. But the proposed normative distinction between nationalism and patriotism is empirically elusive, often defined by the perspective (and nationality) of the evaluator. Patriotism and nationalism both share high degrees of positive group affect and are highly conceptually and empirically correlated (Kosterman and Feshbach 1989). Political psychology further suggests that the empirical distinction between nationalism and patriotism can be situationally primed away, especially under circumstances of threat (Li and Brewer 2004). If patriotism today can be nationalism tomorrow, or nationalism when a political entrepreneur comes to power highlighting threats, then this distinction is not empirically stable. One is left to conclude that nationalism and patriotism are two sides of the same coin – a Janus-faced phenomenon.

Nationalism is not meaningfully distinct from patriotism. And it is here to stay. This is not only because groupness is built into our human psychology. It is also because nation-states lie at the very heart of our global political order. As long as this is the case, the legitimating principles of nationalism will continue to be a usable political resource and political entrepreneurs will possess incentives to invoke nationalism. As the global revitalization of nationalism makes clear, a world without nations and nationalism is not just far from reality, it cuts against the very evolutionary need to feel part of distinct communities of worth and meaning.

Taking seriously the value of human attachment to particular communities, including nations, should lead us to nurture the positive aspects of those relations rather than rejecting those bonds outright because they may lead to violence and aggression. An analogy may be drawn to how we value our own nuclear families. We love our own children particularly and uniquely. Filial love can also veer into violence and aggression, as Shakespeare's Romeo and Juliet teaches us. This danger does not mean that we should not devote thick and particular love to our own children – the world would indeed be a poor place if we each tried to love all children equally. This is what is missing from a line of thought that suggests that if everyone matters equally, then we must therefore have identical moral obligations to everyone. What this reasoning misses, argues Kwame Anthony Appiah, is that "the fact of everybody's mattering equally from the perspective of universal morality does *not* mean that each one of us has the same obligations to everyone .... [I]t would be morally wrong *not* to favor my relatives when it comes to distributing my limited attention and time" (Appiah 2019: 25, emphasis added). This same line of thought can be applied to nations – it is not that my country is better or matters more than yours – it is that my country matters more to *me* and that I may allowed to have a particular love of it. Or in the case of the growing numbers of individuals such as myself who are immigrants or born with multiple citizenships, my multiple countries matter more to me. As one of the greatest thinkers of cosmopolitanism, Martha Nussbaum suggests paying special attention to one's own family is the only sensible way to do good.

Given the enduring nature of groupness in the human psyche, the firm dominance of the nation-state in geopolitics, we need to find ways to positively shape rather than wholly abandon national narratives. A state without a shared identity is more likely to look like modern-day Yemen than a peaceful political unit inhabited by undifferentiated global citizens. At a time when identity politics can challenge the very basis for national belonging, we urgently need to forge bridging identities that can bind citizens together. For without a clear conception of the "we," there can be no conception of the common good, much less the collective action needed to work toward that vision.

Challenges to Shaping New National Narratives

National narratives should thus be made *inclusive* of major social groups *and multiple* so as to both accommodate but still bind citizens in multicultural societies to one another. To be sure, achieving this is difficult in practice because the very thickness of national narratives has historically come at the expense of inclusivity. The first key challenge is thus to forge national identities that help bind majorities and minorities in a manner that allows majorities to celebrate their cultural identities but avoids hierarchy. Koopmans and Orgad's argument that majorities should have normative cultural rights beyond the natural policymaking rights accorded to democratic electoral majorities is a helpful move beyond what has been a historically and normatively compelling focus on minority cultural rights (this volume). At a time when many cultural majorities may start to feel like strangers in their own country, they rightly ask multiculturalists to be more sensitive to the status anxieties of cultural majorities, particularly those whose cultural boundaries seem threatened.

But at the same time, majorities need to be careful that the normative recognition of their cultural rights avoids veering into cultural hierarchy that can be used to politically marginalize. This is particularly true because majorities are by definition armed with the political power to turn a *normative* recognition of majority rights into political hierarchy. The challenge of forging inclusive national narratives is by definition contextually specific and must therefore account not just for the indigenous versus migratory nature of majorities and minorities, but for the extent to which majority culture has historically subjugated minorities. The entirely right normative move toward a recognition of majority rights, and the right to protect majority culture, should be attentive to the fact that majority–minority differentiation, when accompanied by political power, is inherently in danger of becoming hierarchical. And in some cases, that majority–minority difference is so historically suffused with hierarchy that it would be difficult to accommodate majority culture. As Nussbaum points out that "[s]ome forms of difference have been historically inseparable from hierarchical orderings: for example, racial differences in America, gender differences almost everywhere, differences of dialect or of literary and musical taste in many parts of the world" (Nussbaum and Cohen 1996: 138).

The clearest way in which a national identity can be made inclusive is by eschewing ascriptive categories as the basis of the national narrative. This is easier to achieve for what Koopmans and Orgad this volume call migratory majorities because most countries with homeland majorities naturally smuggled in ethnic, racial or religious building blocks during moments of national founding (this volume). Indeed, doing so often made strategic sense: as elites and publics copied and adapted narratives of national belonging to their local contexts, they found it easier to use preexisting communities of belonging as the basis of creating nations, often building what nationalism scholars have historically termed ethnic nationalisms. For this reason, more civic (principled or creedal) national narratives have been the exception rather the rule. Though empirical work has shown that these distinctions are rarely clean and that even civic forms of nationalism can smuggle in ethnic characteristics (witness America's dual racialized and creedal national narrative), the distinction remains important because ethnic national narratives are more likely to legitimate minority targeting. This is because when founding national narratives centrally celebrate such fixed identities as race, religion, and ethnicity, citizens not possessing the central fixed identity are never able to become full-fledged participants in national imaginations. Minorities and immigrants then definitionally become second-class citizens. And when political entrepreneurs can effectively harness these divisions to win elections, they will do so.

While historically, thicker narratives of a national "we" have built on linguistic, racial, and ethnic foundations, this has not always been the case. The case of India shows clearly that when political elites are strategically invested in doing so, it is eminently *possible* to forge an inclusive, nonethnic national narrative – even in cases of what Koopmans and Orgad call homeland majorities, where majorities are historically rooted in and have a special tie to a particular territory (this volume). At the same time, the case of India also underscores how the ideological glue of these inclusive narratives remain perpetually politically *fragile* and subject to fracture by politicians who can gain political currency by trumpeting an alternative, ethnic-majority-based form of nationalism.

A second way in which national narratives can be inclusive is by celebrating ordinary heroes rather than traditional elites. When national narratives centralize what Max Weber would call traditional forms of authority – be they upper castes, sultans, lords, or monarchs – deference to hierarchy is built into the fabric of the national narrative. This vertical hierarchy works at cross-purposes with the horizontal political equality promised to all citizens in a democracy. But, when instead, everyday people are the central protagonists in the national narrative, such hierarchy is more firmly repudiated. Countries like Indonesia and

India that have historically articulated nationalisms primarily based on creeds as well as the stories of everyday heroes are more resistant to an important form of democratic breakdown (Slater and Tudor 2019, Tudor and Slater 2021) than their structurally similar neighboring countries.

And inclusive national narratives can also accommodate *multiple* identities, allowing and even encouraging the hybridity of the national community that enables migratory and indigenous communities alike to see their identities as nested with nation. The ideational basis for Canadian citizenship is an important model here. As many scholars of multiculturalism are wont to do, Tamir highlights the success of Canada's multiculturalism model in her essay. She focuses on Canada's *policy* underpinnings, such as the selection of a diversity of immigrants and a controlled, skills-based immigration process. But the *ideational* underpinnings of the Canadian model are just as crucial, as Canada also actively celebrates a hyphenated-national identity that does not force immigrants to choose between multiple salient identities, especially ethnic and racial cleavages. Unlike the neighboring United States – a country with a similarly migratory majority and minorities – American national belonging is associated with race for a substantial proportion of the population, while Canadian national identity is much more cognitively disassociated from racial and ethnic identities. A comparison of Chinese immigrants in Canada and the Netherlands for example showed that the most salient out-group for Chinese-Canadians were "real Chinese" while the most salient out-group for Chinese-Dutch were the "real Dutch," indicating an implicit ethnic basis for Dutch belonging: that is keenly felt by immigrants. "In contrast to Canada, however, the hyphenated position in the Netherlands was also constructed in opposition to the 'real' Dutch, involving a claim to shared ancestry with the Dutch as *a* people. Being Dutch, unlike feeling and doing Dutch, is all but inaccessible to individuals of Chinese descent if it involves a claim to Dutch blood and ancestry." (Belanger and Verkuyten 2010).

Nation-states whose national narrative has, explicitly or implicitly, absorbed racial, religious, and ethnic identities (which is to say most nations with indigenous majorities) must thus make a particular effort to pluralize the historical underpinnings of national belonging so as to celebrate the contributions of minorities to the national story as well as develop creedal expressions of national belonging. This parallels

Modood's call for a pluralistic thickening of national narratives calling for minorities' collective identities to be added to the national collective identity "by way of an exemption, a parallel provision, inclusion of hybridity, noncoercive assimilation or by broadening, pluralising and synthesising the shared culture." Though hardly homogenous to start with, modern nation-states are increasingly heterogenous through immigration, which challenges the boundary of the national community, as well as organized indigenous movements arguing for their symbolic inclusion in the national imagination.

How Myths, Museums, Monuments and Marvel Can Thicken Inclusive National Narratives

Practically, how is this to be done? How do nation-states, especially those with long-standing indigenous majorities, forge a thick, inclusive, multiple national narrative in practice in a contemporary context? One precondition for forging an inclusive national identity is active state engagement in a thick national storytelling of *some* kind. As the psychologically defining feature of any in-group is an out-group, national narratives will always define themselves in part by who the nations are not – the Scots are not English, the Canadians are not Americans, and the Pakistanis are not Indians. But thick national narratives will move beyond the out-group to fashion identities of belonging that are particular and tractable. Just as successful political parties do not define themselves solely in opposition to governing parties but have particular policy agendas to advance when in power, successful nations will have particular narratives that represent who the nation is – and not just who the nation is not.

Multicultural states can start to pluralize the national identity in a non-zero-sum fashion, by *adding* forms of public commemoration that recognize and celebrate minority contributions to the national story. Pluralizing the national story without taking away symbolically important figures or celebrations for majorities is an excellent starting point because it need not involve a reconsideration of majorities' cultural centrality. Four domains stand out as particularly successful ways to pluralize: national myths, museums, monuments, and a Marvel-like popular culture.

National *myths*, especially as told in national school curricula, can seek to highlight the contributions of minorities. As one of the earliest thinkers on the modern nation, Ernest Renan, argued in his 1882 essay, "Forgetfulness and I would even say historical error, are essential in the creation of a nation" (Renan 1882). This does not mean creating an inaccurate history, but rather involves the careful curation of inclusive figures that encourages the recognition of historical plurality. For example, Amartya Sen's history of India, *The Argumentative Indian*, contends that democratic thinking has distinctively Indian roots by highlighting how an inclusive India's Vedic philosophy was also practiced under India's centuries-long Islamic rule. He posited that the sixteenth century Mughal emperor Akbar created the "foundations of a non-denominational, secular state which was yet to be born in India or for that matter anywhere else" (Sen 2006). His celebration of a Muslim figure helps to authentically ground India's practice of religious tolerance, even though Sen could just as easily have chosen Akbar's grandson and eventual successor Aurangzeb, another Mughal emperor who is renowned for his lack of religious pluralism. This is how to tell an inclusive, syncretic and authentically Indian national myth.

Any modern nation-state embracing universal rights for its citizens will always struggle against the political pull of particularism, especially when founding national narratives legitimated those particularities. This is exactly why actively expanding national identities in history is an important tool for resolving conflicts between majorities and minorities – because it creates a shared basis for belonging. Family feuds between majorities and minorities over national histories does not mean that this history is meaningless. On the contrary, it is because it is so meaningful that capacious states have traditionally spent significant energy ideationally elaborating citizenship and standardizing language to enable communication between members of the imagined national community. Turning Bretons into Frenchman did not happen by accident. It required the kind of active investment in national myth-making that is carried out by all capacious states, from the French Third Republic to the Japanese Meiji restoration.

Pluralizing sites of commemoration for the nation – such as national museums – is another practical way to thicken our conception of the national story in an additive fashion. This has concretely happened in the United States, with the 2016 creation of the National Museum of African American History and Culture and the 2021 creation of a new federal holiday to celebrate the legal emancipation of former slaves.

These new sites and holidays help America's historically subjugated Black community attain greater recognition in the national imagination. The government of Singapore, a country created in 1965 out of severe ethnic and racial animosity, has taken a similarly active role through cultivating a national narrative that recognizes and accommodates its various ethnic communities in its National Museum as well as through a range of policymaking arms such as housing policy. In doing so, Indians, Malays, and Chinese ethnic communities are encouraged to avoid experiencing a tension between their ethnic and overarching national identity.

To be sure, pluralizing the national community is easier when it involves adding celebration and commemoration. It is harder when acknowledging problematic historical chapters in a country's past, which sometimes does require modifying majority symbols. Yet, the difficulties involved in evolving national identities in an inclusive direction are not always insurmountable. Doing so requires cultivating a growth mindset that acknowledges the problematic historical chapters of a country's past while not being wholly defined by such a past. Creating inclusive national identities necessitates an open-ended engagement to sites and subjects of national commemoration which acknowledges that the national story is not uniformly worth celebrating, such as Germany's ubiquitous Stolpersteine, or stumbling blocks which call attention to the last freely chosen place of work/residence of Nazi victims.

Yet as recent public discussions over public monuments – a third domain of pluralization – in Europe and the United States has illustrated, when historic national heroes *primarily* represent the forces of hierarchy or minority mistreatment, it will at least mean contextualizing and sometimes even mean removing majority symbols in the form of historical names and statues. This is as it should be, for sites of public commemoration are not endless: public squares and streets, and statues represent spaces of *celebration*. Who or what is given pride of place in such spaces matters for how nations become symbolically defined. Sites of national commemoration and public spheres are never neutral. Our reaction to them hinges on who is commemorated by whom and for what reason – and they are anyway always being reevaluated by the standards of a new era.

Acknowledging that majorities have cultural rights does not mean majorities can wholly reject minority movements to alter public monuments if they can mount a reasonable public case that these monuments inherently marginalize their communities. But this charge simply misunderstands the always-political role of history and commemoration. Britain's public face changed appreciably during the English Reformation, when many shrines and statues associated with Catholicism were destroyed. The same was true for celebrations of monarchs after the French Revolution, communist leaders after the fall of the Soviet Union, and Saddam Hussein after the US-led invasion of Iraq.

To be sure, these were all violent revolutions which created major ruptures with the past. But any look at the recent historical past within democracies suggests that yesterday's radicals can be absorbed into changing national stories in countries with both migratory and indigenous majorities. The movement to remove statues of slave traders from British public squares, once a fringe movement, now enjoys support of a popular majority, including a plurality of Conservative voters.[2] Whereas an electoral majority did not support the removal of Confederate statues from public spaces in the United States in 2017, an electoral majority in 2020 does support this change.[3] The Confederate flag, a symbol of a system of government that denigrated Black Americans, flew over state capitols until recently, when broad majority support developed for removing it. Martin Luther King Jr was regarded as an utter radical in his time, yet today has been embraced by every major political movement in the United States.

Discussions over why national monuments symbolizing majorities may need to change will always be controversial and critics will argue that changing national monuments erases history. Responding to the social movements that seek to alter the pride of place given to newly controversial figures in the public squares of Britain's cities, British Prime Minister Boris Johnson tweeted in June 2020: "We cannot now try to edit or censor our past. We cannot pretend to have a different history. The statues in our cities and towns were put up by previous generations. They had different perspectives, different understandings of the past. To tear them down would be to lie about our history, and impoverish the education of generations to come" (Johnson 2020).

But statues in public squares inherently venerate. History books could teach the British slave trade and pivotal figures in it without honoring slave traders with prominent statues in public squares. And they could teach the towering leadership of Winston Churchill while acknowledging that his wartime cabinet's policies directly contributed to the Bengal famine of 1943 that killed three million people. Teaching these less savory aspects of British history is an important element of ideationally grounding equal citizenship in increasingly multiethnic societies. Through democratic discussions after independence, India pulled down statues of Queen Victoria, relegating them to dusty corners of colleges or little-used parks with the understanding that such figures no longer deserved to be celebrated in the central spaces of a nation that did not wish to define itself as an imperial subject. As Maya Jasanoff says, "taking down a statue isn't erasing history; it's revising cultural priorities" (Jasanoff 2020).

And finally, at a time when museums and monuments are less salient in the public imagination, state attention as to how to pluralize an inclusive national narrative must move beyond the high culture of museums and monuments to popular forms of nationalism. State sponsored public art is an important form for engaging in this narrative. Ta-Nehisi Coates, a Black American intellectual, has done this through his writing of the first Black-centered comic book and then Marvel superhero movie, Black Panther. His engagement in popular culture helped to elevate the role of Black Americans to a position of admiration and esteem. As Coates said in a recent podcast, "[When] I think about the 2018 movie Black Panther and I think about seeing white kids dress up as the Black Panther. This sounds small. This sounds really, really small .... The symbols actually matter because they communicate something about the imagination, and in the imagination is where all of the policies happen. All the policy happens within there" (Coates 2021).

Squaring the realities of a human need for group belonging, the dominance of the modern nation-state, and the impossibility of a neutral public space requires above all the fashioning of an inclusive, multiple and thick national narrative with space for and celebration of minorities. How we best adapt national history, along with statues, museums, festivals, public spaces, and spaces of public commemoration as the very fabric of the nation changes will be an ongoing struggle, as Tamir's tortellini-of-hospitality example aptly illustrates. Yet as American historian Jill Lepore notes, "Writing national history creates plenty of problems. But not writing national history creates more problems, and these problems are worse" (Lepore 2019).

Notes

1 All data has been taken from Centre for the Study of Developing Societies 2019 National Election Survey.
2 https://redfieldandwiltonstrategies.com/majority-of-brits-support-removal-of-statues-of-slave-traders-through-legal-means/
3 https://thehill.com/homenews/news/503226-poll-majority-supports-removing-confederate-statues-from-public-places

References

Allport, G. (1954). *On the Nature of Prejudice*. Cambridge, MA: Addison-Wesley.

Amira, K., Jennifer, C. W., & Tochetto, D. G. (2021). In-Group Love versus Out-Group Hate: Which Is More Important to Partisans and When? *Political Behavior*, 43: 473–94. https://doi.org/10.1007/s11109-019-09557-6

Anderson, B. (1991). *Imagined Communities: Reflections on the Origin and Spread of Nationalism*. London: Verso Press.

Appiah, K. A. (2018). *The Lies That Bind*. London: Profile Books.

(2019). The Importance of Elsewhere: In Defense of Cosmopolitanism. *Foreign Affairs*, 28/2: 20–26.

Bélanger, E., & Verkuyten, M. (2010). Hyphenated Identities and Acculturation: Second-Generation Chinese of Canada and the Netherlands. *Identity: An International Journal of Theory and Research*, 10(3), 141–63.

Brewer, M. B. (2007). The Importance of Being We: Human Nature and Intergroup Relations. *American Psychologist*, 62/8), 728–38. https://doi.org/10.1037/0003-066X.62.8.728

Coates, T. (2021). Interview on the Ezra Klein Show. July 30. www.nytimes.com/2021/07/30/podcasts/transcript-ezra-klein-interviews-ta-nehisi-coates-and-nikole-hannah-jones.html

Dunn, J. (1979). *Western Political Theory in the Face of the Future*. Cambridge: Cambridge University Press.

Ellemers, N. (1993). The Influence of Socio-Structural Variables on Identity Management Strategies. *European Review of Social Psychology*, 4: 22–57.

Gidron, N., & Hall, P. A. (2017). The Politics of Social Status: Economic and Cultural Roots of the Populist Right. *The British Journal of Sociology*, 68: S57–S84.

Halbwachs, M. (1992). *Collective Memory*. (Edited, translated, and introduction by Lewis A. Coser.) Chicago: University of Chicago Press.

Halevy, N., Weidel, O., & Bornstein, G. (2012). In-Group Love and Out-Group Hate in Repeated Interaction Between Groups. *Journal of Behavioral Decision Making*, 25/2: 188–95.

Hansen, T. B. (2015). Communalism, Democracy and Indian Capitalism. Seminar 674. www.india-seminar.com/2015/674/674_thomas_blom_hansen.htm

Human Rights Watch. (2019). Violent Cow Protection in India: Vigilante Groups Attack Minorities. February 18, 2019. www.hrw.org/report/2019/02/18/violent-cow-protection-india/vigilante-groups-attack-minorities

Jasanoff, M. (2020). Misremember the British Empire. *The New Yorker*. October 26.

Johnson, B. (2020). Tweet. https://twitter.com/borisjohnson/status/1271388182538526721?lang=en

Kahneman, D., & Tversky, A. (1979). Prospect Theory: An Analysis of Decision under Risk. *Econometrica*, 47/2: 263–91.

Kelly, C. (1993). Group Identification, Intergroup Perceptions and Collective Action. *European Review of Social Psychology*, 4/1: 59–83.

Klandermans, B. (1984). Mobilization and Participation: Social-Psychological Expansions of Resource Mobilization Theory. *American Sociological Review*, 583–600.

Kohli, A. (2020). *Imperialism in the Developing World*. Oxford: Oxford University Press.

Koopmans, R., & Orgad, L. (this volume). "Majority–Minority Constellations: Towards A Group-Differentiated Approach." Cambridge: Cambridge University Press.

Kosterman, R., & Feshbach, S. (1989). Toward a Measure of Patriotic and Nationalistic Attitudes. *Political Psychology*, 257–74.

Kymlicka, W. (2001). Western Political Theory and Ethnic Relations in Eastern Europe. In Kymlicka, W. and Opalski, M. (eds), *Can Liberal Pluralism Be Exported?* Oxford: Oxford University Press.

Lawrence, A. (2013). *Imperial Rule and the Politics of Nationalism: Anti-Colonial Protest in the French Empire*. New York: Cambridge University Press.

Lepore, J. (2019). A New America: Why a Nation Needs a National Story. *Foreign Affairs*. March/April.

Li, Q., & Brewer, M. (2004). What Does It Mean to Be an American? Patriotism, Nationalism and American Identity After 9/11. *Political Psychology*, 25/5: 727–39.

Miguel, E. (2004). Tribe or Nation? Nation-Building and Public Goods in Kenya Versus Tanzania. *World Politics*, 56/3: 327–62.

Mylonas, H., & Tudor, M. (2021). Nationalism: What We Know and What We Still Need to Know. *Annual Review of Political Science*, 24.

Nussbaum, M., & Cohen, J. (1996). *For Love of Country: Debating the Limits of Patriotism*. Boston: Beacon Press.

Pinheiro-Machado, R., & Scalco, L. M. (2020). From Hope to Hate: The Rise of Conservative Subjectivity in Brazil. *HAU Journal of Ethnographic Theory*, 10/1: 21–31.

Renan, E. (1882). What Is a Nation. In Giglio, M., (ed.) *What Is a Nation and Other Political Writings*. New York: Columbia University Press.

Richerson, P., Baldini, R., Bell, A., et al. (2016). Cultural Group Selection Plays an Essential Role in Explaining Human Cooperation: A Sketch of the Evidence. *Behavioral and Brain Sciences*, 39.

Samuelson, W., & Zeckhauser, R. (1988). Status Quo Bias in Decision Making. *Journal of Risk and Uncertainty*, 1/1: 7–59.

Sen, A. (2006). *The Argumentative Indian*. New York: Penguin.

Slater, D., & Tudor, M. (2019). Why Religious Tolerance Won in Indonesia but Lost in India. *Foreign Affairs*.

Straus, S. (2015). *Making and Unmaking Nationals: War, Leadership and Genocide in Modern Africa*. Ithaca: Cornell University Press.

Tudor, M. (2013). *The Promise of Power: The Origins of Democracy in India and Autocracy in Pakistan*. New York: Cambridge University Press.

Tudor, M., & Slater, D. (2021). Nationalism, Authoritarianism, and Democracy: Historical Lessons from South and Southeast Asia. *Perspectives on Politics*, 19/3, 706–22.

Walzer, M. (1983). *Spheres of Justice : A Defense of Pluralism and Equality*. New York: Basic Books.

10 Populism and Cultural Majority Rights
An Uneasy Relationship

CHRISTIAN JOPPKE

Ruud Koopmans (2018) recently made a forceful case for cultural majority rights as complementary to already existing cultural minority rights. One justification for this is that to substitute "right v. right" for "right v. might" might help contain "the rise of nationalist populism across Western countries" (p. 1). Koopmans thus follows a common understanding of populism as something negative, with a "tendency to polarize and to escalate" (p. 1) that is damaging to liberal democracy. As Michael Lind (2020: 87) puts it pithily, populism is "a symptom of a sick body politic, not a cure." This is the view I try to defend here. At the same time, I argue that the prescription of cultural majority rights as a "cure" to populism, as suggested by Ruud Koopmans and Liav Orgad (in this volume), overlooks the fact that populism, indeed, is a "symptom" of a deeper malaise, which is the neoliberal restructuring of Western societies.

The chapter proceeds in four steps. First, I argue that populism's inherent illiberalism and anti-pluralism undermine the essentials of liberal democracy, and thus democracy as we know it. Second, populism still responds to real problems generated by the neoliberal transformation of Western societies. The biggest explanatory challenge is to calibrate economic and cultural factors in the rise of populism. While the neoliberal attack on lower middle-class prosperity and future prospects seems to be a principal cause of the populist rage in the West, its proponents tend to articulate their grievance in terms of a culture-focused opposition to cosmopolitan elites and, in particular, immigrants. Third, the move into the cultural terrain, which the advocates of majority rights share with multiculturalists (the inventors of the majority–minority binary), overlooks a more fundamental neoliberal shattering of the social rights of *all*. Fourth, the liberal attempt to temper populism through cultural majority rights not only deflects from some deeper sources of populism; it also underestimates the capacity of existing legal-political arrangements to deal with cultural majority claims.

There is not much new in this. Yet, if there is a message that needs underscoring, it is that a major source of the populist upheaval is neoliberalism, which is a political project with a socioeconomic nucleus, to rescue capitalism from the constraints of democracy. Following the populists into the cultural terrain, which is the gist of the liberal movement for majority rights, is tangential to the problems and fault lines generated by the neoliberal project.[1]

Populism as Threat to Liberal Democracy

Populism's Vertical Axis: Democratic Illiberalism

When populism was born, in form of the late nineteenth-century Populist Party in the American Southwest, it was proud self-designation. Today, "populism" or "populist" is mostly a label attached by others who do not like what they see.[2] Incidentally, "populism" shares this negativity and polemic intent with "neoliberalism," as a response to which, I shall argue, one must understand its contemporary variants in advanced Western societies. Just consider the standard definition by Cas Mudde (2004: 543): populism is "an ideology that considers society to be ultimately separated into two homogenous and antagonistic groups, 'the pure people' versus 'the corrupt elite,' and which argues that politics should be an expression of the *volonté générale* (general will) of the people." The first part of this most-cited definition of populism is at heart a polemic. Because, to conceive of the world as consisting of only two possibilities, "pure" and "corrupt," light and darkness, with nothing in between, is Manichean, resembling a political style that Richard Hofstadter (1964) once diagnosed as "paranoid."

The second, less often quoted half of Mudde's definition appositely refers populism to the Rousseau-Schmittian dark side of democracy, which is radically opposed to liberalism.[3] Carl Schmitt (1926) had radicalized Rousseau's idea that democracy rests on the equality of a homogenous people, always to be reinforced by the "annihilation (*Vernichtung*) of the heterogeneous," and he held it against the idea of parliament as "government by discussion," which he attributed to the "thought world (*Gedankenwelt*) of liberalism." In this sense, populism is both democratic and illiberal, succinctly summarized by Takis Pappas as "democratic illiberalism" (2019: 33). But it is the "paradox of democracy," as Stephen Holmes (1995) has demonstrated, that democracy cannot exist without constraints on majority power, including competitive elections (aka, pluralism) and the protection of individual rights that goes under the name of "liberal constitutionalism": "liberalism is a necessary ... condition for some measure of democracy in any modern state" (p. 9). This is why populism, while pretending to be democratic, is in reality a threat to democracy. As also Nadia Urbinati (2019: 10) concluded, "illiberal democracy" is "*not democracy at all.*"

Of course, this view rests on a certain understanding of liberalism. It is one in which liberalism is not optional and not to be juxtaposed, say, with conservatism or socialism as alternative ideological choices in modern society. And it is one in which liberalism isn't just a "culture," something here but not there, as claimed in some radical or postcolonial views (see Tariq Modood in this volume). Instead, liberalism is necessary for democracy. One could even consider liberalism, with Niklas Luhmann, as the political semantic of functionally differentiated societies to which there is no real alternative.[4]

Michael Walzer (1984) supported such a structural understanding of liberalism in his felicitous notion that liberalism is the "art of separation": "Liberalism is a world of walls, and each one creates a new liberty" (p. 315). The point of "walls" is that "success" in one institutional setting is not "convertible into success in another" (p. 321). In particular, liberalism's challenge is the "confinement of the market to its proper sphere": "the art of separation requires the restraint and transformation of corporate power" (p. 323). No wonder that liberalism thus understood "passes over into democratic socialism" (p. 323). As Stephen Holmes (1995) showed, this is no Social-Democratic era prank, limited to the rosier sections of the twentieth century. Instead, it is grounded in a "deep liberal commitment to psychological security" (p. 37) that already made the classic liberal writers endorse a modicum of public welfare.

Liberalism is thus clearly distinguished from neoliberalism, with which it is often conflated. Neoliberalism is "market fundamentalism," concisely defined by Margaret Somers (2008: 2) as "the drive to subject all of social life and the public sphere to market mechanisms."

Liberalism has been critiqued by left and right alike for separating individuals. In reality, Walzer (1984: 327) insists, liberalism separates "spheres," not "individuals": "A free state, in a complex society, is one ... that is in the hands of its citizens ... just as a free church is in the hands of believers, a free university in the hands of scholars, a free firm in the hands of workers and managers." Importantly, the liberal world of separations is put at risk by the forces of neoliberalism just as much as by the populists who rebel against liberal constraints on power, and thus against "liberty" itself, in the name of the "unity of the collective" (Urbinati 2019: 12).

With respect to the relationship between populism and democracy, it is obvious that populism is both an expression and an enemy of democracy. *Pace* Urbinati (2019), on the expression side, populism harks back to the "ideology" of democracy (Mény and Surel 2002), it is one of its "two faces" (Canovan 1999). Philippe Schmitter (2019) even thinks that populism has a "legitimate place in liberal social democracies," to be shock to the system that saves these democracies from the "likelihood of entropy." On the enemy side, populism threatens the "liberal democratic" synthesis that we have come to take for granted. This synthesis, among other elements (most notably constitutionalism), incorporates the principle of representation, which is not originally a democratic but an aristocratic idea (see Manin 1997). Accordingly, the "will of the people" is not the monist input of the democratic process, as which it is conventionally depicted. Instead, the will of the people is at best a pluralist "answer" to the democratic process; it has "*Antwortcharakter*," as the German constitutionalist Ernst-Wolfgang Böckenförde put it aptly (quoted by Offe 2019a: 6), responding to the multiple options raised within a competitive party system. Moreover, as Robert Dahl (1989) has pointed out, already because of its extended size, a necessarily heterogeneous territorial state requires a liberal-pluralist, "polyarchic" understanding of democracy.

In populist diction, "the people" appear in a variety of guises – as "plebs" connoting ordinariness, which is held against the etiquette ("political correctness") of elites; as "nation" connoting ethnic distinctness, which is mobilized against immigrants; and, of course, as "demos," the source of sovereignty in a "democratic" state, which is populism's Sunday dress (see Brubaker 2019). To this list must be added, pertinent to this volume, that the people may also appear as the "majority," partially as an artefact of the majority principle of electoral democracy,[5] but also as the logical other of "minorities." The constant in all these various appearances is that for populism the people are always one.

Social choice theory has demonstrated that "oneness" is technically not possible (especially Riker 1982). If there are more than two alternatives in an election, the majority principle fails to produce a consistent result because the principle of "transitive" preferences no longer applies and no clear hierarchy of preferences can be established. It is thus quite literally impossible to know "what the people want." William Riker (1982: 9) concludes:

> Populism as a moral imperative depends on the existence of a popular will discovered by voting. But if voting does not discover or reveal a will, then the moral imperative evaporates because there is nothing to be commanded. If the people speak in meaningless tongues, they cannot utter the law that makes them free. Populism fails, therefore, not because it is morally wrong, but merely because it is empty.

For Riker, "populism" is not the name for a movement but for a Rousseauian understanding of democracy, which he juxtaposes with a "liberal" or Madisonian understanding. While in both approaches voting is "the central act of democracy," only the liberal approach passes the formal test of preference aggregation and produces a consistent outcome. As a result, "the function of voting is to control officials, and no more" (p. 5). Riker's sober conclusion, which echoes Joseph Schumpeter`s "realistic" understanding of democracy, must displease the political romantic, which the populist is by definition.

The "pure people" is obviously a poor compass for the workings of real-existing democracy. But what about populism's perceived other, which in Mudde's classic definition (2004: 543) is the "corrupt elite"? In its 2016 program, the populist Alternative for Germany (AfD) described the despicable "secret sovereign" of the political process as a rent-seeking "political class of professional politicians," and they called it a "political cartel" (AfD 2016: 8). This part of the populist imagination has more traction than the purified "people." Indeed, "cartel" is also the central concept in the one theory of contemporary party systems that best explains the political conditions for populism. "Cartel parties" (Katz and Mair 1995) grow out of a long-standing trend of political parties to be relocated from civil society to the state, partly pulled by the "taste of office" (p. 12), but also pushed by an "individualized" social structure in which there are no longer fixed groups or classes that might be recruited *en bloc*. At the end of the process, "colluding parties become agents of the state" (p. 5). In a restatement of the cartel party thesis, Richard Katz and Peter Mair (2009) identified the decline of the left-right ideological divide after the fall of communism and the rise of "technocratic" governance, particularly in the European Union, among other elements, as the larger political context of a transformed party system. The world of cartel parties is one without major political alternatives. In short, the depoliticization brought about by neoliberalism, famously expressed by Margaret Thatcher as "there is no alternative," is the backdrop to the rise of cartel parties. Tony Blair, whose "Third Way" New Labour was emblematic of the trend, retrospectively said that he "never really (was) in politics" (Luce 2017: 91), which is a truly astounding statement for the politician that he surely was.

Blair did not just say that technocracy has replaced politics, but that it is better this way. Populists beg to disagree. If they rally against a "political cartel," they are also up against technocracy. In a look at the United States, Michael Lind (2020: ch. 1) even speaks of a "new class war," in which "native working-class populists" oppose "technocratic neoliberalism." For Europe, Michael Gove, a leading Brexit advocate, famously quipped that "People in this country have had enough of experts," thus dismissing economists' warnings that leaving the European Union would slow down growth in the United Kingdom and come at considerable cost.

What populists overlook is that "technocracy" strangely resembles them in their distaste for representative party government, which both of them help dismantle. Daniele Caramani has shown (2017: 54) that technocracy is not unlike populism in advocating an "unmediated politics," in which no parties are required to mediate between the common interest of society and the elites – only that "reason" takes the role for technocrats that the "common will" takes for populists. But party democracy is the properly liberal way of democratic government, because it alone acknowledges the pluralism of groups and interests in a modern society. In party democracy, "the common good that ought to prevail and therefore be translated into public policy is the one that is simultaneously constructed and identified through the democratic procedures of parliamentary deliberation and electoral competition"

(Bickerton and Azzetti 2017: 189). In liberal understanding, the common good is indeterminate and changeable, and the only certainty that exists is about the procedures and the rules to approximate it. By contrast, both populism and technocracy convene in the illiberal assumption that the common good is a fixed matter that is objective and stands to be discovered, like a truth. But they do this in different ways: through rational insight on the side of technocrats, and through a mysterious unity of ruler(s) and ruled on the side of populists. Technocracy and populism thus share a non-pluralistic, even anti-political view of society and politics. The bottom-line is that populism and technocracy jointly dismantle the liberal core assumption of representative party government, which is that "society" can never speak for itself directly, be it through "will" or through "reason."

Populism's Horizontal Axis: Against Immigrants

If populism were just that: the vertical confrontation between the "pure people" and a "corrupt elite," to reiterate one last time Mudde's definition (2004: 543), it would be of interest to the students of democracy, yes, but of no relevance for majority–minority relations, the topic of this volume. However, there is also a horizontal axis to populism, which posits the "people" against conspicuous "others," typically immigrant minorities (see Brubaker 2017). A vertical ordering, of course, is not absent on the horizontal axis, as these "others" are simultaneously placed below the natives in the social hierarchy. Conversely, a horizontal ordering is also present on the vertical axis, as the despised elites are suspected of being cosmopolitan and having ruptured the ties with their home countries, and of being allied with "tribal-minded immigrants" (Krastev 2017: 15). Only if this horizontal axis is factored in, carving out a "space of difference" in addition to a "space of inequality" (Brubaker 2019: 12–14), one can account for the fact that populism may be either right or left. John Judis (2016) put it succinctly that left-wing populism is "dyadic," positing people against (political-economic) elites. By contrast, rightwing populism is "triadic": "It looks upward, but also down upon an out group" (p. 15).

In response to globalization, one can observe both expressions of populism, right and left. In a rare attempt to explain this variation, economist Dani Rodrik (2018: 2) grounds it in the "forms in which globalization shocks make themselves felt in society." If globalization is experienced primarily in the form of immigration, as in northwestern Europe, it leads to political mobilization around a cultural cleavage. Rodrik connects this mobilization to the fact that well-developed welfare programs, which northwest European states have offered in compensation for the social risks of their export-led growth strategies, are seen as being under threat by abusive immigrants – commonly referred to as "welfare chauvinism." By contrast, if globalization is primarily experienced in the form of foreign investment and financial dependence, and where welfare states are either weak or insider-oriented and sealed from immigrants by clientelism, political mobilization will pivot around a class cleavage, as can be observed in the leftwing populisms of Latin America and, to a degree, southern Europe. In a nutshell, rightwing populism is a response to the globalization-caused loss of sovereignty over *borders*, whereas leftwing populism is response to the loss of sovereignty over *money*. Building on Rodrik, Philip Manow (2018) has proposed a political-economic explanation of the varieties of contemporary populism, and he juxtaposed his own favored approach to competing approaches that are either purely politics-focused (for instance, with populism figuring as "style") or culture-focused (in which populism revolves around a new cleavage between "cosmopolitans" and "communitarians").

The problem is that these approaches are complementing rather than excluding one another, and it makes little sense to play out one against the other. Instead, one needs to disentangle and recombine the factors – at a minimum: political, economic, cultural – that drive contemporary populisms. Unfortunately, in most accounts one-sidedness prevails (an exception is Brubaker 2017). Takis Pappas (2019: 126), for instance, opts for an endogenous, politics-focused explanation of populism that explicitly discards the reference to economic factors, and culture goes entirely unmentioned. For Pappas, populism is all about "liberalism's decay," which he describes as "(i)ncreased bureaucratization and institutional rigidity in politics, the recycling of political elites and the rise of technocracy, the entrenchment of interest groups, the lack of transparency, widespread corruption, and spreading cynicism" (p. 262). However, if populism is mainly a response to a "(d)emocratic representation crisis," as Pappas argues (p. 124), the left v. right distinction becomes impossible to account for; it simply fades from view. Pappas' exclusively vertical, that is, people-v.-elite focused view of populism, also leads to questionable classifications. "Nativists," in his view, are not populist at all. A similar divorce between "populism" and "nationalism" is suggested by De Cleen and Stavrakakis (2017), though their intention is mainly political, to rescue populism's progressive possibilities by separating it sharply from a rightwing nationalism that they dislike. As a result of distinguishing populism from nativism, the gamut of Western Europe's radical right parties is all "non-populist" (Pappas 2019: 63–78): the French National Front, the Austrian FPÖ, the Dutch List Pim Fortuyn and the follow-up PVV led by Geert Wilders, the Danish People's Party, Norway's Progress Party, the Sweden Democrats, the True Finns, the Swiss SVP, the British UKIP, and the German AfD. In Pappas' account, this narrowing of the populist family is based on the questionable assumption that nativists are not "illiberal" but "abid(ing) by the rules and principles of political liberalism" (p. 72), and all they want is "liberal democracy for the natives" (p. 71). That is a rather strange notion. It is true that some of the parties mentioned by Pappas, especially the Dutch and Danish, have taken on a surprisingly "liberal" or "civic" coating (see Halikiopoulou and Vlandas 2019). However, this "liberalism" is only skin-deep, a strategic stick to beat Muslims, who constitute the large majority of immigrants in Europe (see also Marzouki et al. 2016). And it is simply too early or perhaps generally impossible to know what any of these "nativist" parties would do in power, because for the moment they are all minority or niche parties and none has ever exercised power *alone* – and probably never will, not least because a self-corrective "clown ceiling" prevents them from becoming majority parties.[6]

Searching for Root Causes: The Economy-Culture Conundrum

Takis Pappas (2019) is right that a political lens provides a minimal definition and point of entry for comprehending populism across its historical incarnations. However, if one wants to explain its contemporary formation in the West, the biggest challenge is the calibration of economic and cultural factors, in addition to the political. Ernest Gellner (1983: 129) once quipped about the outbreak of World War I, when German socialists abandoned their internationalist commitments in favor of imperial nationalism: "(T)he awakening message was intended for classes, but by some terrible postal error was delivered to nations." Something quite similar applies to the nationalist populisms that are gaining ground in the developed West in neoliberal times. A major source of their grievance *must* be economic, if one accepts Barry Eichengreen's plausible conclusion, derived from a review of a hundred years of populist movements in America and Europe, that "(p)opulist revolts rarely arise in good economic times" (2018: x). However, economic grievance tends to be sidestepped today in favor of culture-focused opposition to immigrants and other minorities. As Claus Offe expresses the paradox, "Fear of the uncertainties of one's socioeconomic future is … being reframed as fear of 'the other'" (2019b: 33).

The long-term economic causes of populism's sudden breakthrough in the West, which occurred in 2016 with the Brexit referendum and the Trump victory in the United States, are to be found in Branko Milanovic's famous "elephant curve" (2016). It reveals in one line the winners and losers of the new globalization, and thus the sociodemographic basis of the nationalist populism that is raging in the West. Showing relative per capita income gains between 1988 and 2008 at all points of the global income distribution, the graph visualizes the two most remarkable features of the globalization that has happened over the same period. First, it has narrowed the wealth gap between the global South and the global North, lifting large parts of the developing world, like India or China, out of acute poverty. Richard Baldwin thus called it the "great convergence" (2016), in contrast to the first, late nineteenth-century globalization that had the West run away from the Rest. But secondly, and decisive for our purposes, the new globalization has also enormously increased the internal wealth gap within the global North, with the top one percent of global earners, most of them in the West, experiencing truly spectacular income increases. Conversely, between the sixth and ninth global income deciles, Milanovic's elephant curve shows only small income increases or even income losses. Globally, the people in this segment are all "rich." Domestically, however, they are mostly the rich societies' lower-middle or working classes. On the one hand, they profit from the "citizenship premium" that is derived from the sheer fact of being born or residing in a rich country. On the other hand, they have seen their income stagnate or even shrink over the past three decades. These are the proverbial losers of globalization, who feed the ranks of the populist-nationalist parties and movements across Western countries.

A curve is not a story, and several stories can be read into it, not the least of which is about the productive possibilities unleashed by the IT revolution (as suggested by Baldwin 2016). However, the elephant curve also tells the story of the "restoration of (capitalist) class power" (Harvey 2005: 16). The latter ended an interim of three decades, ca. 1945–1973, in which capitalism and democracy in the West were locked into a "shotgun marriage" (Streeck 2016: 2). Various names have been given to this relatively short but happy moment in history, such as "embedded liberalism" (Ruggie 1982) or "*Trentes Glorieuses*" (Fourastié 1979). They flag a combination of social rights, economic growth, and dramatic improvement of general living conditions that had never before or after been achieved in the history of Western societies, indeed any human society. In a celebrated work, French economist Thomas Piketty (2014) showed this moment to be the tail-end of an exceptional 60-year period, starting in 1914, in which income inequality and the stock of wealth had dramatically declined across Western societies. It interrupted a 300-year trend in the history of capitalism for wealth to become ever more concentrated. By contrast, the post-1970s era, shortly after the enthroning of neoliberal supply-side economics, saw the return of the default mode of wealth-rewarding "patrimonial capitalism," as Piketty calls it. For Piketty, this is a condition in which the rate of return to wealth is higher than the rate of economic growth, resulting in steadily widening inequality. Accordingly, by the early 2000s, the wealth gap returned to its early twentieth-century heights, when, in Europe, the top 10 percent of households had controlled 90 percent of total wealth in society. In 2004, the wealth of the top 100 households in the United States, if compared to that of the bottom 90 percent, was at the staggering ratio of 100.000 to 1. This "corresponds roughly to the difference in material power between a senator and a slave at the height of the Roman Empire" (Streeck 2016: 29). Donald Trump, the populist, is right: "Globalization has made the financial elite ... very wealthy. But is has left millions of workers with nothing but poverty and headache" (quoted by Holmes 2019: 10). As the restoration of capitalist class power largely occurred by way of regressive taxation (see Piketty 2020: 33), it was only fitting that Trump, the plutocrat, would crown this development with a tax reform that made the 400 richest Americans pay less income tax (averaging 23 percent in 2018) than the bottom half of the income distribution (averaging 25 percent).[7] "For the first time in the last hundred years," economists Emmanuel Saez and Gabriel Zucman (2019: Introduction) comment on this, "billionaires have paid less than steel workers, schoolteachers, and retirees."[8]

At the same time, there is a consensus among social scientists that not economic concerns but immigration and the ensuing cultural changes are central to the agenda of nationalist populism (most recently, Piketty 2020: 959), which in Europe is carried by fast-growing radical right parties. In one of the earliest and best analyses of the radical right phenomenon, David Art (2011: 11) finds that "culture has trumped economics as (radical right parties') singular feature." A few years and many more radical right successes further on, David Goodhart (2017: 2) agrees, and he depicts populism's "coming of age" with Brexit and Trump as the result of "unhappy white working class voters (plagued) more by cultural loss, related to immigration and ethnic change, than by economic calculation." The paradigm-setting analysis is by Ronald Inglehart and Pippa Norris (2016: 3), who conclude that "the classic economic Left-Right cleavage in party competition is overlaid today by a new cultural cleavage, dividing Populists from Cosmopolitan Liberalism."[9] In particular, their global survey of voters' preferences finds concerns about "economic insecurity" to be less important than "psychological factors" when explaining support for populist parties: "Older birth cohorts and less-educated groups support populist parties and leaders that defend traditional cultural values and emphasize nationalistic and xenophobic appeals, rejecting outsiders, and upholding old-fashioned gender roles" (p. 30).

If economic concerns apparently take the backseat to cultural concerns, both in the programs of populist right parties[10] and in their voters' preferences, this is not to say that both types of concern are not intertwined. For instance, in Katherine Cramer's ethnography of "rural consciousness" in the American Mid-West, "people mak(e) sense of economics by putting themselves against their fellow citizens along social and cultural lines" (2016: ch. 8). Rural folks, often harmed by the financial crisis of 2008, still vote for less government even if they would profit from more government, because they (mistakenly, as Cramer shows) see their tax dollars not flowing back to them but sent to "urban areas that are home to liberals and people of color." Rural consciousness is thus "resentment against cities," which intricately mixes economic and cultural concerns.

In a twenty-country inquiry about "why ... the populist right win(s) working-class support on identity issues," Noam Gidron and Peter Hall (2017: S61) identify "status anxiety" as the chief cause, which likewise mixes economic and cultural concerns. As they observe, status anxiety afflicts not the very poor or the unemployed, but those "who still have a significant measure of status to defend" (p. S66). In this analysis, white male working class members see their "subjective social status," which is materially battered by depressed incomes and job insecurity, further diminished by "cultural frameworks" that upgrade minorities and women.[11] In this way, "(e)conomic and cultural developments" work in tandem, in a logic of insult added to injury, to boost the populist right (p. S58).

It is fact that the very poor or unemployed are not among the typical support groups of populist right parties; instead, they stay out of the political process altogether. This sits oddly with the standard view that the "losers of globalization" fill the populist ranks. This is exactly why some, like Goodhart (2017), have proposed a culture- rather than economics-focused approach. The economic linkage still exists, if one considers that it is more the *prospect* than the actual *experience* of falling down (as shown by Mounk 2018: ch. 5), particularly in regions hit hard by deindustrialization or left out by globalization gains (as shown by Rodriguez-Pose 2017), which makes people support populist parties. Accordingly, a perceptive survey of the "new populism" in Europe has found that it "represents not the losers of today but the prospective losers of tomorrow" (Krastev 2017: 81). In a similar vein, "societal pessimism" and a concern that "society is in decline" has been identified as the "possibly overarching characteristic of populist radical right voters" in a study of eight of Europe's richest countries (Steenvoorden and Harteveld 2018: 281).

Recent work exploring the link between a changing employment structure and electoral behavior affirms the diagnosis of a middle class in fear of falling. Thomas Kurier and Bruno Palier (2019) pointed out that technological change increasingly hits the "middle of society," whose votes turn out to be the "electoral game changer" towards the radical right. Importantly, automation and digitalization do not make "routine work" disappear right away, but only with a delay, through "natural turnover." As a result, the "large majority of routine workers is doing relatively well" (p. 3). But they are still given to "perceptions of insecurity and loss of control" that express themselves in "social conservatism," "authoritarianism," "societal pessimism," and "nostalgia" – the signature themes of the populist right. Echoing Gidron and Hall's (2017) notion of "status anxiety," Kurier and Palier (2019: 5) conclude that "routine workers' grievances are not primarily about material concerns," not even about "expanding social security," but about "dignity" and "social status."

The paradox remains. Those who have seen their fortunes stagnate or decline over the period of neoliberal globalization, and for whom "progress" is no longer part of their or their children's life experience and expectations, are prone to express their grievance in cultural or identity terms, and they largely spare the economic elites who are responsible for their dimming prospects. Wolfgang Merkel (2017) describes the paradox: "not the ... containment of inequality-generating markets is high on the populist agenda, but the fight against Otherness or even the Others."

The Battered Majority: Demise of Social Citizenship

Multiculturalists, like Will Kymlicka in this volume, but also the liberal supporters of majority rights (Koopmans and Orgad, in this volume), operate with a simplistic and static majority–minority binary, which conceals the internal heterogeneity and downward trend of the majority. This majority is treated much like a black box or unchanging entity.[12] As a result, another distinction, more at home in liberal nationalism theory (Tamir 1993; Miller 1995), but also evoked by Kymlicka under his hat of liberal nationalist: that between thick "membership" obligations and thinner "humanitarian" obligations, loses traction. Kymlicka refers to membership obligations as "the idea of citizenship rights" (in this volume). Its classic expression is what T. H. Marshall called the "social citizenship rights" of the welfare state, which he saw grounded in "a direct sense of community membership based on loyalty to a civilization that is a common possession" (1950: 96), in short, nationhood. Half a century of hollowing-out the welfare state has eaten large holes into the distinction between "membership" and "humanitarian" obligations, which Kymlicka retains as if nothing had happened. In reality, citizenship has been thinned of its social rights dimension, and the liberal "right to have rights" (Arendt 1948) has given way to the neoliberal notion of "earned citizenship" (Joppke 2021a), which is inflicted on immigrants and citizens alike.

Consider for this a striking decision of the German Constitutional Court, in 2012, about the social rights of asylum-seekers. The court ruled that asylum-seekers, however unfounded their claims might be, and even if they are merely "tolerated" (*geduldet*) and subject to expulsion, have exactly the same social aid entitlements as any German (or permanent resident) after one year of unemployment. After one year of being out of work, according to the austere Hartz IV (or Unemployment Money II) rules imposed a decade earlier, the unemployed are demoted from status-based compensation to flat-rate minimal social aid (*Sozialhilfe*), to secure their bare existence (*Grundsicherung*). Hartz IV may be a fortune for migrants from Macedonia (whose asylum applications, overwhelmingly rejected, incidentally skyrocketed right after the 2012 court decision); but it means the descent into poverty for German citizens. According to the court, "[h]uman dignity," protected by Article 1 of the Basic Law, "cannot be relativized for the purposes of migration policy" (*Menschenwürde ist migrationspolitisch nicht zu relativieren*).[13] This is a fine dictum for asylum-seekers but not for downgraded post-citizens in one of the world's richest countries, who are no longer treated as privileged "members" but in accordance with the "humanitarian" minimum.[14]

It is a moot question whether the German constitutional court's 2012 asylum decision should be regarded as an upgrading of migrant rights, as which it was hailed by the pro-migrant lobby, or as an indirect downgrading of citizen rights, which had gone largely unnoticed. The important matter is that under neoliberalism, citizenship, while lauded in current state rhetoric as the "highest prize" and "privilege" that needs to be "earned" (first observed by Houdt et al. 2011), has become massively devalued. In the liberal era, the standard movement was for migrant rights to be "levelled-up" to citizen rights – Yasemin Soysal (1994) memorably called it the rise of "postnational membership." More recently, the movement has shifted in the opposite direction, citizen rights being "levelled-down" to migrant rights, while the yardstick for both are increasingly universal human rights, as in the German asylum rights decision.

The main instance of levelled-down citizen rights is the neoliberal depletion of social citizenship,[15] which figured prominently in the 2012 German asylum decision. This outcome, incidentally, also has a liberal aspect: it attests to the difficulties of "welfare chauvinism" being implemented in a liberal-constitutional state (see also Koning

2019: ch. 5). One of the main planks of populist radical right parties, "welfare chauvinism" may be defined as "a political view that promotes nativism as the main organizing principle of social policy" (Ennser-Jedenastik 2018: 294). However, the territoriality principle of the welfare state sets narrow limits to this endeavor. Interestingly, radical right parties have adjusted to this liberal constraint by demanding, not to exclude immigrants from welfare benefits completely, but to greatly increase the residence-time requirement before welfare can be accessed. The Dutch PVV, for instance, the party of populist maverick Geert Wilders, wants immigrants to live and work in the Netherlands for 10 years before they become eligible for social benefits; this is five years more than the residence time required for legal permanent residence status (that usually triggers equal treatment). Laurenz Ennser-Jedenastik's (2018) analysis of populist party manifestos in four European countries with a notorious radical right presence: Sweden, Netherlands, United Kingdom, and Switzerland, found that their restrictive claims are mainly "directed at groups that have no contribution history" (p. 307), such as asylum-seekers and illegal immigrants. By contrast, social policy areas that operate strictly or mainly on the basis of individual contributions, such as unemployment compensation or old-age pensions, have seen no or little welfare chauvinist claims. Real-existing welfare chauvinism apparently operates less on an ethnic or racial agenda, which is usually attributed to it, than on a strong sense of "equity" or "reciprocity," that is, the notion that merit or desert, and not need, triggers social rights (p. 296).

But merit and strict reciprocity, or the idea that the "benefit one receives from the community should be in proportion to one's contribution" (Ennser-Jadenastik 2018: 296), belongs to the austere ethics of neoliberalism. It centers around "personal responsibility" (Mounk 2017), which has been pirated in this instance by notionally "welfare chauvinist" populists. Strict reciprocity and personal responsibility are also the basis of a new nationalism of "hard-working people" that not only populists but the former British Prime Minister David Cameron adopted, under the umbrella of Britain as an "aspiration nation." Cameron's two welfare reform acts, in 2012 and 2016, which introduced a so-called Universal Credit system, represent the apex of demolishing social citizenship through neoliberal welfare reform. This reform was meant to leave behind the "Age of Irresponsibility" in favor of a strangely positively valued "Age of Austerity."[16] Welfare reform under the lodestar of "responsibility," that central plank of "neoliberal reasoning" (Brown 2015), meant tying welfare closely to a duty to work, because "work is the best form of welfare," to quote Cameron's predecessor Tony Blair (in Macnicol 2010: 3). In fact, Cameron merely followed a path carved out by Blair, according to whom "you can't build a community on opportunity or rights alone. They need to be matched by responsibility and duty."[17] What Cameron radicalized was the harsh sense of reciprocity, according to which "real fairness ... is about the link between what you put in and what you get out."[18] Fairness, above all, is fairness to the "Taxpayers," who under neoliberalism have replaced the citizenry as the (ethnically anonymous) collective subject to whom public policy is accountable.

While political rhetoric conjures up an idealized "fantasy citizenship" (Anderson 2015: 196) as precious good, the "highest prize" as a Dutch immigration minister memorably put it, the opposite reality of neoliberal welfare is to blur the line between citizen and immigrant. David Cameron tellingly depicted welfare reform and immigration restriction as "two sides of the same coin." The "'something for nothing' culture" of freeloaders, which involved both immigrants and citizens, had to be put to an end: "Migrants are filling gaps in the labour market left wide open by a welfare system that for years has paid British people not to work ... (W)e will never control immigration properly until we tackle welfare dependency."[19] Cameron thus subtly combined anti-welfare with anti-immigrant resentment, with cleverly inverted roles to neutralize any charge of racism or of ethnic favoritism. On the welfare front, the "go-getting migrant" was extolled over the "lazy Brit" (Anderson 2015: 189), while on the immigration front the "genuine concerns of hard-working people" about "uncontrolled immigration" had to be heard.[20] But this deliberate double game cannot hide the fact that the "experience of citizens and migrants moves closer together" (Morris 2016: 696), because the rights or prerogatives of both are now subject to restriction, for the sake of "fairness to the taxpayer" (p. 703). As Lydia Morris has shown in an intriguing analysis of British court cases that involved both immigrants and citizens as plaintiffs against restrictive welfare reform, citizenship rights no longer serve as "normative yardstick" for immigrant rights; instead, legal contestation is increasingly expressed in terms of "human rights ... for both groups" (p. 696).

The Universal Credit system, created by the British Welfare Reform Act of 2012, is emblematic for the neoliberal devolution from welfare to workfare, or from "social citizen" à la Marshall to "worker citizen," as Bridget Anderson (2015) aptly calls the reductive form of neoliberal membership that includes or excludes citizens and immigrants alike. Its core is a "strong system of conditionality," that is, of strict behavioral requirements backed up by an aggravating scale of sanctions for repeat violators, to ensure that "unemployed people who can work will ... take all responsible steps to find and move into employment" (DWP 2010: 4). The ethos of neoliberal welfare reform is to "hold individuals," and not society, "as primarily responsible for the adverse life situations they experience" (Dwyer and Wright 2014: 30). In a pure application of the "perversity thesis" that has undergirded anti-welfare rhetoric since Thomas Malthus (Block and Somers 2005), "welfare dependency" is said to be the self-generated result of having received too many social benefits in the past – hence the need for moving towards self-disciplining workfare.[21]

Like under a microscope, the Universal Credit scheme allows to see in augmented size the neoliberal demolition of social citizenship. Merely consider one of its central measures, the Household Benefit Cap, which imposes an absolute limit on the cash benefits a household may receive per week, irrespective of the number of children. An extremely popular measure, presumably because it mostly hit (usually larger) minority families, this cap was meant to ensure "greater fairness in the welfare system," so that "people on benefits can no longer receive more from the state than the average wage of a hardworking family" (DWP 2014: 21). This is the "Victorian" baseline of the entire reform effort.[22] Lydia Morris (2016: 706) observed that, in breaching the principle of a guaranteed subsistence income, the Household Benefit Cap has undone the central plank of social citizenship, defined by Marshall as "the right ... to live the life of a civilized being according to the standards prevailing in the society" (1950: 11). Justice Lady Hale, dissenting in a High Court judgment that upheld the measure, acknowledged this fact: "The prejudicial effect of the cap is obvious and stark. It breaks the link between benefit and need. Claimants affected by the cap will, by definition, not receive the sums of money which the state deems necessary for them adequately to house, feed, clothe, and warm themselves and their children."[23]

In the land of Thomas Marshall, social citizenship is no more, and the line between thick "membership" obligations and lesser "humanitarian" obligations, between citizen and migrant, is being eroded. In an often-ignored side argument, Marshall (1950: 96) grounded social citizenship in shared nationhood. Social citizenship's demise also casts doubt on Will Kymlicka's optimism, expressed in this volume, that the "battery of nationhood" is alive and well.

Cultural Majority Rights?

Acknowledging its root causes across the politics-economics-culture spectrum does not make populism any bit more legitimate as a form of political action. This is because "democratic illiberalism" (Pappas 2019: 33), which is perhaps the most concise definition of populism, is a threat to liberal democracy as we know it. Give in to it, and the ladder that helped populists into power will be pulled up. This has unfailingly been the experience. Steven Levitsky and Daniel Ziblatt (2018: 5) called it the "electoral road to breakdown." They chillingly showed that Donald Trump, after only one year in office, had fulfilled, point by point, Juan Linz's poisonous road-to-authoritarianism quartet of rejecting the democratic rules, denying the legitimacy of political opponents, encouraging violence (notably *before* the storming of the Capitol in early January 2021), and curtailing civil liberties – only that American political institutions happen to be more robust than those of Venezuela or Hungary (Levitsky and Ziblatt: chs. 1 and 8).

Some liberal scholars are tempted to follow the populists onto their preferred cultural terrain, not to agree with them, but on the commendable assumption that it would be a "tragedy if nationalism ... be left in the hands of extremists" (Tamir 2019: 181). The most daring version is by Eric Kaufmann (2018: 1), who has argued for a symmetrical multiculturalism in which "white identity" is acknowledged and protected as "an ethnic identity like any other." In practical terms, this would mean an immigration policy that operates with "cultural points," in addition to economic or humanitarian criteria, to recruit immigrants "who are more likely to assimilate into the existing ethnic constituencies in a country" (p. 523). This is not meant to be a return to the racist immigration policies of the past, because Kaufmann *also* defends the ultra-liberal idea of a strictly neutral state, asking the latter to "de-centre itself from the ethnic majority and treat it as just another stakeholder" (p. 524). The result would be a multicultural yet "national origin" – selective immigration system, apportioning quotas according to the ethnic composition of a country, with the post-racist difference that no minority is categorically excluded (as Asians and Africans were under the United States national origins system, which was in place from the 1920s to the mid-1960s); instead, each group, the minorities included, is given its due share of immigrants.

This courageously iconoclastic proposal fails over the assumption that "white" or "majority" identity could ever be like any other identity, to be adjudicated by a neutral state that "doesn't play favourites, but must carry out its duty to represent the cultural interests of its stakeholder communities" (Kaufmann 2018: 523).[24] It is the nature of identity politics to defy compromise. This can only be aggravated in the case of a group that once had the privilege not to be in need of an "identity" and thus not being a "group" in the first place. It is not obvious how a liberal and nondiscriminatory immigration policy could follow from giving identity politics a free run.

Can there be legitimate, that is, liberal-democratic "white identity" politics? Another way of putting this question is to ask whether the "myths of descent, symbols and traditions," which is Kaufmann's (2018: 1) description of the content of "ethnic identity," could ever be innocent in the case of "white" identity. This is unlikely because "white" is a racial, not ethnic category, and as such is primarily defined by a negative demarcation from the "conspicuously different" (*auffällig Andersgeartete*), to follow Max Weber's (1976: 234) classic understanding of "race membership." Unlike ethnicity, Weber seems to suggest, race is not in the first place a positive and self-referential marker, but springs from a pejorative, discriminatory intention by a putatively superior out-group.

The same conflation of racial and ethnic identity plagues Ashley Jardina's (2019) empirical claim that a positive and nondiscriminatory "white identity" exists in the United States: "Many whites identify with their racial group, without feeling prejudice toward racial and ethnic minorities" (p. 5). Building on Tajfel's social identity theory, she argues that "racial identity," be it that of whites or of blacks, is simply "a conscious favoritism for one's in-group and recognition that one's group has shared interests" (p. 47–48). However, somewhat dissonant with this symmetry assumption, she concedes that in the case of "whites" one is dealing with "*dominant* group identity," which in the United States is actualized by the realistic "threat" of becoming a numerical minority by mid-century (p. 42). If one probes into this dominance, "white" loses its innocence as just another ethnic identity, and it reveals its historical truth as referring to America's *Herrenrasse*. Moreover, the very fact that "so many white Americans (were) drawn to a candidate like Donald Trump, who was often derisive of racial and ethnic minorities" (p. 3), suggests that the distinction between in-group favoritism and out-group hostility, which for Jardina is strong and categorical, *must* be more blurred than she would have it.

In Europe, where race talk is eschewed, some liberal scholars prefer to speak of "cultural majorities," whom they deem demographically and politically endangered and in need of moral or even legal support. In a paradigm-setting work, Liav Orgad (2015) has argued that, complementary to a "liberal theory of minority rights" (Kymlicka 1995), the time has come for a "liberal theory of majority rights." Indeed, is it not true that the concept of minority, which the liberal world has held high like a monstrance for half a century or more, logically requires the concept of majority? But "majority," Orgad argues, remains legally uncharted, even morally despised, despite the fact that majority existence has never been more precarious than in the global age of mass migrations and its diversity doxa. This empirical diagnosis notwithstanding, for good liberal reasons, Orgad (2015: ch. 6) radically narrows down the legal scope of majority protection to what he calls "national constitutionalism," which strongly resembles Jürgen Habermas' "constitutional patriotism" and does not go much beyond the standard precepts of liberal constitutionalism.

Ruud Koopmans (2018) has made an edgier case for legally protecting liberally suspicious majority claims. He shows sympathy not only for the innocent Dutch Black Pete pre-Christmas ritual, which is under attack by a militant multiculturalism squad, but also – albeit more implicitly – for liberally problematic cases like the Swiss minaret ban and the French burka prohibition.[25] Not unlike Orgad's (2015), Koopmans' argument for cultural majority rights is essentially by analogy: if minorities enjoy such protections already – especially "national minorities," as argued incisively by Kymlicka (1995) – it is only a matter of "normative and logical consistency" (Koopmans 2018: 18) to grant the same legal treatment to majorities also, given their demographically diminished and morally ostracized status today.

Koopmans rejects the usual counterargument, which is that majorities have the electoral process at their disposal, for the pragmatic reason that the lack of "normative legitimacy" of cultural majority claims unnecessarily "polarizes and poisons the public debate," breeding "nationalist populism."

However, the same Dutch Black Pete controversy, which figures prominently in Koopmans' case for cultural majority rights (2018), may also be turned into an argument against the need for special legal protection. Should constitutional majority protection, whatever that might mean concretely, and particularly in this instance, silence the freedom of expression of those who find fault with Santa's black-faced assistant? This is not just problematic for liberal reasons. To legally silence this opposition would be a deep affront to what it has traditionally meant to be "Dutch," a world-open, seafaring liberal people at least since the pre-Reformation days of Erasmus, when obscurantism and freedom-stifling Catholic Church orthodoxy were rampant in the rest of Europe. A speech prohibition would surely be a deeper affront to "Dutchness" than allowing Black Pete to be attacked by a farcical truth squad. Incidentally, the very fact of controversy revitalized the majority's insistence on not having their children's pre-Christmas ritual taken away by a remote United Nations bureaucrat and Jamaican academic who bizarrely admonished the Dutch that "you people (do not) need two Santa Clauses anyway" (Verene Shepherd, chairwoman of the UN Working Group of Experts on People of African Descent, quoted in Koopmans 2018: 6). Even the legal system, suspected by Koopmans to be chronically minority-friendly and majority-bashing, worked as it should: a lower court decision that had prohibited a Sinterklaas parade in Amsterdam, on the obscure legal argument that such a parade would negate the privacy rights of "black people" under the European Convention of Human Rights, was simply overturned by an appeal court.

It is true: Dutch children are still deprived of their Black Pete, and game half-won by the "anti-racists." However, this outcome is not due to the anti-racists having won their case legally, but because an apparently controversy-shy and "politically correct" Dutch national television decided to phase-out Black Pete; and like-minded storeowners quietly removed his picture or imitative toys from their shop windows and shelves. In light of this outcome, Ruud Koopmans now thinks that the "issue of majority and minority rights is first and foremost a normative, moral one, and only partially and secondarily a legal one."[26]

But then the matter is no longer one of rights, but of prudence – or unstoppable craziness. This may be an acceptable move with respect to majorities, who still have the electoral process at their disposal. However, if applied to minorities, it would subject them to considerable vulnerabilities to protect from which "rights" are there in the first place.

Multiculturalists and majority rights advocates, who are sometimes of one cloth (as in Patten's [2020] cautious and qualified defense of majority rights), are to be equally rebutted in their strangely symmetric claims to have their "cultures" placed under legal protection. In his famous exchange with Charles Taylor, Jürgen Habermas ridiculed the idea as "species conservation" (1994: 30). With an eye on the workings of liberal law, German constitutionalist Christoph Möllers observes that "many questions, which are handled under the register of cultural difference, are legally speaking traditional individual rights problems" (2008: 235), so that there is no need for a "new multiculturalist constitutional paradigm" (p. 223). But then the case for cultural majority rights collapses, too. "Culture," Möllers acutely notes, has the paradoxical double face to be both "contingent" and "fundamental": *contingent*, because the concept implies a plurality of cultures and that things can always be different; *fundamental*, because "culture" points to "differences that cannot be otherwise explained" and that are immune to "intentional change" (p. 227–28). From this follows a compelling understanding of culture(s) as "non-malleable differences" (*nicht gestaltbare Differenzen*). The state, as it operates by way of positive law and coercion, is by definition the wrong agent and medium to deal with things that are *nicht gestaltbar* (non-malleable).

A separate problem is the majority rights defenders' confounding of the tricky but important distinction between ethnic group and nation. Following Max Weber's classic account, a group is "ethnic" when self-defined by a "subjective belief in common origins," while at the same time "renouncing 'power'" (*Verzicht auf die "Macht"*) (1976: 237, 243). The same group becomes a "nation" when common-origin beliefs are connected to "the idea of having or aspiring to have a state of their own" (p. 244). However, beyond Weber, it needs to be stated that having a state, and not being challenged in this by a competing group, changes the game. A liberal-democratic state, for the sake of symmetry between the subjects and objects of power, *must* admit all residents into the citizenry, if certain conditions are fulfilled, most notably a period of legal residence (Dahl 1989: ch. 9; see also Walzer 1983:

ch. 2). A modicum of civicness and weakening of ethnic particularity is the price to pay for having a state – in fact, the very idea of "owning" the state has to be given up. This is why the following statement by majority rights defenders sounds wrong: "If Quebecois, Pueblo Indians, and Frisians can claim cultural rights, so should the Danes, the Dutch, and the Italians" (Koopmans and Orgad, in this volume). Long in possession of a state, not challenged in this by a competing group, and subscribing to the tenets of liberal democracy, "Danes," "Dutch," or "Italians" are no longer a "group" in any meaningful sense. These are simply names for different state citizenries, which are open to members of any ethnic group by the standardly nondiscriminatory citizenship laws of a liberal state.[27] Technically, a Dane can be of any group or ethnic background, while the Pueblo Indian cannot. Put differently, a Pueblo Indian[28] can become a Dane while the reverse is not possible. There is a difference in quality, not just in size, between an ethnic group and a state-bearing national "group" that can retain its groupness only by renouncing the liberal-democratic credentials of "its" state, *or* by not admitting any immigrants, including refugees and asylum-seekers – which, in effect, may amount to the same thing. Koopmans and Orgad (in this volume) have conceded as much by limiting cultural majority claims to highly specific types,[29] labelled "dwindling majority," "regional-minority majority," "victimized majority," and "minoritized majority." None of these types, including that of "dwindling majority," remotely resembles the situation in a long-established, developed Western nation-state.[30]

Conclusion

In his sweeping comparison of "inequality regimes" in global history, Thomas Piketty (2020: 962–63) discards the concept of populism, because of its "lack of precision" and polemical nature. He even denounces it as the "ultimate weapon in the hands of the objectively privileged social classes." Instead, Piketty prefers to speak of "social nativism," whose rise in post-1980s Europe and the United States, in his view, is caused less by "racism" on the part of workers than by the "ideological failure" (p. 40) of leftist parties to address the inequalities of global capitalism. These parties, in fact, have turned from being the "part(ies) of workers" into being the "part(ies) of the educated," dubbed the "Brahmin Left" (p. 744).[31] Only this transition provided the space for nativism to unfold:

"identity conflicts are fueled by disillusionment with the very ideas of a just economy and social justice" (p. 831). In turn, "as the identity cleavage deepened, the class cleavage receded. This is surely the main reason for the rise of inequality since the 1980s" (p. 959).

This is not to endorse a vulgar Marxism in new cloth, where it is always "the economy, stupid."[32] And Piketty may well be wrong in blaming the left for the rise of "hypercapitalism," in which the underprivileged fret over "borders" and identity while "property" and rising inequality go untouched. Commendable, however, is the attempt to link the ebb and flow of conflict in both dimensions, the cultural and the economic, rather than seeing each in isolation. Brian Barry, in his furious early millennium diatribe against multiculturalism, objected that the "'culturalization' of group identities" was at the cost of the "systematic neglect of alternative causes of group disadvantage" (2001: 305), and that the obsession with "culture" implied losing sight of "equality" (pp. 317–28). A similar objection may be raised against the more recent quest for cultural majority rights. It is unlikely to put populism to rest, as the latter feeds on deeper sources, to be found in the ongoing neoliberal transformation of Western societies.

Notes

1 On the neoliberal project and its stunning successes, see Mierowski and Plehwe (2009), especially the concluding chapter by Philip Mierowski.

2 A rare self-identifying "populist" on the American scene today, Thomas Frank (2020: ch. 4), has outed a reflex-like "anti-populism" as "tool for justifying unaccountable power."

3 But see Nadia Urbinati (2019: 48), who finds the reference to Rousseau's volonté générale in the definition of populism mistaken: "The root of populism is the nonelite people, or the masses minus the elites: it is anti-establishment." Her valid point is that populists are not universalists but particularists, who exclude the nonelites from the ambit of an essentialized and unchanging "people" (that is always less than the whole, and thus inevitably "factionalist"). In her impressively learned account, spanning many of the political writings from Aristoteles on, populism is not direct democracy but a form of representative democracy, in which the logic of *pars pro parte* has replaced that of *pars pro toto*. With considerable more philosophical investment and sophistication than can be proffered in this paper, Urbinati comes to the same conclusion: "Populists cannot answer the problems that populists are reacting against" (p. 207).

4 Luhmann (1995: 245–46) considers "freedom" and "equality," liberalism's two core values, as constitutive of the semantics of "inclusion" into the functionally differentiated subsystems of modern society.
5 But see again Urbinati's sharp observation (2019: 24), that in democratic theory the "majority" is procedural and forever in flux, while for populists it is fixed and unchanging.
6 "The Clown Ceiling," *The Economist*, January 9, 2021, p. 23.
7 For the strange amalgam of "plutocratic populism," which has characterized the US Republican Party already preceding Donald Trump, see Hacker and Pierson (2020).
8 However, the quoted tax rate of low-income Americans does not include transfer payments to the very poor. See the debate over "measuring the 1%" in *The Economist* ("Economists are Rethinking the Numbers on Inequality," November 28, 2019).
9 The most complete empirical analysis along such lines is Maria Sobolewska and Robert Ford's *Brexitland* (2020). They depict the dynamics leading to Brexit as polarized conflict between (lowly educated) "identity conservatives" and "graduate conviction liberals" (the latter in alliance with "ethnic minority necessity liberals").
10 This is not to deny the rise of "national social" and "anti-austerity" positions in a number of European radical right parties, east and west, which are brilliantly explored by Melinda Cooper (2020). Cooper also draws interesting parallels with 1930s to 1940s German "National Socialism," described by her as "anti-capitalism divested of class conflict" (Cooper 2020: 122).
11 Economic distress upped by a sense that minorities are unjustly favored, is also the gist of Arlie Hochschild's "deep story" (2016: ch. 9) that summarizes, to the point and with great imagination, why white working-class Americans in Louisiana would support the right-wing populist Tea Party movement, which is anti-government and anti-tax and thus detrimental to their interests.
12 That not all majorities are alike is one of the main points raised in the chapter by the editors of this volume (Koopmans and Orgad 2020). Their distinction between "homeland" and "migratory" majorities is indeed helpful for adjudicating the legitimacy of majority claims. However, even within its respective category, a "majority" is still seen as homogenous and unchanging, and set apart from "minorities." It is this static view and distinction, which is oblivious of internal divisions and implies a principled privileging of the "majority" (either criticized, as by multiculturalists, or affirmed, as by majority rights advocates), that I would like to question. See also the compelling (and rather more complex) critique by Bauböck (in this volume).

13 1 BvL 10/10 and 1 BvL 2/11, decision of 18 July 2012, at para. 95.
14 For the strange coincidence between human rights advocacy and galloping inequality in neoliberal capitalism, see Moyn (2018).
15 For other instances of demoted citizen rights, caused by the invasion of migration control imperatives into the citizenship domain, see Joppke (2021b: ch. 3). Particularly noteworthy in this respect are income-dependent, and thus class-selective family formation and reunification rights, which even tend to prioritize certain (high-skilled) immigrants over (low-income) citizens (see Staver 2015 and Kofman 2018).
16 David Cameron, The Age of Austerity, speech to the Conservative Party on April 26, 2009 (https://conservative-speeches-sayit.mysociety.org/speech/601367).
17 Tony Blair in 2000, quoted in Morris (2007: 43).
18 David Cameron, in Morris (2018: 7).
19 David Cameron, in Morris (2016: 693).
20 David Cameron, Speech on Immigration and Welfare Reform, March 16, 2016 (www.gov.uk/government/speeches/david-cameron-immigration-speech).
21 See the foreword by Ian Duncan Smith, Secretary of State for Work and Pensions, in DWP (2010: 1).
22 See "The Politics of Virtue," *The Economist*, January 11, 2020.
23 Supreme Court (UK), R v. Secretary of State for Work and Pensions, [2015] UKSC 16, March 18, 2015, at para. 180.
24 This echoes Alan Patten's case of justifying minority rights on grounds of a perfectly neutral state (2014). Patten (2020) promptly comes out in favor of (a moderate range of) majority rights.
25 All three incidents are listed as delegitimized "rights claims by … cultural majorities" that call for a friendlier reception (Koopmans 2018: abstract).
26 Personal communication, February 7, 2020.
27 A similar problem mars Eric Kaufmann's concept of "dominant ethnicity," a precursor to the cultural majority rights notion, if applied to the British, the French, or the Americans (as can be found in Kaufmann 2004).
28 The case of the Quebecois does not quite fit here, because Quebec has state-like powers, including immigration powers, within the Canadian federation.
29 For an even narrower list of legitimate cultural majority claims, derived from his multiculturalism-grounding principle of "equal recognition," see Patten (2020).
30 For the US, and the claim of an emergent white "majority-minority," see the rebuttal by Alba (2020).

31 For a critique, see Hicks and Abou-Chadi (2021), who argue that the highly educated mainly support the new "green/left-libertarian" parties rather than the classic leftist parties, while simultaneously espousing pro-redistributionist views.

32 "The economy, stupid" was the successful 1992 United States presidential election slogan used by the Democratic challenger, Bill Clinton, against the Republican incumbent, George Bush, Sr.

References

AfD. (2016). *Programm für Deutschland*. Stuttgart.

Alba, R. (2020). *The Great Demographic Illusion: Majority, Minority, and the Expanding American Mainstream*. Princeton: Princeton University Press.

Anderson, B. (2015). "Heads I Win. Tails You Lose": Migration and the Worker Citizens. *Current Legal Problems*, 68: 179–96.

Arendt, H. (1948). *The Origins of Totalitarianism*. New York: Harcourt Brace Jovanovich.

Art, D. (2011). *Inside the Radical Right: The Development of Anti-Immigrant Parties in Western Europe*. New York: Cambridge University Press.

Baldwin, R. (2016). *The Great Convergence: Information Technology and the New Globalization*. Cambridge: Harvard University Press.

Barry, B. (2001). *Culture and Equality: An Egalitarian Critique of Multiculturalism*. Cambridge: Polity Press.

Bauböck, R. (in this volume). Are There Any Cultural Majority Rights?

Bickerton, C., & Accetti, C. I. (2017). Populism and Technocracy. *Critical Review of International Social and Political Philosophy*, 20/2: 186–206.

Block, F., & Somers, M. (2005). From Poverty to Perversity. *American Sociological Review*, 70/2: 260–87.

Brown, W. (2015). *Undoing the Demos: Neoliberalism's Stealth Revolution*. New York: Zone Books.

Brubaker, R. (2017). Why Populism? *Theory and Society*, 46/5: 357–85.

(2019). Populism and Nationalism. *Nations and Nationalism*, 1–23, https://doi.org/10.1111/nana.12522

Canovan, M. (1999). Trust the People! Populism and the Two Faces of Democracy. *Political Studies*, 47: 2–16.

Caramani, D. (2017). Will vs. Reason: The Populist and Technocratic Forms of Political Representation and their Critique to Party Government. *American Political Science Review*, 111/1: 54–67.

Cooper, M. (2020). Anti-Austerity on the Far Right. In Wallison, W. and Manfredi, Z., eds. *Mutant Neoliberalism*. New York: Fordham University Press.

Cramer, K. (2016). *The Politics of Resentment: Rural Consciousness in Wisconsin and the Rise of Scott Walker*. Chicago: University of Chicago Press.

Dahl, R. (1989). *Democracy and Its Critics*. New Haven: Yale University Press.

De Cleen, B., & Stavrakakis, Y. (2017). Distinctions and Articulations: A Discourse Theoretical Framework for the Study of Populism and Nationalism. *Javnost-The Public*, 24/4: 301–19.

DWP (UK Department of Work and Pensions). (2010). *Universal Credit*. London: HMSO.

(2014). *The Benefit Cap*. London: HMSO.

Dwyer, P., & Wright, S. (2014). Universal Credit, Ubiquitous Conditionality and its Implications for Social Citizenship. *Journal of Poverty and Social Justice*, 22/1: 27–35.

Eichengreen, B. (2018). *The Populist Temptation*. New York: Oxford University Press.

Ennser-Jedenastik, L. (2018). Welfare Chauvinism in Populist Radical Right Platforms. *Social Policy and Administration*, 52/1: 293–314.

Fourastié, J. (1979). *Les Trente glorieuses ou La révolution invisible de 1946 à 1975*. Paris: Fayard.

Frank, T. (2020). *The People, No: A Brief History of Anti-Populism*. New York: Metropolitan Books.

Gellner, E. (1983). *Nations and Nationalism*. Ithaca: Cornell University Press.

Gidron, N. & Hall, P. (2017). The Politics of Social Status: Economic and Cultural Roots of the Populist Right. *British Journal of Sociology*, 68/S1: S57–S84.

Goodhart, D. (2017). *The Road to Somewhere*. London: Hurst.

Habermas, J. (1994). Struggle for Recognition in the Democratic-Constitutional State. In A. Gutmann, ed. *Multiculturalism*. Princeton: Princeton University Press.

Hacker, J., & Pierson, P. (2020). *Let Them Eat Tweets: How the Right Rules in an Age of Extreme Inequality*. New York: Norton.

Halikiopoulou, D., & Vlandas, T. (2019). What Is New and What Is Nationalist about Europe's New Nationalism? *Nations and Nationalism*, 25/2: 409–34.

Harvey, D. (2005). *A Brief History of Neoliberalism*. New York: Oxford University Press.

Hicks, S., & Abou-Chadi, T. (2021). Brahmin Left versus Merchant Right? *British Journal of Sociology*, 72/1: 79–92.

Hochschild, A. (2016). *Strangers in Their Own Land: Anger and Mourning on the American Right*. New York: The New Press.

Hofstadter, R. (1964). The Paranoid Style in American Politics. *Harper's Magazine*, November: 77–86.

Holmes, S. (1995). *Passions and Constraint: On the Theory of Liberal Democracy*. Chicago: University of Chicago Press.

(2019). On Populism. *Sociologica*, 13/2: 9–10.

Houdt, F. et al. (2011). Neoliberal Communitarian Citizenship. *International Sociology*, 26/3: 408–32.

Inglehart, R., & Norris, P. (2016). *Trump, Brexit, and the Rise of Populism*. HKS Faculty Research Working Paper RWP 16-026, Harvard Kennedy School, Cambridge.

Jardina, A. (2019). *White Identity Politics*. New York: Cambridge University Press.

Joppke, C. (2021a). Earned Citizenship. *European Journal of Sociology*, 62/1: 1–35.

(2021b). *Neoliberal Nationalism: Immigration and the Rise of the Populist Right*. Cambridge: Cambridge University Press.

Judis, J. B. (2016). *The Populist Explosion*. New York: Columbia Global Reports.

Katz, R. S., & Mair, P. (1995). Changing Models of Party Organization and Party Democracy. *Party Politics*, 1/1: 5–28.

(2009). The Cartel Party Thesis: A Restatement. *Perspectives on Politics*, 7/4: 753–66.

Kaufmann, E. (2018). *Whiteshift*. London: Allen Lane.

Kaufmann, E., ed. (2004). *Rethinking Ethnicity: Majority Groups and Dominant Minorities*. London: Routledge.

Kofman, E. (2018). Family Migration as a Class Matter. *International Migration*, 56/4: 33–46.

Koning, E. A. (2019). *Immigration and the Politics of Welfare Exclusion*. Toronto: University of Toronto Press.

Koopmans, R., & Orgad, L. (in this volume). Majority-Minority Constellations: Toward a Group-Differentiated Approach.

Koopmans, R. (2018). *Cultural Rights and Native Majorities Between Universalism and Minority Rights*. Wissenschaftszentrum Berlin (WZB): Discussion Paper SP VI 2018–106.

Krastev, I. (2017). *After Europe*. Philadelphia: University of Pennsylvania Press.

Kurier, T., & Palier, B. (2019). Shrinking and Shouting: The Political Revolt of the Declining Middle in Times of Employment Polarization. *Research and Politics*, 1–6. https://doi.org/10.1177/2053168019831164.

Kymlicka, W. (1995). *Multicultural Citizenship: A Liberal Theory of Minority Rights*. Oxford: Oxford University Press.

(in this volume). Nationhood, Multiculturalism and the Ethics of Membership.

Levitsky, S., & Ziblatt, D. (2018). *How Democracies Die*. New York: Crown.
Lind, M. (2020). *The New Class War: Saving Democracy from the Managerial Elite*. New York: Penguin.
Luce, E. (2017). *The Retreat from Western Liberalism*. London: Little Brown.
Luhmann, N. (1995). Inklusion und Exklusion. In N. Luhmann, ed. *Soziologische Aufklärung 6*. Opladen: Westdeutscher Verlag.
Macnicol, J. (2010). *New Labour's Anti-Poverty Strategy*, 1997–2019. Paris: SciencesPo and CERI/CNRS (www.sciencespo.fr/ceri/sites/sciencespo.fr.ceri/files/art_jm_0.pdf).
Manin, B. (1997). *The Principles of Representative Government*. New York: Cambridge University Press.
Manow, P. (2018). *Die Politische Ökonomie des Populismus*. Berlin: Suhrkamp.
Marshall, T. H. (1950). *Citizenship and Social Class*. Cambridge: Cambridge University Press.
Marzouki, N. et al., eds. (2016). *Saving the People: How Populists Hijack Religion*. London: Hurst.
Mény, Y., & Surel, Y. (2002). The Constitutive Ambiguity of Populism. In Mény, Y. and Surel, Y., eds. *Democracies and the Populist Challenge*. Basingstoke: Macmillan.
Merkel, W. (2017). Kosmopolitismus versus Kommunitarismus. In Harfst, P. et al., eds. *Parties, Governments and Elites*. Wiesbaden: Springer VS.
Mierowski, P., & Plehwe, D. (2009). *The Road from Mont Pèlerin: The Making of the Neoliberal Thought Collective*. Cambridge: Harvard University Press.
Milanovic, B. (2016). *Global Inequality*. Cambridge: Harvard University Press.
Miller, D. (1995). *On Nationality*. Oxford: Oxford University Press.
Möllers, C. (2008). Pluralität der Kulturen als Herausforderung an das Verfassungsrecht? *Archiv für Rechts- und Sozialphilosophie*, 113: 223–44.
Morris, L. (2007). New Labour's Community of Rights. *Journal of Social Policy*, 36/1: 39–57.
(2016). Squaring the Circle: Domestic Welfare, Migrants Rights, and Human Rights. *Citizenship Studies*, 20/6–7: 693–709.
(2018). "Moralising Welfare" and Migration in Austerity Britain. *European Societies,* https://doi.org/10.1080/14616696.2018.1448107
Mounk, Y. (2017). *The Age of Responsibility: Luck, Choice and the Welfare State*. Cambridge: Harvard University Press.
Moyn, S. (2018). *Not Enough: Human Rights in an Unequal World*. Cambridge: Harvard University Press.

(2018). *The People v Democracy*. Cambridge: Harvard University Press.
Mudde, C. (2004). The Populist Zeitgeist. *Government and Opposition*, 39/4: 541–63.
Offe, C. (2019a). *The "Liberal Democracy Cube" under the Onslaught of Populist Parties*. Unpublished manuscript (in author's possession).
(2019b). Wille und Unwille des Volkes. In C. Offe, *Liberale Demokratie und soziale Macht*, vol. 4. Wiesbaden: Springer VS.
Orgad, L. (2015). *The Cultural Defense of Nations: A Liberal Theory of Majority Rights*. New York: Oxford University Press.
Patten, A. (2014). *Equal Recognition: The Moral Foundations of Minority Rights*. Princeton: Princeton University Press.
(2020). Populist Multiculturalism: Are There Majority Cultural Rights? *Philosophy and Social Criticism*, 46/5: 539–52.
Pappas, T. (2019). *Populism and Liberal Democracy*. Oxford: Oxford University Press.
Piketty, T. (2014). *Capital in the 21st Century*. Cambridge: Harvard University Press.
(2020). *Capital and Ideology*. Cambridge: Harvard University Press.
Riker, W. (1982). *Liberalism against Populism*. Prospect Heights: Waveland Press.
Rodrik, D. (2018). Populism and the Economics of Globalization. *Journal of International Business Policy*, 1/1–2: 12–33.
Rodriguez-Pose, A. (2017). The Revenge of the Places that Don't Matter. *Cambridge Journal of Regions, Economy and Society*, 11/1: 189–209.
Ruggie, J. (1982). International Regimes, Transactions, and Change. *International Organization*, 36/2: 379–415.
Saez, E., & Zucman, G. (2019). *The Triumph of Injustice*. New York: W.W. Norton.
Schmitt, C. (1926). *Die geistesgeschichtliche Lage des heutigen Parlamentarismus*. Berlin: Duncker & Humblot.
Schmitter, P. (2019). The Vices and Virtues of "Populisms." *Sociologica*, 13/1: 75–81.
Sobolewska, M., & Ford, R. (2020). *Brexitland: Identity, Diversity and the Reshaping of British Politics*. Cambridge: Cambridge University Press.
Somers, M. (2008). *Genealogies of Citizenship*. New York: Cambridge University Press.
Soysal, Y. (1994). *Limits of Citizenship*. Chicago: University of Chicago Press.
Staver, A. (2015). Hard Work for Love: The Economic Drift in Norwegian Family Immigration and Integration Policies. *Journal of Family Issues*, 36/11: 1453–71.
Steenvoorden, E., & Harteveld, E. (2018). The Appeal of Nostalgia. *West European Politics*, 41/1: 28–52.

Streeck, W. (2016). *How Will Capitalism End?* London: Verso.
Tamir, Y. (1993). *Liberal Nationalism*. Princeton: Princeton University Press.
(2019). *Why Nationalism?* Princeton: Princeton University Press.
Turner, B. S. (2016). We Are All Denizens Now: On the Erosion of Citizenship. *Citizenship Studies*, 20/6–7: 679–92.
Urbinati, N. (2019). *Me the People: How Populism Transforms Democracy*. Cambridge : Harvard University Press.
Walzer, M. (1983). *Spheres of Justice*. New York: Basic Books.
(1984). Liberalism and the Art of Separation. *Political Theory*, 12/3: 315–30.
Weber, M. (1976). *Wirtschaft und Gesellschaft*. Tübingen: Mohr Siebeck.

11 *Legitimate Populism and Liberal Overreach*

DAVID GOODHART

We are all liberals now. The vast majority of mainstream politicians and voters in Western societies sign up to what Nick Timothy (2020) has called "essential liberalism," meaning the rule of law (and equality before the law), free elections and universal adult franchise, freedom of speech and assembly, and individual and minority rights.

Essential liberalism has evidently not prevented much dissatisfaction with the modern world. This is more surprising than is often recognized. Notwithstanding financial crises and pandemics, never have people living in Western societies enjoyed such an extraordinary combination of health, wealth, and freedom.

But we humans are restless creatures, easily discontented, and with a strong tendency to compare ourselves to others. And while essential liberalism has provided the framework for the largely peaceful management of power in Western societies, underpinning state machines's that are neither too strong nor too weak, it has been supplemented in recent decades by what might be called an Anywhere liberal ethos (Goodhart 2017).

The Anywhere liberal ethos has been a dominant force in most Western countries for several decades regardless of the party in power. It is often what politicians mean by modernization or (for those on the left) progressivism, and it includes a preference for the mobile over the settled, for change over stability, for the open over the protected, for reason over tradition and authority, for academic training over practical know-how, for global or European regulation over national sovereignty, and greater concern for the noneconomic inequalities (of race, gender, sexuality, etc.) than for economic inequalities (Goodhart 2017).

Populism, at least in its mainstream, legitimate form, has been a reaction against this increasingly pervasive Anywhere liberal ethos, especially where the mainstream parties of the center-right have been partly captured by that ethos. It has been a more militant, and plebeian, resistance to the over-reach of modern liberalism than that provided by most forms of conservatism, although its critique sometimes overlaps.

I will later describe in more detail the three main clusters of policy where liberal over-reach has had most impact. But the three are in broad outline: the enthusiastic embrace of change and openness, most visibly in the case of immigration; the promotion of cognitive-professional employment and academic training as the main route to a successful life; and the devaluation of family life and domesticity with a view to transcending any kind of gender division of labor.

This over-reach has provided the fuel for much of mainstream populism. But the populist critique is not just about resisting the policy priorities of the Anywhere liberal graduate class, it is also an objection to the legal-professional form of the modern political process.

The American writer Christopher Caldwell (2020) has talked about the "two constitutions." The first constitution is the traditional democratic constitution of political parties and elections with new legislation based on majorities in democratic assemblies. The second constitution is the legal-regulatory constitution which has emerged so powerfully in recent decades in which an increasing number of key decisions – from gay marriage (in the United States) to immigration and asylum rules are taken by judges and sometimes by judges belonging to international institutions, thereby by-passing national electoral democracy.

Populism bases itself firmly in the first constitution and objects to the rising authority of the second constitution which is seen as lacking democratic legitimacy.

These objections to some of the dominant trends in modern politics seem to me legitimate and are widely shared by a variety of non-populist politicians and writers, even if less raucously expressed.

So, on what grounds do critics, such as Christian Joppke, declare modern mainstream populism as offered by leaders such as Marine Le Pen and Nigel Farage to be illegitimate? There are two main objections: one is populism's alleged lack of pluralism and the other is the manner in which it redirects economic discontent into cultural channels.

The pluralism point is common ground among many liberal and left critics of populism. The argument is that populists have a simplistic idea of "the people" (and the "general will") as a coherent entity with a common interest, pitted against the economic elites (in the case of left populists) and against the cosmopolitan elites and immigrants (in the case of right populists).

I find this unconvincing on two grounds. First, there is a sense in which all democratic politics is populist and all democratic politics is un-pluralistic in the simple sense that all parties and movements want to win, which means imposing their vision and their policy solutions on many people who object to them. When Tony Blair's Labour Government decided to allow free movement for East Europeans in 2004 or when it opted in 1999 for a target of sending half of all school-leavers to university – two policy positions strongly opposed by a large minority if not a majority of voters – was that not un-pluralistic?

In a democratic, rights-based polity like the United Kingdom, the opponents of those policies were free to argue and campaign against them but they could not stop them. In adversarial, democratic politics too great a value accorded to pluralism and too much respect for the positions and values of one's political opponents, would lead to stasis. Moreover, when politicians, especially of the left, talk of being for "the many, not the few," is that not populist? Tony Blair even famously talked about New Labour being the "political wing of the British people."

My second objection to the alleged "general will" thinking of naive populists is that no evidence is ever provided for it. No doubt, occasionally a Le Pen or a Farage will talk loosely about "the people," implying it is a single entity with a common interest, but so do almost all democratic politicians.

In reality, modern populists are only too aware of the fractured and fragmented nature of democratic majorities and the complex and often conflicting interests within those majorities. They regard themselves, rightly or wrongly, as speaking for groups of people mainly in the bottom half of the economic system who feel culturally and economically marginalized.

No political strategy based on a simplistic account of a single general will could hope to be successful in modern politics, and yet Nigel Farage has some claim to being the most successful British politician of recent decades and Marine Le Pen is a sophisticated political operator capable of finessing her political message to maximize its appeal.

The second objection to populism is that is converts discontent that is at root economic and redirects it down a cultural cul-de-sac. This objection has strong echoes of Marxist economism and of the idea of a false consciousness dividing and distracting the working class from its true goal of socialist liberation.

There is plenty of survey evidence for the cultural priorities of populist voters and also for their economic discontent, but it is impossible to speculate with any accuracy about which is the prime mover. The truth is that on many issues it is conceptually difficult to disentangle economics and culture. For example, is the complaint about the declining status of much nongraduate employment, a cultural complaint or an economic one? And objections to immigration surely have both a cultural and an economic dimension.

If populism really was first and foremost an economic phenomenon, then surely it would rise in periods of economic strife and be concentrated among the poorest or most disrupted economic actors, but there is no evidence for either of these connections. And populism has been thriving in Scandinavian countries such as Sweden, which have seen healthy economic growth in recent years and remain models of egalitarianism.

Nevertheless, Joppke blithely asserts that populists are driven by economic discontent. He also asserts that neoliberalism has shattered the rights of all citizens in its quest to rescue capitalism from the constraints of democracy. Yet there is precious little evidence provided for the claim that Western societies are becoming less democratic, except in the sense of more important decisions shifting from the first constitution to the second which is a populist but not usually a liberal complaint.

And there is even less evidence for the shattering of social rights. Joppke provides a cartoonish account of how a rather technical welfare reform in the United Kingdom, Universal Credit, has allegedly caused the demise of social citizenship. Universal Credit was inspired by the goal of simplifying a highly complex welfare system and although it has had some quite serious teething troubles, mainly concerned with the time it takes to make initial welfare payments, it cannot possibly be accused of undermining social citizenship.

Universal Credit, like its many predecessors, is based on various principles, including welfare conditionality and the idea of reciprocity – one pays into the system when one is earning and then draws out from it when one is not – which are both popular and long established. Joppke seems to be arguing that the only legitimate form of social welfare is a universalist one, which would involve no means-testing and no conditionality. He is entitled to his preference but to declare that other forms of welfare are undermining social citizenship seems peculiar.

More broadly the claim, often made from the left, that the social state is in decline is hard to fit with the facts of increased public spending including continued rises in social spending, albeit with a pause in the post-financial crisis austerity period. In the United Kingdom, social rights increased in the early 2000s with the introduction of the tax credit system and income top-ups for low paid workers. The minimum wage in the United Kingdom is one of the highest in Europe and poverty levels have recently been falling. Moreover, the generous furlough schemes and welfare support provided during the pandemic has shown the modern welfare state and social citizenship to be alive and well in most rich countries.

Majority Rights

One answer to populism favored by Koopmans and Orgad (this volume) is a greater focus on majority rights. Joppke, by contrast, thinks that majorities are already well served by current legal-political arrangements. I think both are right. I find majority rights helpful as a kind of political metaphor rather than a legal or political concept, but there are some circumstances where it might be reasonable to talk about reinforcing majority rights.

A weakening of majority ethnic favoritism is one of the bases of essential liberalism and the rule of law. If majorities favor those like themselves, minorities will potentially suffer, hence the need for minority rights and antidiscrimination laws. But as majorities shrink in size and the common norms forged by majorities are no longer taken for granted, do majorities themselves need some kind of protection? Certainly, some members of the ethnic majority may be attracted to populist parties by their implicit, and sometimes explicit, promise to restore a kind of "majority common-sense."

It is true, as Koopmans, Orgad (this volume), Kaufmann (2019), and others have argued that majorities are the absent center in most liberal democratic thinking. Political progress and much political theorizing for the past two centuries has been focused on limiting and spreading power and thus, in part, on preventing majorities from abusing their dominance.

But two of the great progressive causes of the nineteenth century were extending the electoral franchise to all classes (and to women) – so creating the modern democratic majority – while also securing the equal rights of minorities, Catholics, Jews, and non-conformists in Britain. So, historically speaking, majority and minority rights have not been seen as in conflict.

Yet, once the right of minorities to join the majority in full citizenship had been achieved, the focus shifted in the mid and later twentieth century to the right of minorities to be *different* to the majority. The universalist shift of the mid-twentieth century, exemplified by the United Nations Declaration of Human Rights (1948), proclaimed the moral equality of all human beings and, implicitly, the right of individuals to practice a religion or a distinct cultural life wherever they might find themselves.

In the context of significant non-Western immigration into Western societies in the 1960s and 1970s, the message of liberal multiculturalism was "come here and be oneself." As all cultures were valid and worthy of respect, it was argued, it was wrong to force newcomers to adopt the common norms of the majority society beyond obeying the law and paying their taxes.

This may have helped provide a psychological soft landing to minority individuals, especially from traditional societies, arriving in increasingly pluralistic and liberal Western societies but it was also creating, in Eric Kaufmann's phrase (2019), an "asymmetrical multiculturalism."

Asymmetrical multiculturalism means that minorities have a way of life and a culture that is important to them, indeed is part of their identity as human beings, and this needs legal protection and recognition in liberal democracies, but majorities do not need the same protection for *their* way of life.

Two reasons are usually given in defense of this asymmetry. First, majorities do not need special rights or protections in the way that minorities do because their culture and way of life are already pervasive: the language that is spoken everywhere, the national ceremonies and rituals, the culture and history that is transmitted through the school system, and so on.

Second, while ethnic majorities may share common ancestry in some rather abstract sense, there is no real majority culture or way of life, there is too much value and life-style diversity, too many different sociological tribes, in a county like modern Britain.

Joppke makes both of these points in an earlier paper (2019). He rejects the idea that there is a dominant ethnicity in a country like France or Germany but then also argues that majorities do not in any case need protection. "Majorities by definition have the democratic process at their disposal, they do not need the legal process which is the domain of rights" (2019).

There is, however, a certain tension between the argument that majorities do not really exist and that their culture is so pervasive that it needs no protection in the way that minorities are protected.

In any case I think the traditional defense of asymmetrical multiculturalism has been weakened by the demographic facts, with the majority status of whites gradually being eroded, especially in the Anglosphere (Kaufmann 2019). In an increasing number of cities, towns, and neighborhoods, the majority way of life and its institutions – the shops, pubs, and churches – is no longer dominant.

The issue of whether a dominant culture or a national way of life persists in modern Britain is complex. The forces that make integrating minorities harder – liberalism, multiculturalism, identity politics and so on – also increasingly fragment the majority. Think of the gulf between a Brexit supporting 65-year-old grandmother living in a small town in the north of England and a *Guardian*-reading, gay, web designer living in central London. We have always been a country of many tribes but do we still recognize something in common behind our particularist colorings?

It seems that many of us do. We no longer think ethnically, except in the haziest of ways, and we would be horrified if Boris Johnson started talking about promoting white British values. Yet we do not want newcomers to join a race or even an ethnicity but a *society*, albeit one shaped historically by the ethnic majority.

If there was no such thing as an ethno-cultural majority then presumably nobody would care about the disappearance of the majority way of life but it is pretty clear that a large minority or even a majority of citizens of the majority group do care about this erosion. This can be ascertained by just asking people or watching their behavior.

Opinion polls suggest that national identities remain strong and that large majorities want significantly lower immigration (see British Social Attitudes polling on immigration over the past two decades), while significant numbers of people complain of feeling a stranger in their own land. Moreover, if one observes patterns of settlement and segregation, it is clear that members of the ethnic majority tend to move to areas where their groups are dominant just as minorities tend to cluster together.

The claim that majorities are already protected is also weakened by the fact that majorities are not self-conscious agents in the democratic process. There are, thankfully, no ethnic majority and minority political parties (though the latter are emerging in some European countries), there are Labour, Conservative, Liberal Democrat, and so on, parties. Majorities have a low political self-awareness, albeit one that is probably rising as their majority status becomes threatened.

In any case, the fact that majority interests are hard to define and hard to represent in a liberal political system, does not mean they do not exist. So how should liberal societies think about majority concerns?

People of white European background have similar psychological attachments to cultures and ways of life as the ethnic minorities in European societies. It is true that these ways of life are very diverse but that is increasingly true of minorities as well, and the strongest attachment to a way of life is usually expressed by the least mobile and least educated members of both majority and minority groups.

But Joppke is probably right that legal rights is not the way forward. The state does not belong to the majority and the legal system, although granting group rights to minorities in some rather exceptional cases (e.g., the Sikh motorcycle helmet exemption), should remain broadly indifferent to majority or minority status.

A legal claim to indigenousness is potentially divisive, though it is not impossible to imagine laws to protect the majority language from being overshadowed in certain places and even to protect certain national rituals. It is more appropriate, however, to think of legitimate majority concerns as *interests* rather than legal rights, interests to which democratic politics should give voice and accommodate more than is usually the case at present under the influence of Anywhere liberalism.

What those legitimate interests are will be worked out as part of national democratic conversations that depend on national circumstances (e.g., if Israel is to remain Jewish and democratic, there will have to be some degree of demographic engineering to ensure a permanent Jewish majority).

The key interest of anxious majority groups is to maintain a degree of stability in the way one lives. The right to remain the dominant, tone-setting group in any particular neighborhood is obviously not a right that any liberal society could grant as it would require restrictions on where people live, something that smacks of the Soviet Union or apartheid South Africa. And there is a distinction to be drawn between preserving a majority way of life in specific places, even as the majority loses its majority status, and preserving the overall numerical dominance of the majority which is clearly not a feasible goal.

Yet the idea of a settled life and a degree of control over one's environment is precisely the goal that modern politics does hold out to citizens, both majority and minority. Stability need not necessarily mean homogeneity and stability is not only desired by majorities – look at the resentment among British Caribbeans at the way they are being driven out of "their" Brixton by affluent, liberal whites.

Policies to reassure majorities and support their interest in preserving familiar ways of life both locally and nationally could include the following: lower immigration to ensure a degree of demographic stability, more emphasis on integration of newcomers into common norms than on diversity and difference, managing ethnic settlement so that minorities are well spread out and do not cause the majority to decline too rapidly in particular places, sons and daughters' preferences in public housing allocation, public subsidy of pubs and other traditional majority institutions that are disappearing.

One might add the encouragement in the public sphere (and in schools) to celebrate a non-chauvinistic version of the national story, much as minorities are encouraged to celebrate their story. Not all these things are easily subject to legislation, but there are other ways of promoting desirable things than through law. Well-designed "nudges" may be more effective than legislation in encouraging people to integrate around broad common norms and think of each other as sharing common interests as citizens.

The desire to retain a majority way of life is usually a defensive not an assertive sentiment and need not be hostile to minority groups and minority rights. Indeed, majorities and minorities usually want the same thing, as the Brixton example shows. And as Koopmans, Orgad (this volume), and Kaufmann point out, the personal autonomy, cultural preservation and group identity that matters to minorities matters also to individuals from majorities.

The failure of mainstream liberal politics to adequately recognize this common interest has been exploited in recent years by illegitimate populists of the far right who have invoked multiculturalism to defend whites in areas of rapid ethnic change. Meanwhile Donald Trump's appeal in the United States was surely based in part on the demographic anxiety of lower-status whites – non-Hispanic whites now make up just 60 percent of the United States population – the sort of people who are irked to have to press one for English on automated phone systems.

Liberal Overreach

I have sympathy for Koopmans and Orgad's (2021) focus on the sense of loss that helps to power populist parties and with their wish to reinforce cultural majority interests, and possibly even rights, as a response to legitimate populism. But in this final section I want to unpack that sense of loss by returning to the three areas of liberal overreach I mentioned earlier. The policy areas, values, and beliefs I pinpoint are all perfectly decent and legitimate but they tend to be those of the mobile, university-educated dominant group and often conflict with the priorities and values of more traditional, conservative-minded voters of all classes. The first is change and openness. One of the contradictions of modern Anywhere liberalism is the belief that the goal of politics is about, on the one hand, giving people as much autonomy and control over their fate as possible while, on the other hand, demanding that people adapt themselves to the tides of change and modernization whether economic or cultural.

The locus classicus of the latter position was Tony Blair's Labour conference speech of 2005 in which he stated: "I hear people say we have to stop and debate globalization. You might as well debate whether autumn should follow summer" (Blair 2005).

Self-evidently, change is often necessary and refreshing and market economies are dynamic systems in which companies and whole industrial sectors die and others arise, and this causes disruption to many lives even while the system as a whole may be raising living standards and increasing well-being.

But in recent decades, the pace of both economic and cultural change has been uncomfortably fast for large minorities, or even majorities, in rich Western countries. In secular societies where meaning and purpose in life are often strongly associated with productive labor, especially for men, the psychological impact of deindustrialization has often been underestimated.

Clearly, there have been choices about the speed of deindustrialization, one just needs to compare the experience of the United Kingdom with that of Germany. The political class in the United Kingdom (and the United States) has broadly been happy to encourage very rapid change. From Margaret Thatcher to Tony Blair, market-led modernization has been pursued with some success and with genuine concern for the losers from this process. Nevertheless, the pace could have been slower.

Cultural change is something that politicians have even less control over than economic change. But the liberal baby boomer generation in power across the rich world came of age in an era where progress was associated with throwing off the moral constraints of the past in the pursuit of happiness and self-actualization.

The great liberal reforms of the past fifty years providing women with more freedom and autonomy, protecting the rights of minorities of many kinds, and ending almost all constraints on personal behavior and artistic expression, are now largely absorbed into essential liberal common-sense.

But other aspects of recent change and openness have been much more divisive and driven by Anywhere liberal assumptions that have shown scant pluralistic respect for the many who have felt discomforted by rapid change and openness.

Here are a few of them. Mass immigration and rapid demographic change has not been popular. The European Union's freedom of movement in big receiving countries like the United Kingdom has also offended against the notion of fellow citizen favoritism, the idea that national citizenship should trump universal rights.

Although racism has become one of the central moral taboos in all Western countries, the tendency of political elites to prioritize minority rights and minority equality before the much more complex question of minority integration into common cultural norms has run counter to the intuitions of a large slice of citizens. This latter point also overlaps with popular hostility toward the "legalization" of politics, to the challenge to the first constitution of democratic elections from the second constitution of decisions taken by courts, including international ones. Joppke cites an interesting example in the 2012 decision of the German Constitutional Court which ruled that even failed asylum seekers had the same social rights as German citizens.

Anywhere liberalism has been far more relaxed about trading off national sovereignty for other benefits, from economic efficiency to freer movement across borders, than the average citizen: one of the core reasons behind the Brexit vote.

There are many examples of unpopular change in the cultural sphere as well. To name just one: the top-down redevelopment of many towns and cities usually following a modernist aesthetic much more popular with elites than with ordinary citizens.

The second area of liberal overreach concerns the promotion of cognitive-professional employment and academic training as the main route to a successful life. This is a relatively recent phenomenon in Western societies and coincides with the big expansion of higher education and the promotion of the idea of a cognitive meritocracy.

Sending more young people to university certainly made sense in the final decades of the twentieth century as both business and the public services demanded more academically trained professionals from doctors to the IT experts of the knowledge economy. But little thought was given to those who did not take the chosen path of university and professional employment and a status gap opened up between the best educated quarter to one-third of the population and the rest, many of whom were also losing relatively well paid skilled manual employment.

The single ladder up to safety and success via the modern university on the one hand and the declining status of nongraduate employment on the other has exacerbated the value divide in Western societies. A new gulf of incomprehension has opened up between a graduate class favoring mobility and openness, which is happy surfing rapid change, and a less well-educated and more rooted group, which draws its identity not from academic and professional achievement but from place and group.

Moreover, the fact that the political class and the wider social elites are drawn almost entirely from the graduate class, and have then tended to promote their own priorities in the rapid expansion of academic education, in relatively open borders, and in protecting the interests of professional lobbies, has further deepened the divide.

Some of the superior rewards and status of cognitive professional employment are set to decline in coming decades as Artificial

Intelligence replaces some of the more routine cognitive work and more practical technician type skills and caring work will come to be more highly valued. But the divide has left a deep scar in rich democracies leaving many people feeling that their own contribution is not valued.

The third area of liberal overreach concerns the devaluation of family life and a desire to abolish, rather than reform, the gender division of labor in the name of a new androgynous fluidity.

Politicians tend to talk glowingly about the family but the policy drift in recent decades in most rich countries has been one of neglect. Family and gender policy (with the exception of paternity leave) has mainly been about making it as easy as possible for both parents to spend as much time as possible at work and away from the family. And the idea of using public policy to try to encourage couples with children to stay together in the stressful early years of child rearing has generally been considered old-fashioned.

This partly reflects the ambivalence of modern, professional-woman-dominated feminism about family life which has stressed equality with men in professional work and *escaping* from care roles, rather than raising the pay and status of such roles. The wider public in most countries favors doing both.

Rebooting domesticity for an age of gender equality is popular. And support for gender equality can happily coexist with support for modern domesticity. The public in most rich countries does not want to go back to the old gender division of labor, or stigmatizing single parents. But in the United Kingdom there is strong support for what is called the "modified male breadwinner model," meaning the man working full-time and the woman part-time when children are young. In a 2018 survey (British Social Attitudes 2018) only 6 percent supported both the mother and father working full-time when children are pre-school. "Watching children grow up is life's greatest joy" has remained at more than 80 percent agreement for more than three decades in the United Kingdom.

These three examples of liberal overreach are by no means exhaustive but they point to the real roots of legitimate populist dissatisfaction with modern politics. And the success of populist parties in many countries is causing some of the Anywhere liberal priorities of the past two or three decades to be reined in. The best example is probably the way the Conservative party in the United Kingdom has absorbed the populist UKIP/Brexit party into mainstream politics while reflecting in muted form some of its populist concerns.

Orgad, toward the end of his book on majority rights (2016, 235), raises the interesting question of whether the quest for majority rights is a swan song for an old idea of national identity. Perhaps as people become more educated and mobile, they will draw their identities less from place and group and more from inside themselves, from their personalities and temperaments, making them less concerned with maintaining stable communities. I doubt it.

But if ethnic majorities are destined to become minorities throughout the West, we are left with another question: is it possible to retain a strong sense of common interest and mutual regard in a society that is not grounded in an ethnic majority?

Nobody knows. So, it is best to move with caution and recognize that significant sections of the majority group have a legitimate interest in preserving their culture and way of life. Mainstream politics should reflect not suppress this interest.

References

Blair, T. (2005). Conference Speech (September 27, 2005), available at www.theguardian.com/uk/2005/sep/27/labourconference.speeches.

British Social Attitudes. (2018). Family Life, Attitudes to Non-Traditional Family Behaviours, available at https://bsa.natcen.ac.uk/latest-report/british-social-attitudes-37/family-life.aspx.

Caldwell, C. (2020). *The Age of Entitlement: America Since the Sixties*. New York: Simon & Schuster.

Goodhart, D. (2017). *The Road to Somewhere: The New Tribes Shaping British Politics*. London: Penguin Books Ltd.

Joppke, C. (2019). The Neonationalist Defense of Majority Culture: Themes, Actors, Policies. *Justice* 62: 22–27.

Kaufmann, E. (2019). *Whiteshift: Immigration, Populism and the Future of White Majorities*. Penguin.

Koopmans, R., & Orgad, L. (this volume). Majority–Minority Constellations: Towards a Group-Differentiated Approach. Cambridge: Cambridge University Press.

Orgad, L. (2016). *The Cultural Defense of Nations: A Liberal Theory of Majority Rights*. Oxford: Oxford University Press.

Timothy, N. (2020). *Remaking One Nation: The Future of Conservatism*. Cambridge, UK: Polity.

12 *The Causes of Populism and the Problem of Cultural Majority Rights*

DANIEL ZIBLATT

Few topics have been more well-studied in the social sciences in recent years than the causes of populism. One central pivot of the debate is whether its roots are cultural or economic (see Gidron and Hall 2017). The implications of this debate are important. If, as Christian Joppke (this volume) contends, populism is a bottom-up reaction to globalization-induced socioeconomic displacement, the call for majority cultural rights as a device to defeat the appeals of populism founders. In that case, as Joppke argues, such a strategy merely "deflects" from the deeper socioeconomic sources of populism.

This chapter begins by agreeing with Joppke's assessment of the socioeconomic roots of populism. But it parts company with him in the diagnosis of the precise mechanisms linking socioeconomic change to populism. A strictly "demand-side" bottom-up narrative of vulnerable voters tempted by the appeals of populism needs to be supplemented with a top-down political account of populism. Rather than assuming voters' preferences autonomously drive politics, we can ask an alternative set of questions: What leads mainstream political parties, and ultimately radical right parties, to make nationalist appeals in the first place? And what is the effect of these appeals on voters' preferences?

The answer offered here is that the strategies of political parties, especially center-right parties, over the long run help *create* populist sentiment, in a kind of "boomerang effect," unintentionally paving the way for the rise of their own radical right party challengers. Based on historical and contemporary cross-national evidence, this chapter argues that the rise of populism does not simply reflect the autonomous preferences of voters shocked by the pressures of globalization. Rather, voters express right wing identity issues in some instances only after politicians – especially mainstream center-right politicians – have accentuated these issues in their own electoral campaigns. Broadly speaking, then, the identity appeals of populism including calls to defend a national "cultural majority" emerge as a product of mainstream political parties' efforts to cope with the contradictions of capitalism and democracy in an age of high socioeconomic inequality.

In short, I agree with Joppke that calls for protections for "the cultural majority" may be aimed at the wrong target. But the account here posits an additional point: The very notion of a cultural majority is itself a *politically constructed* category – an imagined community of ephemeral democratic normative weight, crafted by center-right political parties as they scramble to try win electoral majorities in an age of heightened socioeconomic inequality.

A Top-Down Account of Populism's Rage

There is no shortage of accounts seeking to locate the origins of the surge of populist parties, rhetoric, and candidates in advanced democracies. After all, few phenomena have been regarded as more pressing for democracy today than the over-decade-long emergence of new and successful radical right political parties (e.g., the AfD in Germany), the renewed success of far-right parties (e.g., the Freedom Party in Austria), or the capture of traditional center-right parties by a radicalized right (e.g., the Republican Party in the United States). Most scholarships tend to focus on one of several factors: the economic roots of far-right success (e.g., slow economic growth, stagnant wages, inequality), the cultural roots of this same phenomenon (e.g., perceived threats of immigration), or some combination of the two (Gidron and Hall 2017). Despite differences in emphasis, all of these approaches share two common presumptions. The first is that the drivers of the phenomenon are mostly bottom-up emerging directly from the shifting preferences of voters. The second is that illiberal nationalist right represents a "new" departure from some "normal" baseline.

The central claim here is different. The current moment is most usefully thought of as the outgrowth of the *return* of an old, and reoccurring dilemma of modern conservatism itself. It is a dilemma that was eclipsed from view for a variety of reasons in the last half of the twentieth century (roughly 1950–2000) but has now, in the twenty-first century, returned with a vengeance. What is the dilemma?

In 2017, I wrote a book, *Conservative Parties and the Birth of Democracy* in which I explored the foundational period of modern democracy (1830–1933) in the North Atlantic world arguing that in that period, the forces of property, power, and privilege made peace with democracy by assuring that they *could win elections,* if not most of the time, at least a lot of the time. In the concluding paragraphs of that book I asked,

> What ransom [must] the advocates of democracy pay to property for its willingness to accommodate itself to democracy?

I gave a grim answer,

> In simplest terms, this study has argued that the price that advocates of democracy must pay is that the propertied and powerful not only have a diffuse but disproportionate influence on society all the time, but also that it be protected by organizationally strong and well-endowed political parties that have the chance of winning elections at least some of the time.

This is – I admitted even then – not only where my normative predilections led me but rather where the evidence had led me: a relatively "dismal science" view of democracy's birth, in which property's relationship with democracy is conditional and contingent.

But this perspective, if correct, exposes a dilemma in the age of mass democracy. It is easy to explain how a conservative political party with a core founding constituency of affluence and privilege could win in the mid-nineteenth century when suffrage was limited to the wealthy alone. But the democratic age opens a new challenge: How can defenders of affluence, power, and privilege win elections in the face of an expansive, more inclusive, and hence poorer electorate? This is the heart of what I called the conservative dilemma. And it is a dilemma that is exacerbated under conditions of extreme socioeconomic inequality.

When 2012 U.S. presidential candidate Mitt Romney famously was caught on camera confessing in a closed-door fundraising event (in a losing election campaign) that he had no ambitions to appeal to the "47 percent ... these are people who pay no income tax," this was more than an embarrassing gaffe. He was revealing a fundamental dilemma or tension that conservative politicians have felt at key moments in history, including in the last Gilded Age – the late nineteenth century. In the 1860s, Tory British Prime Minister Lord

Salisbury, presaging Romney's sentiments, warned about the perils of democracy when he quipped that democracy was the mere "right of eight beggars to govern seven Rothschilds, and what is more, to tax them!"

The enduring dilemma of conservative political parties is this: Under conditions of high socioeconomic inequality – of the sort that wracked the North Atlantic world both before World War II and that has returned since the 1980s – a political party cannot represent the wealthy alone and hope for a secure path to electoral majorities. How, then to, win? There are multiple, alternative possible strategies for conservative or center-right parties, which represent different challenges for democracy: repress the vote of the poor, abandon the rich as a core constituency, or, as I discovered in my account of early democratization, the option most often pursued in *stable* democracies: Economic conservatives figure out how to win elections by emphasizing nonclass or noneconomic issues in their electoral appeals to mobilize voters and activists.

In particular, the historical record makes clear that conservatives won middle-class and even working-class Tory voters by inventing, or at least, highlighting cleavages that were powerful, enduring, and above all premised on *social identities* that sharply divide between "us" and "them." These sorts of social divisions include appeals to nationalism, religion, ethnicity, race, and patriotism. Historically, conservatives made appeals to empire, nation, monarchy, and establishment religion. Today, these appeals take a different form but frequently include patriotic calls to defend traditional values or calls to defend the national culture from immigrants and other "outsiders."

To put the point more directly, center-right parties, under conditions of higher socioeconomic inequality are placed at an electoral disadvantage: If socioeconomic issues remain the central cleavage of politics, a basic one-dimensional spatial model of electoral politics predicts loyal parties representing upper classes would lose elections repeatedly (Downs 1957). Those voters at the lower income end of the income distribution who constitute a majority of voters under universal suffrage would find the socioeconomic programmatic appeals of center-left parties more and more attractive as inequality increases (Acemoglu and Robinson 2006). So, to block the possibility of the formation of a new broader center-left majority coalition, as socioeconomic inequality increases, the center-right must find new issues. It is a classic "heresthetic maneuver," described by William Riker (1986) in these terms,

> .... [For] a person who expects to lose on some decision, [a] fundamental ... device is to divide the majority with a new alternative, one that he prefers to the alternative previously expected to win. If successful, this maneuver produces a new majority coalition composed of the old minority and the portion of the old majority that likes the new alternative better.

As a result, in the two-dimensional electoral space of modern democracies, where economic issues run at cross-purposes to "social identity" issues, center-right politicians and parties, under conditions of high inequality, will find it tempting to make values-based or identity-based "talk" central to their campaigns and public appeals. The content of the appeal will vary from country to country but to hold together their increasingly fractious coalition, center-right parties will find public discussions about race, immigration, religion, and national cultural values increasingly useful. While these appeals may have always been part of some voters' genuine social identity, the core prediction here is that the salience and importance of these issues grow as socioeconomic inequality grows.

To be clear: This is not an argument about "false consciousness," nor is it an argument that the rich can "distract" the poor by *inventing* issues from whole cloth (e.g., Roemer 1998). Instead, the argument contends that voters have multiple genuine preferences on multiple dimensions of politics. And, if a political party primarily represents rich voters, this creates a challenge or a dilemma – under inclusive, democratic elections, for which noneconomic identity issues provide a useful solution.

The question remains: What explains why the right radicalizes, or why *new* radical right parties emerge? A final step in the causal chain is necessary. Here, I follow in a tradition of political science that grants political leaders great consequence in their words and actions for voters' mass opinion (Lippman 1922; Zaller 1992). While voter preferences shape politician strategies, the converse is also true. The strategic shift in the emphasis of elite discourse of center-right politicians (and media) away from socioeconomic themes to identity-related themes, over time, leads to the growth in the salience in many voters' minds of the issues of race, immigration, social identity, and national culture. That is, voters begin to rank identity issues as more important than socioeconomic issues. Naturally objective "facts on the ground" shape what issues voters rank as important issues, but so too, does the way in which politicians frame issues.

There is growing evidence that elite cues matter in exactly this way. As mainstream politicians talk about social identity issues – religion, nation, and race – all else equal, voters begin to list these issues as more important in surveys. In careful empirical work, Lenz (2012) makes clear, for example, that voters often do not choose politicians based on policy stances but rather the opposite: Once they choose a politician, they then adopt the politician's policy stances. Similarly, empirical work shows that talk of extremist politicians alters respondents' willingness to express previously stigmatized nationalist views (Bursztyn et al. 2020) as does the electoral success of such candidates (Valentim, 2021). In other words, politicians' own words and their electoral success can alter what voters *say* they think is important. For this reason, it is possible to regard voters' stated attachment to a "national culture under siege" as an endogenous outgrowth of the mobilizational strategies of politicians themselves.

Some Tentative Evidence

To confirm this general proposition would require extensive and difficult-to-muster evidence – a project, I am just beginning. But consider the following tentative evidence as a first step. First, I draw on national election studies from Britain, the United States, as well as Germany's more recent Socioeconomic Panel from the earliest date available to the present. The analysis uses self-reported income and party leanings of respondents to present a disaggregated picture of levels of income inequality within the voting base of major parties in Germany, Britain, and the United States from the 1950s to the present. Confirming the conventional wisdom, Figure 12.1 shows that income inequality has broadly risen over the past forty years, in all parties, including center-right parties between the richest and poorest voters of each party in Britain, the United States, and Germany.

The gap is in some instances greater in center-left parties than center-right parties, which poses its own challenges. But given the notion of a "conservative dilemma," we can narrow our focus on

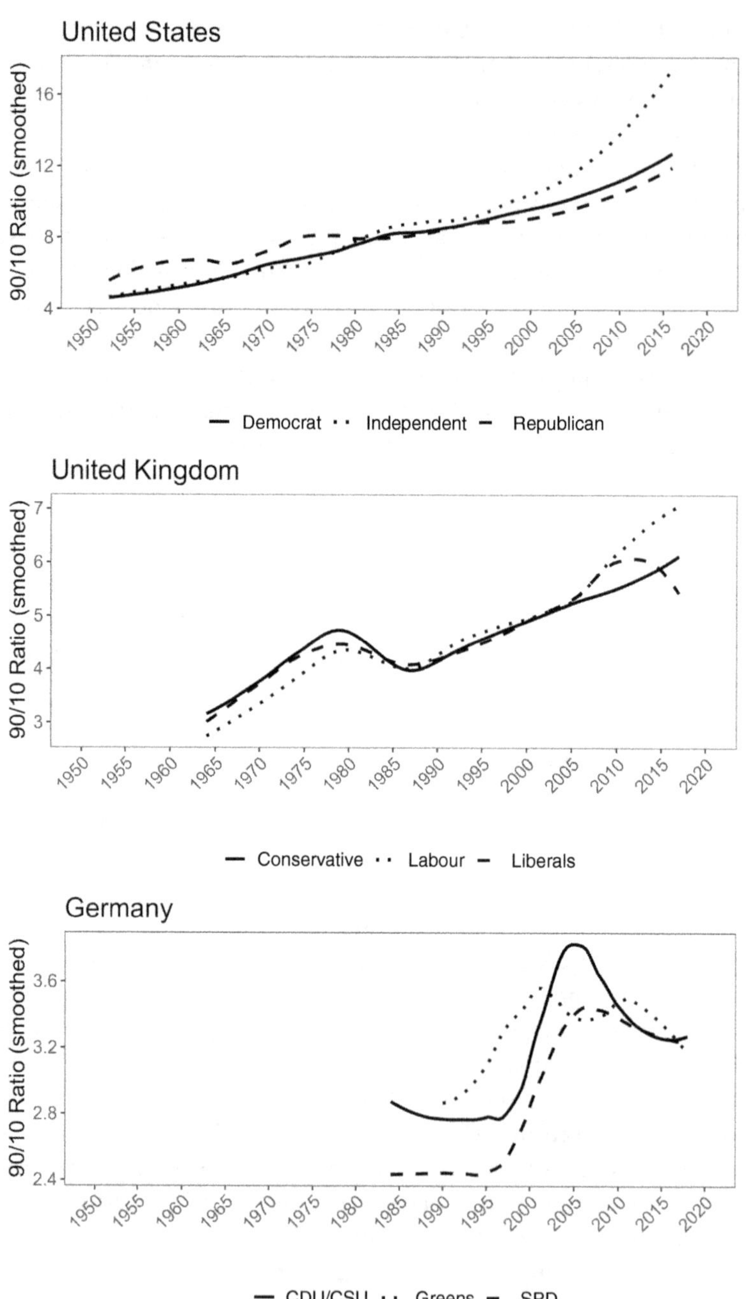

Figure 12.1 Income inequality of political parties voting base, 1950–present
Notes: National Election Study; British Election Study; Socioeconomic Panel (Germany)

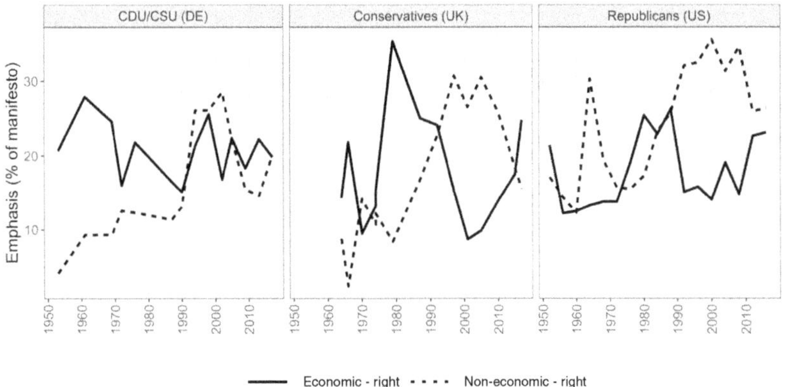

Figure 12.2 Themes in party programs by share of emphasis
Notes: Data from Comparative Manifestos Project (https://manifesto-project.wzb.eu/)

the dynamics within center-right parties, to ask: Has this increase in within-party inequality within center-right parties led them to increase their emphasis on right-wing social identity issues over time? Tavits and Potter (2015) in an earlier study note that heightened aggregate national levels economic inequality leads to greater reliance on identity themes in party manifestos across all parties, using the Comparative Manifestos dataset. I replicate that analysis here but, given the findings in Ziblatt (2017), I focus on how within-party income inequality relates to changes in center-right party programs over time. I follow the coding scheme of Abou-Chadi and Krause (2020) who categorizes party manifestos' inclusion of positive assessments of "national way of life" or "traditional values," and negative assessments of "multiculturalism" – all as "right-wing social identity" themes. With this as a basis of analysis, we can see in Figure 12.2 that over time the three center-right parties under evaluation here (Germany, Britain, and the United States) have generally increased their reliance on such themes.

But is this correlated in any systematic way with increases in income inequality among center-right voters? Figure 12.3 shows that within-party income inequality, as noted above, is associated with an increased emphasis on radical right identity themes in party programs. And Figure 12.4 shows this effect holds even holding constant time trend factors.

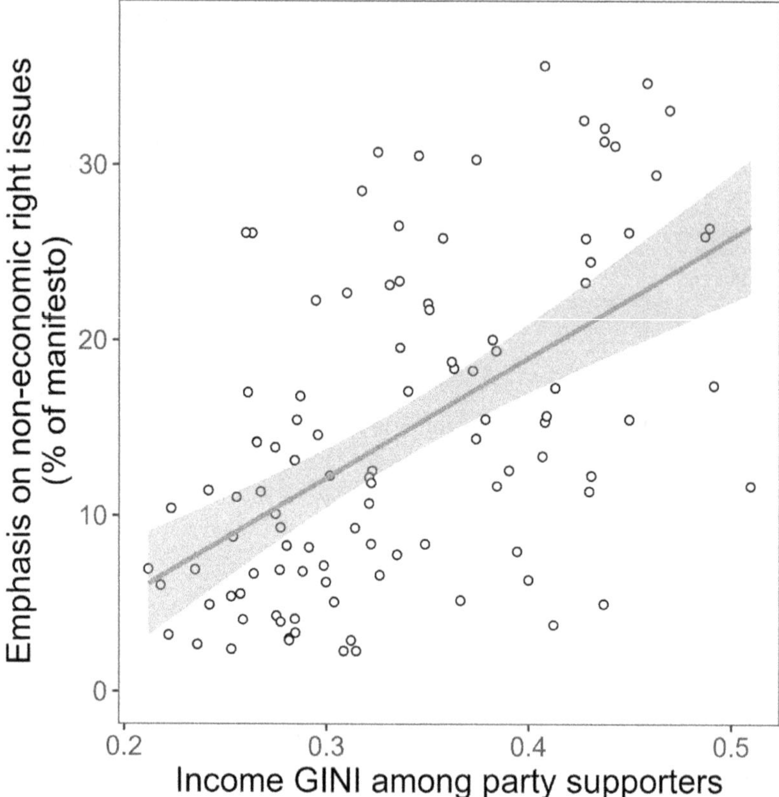

Figure 12.3 Bivariate relationship of economic inequality and noneconomic right issues among center-right parties (Britain, Germany, and the United States)

Now, certainly part of this shift to identity themes is driven by politicians' efforts to respond to where they think voters themselves are. But, as noted above, recent experimental work has bolstered the expectation that public opinion shifts in response to how politicians themselves talk. Politicians normalize certain attitudes and can certainly raise the salience of certain themes in voters' minds. During campaign time, politicians can distract or refocus voters' attention, and can in turn shape the agenda of what voters think is important.

The cumulative effect of these efforts over time can plausibly be linked to long-run opinion shifts. Again, it is worth noting here that

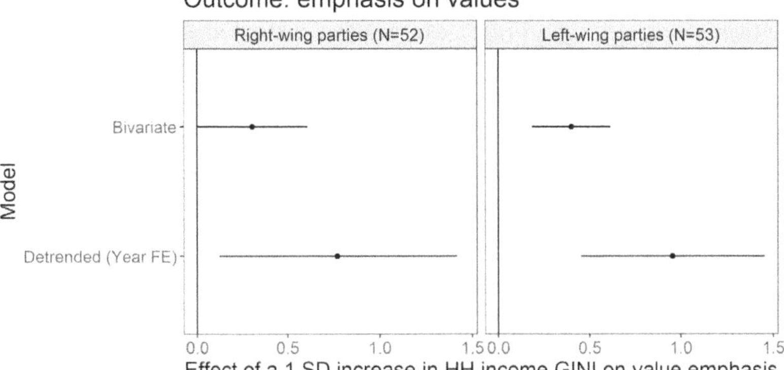

Figure 12.4 Relationship of income inequality and emphasis on right identity themes, 1950–present

my argument is self-consciously theoretically modest: I am not suggesting that politicians' talk *creates* preferences among voters where they previously did not exist. Rather, I am making the less ambitious argument that multiple competing strands of beliefs and attitudes – about economics, identity, race, immigration, etc. – are always present in voters mind in what we can think of as a complex "primeval soup" of preferences. What politicians (and media) can do is activate how relatively *important* voters think issues are.

This account suggests that voters perception of a "culture under siege" may in part be political constructed. These sentiments furthermore may reflect the strategies of politicians in their effort to carve out winning electoral majorities. And if cultural majorities are "politically constructed" in this way, then this suggests uncertainty about the normative significance of majority cultural rights.

Conclusion: What Does This Mean for the Cultural Majority Rights Agenda?

One reason the notion of "electoral majorities" has particular normative value in democratic theory is that majorities can be easily counted. A singular "public will" or "will of the people" is infamously inscrutable for a variety of reasons that democratic theorists have long identified. As Joseph Schumpeter long ago clarified, it is impossible to discern a single coherent "will of the people"

(Schumpeter 1946). Additionally, mechanisms of translating preferences of voters into policy are always distorted if not biased by varying systems of electoral representation (Aachen and Bartels 2017). But electoral majorities, however imperfect, with a real numerical value are nonetheless discernable via elections. Elections allow us to count-up preferences. Hence, they have a normative value; they give us a reasonably plausible approximation of the public will.

Even James Madison, famously alert to the dangers of majority tyranny was himself an advocate of the normative value of majoritarianism. In the 1830s, toward the end of his life, frustrated by John Calhoun's efforts to secure special rights for South Carolina in tariff disputes of the day, Madison wrote,

> The vital principle of republican government is the *lex majoris partis*, the will of the majority. (Meyers 1973)

But the idea that electoral majorities have rights is different from the notion that a single "cultural majority" has rights. First, the size of the latter cannot be counted-up in any reliable way as part of a democratic political process. In this sense cultural majorities are – unless one uses hard-to-justify ascriptive criteria – "imagined communities" or fictive. There are undoubtedly citizens who intensely associate themselves with a particular cultural group that they imagine constitutes a "cultural majority." But it is very difficult to develop institutional mechanisms to "count" the intensity of preferences in modern democracies (Dahl 1956; Hirschman 1982). Hence, a smaller faction of a cultural majority may *claim* to speak on behalf of a self-perceived cultural majority, but with no electoral mechanism in place to assess this, their right to speak on behalf of the "majority" possesses a normative value that is difficult to sustain.

Additionally, Madison's justification of the importance of electoral majorities runs at cross purposes to the notion of a singular cultural majority. A singular cultural majority is premised on the idea of a relatively fixed group; after all, there can, logically speaking, only be one cultural majority in a country. Madison's notion of electoral *majorities* (note the plural) is premised on the opposite grounds: Membership in majorities must be fluid for democratic stability to be achieved. In *Federalist 10*, for example, Madison argues that majority rule can only avoid tyranny if the individuals and interests that constitute any temporary majority themselves regularly shift, rotate, break away, and realign themselves, from issue to issue. In short, the essence of pluralism as a mechanism of sustaining social order is that majorities are neither fixed nor essentialist. By contrast, the notion of a single cultural majority – itself, as I have argued here, a politically constructed category – appears to be both fixed and essentialist in a way that would seem to pose serious problems for political stability in Madison's framework.

In sum, while the perception of "cultures under siege" undoubtedly fuels populism and its roots are found in shifting economic conditions, there is some reason for skepticism that granting rights to self-proclaimed "cultural majorities" offers a way out of our current predicament. In the realm of public policy, more promising – though themselves admittedly not unproblematic – avenues include: (1) developing mechanisms for addressing underlying conditions of socioeconomic inequality, and (2) constructing the definition of national communities in ways that are premised on a notion of *civic equality and rights*, no matter the background, ethnicity, religion, or race of a country's citizens.

References

Abou-Chadi, T., & Werner K. (2020). The Causal Effect of Radical Right Success on Mainstream Parties' Policy Positions: A Regression Discontinuity Approach. *British Journal of Political Science*, 50/3: 829–47.

Acemoglu, D., & Robinson, J. A. (2006). *Economic Origins of Dictatorship and Democracy*. Cambridge: Cambridge University Press.

Achen, C., & Bartels, L. (2017). *Democracy for Realists*. Princeton: Princeton University Press.

Bursztyn, L., Egorov, G., & Fiorin, S. (2020). From Extreme to Mainstream: The Erosion of Social Norms. *American Economic Review*, 110/11: 3522–48.

Dahl, R. A. (1956). *A Preface to Democratic Theory*. Chicago: University of Chicago Press.

Downs, A. (1957). *An Economic Theory of Democracy*. New York: Harper & Brothers.

Gidron, N., & Hall, P. A. (2017). The Politics of Social Status: Economic and Cultural Roots of the Populist Right. *The British Journal of Sociology*, 68/51: 57–84.

Hirschman, A. O. (1982). *Shifting Involvements: Private Interest and Public Action*. Princeton: Princeton University Press.

Lenz, G. S. (2013). *Follow the Leader?: How Voters Respond to Politicians' Policies and Performance*. Chicago: University of Chicago Press.

Lippmann, W. (1922). *Public Opinion*. New York: Harcourt, Brace and Company.

Meyers, M. (1973). *The Mind of the Founder: Sources of the Political Thought of James Madison*. Indianapolis: Bobbs-Merrill Co.

Riker, W. H. (1986). *The Art of Political Manipulation*. Vol. 587. New Haven: Yale University Press.

Roemer, J. E. (1998). Why the Poor Do Not Expropriate the Rich: An Old Argument in New Garb. *Journal of Public Economics*, 70/3: 399–424.

Schumpeter, J. A. (1946). *Capitalism, Socialism and Democracy*. New York: Columbia University Press.

Tavits, M., & Potter, J. D. (2015). The Effect of Inequality and Social Identity on Party Strategies. *American Journal of Political Science*, 59/3: 744–58.

Valentim, V. (2021). Parliamentary Representation and the Normalization of Radical Right Support. *Comparative Political Studies*, 54/14: 2475–511.

Zaller, J. R. (1992). *The Nature and Origins of Mass Opinion*. Cambridge: Cambridge University Press.

Ziblatt, D. (2017). *Conservative Parties and the Birth of Democracy*. Cambridge: Cambridge University Press.

Index

Lightning Source UK Ltd.
Milton Keynes UK
UKHW021833091222
413661UK00015B/340

9 781009 233354